THE GREAT KANSAS BOND SCANDAL

The Great Kansas Bond SCANDAL

Robert Smith Bader

UNIVERSITY PRESS OF KANSAS

© 1982 by Robert Smith Bader
Printed in the United States of America
First paperback edition, 1984

Library of Congress Cataloging in Publication Data
Bader, Robert Smith, 1925–
The great Kansas bond scandal.
Includes bibliographical references and index.
1. Securities fraud—Kansas. 2. Kansas—History—20th century.
I. Title.
HV6770.A2K23 1982   364.1'68'09781   82-9056
ISBN 0-7006-0248-8   AACR2

Produced digitally by Lightning Source Inc.

Published by the University Press of Kansas (Lawrence, Kansas 66045), which was organized by the Kansas Board of Regents and is operated and funded by Emporia State University, Fort Hays State University, Kansas State University, Pittsburg State University, the University of Kansas, and Wichita State University.

To the people of Kansas
Who have ofttimes found
That the journey to the stars
Can be of inordinate difficulty

Contents

	List of Illustrations	ix
	Preface	xi
1	The Summer of 1933	1
2	The Bubble Bursts	19
3	Gross and Enormous Irregularities	43
4	Impeachment	61
5	*Homo Sapiens Kansensis*	79
6	The Blood Line	99
7	His Father's Son	121
8	The Sins of the Father	141
9	Crime and Punishment	163
10	A Brother's Trust	185
11	The First Lieutenant	205
12	Honest, But . . .	215
13	A Most Helpful Office	247
14	Politics	275

15	Victory	297
16	Redemption	313
17	Epilogue	343
	Appendix	349
	Notes	353
	Index	387

List of Illustrations

Map of Kansas	8
William Allen White	10
William L. White	12
Sardius M. Brewster	20
Ronald Finney	22
Alf Landon, Arthur Capper, and John D. M. Hamilton	25
Martial Law at the State Treasury	27
Fred Harris	31
Lester Goodell	33
Schuyler C. Bloss	37
Landon Addressing the Legislature	68
Hellen and David Finney	103
Warren W. Finney as Legislator	105
The W. W. Finneys' Twelfth-Street Home	113
Warren W. Finney, about 1930	116
Farmers State Bank, Neosho Falls	123

Commercial Street, Emporia, 1932	143
Clarence V. Beck	150
Hugo Wedell	151
A Forged Logan County Bond	166
Zula Bennington Greene	172
Winifred and Ronald Finney	178
Tom Boyd	186
The National Bank of Topeka	190
Leland C. Caldwell	206
Roland Boynton	216
Clif Stratton	221
Frank J. Ryan	226
Leon N. Roulier	233
Will J. French	248
Landon on Kansas Day	278
Ronald Finney as a Prisoner	315
Christmas Card from Ronald Finney	318
William A. Smith	325
Landon and William Allen White	333
Ronald Finney, about 1955	340

Preface

ooooooooooooooooooooooooooooooooooooooooooooooooooooo

AT THE NADIR of the Great Depression, in the summer of 1933, the state of Kansas was shocked to the depths of its puritanical soul by the greatest public scandal in its history. The shock was all the greater since the million-dollar bond scandal involved one of the state's leading families—father and son—and several of the state's constitutional officers, including the treasurer, the attorney general, and the auditor. Profoundly shaking the confidence of the people in their state government at a time of great economic stress, it became a Kansas Watergate, with a character distinctively its own.

When the prairie air eventually cleared following the initial "startling and appalling discoveries," the total financial, political, psychological, and personal costs of the tragic affair became almost impossible to calculate. A million and a quarter in forged bonds and warrants had been discovered in the state treasury and in bond brokerage houses. An "amazing" story of "gross and enormous irregularities" in several Statehouse offices had been revealed, stemming principally from the infamous activities of the charismatic confidence man Ronald Finney. Governor Alfred M. Landon had, unprecedentedly, placed the treasury under martial law after ordering the arrest of Finney and the state treasurer. Payment of the interest and principal on all public-body bonds had been suspended for months. Four criminal convictions had been effected, including the three longest sentences in the state's penal history. Two state officers had been impeached at a special session of the legislature. Six federal indictments had been brought against seven defendants, who included the president of one of the Midwest's leading banks. A record number of civil suits jammed the courts. Three banks had closed permanently, with consequent heavy losses to their hard-pressed depositors. A major Chicago brokerage firm had gone bankrupt. One of the principals had committed suicide, and several other scandal-related deaths had occurred. Political alliances had re-formed and regrouped, particularly in the progressive faction of the Republican Party. The honor, pride, and image of the state had been seriously, though not permanently, damaged. And finally, the multifaceted affair had concluded with the dramatic behind-the-scenes attempts by the friends of Ronald Finney to obtain his release from the state penitentiary—efforts of a decidedly political nature.

The hard-nosed and thorough handling of the affair by Governor Landon—even though it required him to prosecute some of his closest friends and political allies—became a necessary condition for his successful bid for a second gubernatorial term and for his subsequent nomination as a candidate for president of the United States of America. The vigorous prosecution of the bond-scandal defendants enabled an obscure small-town lawyer to be named to the Kansas Supreme Court at the governor's next opportunity and enabled an equally obscure county attorney to become the state's attorney general at the next general election. The William Allen White family's intimacy with the principal culprits added a fascinating dimension to the drama. Despite the harsh economic and climatic conditions of the day, the bond scandal and its several ramifications held a central place on the Kansas stage from its explosive beginning in August, 1933, through the summer of 1935.

In this book I have attempted to do two things: to relate the swirl of events in a balanced, even-handed, "objective" fashion—"without fear or favor," to use a favorite expression of the time—and, simultaneously, to look at a narrow time slice of Kansas cultural history along the way. My purpose is not only to relate what happened and how it happened—the action—but also to record the response of the people of the state to the strange and alarming circumstances that had suddenly been thrust upon them—the reaction. To further both these goals I have given the contemporary "actors" a chance to speak whenever possible rather than having attempted a personal and probably jaundiced interpretation on every page or in every paragraph. The world wearies of academic tomes overflowing with sterile and tendentious interpretations of historical events, piled high upon a fragile factual base.

In preparing the manuscript, I have kept in mind the interests of the more general reader as well as those of the academician. I retain a fond hope—hope is still free—that the book will be widely read (even if not bought), especially by Kansans. Why should they give up a few hours of television time for such an endeavor? Simply because it is a part of their cultural heritage. To understand something of the action and reaction of those days is to understand something of themselves. The discerning reader will be able to distinguish an occasionally satirical style from the underlying sympathetic substance. If there is a wry smile here and there, it is always a smile (occasionally teary-eyed) with Mother Kansas and her people and never a laugh at them. They are laughed at enough by others. They are my people, and I love them—warts, scandal, and all.

Since recent years have seen a sharp inflationary rise in both prices and wages, some economic calculations and perceptual adjustments may be necessary in order to appreciate fully the impact of the bond scandal on the state in 1933/34. The consumer price index for 1933 was estimated at 38.8; the index at the end of 1981 stood at approximately 285, an increase of almost 750 percent.[1] The $1.35 million in bogus securities generated by the Finney operations would be the equivalent of nearly ten million in 1981 dollars.

On the price side, a substantial house could be purchased for $5,000 or thereabouts; a new Ford cost $500; a refrigerator, $75. A quarter would buy a pound of round steak, butter, or coffee; six quarts of milk; a haircut; a ticket to your favorite movie; a Thanksgiving Day turkey dinner with all the trimmings at Emporia's Broadview Hotel; or a barrel of oil.[2]

For federal income-tax purposes, only twenty Kansans in 1933 reported net incomes greater than $40,000. Salaries in the $2,000 to $3,000 range were considered substantial. The governor's salary was $3,750 (reduced as an economy measure from $5,000); that of other major state officers, about $3,000. An unofficial "minimum wage" for unskilled labor averaged about twenty-five cents an hour, or $600 a year.[3]

Legislative appropriations for state government for fiscal 1933 were only $9 million. In 1933, the first year of the state income tax, about $0.5 million came in from that source.[4] Ronald Finney's antisocial activities, then, represented nearly 15 percent of the state's total appropriations and over twice the revenue derived from the state income tax.

In a previous incarnation as a biologist, I published under the name of Robert S. Bader. In this work I have chosen to use my full name, Robert Smith Bader. I have done so for two reasons. The middle name—Smith—is my mother's family name, and since the Smiths were kinfolk of the Finneys, it seemed particularly fitting that I use it. The second reason derives from what I believe to be an especially astute observation of mine—namely, that one's chances of success as a historian improve markedly if one but writes under three full names. I offer in evidence Frederick Jackson Turner, Henry Steele Commager, Walter Prescott Webb, and Arthur Schlesinger, Jr.

I am indebted to many institutions and individuals for helping to make this work possible. The University of Missouri–St. Louis (UMSL) approved a sabbatical leave for me in 1978/79, during which time I completed the bulk of the research. The Graduate School of that institution helped to defray part of the cost of the research. The research was carried out primarily in the Kansas Collection of the Spencer Research Library, University of Kansas, and at the Kansas State Historical Society, Topeka. The curators and librarians of both institutions were unfailingly competent, cheerful, and helpful. The Department of History, University of Kansas, made an office available to me and otherwise extended many considerations and courtesies during 1978/79. I interviewed more than one hundred Kansans, including Governor Landon, during the course of the work. A very special thanks is extended to them, and most particularly to Kathrine White of Emporia, with whom I spent many pleasant and edifying hours. From the outset I had the sage advice and strong encouragement of two of Kansas' most eminent historians, Donald R. McCoy of the University of Kansas and Homer E. Socolofsky of Kansas State University. Jean Kennedy of Washburn University very kindly furnished copies of useful materials from the Library of Congress, as did Patricia Michaelis from the Kansas State Historical Society. Several members of the faculty of the UMSL College of Arts and Sciences contributed useful suggestions and responded promptly to my quest for specific information. Kathrine White, Eugene Murray (UMSL), and Thomas Averill (Washburn University) read several chapters and offered valuable substantive and stylistic criticism. My deep appreciation goes to the typists, Theresa Orso Smythe and Barbara Harrington, and most especially to my secretary, Anne Butler, whose interest has been unflagging. Finally, I would like to thank my entire family for their aid and encouragement during the course of the work, especially my wife, Joan Larson Bader, who listened to more Finney stories than any mortal should be subjected to in a dozen lifetimes.

1

The Summer of 1933

IT WAS THE SUMMER of 1933. The Great Depression held the nation, especially its heartland, in a viselike grip. Fully one-third of the people found themselves unemployed or severely underemployed as the national economic machine nearly ground to a halt. The New Deal medicine prescribed by the recently inaugurated Franklin Roosevelt had only lately and barely begun to revive the critically ill patient. Surprisingly, revolution was not in the air. Something more akin to resignation, undergirded by a grim and defiant determination to survive, marked the public mood. That greatest irony of the human spirit filled the countryside—the feeling of guilt engendered within those most victimized by the crushing events. "Times are hard," lamented William Allen White, the Sage of Emporia, "bitter hard."[1]

Since it was so difficult to make an honest living, some imaginative fellows had turned to other means of earning their livelihoods. As an escape from the harsh controlling realities, the good folks of the southern plains read with eager fascination the accounts of the escapades and escapes of such as Al Capone, John Dillinger, Harvey Bailey, and those all-American sweethearts Bonnie and Clyde. On Decoration Day, eleven convicts had forced their way out of the Kansas State Penitentiary, taking the warden and two guards as hostages. Convict Frank Nash and four police officers lay slain in the aftermath of the Kansas City Union Station massacre in mid June. Kansas had been hit by the greatest wave of bank robberies in its seventy-two-year history. In the first six months of the year, forty-one bank holdups had yielded a total of over $150,000. The culprits, with their loot, usually made a clean break, heading straight for the secluded haven afforded by the rugged hills of northern Oklahoma.[2]

The weather was bad and getting worse. The plains states had suffered about halfway through a six-year period of cruel heat and drought, with the torridly hot summers of 1934–36 and the attendant dust storms yet to come. And in ironic counterpoint, devastating spring floods frequently inundated the flood-plain crops on the most fertile land of the region.[3]

IN THE GREAT AND SOVEREIGN STATE of Kansas, Governor Alfred Mossman Landon enjoyed a few days of well-deserved rest and relaxation at midsummer after a hectic, but most successful, legislative session earlier in the year. That the forty-six-year-old Landon was in the Statehouse at all was a minor miracle. Like the phoenix, he had risen from the ashes of the bitter defeat in the 1930 Republican primary of incumbent Governor Clyde Reed, whom he had served as campaign manager. Landon had even had to suffer the ignominy of being rejected as precinct committeeman in his own hometown of Independence. The Democratic candidate, Harry Woodring, had nosed out the victor in the Republican primary, Frank ("Chief") Haucke, in a photo-finish general election that fall of 1930—the most controversial gubernatorial contest in Kansas history. The goat-gland charlatan, Dr. John R. Brinkley, ran a disturbingly close third as a write-in candidate. In the 1932 primary, Landon recovered to run successfully as a "harmony" candidate for the badly divided Republicans. The campaign featured Alf's "common as an old shoe" approach, which often found him—in a slouchy old hat and well-used oil-field boots—accepting a cigarette from the nearest obliging citizen at rallies in courthouse towns the length and breadth of the state. Bucking the national Democratic flood tide, he edged out Woodring—with Brinkley again scaring the pants off both of them—to become the only Republican governor elected west of the Hudson River that year.[4]

Through sage counseling and the deft timing of patronage appointments, Landon had been able to guide a record proportion of his major proposals through the legislature, even though the Republican majority in each house was, for Kansas, uncharacteristically small. In a rare spirit of cooperation fathered by the economic emergency of the day, legislators on both sides of the aisle laid aside partisan and factional disputes in order to work together to produce a series of measures aimed principally at governmental economy and tax reduction. In response to the governor's plea "to do away with waste, extravagance, duplication and unnecessary service," direct appropriations were pared almost 25 percent, state and local governmental payrolls were cut 10 to 40 percent, and taxes were decreased by upwards of $20 million. "Let us cut out the red tape," Landon told the legislature, ". . . and see that the state receives honest values for every dollar spent. Let economy be the watchword." He had taken a very special satisfaction in putting Kansas' finances—which included the municipal bonds of its several governmental units—on a sound basis. His pet measure—the cash-basis law—required that local units immediately refund (convert) all outstanding obligations into bonds and that, subsequently, no debts of any nature whatsoever could be obligated unless there were cash in hand or specific approval from the voters.[5] "If we have succeeded in keeping public spending down," Landon later remarked, "it is chiefly because Kansans have a passion for paying their bills and in not spending that which they do not have."[6]

The governor had kept the fiscal ship of state afloat during the national banking crisis for a dramatic seventy-two-hour sleepless period, during which he refused to honor the request of the federal comptroller of the currency that banks in Kansas be closed, thus necessitating the national bank holiday that began on March 6. Consequently, the first press release of that national moratorium was datelined Topeka, not Washington, D.C.[7] But Landon's most poignant experience came in listening to the pathetic stories of the never-ending stream of determined job seekers. "The tragic part about it," he wrote to a friend a month after the election, "is that I am able to take care of only such a small fraction of those who asked me to. I lie awake nights worrying and thinking of the pitiful stories I hear everyday—of men in middle age begging for a job in order to keep them off the county this winter."[8]

During this crisis, the governor—no less than the president at the national level—attempted to lead the people, to assuage their despair, to heal their wounds, and to point the way out of the wilderness. If Landon was not always sure whither he and the people tended, he was always and forever sure that faith in hard work, frugality, and respect for the law would deliver them all ultimately to the Promised Land. Thus, at the end of his first six months as chief executive, though he was something less than a charismatic charmer at the lectern or an electrifying spellbinder on the stump, Landon emerged as an honest, hard-headed, no-nonsense businessman who had put Kansas government on a solid pay-as-you-go basis while all the world was going to hell in a handbasket, down the road of deficit spending.[9]

Never have intoxicating beverages, or the absence thereof, been far from the center of the psyche of puritanical Kansas; the summer of '33 was no exception. Kansas had been settled in the territorial days of the mid nineteenth century principally by northern European Protestants, most of whom were fervent opponents of slavery and zealous prohibitionists in equal proportion. Its early prohibitionary laws were later tightened to produce a state as "dry" as its recurrent summer droughts.[10] A mixture of joyous cries and anguished screams filled the air in mid July when the Kansas Supreme Court decided that the state's prohibitionary laws did not clearly define 3.2 beer as an intoxicating beverage. The high tribunal left it up to each local court to establish the status of beer in its community. The thirsty looked hopeful, bootleggers scowled, and confusion reigned.[11]

Primary responsibility for enforcement of the Kansas liquor laws rested with the attorney general. Since 1930, that position had been filled by the rotund, easygoing Roland Boynton of Emporia. Boynton had the good fortune to be both the cousin and the protégé of Kansas' most famous and respected citizen, William Allen White. After the 3.2 beer decision, rumors surfaced of plans to flood Kansas with large amounts of the brew from neighboring states, rumors that were disturbing enough to the conscientious attorney general who had become the darling of the WCTU and the Anti-Saloon League. When he wasn't worrying about the liquor statutes, Boynton busied himself with rigidly enforcing the anti-slot-machine laws, ousting wayward sheriffs and other erring public officials from office, and generally doing his imperturbable, good-natured best to make the commonwealth a fit place for decent folk to live and rear their children.[12] Boynton enjoyed the respect of most Kansans, but with no one was his stock higher than with his famous cousin. Just a year earlier—in an adulatory outburst stemming less from detached objectivity than from familial pride—Mr. White had declared that "Kansas hasn't had for twenty years an attorney general with more intellectual and moral equipment than Roland Boynton."[13]

Toward the end of July the dieting attorney general made plans to visit his mother in southern California for two weeks. The day before he packed his moral and intellectual equipment and headed west, Boynton received a timely visit in his Statehouse office from his long-time Emporia friend, the bond broker Ronald Finney. Finney plunked down $700 in crisp new $20 bills on Boynton's desk, which, he solemnly declared, represented the latest profit on Boynton's recent $400 investment in the commodity market. The grateful attorney general thanked him kindly and instructed him to let ride the $1,000 that remained in the account, in anticipation of future profits. How fortunate he was to have an old friend like Ronald Finney, who was just like family, so knowledgeable about the market that he could virtually guarantee tidy profits, which came in especially handy just a few months after a "voluntary" 10 percent salary cut. And how thoughtful it was of Finney to supply the extra cash on the eve of one's summer vacation.

Ronald always seemed to be giving, never asking or taking for himself. After dutifully filing with the Kansas Supreme Court for a rehearing in the beer case, a self-satisfied and relaxed Rolie Boynton—proudly sporting a thinner waistline and a fatter wallet—caught the Santa Fe's Grand Canyon Limited on the afternoon of July 26 and headed west to golden California.[14]

State Treasurer Tom Boyd had just returned from his annual vacation at the Colorado ranch of his very close associate Ronald Finney. Boyd, a flatlander, never tired of recounting the delights of the ranch out near Lake City—the bracing Colorado air, the fish-laden streams, and the majestic stony mountains. The fact that someone else picked up most of the tab didn't hurt either. A Topeka native, Boyd had risen in middle age to become one of the most popular and powerful politicians in recent history around the courthouse and the Statehouse, having been reelected again and again with huge pluralities. A valedictorian of the good-old-boy school of politics, Tom hugely enjoyed an occasional libation and a night out with the boys. Financially hard pressed, he hadn't taken very kindly to the "voluntary" salary reduction that had been pressed by the bachelor Governor Woodring in 1932. "I'm no bachelor," Boyd protested, ". . . I have six children to support, and I don't get an automobile and a mansion to live in."[15]

Tom Boyd and Ronald Finney had been intimate friends for some time. As a bond broker, Finney was a frequent visitor in and around the fiscal agency—that part of the Treasurer's Office which handled bond and coupon payments—and the treasurer's vault, which housed the bonds put up for security by banks that received deposits of public funds. The office staff had been instructed to give him and his subordinates every accommodation. In recent weeks some unkind rumors had been whispered in the Statehouse corridors about possible irregularities involving the treasury. The treasurer, it is true, had had to be firm on several occasions with unauthorized outsiders, including federal agents and bank examiners, who had tried to gain access to the vault. But this was nothing to worry about really, and besides, it was the good old summertime, when Boyd spent every free hour on his recently purchased 200-acre farm just outside of Topeka. Despite his financial problems and the salary cut, he had recently been able to buy two farms with money from "investments" that Finney had made for him on the commodity market.[16] That Ronald Finney certainly was a character—a great party man and a financial genius to boot—a freewheeling, charismatic crony who could sure do you a lot of good.

On the second floor of the Statehouse, in a suite of rooms directly across the corridor from the state treasury, the state auditor, with a staff of fifteen, carried out his several functions. His duties included certifying new bond issues, recording bond and coupon payments, issuing checks and warrants, housing bond transcripts in his vault—in other words, serving generally as the state's fiscal accounting center. Now forty-four years old, Will J. French had first been elected state auditor in 1926 and had thrice been reelected by comfortable margins. His name had arisen early as a possible opponent to Landon in the 1932 primary, but nothing had come of that. A strong family man, the teetotaler French held to rigid personal standards of morality.

Since his staff included his brother-in-law, the son and daughter-in-law of his private attorney in his hometown of St. John, and other long-time hometown friends and residents, French obviously believed with some fervor in the redeeming virtues of blood and geography when staffing his office. The auditor had had enough of the Democrats by 1932 and, though he was a conservative, had pledged his full support to the progressive gubernatorial candidate in the fall campaign. Over the years his detractors had accused him of manipulating the release of fiscal data in a manner calculated to bring maximum damage to his opponents—that is, of running a bureau of political statistics. To some extent French took the criticisms as a compliment. "I probably had as much to do with your election as any other one person," he wrote to Landon in self-congratulation after the election.[17]

French did not share in the esteem that his fellow state officers felt for Ronald Finney. He and Finney hadn't liked each other for at least two years, though, on frequent occasion, bond matters brought them together. But if the boss didn't hold much truck with Finney, the same could not be said of French's subordinates. The former assistant auditor Joe Voorhees had been as helpful as he could be, for on more than one occasion he had returned on a Sunday from out of town just to let Finney into the Auditor's Office to conduct what Finney claimed was urgent business. Finney tried to express his appreciation by asking Voorhees's opinion on the Federal Reserve's fiscal policy and other esoteric financial subjects. When Voorhees, though flattered, pleaded ignorance of such matters, Finney showed his gratitude in a more orthodox and tangible fashion. Finney's approach to Voorhees's successor, Ray Hardin, was even more direct: Hardin received an apartment rent-free in a building owned by Finney, as well as gratis vacations at the Colorado ranch. When French made an emergency call to his assistant in early August, urging him home forthwith, Hardin and his family were at Lake City enjoying the mountain air.[18]

DOWN IN EMPORIA, the "Athens of Kansas," the weather had been so hot and dry that even the crabgrass was dying. The "longest tax delinquency list ever" in Lyon County had recently been published. But the 12,980 denizens of the self-proclaimed intellectual and moral capital of Kansas had plenty besides the weather and taxes to occupy their minds. After the Supreme Court's decision on beer, the open selling of the brew in the driest town in the state had led to a quick arrest. The subsequent trial resulted in a not-guilty verdict by the man's peers, which was announced to a "crowded and excited" courtroom. The animated townspeople could think of little else. The *Gazette* reported, with a disapproving frown, that "night life in Emporia . . . last evening was a dizzy whirl, what with half a dozen stores selling 3.2 beer."[19] One chagrined citizen sheepishly acknowledged that the noise he had been hearing in the nether regions of his car, which he feared might be differential trouble, had turned out to be an empty 3.2 bottle rolling around in the trunk.[20]

Two other raging moral issues had lately been troubling the Emporia mind: the showing of movies on Sunday and the use of the high-school gym for school dances. The Sunday-movie question had become an open town controversy in 1931. A march on city hall in 1932 by a group of outraged burghers that included the town's two leading citizens, W. A. White and W. W. Finney, had been followed by a negative vote on the Sunday-movie proposition. An obstinate theater manager, however, continued the Sunday movies and was promptly arrested and rearrested for his trouble; by October the number of separate warrants stood at fifteen. The issue of high-school dances had been cussed and discussed throughout the academic year, but in the spring, evil forces carried the day. Emporia High School held its first official dance in mid April, 1933. This could be counted as progress compared with the moral milieu of a generation earlier, when the county attorney had asked the school superintendent for a list of the boys who had been caught smoking, indicating that he intended to prosecute them for violating the state law of Kansas.[21]

Some commentators on the Kansas scene expressed mock horror at the goings on in "poor ole Empory." Jack Harris, in the *Hutchinson News*, observed: "Road houses seem to be springing up in Kansas. But no one expected the hell-joints to invade the sacred precincts of the Athens of Kansas, where Sunday movies are banned and the higher arts flourish."[22]

The excitement created by the sight of two young women pedaling their bikes down Commercial Street in shorts had almost been equaled in the spring by the daylight holdup of the town's largest bank, the first bank robbery ever to occur in Emporia. The *Gazette* said not to worry—it was a good antidote to the long, depressive winter. The sessions at the kiddies' wading pool at Peter Pan Park, as well as the storytelling hours, took eight separate one-hour periods per day to accommodate the segregation by age,

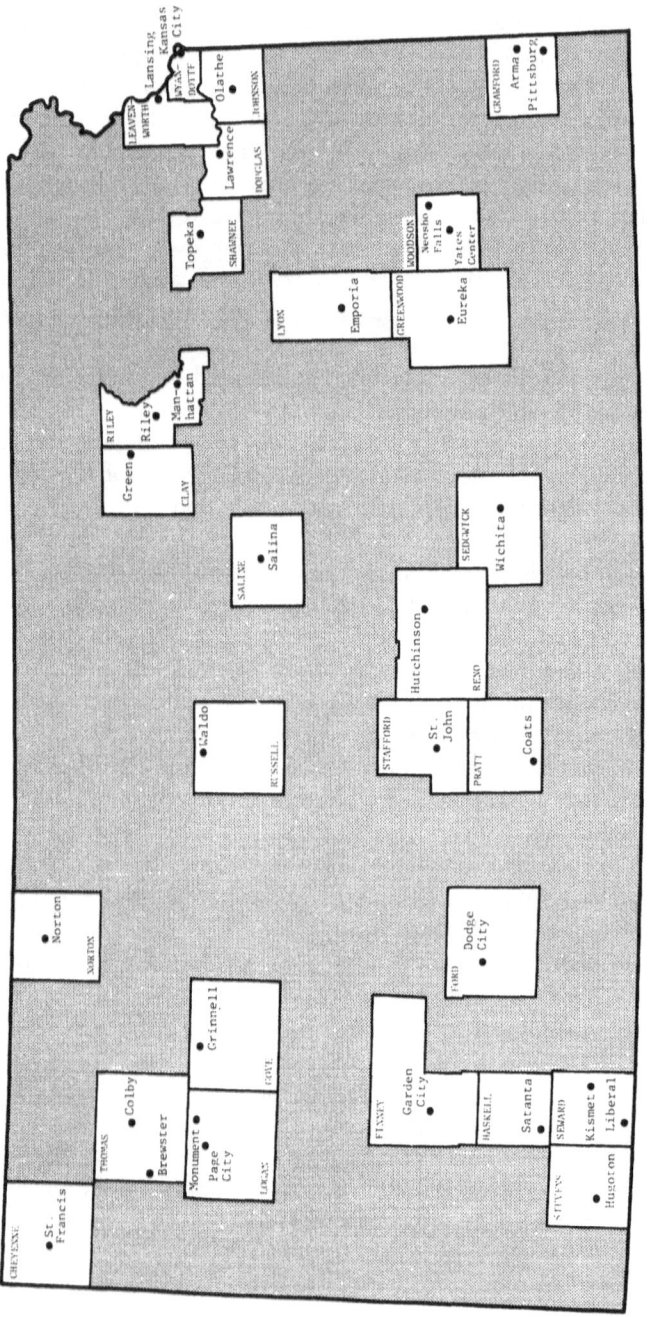

Map of Kansas, showing sites that played a prominent role in the bond scandal (Lewis A. Armstrong)

by sex, and by race. (Blacks and Mexicans were allowed to attend the same session to avoid the necessity of twelve separate daily periods.) In 1931, when that wading pool had been dedicated in the park that the Whites had donated, it drew to the ceremonies the vice-president of the United States, a U.S. senator, a U.S. congressman, a U.S. circuit judge, and the governor. This led a local wag to comment that had it been a full-size swimming pool, President Hoover and King George would surely have been there.[23]

If business was bad in most establishments, it was otherwise in the courts of justice. Judge Lon McCarty, of the district court of Lyon County, sadly proclaimed that lawsuits were on the increase in these stressful times. Without trying to make a pun, the good judge solemnly declared that "this is a place beset with trials and tribulations in times like these."[24] But the judge, Lyon County, and the state of Kansas hadn't seen anything yet.

All was not gloom and despair across the troubled land, however. The bright glow of eternal optimism could still be found in the rural precincts. Twenty miles east of Emporia the bustling community of Lebo, population 564, proudly crowed on the Fourth of July that now that the lights had been installed at their flying field, they had, without doubt, one of the finest, most modern airports to be found in all these United States.[25]

BENIGNLY PRESIDING over the local Emporia scene, recorder and interpreter, if not the master, of all he surveyed, reigned the cherubic William Allen White. Hale and hearty, though somewhat mellowed at the age of sixty-five, the jolly but wily editor still commanded the *Gazette,* which he had long since made into the most renowned and oft-quoted small-town daily on the planet. An admixture of liberal idealism and hard-headed political practicality, White had become the undisputed national champion and spokesperson for middle America, the middle class, and the middle way. He continued vigorously to pursue his lifelong threefold career as editor, author, and politician. On a given day the White typewriter might produce a caustic diatribe warning of the inherent danger in the likes of Doc Brinkley, a poignant vignette vividly portraying his beloved Kansas, a feisty polemic touting the virtues of hometown Emporia vis-à-vis Topeka or Atchison, or a whimsical piece extolling the redeeming social value of eating papaws. He continued to use his impressive vocabulary and his witty, vigorous style—which he no longer employed to write fiction as he had during the first two decades of the century—to create magazine articles and nonfictional books that rolled from the Emporia word factory at a rate that would be considered prodigious for one who was half his age.[26]

White continued to be what he had been for the past thirty years: the

William Allen White (Bernard Hoffman, *Life Magazine*, copyright 1937 by Time, Inc.)

most powerful single personage on the Kansas political scene. Though the only elective political office he had ever held was as precinct committeeman of the Fourth Ward, he had become over the decades the self-styled leader of the forces of goodness and light—that is, the liberal or progressive faction of the Kansas Republican party—as it jousted every two years with the forces of darkness and evil—that is, the conservative or standpat faction. There was no more personal political campaigning after his whirlwind anti–Ku Klux Klan gubernatorial race of a decade earlier, but he continued to participate actively in the affairs of the party at the state and local as well as national levels. And in his spare time, the irrepressible editor tried to help Alf run the state of Kansas. This lifetime of service to God, society, and man had produced a rich harvest of well-deserved honors, which were now being showered on the appreciative Sage.[27] (Nearly fifty years later his bigger-than-life statue could be found in an honored niche in the Statehouse rotunda. That honor, coming from his fellow Kansans, would have pleased him more than his Pulitzer Prizes or his honorary degree from Harvard.

He shares his place in the pantheon of Kansas gods with Amelia Earhart, Arthur Capper, and Dwight David Eisenhower.)

IN LATE MAY, Mr. and Mrs. White, accompanied by Mary Jane Finney, the nineteen-year-old daughter of Mr. and Mrs. W. W. Finney and sister of Ronald, left for a European tour of several months' duration. That the elder Whites had asked young Mary Jane to join them on the long trip was not surprising in view of the longstanding and intimate association of Emporia's two leading families. (One could speculate that Mary Jane represented a surrogate for Mary White, their seventeen-year-old daughter who had been tragically killed in a fall from her horse in 1921. Her obituary, appearing in the *Gazette* the day after her funeral, entitled "Mary White," has proved to be the most popular of all of White's writings.)[28] The front door of the *Gazette* opened directly across Merchant Street from Mr. Finney's telephone company. Mr. White and Mr. Finney had for years been closely associated with virtually every major civic endeavor in Emporia. Both were staunch pillars of the Congregational Church, the town's wealthiest, whose rolls included many of Emporia's leading citizens—direct descendants of the ardent, puritanical New Englanders who had fought during the 1850s to make Kansas a Free State. Finney tended to follow White's lead in politics, preferring to remain a power behind the unofficial White throne, which the publisher had built for himself over the years.[29]

After a bumpy beginning, which stemmed from a difference of opinion over telephone-company policies, the two leaders had become fast friends. They sometimes traveled about the state together on political business. On one such occasion they had had a one-car accident out in a remote spot in the Flint Hills, and both had ended up "looking at the stars through the wheels." Finney, who had been asked to serve as one of the pallbearers at Mary White's funeral, was described as "W. W. Finney, her friend" in the famous obituary. "When I use the term, 'my friend' with Mr. Finney," White had written several years earlier, "I mean something real and close and intimate."[30]

Not content to be just a close friend of Finney's, White had become his sponsor as well. The celebrated editor rarely missed an opportunity to tout the virtues of his friend, to recommend him for an important position, or publicly to laud his character and devotion to mankind. Only recently, in a mid-June radio broadcast from London, after describing the machinations at the International Economic Conference that he was covering, White grandly declared to the national NBC audience that "if Warren Finney . . . could put the London telephone system in as good condition as he has the

Emporia telephone system, then he would have done as much for England as Columbus did for America."[31]

The Whites and the Finneys had essentially become "family" to each other, socializing in an almost infinite series of public and private events. Sallie White and Mabel Finney had worked closely together for decades on innumerable civic, church, and YMCA projects, doing their kind-hearted best for the unemployed, the needy, and the downtrodden, as became the spouses of the town's two leading progressives. A current project found them overseeing the canning of vegetables for the unemployed families of Emporia ("Wanted: Beets to can for our neighbors who will need them next winter.... Call ... Mrs. W. A. White or Mrs. W. W. Finney").[32]

When Mr. White went to Europe, he left the paper in the capable hands of his thirty-three-year-old son, William Lindsay White. "Young Bill," as

William L. ("Young Bill") White (Kansas State Historical Society)

he was always known around Emporia and throughout Kansas, had transferred to Harvard after a year at the University of Kansas and had graduated in 1924. When he returned to Emporia, he held positions of increasing responsibility on the *Gazette* for the next ten years. After the death in 1932 of Walter Hughes, the long-term financial manager of the paper, Bill had been promoted to business manager.[33]

There was a time not so long before when the town hadn't been so sure about Bill. Back in the twenties, during his coonskin-coat phase, when he affected the manners and speech of Harvard, Emporians doubted that he had the sense that God had given geese, and some were bold enough to say so, even to Mr. White. But that conventional wisdom begrudgingly had to be changed as Bill came to manifest the sound business acumen and caustic editorial wit of his father. His occasional unsigned editorials, which often were assumed to have been written by his father, began to evince more and more the inimitable White stamp. Bill's personal identity crisis and his penchant to disdain the parochial Kansas scene both decreased markedly after he was elected to the Kansas House of Representatives in 1930. A leader in obtaining passage of the state income-tax bill, he had had the opportunity to witness at close range the activities of his friend Ronald Finney, who had lobbied his pet bond bill through that legislative session.[34]

Only two years apart in age, Bill White and Ronald Finney had known each other from their early teens, having been thrown together at innumerable family gatherings. Though of markedly different temperaments and backgrounds, they had developed a genuine fondness for each other. The serious and studious young White was given to discoursing on the momentous political, social, and economic events of the day. As a teenager, he had accompanied his father to the Versailles Conference at the close of World War I, had studied French with a tutor in Paris, and over the years had listened to many famous personages holding forth on socioeconomic conditions in the White's home. For his part, the spirited young Finney bent the ear of his impressionable younger friend about how rich he was going to become and about how quickly and easily he was going to do it. Ronald had only been to Neosho Falls, Kansas, not to Paris, France, and his reading hadn't often gone much beyond the newspaper level. The talk in his home tended to phone companies, banks, taxes, mortgages, and money, money, money.[35]

In 1931 Bill had married a young reporter for *Time,* Kathrine Klinkenberg, a Kansas girl who had been born in Cawker City and reared in Ottawa. Bill and Kathrine didn't run much with the Junior Chamber of Commerce crowd that the Ronald Finneys socialized with, though they did see young Finney and his wife with some frequency. The younger

Whites preferred to stay closer to home, reading and discussing books, perhaps lighting a furtive cigarette or having an occasional drink (the elder Whites wholeheartedly disapproved), and asking themselves how they could be so unfortunate as to be stuck in the dullest town in the U.S.A. Ronald Finney helped to brighten the scene though, for with Ronald one was never bored. How could you be bored by someone who would climb through a hospital-room window to deliver a jar of caviar and a bottle of champagne in a bucket of ice? That wasn't, after all, your standard Kansas fare. And so Kathrine came to "adopt" Ronald in the same way that the rest of the White family had done.[36]

IT HAD BEEN nearly thirty years since Warren Finney, as the new owner of the Emporia Telephone Company, had moved the fifty miles up the Neosho River from the village of Neosho Falls. A pioneer in the telephone business in Kansas, Finney, now aged fifty-nine, had acquired control of a string of small-town phone companies in southeastern Kansas; had invested prudently in land, cattle, and the stock market; and after World War I had bought banks in Emporia and Neosho Falls. Hard work and sharp bargaining had paid off so handsomely that at the time of the March bank holiday he could list his total assets at $800,000. "W. W.," as his close friends called him, was over six-feet tall, handsome, immaculately groomed, confident to the edge of cockiness, and self-destructively proud. Pious and strait-laced, he abstained from alcohol, tobacco, dancing, and card playing, though he could cuss a bit when provoked. "His constructive imagination as our small town talent goes," Mr. White raved, "was genius."[37]

To White and the town—indeed to all of Kansas—the accomplished and moneyed Mr. Finney had come to represent the very quintessence of what a successful country-town businessman should be and do. He had unstintingly placed his considerable energy and resources at the service of the civic, charitable, and religious concerns of his hometown and his state. "When Emporia, or Kansas, wants anything done that requires energy and ability and enthusiasm," exclaimed former governor Clyde Reed, "Warren Finney is almost sure to be drafted as one of the men to do the job. . . . He is one of the most democratic citizens we have. Burdened with widespread activities of his own he never fails to respond to the public need. . . . Warren W. Finney . . . would be included in any list of the dozen most useful citizens of Kansas."[38]

Finney had been married for over thirty-five years to Mabel Tucker of Eureka. Mabel's father had founded Eureka, and her family continued to be the town's most prominent—owning the Eureka Bank and having acquired extensive land and cattle holdings in the area. A tall, intelligent, somewhat severe woman, Mabel Tucker had both puritanical and aristocratic inclinations. The marriage proved to be a most sound partnership, withstanding, as it was destined to do, the most severe of human tests. Just two years earlier, the senior Finneys had moved from their comfortable home on State Street to a twenty-five-room English Tudor-style mansion on Twelfth Street, the largest and most pretentious home in Emporia. In mid July the Finneys' bank at Neosho Falls was robbed, and the culprits made off with the safe, which contained the bank's charter and an undisclosed amount of cash. Preoccupied with his farms, his prize Holstein herds—and his son Ronald—Finney told his friends not to worry, that everything "was covered by insurance."[39]

Ronald Finney had returned to Emporia in the late twenties after spending most of the decade running that same Neosho Falls bank. After a year of desultory dabbling in this and that, he had launched a meteoric career in the bond-brokerage business, which made him and his subordinates well known throughout the state. At the time of the bank moratorium he had gone on a wild buying spree in land, cattle, and commodities, fully confident that inflation and prosperity lurked just around the corner. "If you have any money," he confided to the Boyntons, "you better buy something. There is no time like this to do it."[40]

Pyramiding his profits from daring but well-informed speculation on the commodity futures market, he had become by this fateful summer, at thirty-four, the most talked-about young man in the state and, arguably, its richest. His headquarters—a suite of rooms located on the fifth floor of the Jayhawk Hotel in Topeka—included both working and living quarters. He continued to maintain his official residence and his family in their large home in Emporia. Overseeing a staff that varied from twelve to fifteen was Finney's first lieutenant, the dapper thirty-one-year-old Leland Caldwell. Finney's rooms had developed a reputation of being the most exciting night spot in Topeka, if not in all of Kansas, which perhaps wasn't saying so very much. On winter evenings, especially during the legislative sessions, the Jayhawk suite was often crowded with many of the leading political and business figures of the state. Nearly everyone who was anyone (and some who weren't) showed up there at one time or another—excepting, of course, the saintly Senator Arthur Capper—for a little libation, a fast game of "keen-ball," some juicy political gossip, or a promising "inside" tip on the market.[41]

The six-foot-tall Finney was given to fleshiness, having had a weight problem since childhood. His brown eyes conveyed an explosive combination of high nervous energy and pure devilment. Full of daring like his father, the dark-haired financial highflier had the instincts and nerve of a professional gambler. He had inherited his father's confidence and authoritative temperament, though not his father's polish. There remained something of the small-town rowdy about him—a good-natured, gregarious bull in the Kansas bond shop. Ronald was a born salesman, of the true ice-box-to-eskimos type. An old Neosho Falls farmer admitted that "whatever Ronald was sellin', we were buyin'." A keen though untutored student of human behavior and motivation, the likable younger Finney developed a genius at convincing others to do his bidding. Unfortunately, something that Mr. White had once said about Huey Long would prove true for Ronald: having been through the human heart with a lantern, he knew its dark places all too well.[42]

Ronald had been married for ten years to his childhood sweetheart, Winifred Wiggam. The chic, slim-figured "Win," who was from a prominent Emporia family, was one of the best-looking young women in town. Extremely popular with the more affluent crowd of young marrieds, Ronald and Winifred threw frequent and lively parties, sometimes with lobster and champagne as the chief attractions. They were "lavish spenders by Kansas standards," and their popularity hadn't suffered any in the early summer when a lighted tennis court had been completed behind their house. Lately there had been gay trips with friends and their children down to Eureka to enjoy private performances of the 101 Ranch Wild West Show, complete with cowboys, buffaloes, and five elephants, which Ronald had bought as a lark in the spring and which now occupied star billing at the Greenwood County Fair.[43]

DURING THE WEEK of July 31 Governor Landon combined business with pleasure as he toured the CCC camps of southeast Kansas, getting in a little fishing and a few games of pitch on the side. In the late afternoon of August 2 (a Wednesday) the governor rolled into Emporia with his sixteen-year-old daughter, Peggy Anne, at the wheel of his 1932 coupe. They headed straight for 310 West Twelfth, where they and the younger Whites enjoyed a splendid dinner, featuring Mrs. Finney's veal roast with spinach and browned potatoes. After dinner, Alf, W. W., and Young Bill chatted amiably about oil wells, state politics, and the limited efficacy of bank examiners.[44]

On a torrid afternoon two days later, a group of veteran newspaper reporters, who were assigned to the Statehouse beat, half-heartedly made the rounds of the state offices for scraps of news. (The journalists included W. G. Clugston, *Kansas City Journal-Post;* Cecil Howes, *Kansas City Star;*

A. L. ("Dutch") Shultz, *Topeka State Journal;* and Clif Stratton, *Topeka Capital.*) The attorney general was still on vacation. The apprehensive auditor nervously assured them that he had nothing newsworthy to report. They ended up in the Governor's Office, bantering good-naturedly about their relative skills as poker players and making arrangements to accompany him on his inspection trip that weekend to the National Guard encampment at Fort Riley.[45]

On Monday morning, August 7, Landon returned to his office, refreshed by the convivial festivities at Fort Riley and the cordial hospitality of Adjutant General McLean. His 9 A.M. appointment was with the United States district attorney for Kansas, Sardius Mason ("Sard") Brewster. Landon knew nothing of Brewster's purpose. What he would hear that morning from the federal official would shake him and the state to their foundations and would alter the course of Kansas history.

2

The Bubble Bursts

SARD BREWSTER quickly briefed the governor on what he knew and what he suspected. During a routine examination of the National Bank of Topeka in late June, federal examiners had become suspicious of a series of Kansas municipal bonds totaling over $100,000, which had been placed in the bank by Ronald Finney as collateral for a loan. At the examiners' request a local bond broker had checked the list of serial numbers in the state Auditor's Office, and he had discovered that bonds of identical description were, according to the record, held in the state treasury for the state's School Fund Commission. The bank demanded that Finney remove the bonds, which he did forthwith, eventually selling them to brokerage houses in Chicago.

The bank examiners' report had passed through the bureaucratic channels in an orderly but unhurried fashion, arriving about mid July on the desk of the U.S. district attorney. Armed with photostatic copies of the questionable bonds, supplied by federal agents in Chicago, the Justice Department's investigators had attempted to gain entry into the vault of the state treasury to make a direct comparison. But treasurer Tom Boyd was having none of that. At the very hour of the Brewster-Landon meeting, Boyd was rebuffing the latest attempt by the federal investigators to gain entry to the vault. The investigators' initial suspicion was that Boyd—or someone else—had loaned Finney the bonds, or, less probably, that Finney had stolen them. Now they had come to believe that the bonds sold in Chicago were forgeries, though how this had been effected remained a mystery, since the originals had "Property of School Fund Commission" stamped on them in red ink and had never been in commercial channels.

THE GREAT KANSAS BOND SCANDAL

Sardius M. Brewster, United States district attorney *(Builders of Topeka)*

At that moment the possible forgeries appeared to total approximately $400,000.

Brewster told Landon that he had hoped to forestall arrests until the general outline of the case had become evident and until all the principals had been positively identified. However, since there was reason to believe that additional forgeries in substantial volume were being pushed out into the stream of commerce almost daily, he had reluctantly decided to lay the case before the governor and to request action at once. He urged the governor to take immediate steps while the Federal Bureau of Investigation continued to perfect its case.[1]

Governor Landon was shocked. The Finneys were, of course, his very good friends—he had eaten veal roast in their magnificent home just last Wednesday. And they were so close to the man he admired more than any other in this world, William Allen White. But Alf reacted instinctively—

and angrily. He had worked so very hard during the legislative session to put the finances of the state and its municipal units on a sound basis, thus ensuring that Kansas municipal bonds would be as sound as any in the country. All that was now threatened—and by his own friends! The temperature that sweltering August day hit 100° about noon, but Alf Landon's had reached the boiling point by 9:15 A.M.[2]

Landon immediately sent for Treasurer Boyd, then ordered him to permit the federal investigators to enter the vault at once and told him that he wanted an immediate and complete check on the bonds held by the School Fund Commission. An apprehensive Boyd, still stalling for time, coolly responded that the request would have to be presented to the School Fund commissioners for their approval. An angry Landon retorted: "That won't be necessary. I am issuing the order now and if you cannot see your way clear to grant it I shall put the school fund under martial law." Boyd blinked a couple of times, swallowed hard, and underwent a sudden change of heart. He reluctantly consented to Landon's demand.[3]

After a hurried conference with close advisors, including his legal counsel, the governor dictated a terse and urgent letter to the Shawnee County attorney, Lester Goodell:

> Information has come to me which seems to make it imperative that Ronald Finney of Emporia, Kansas be prosecuted at once for uttering forged municipal bonds. I therefore direct that you institute prosecution against the said Ronald Finney.[4]

The warrant charged Finney specifically with uttering (selling) $20,000 in Kansas City, Kansas, paving bonds, which were now owned by the School Fund. The charge comprised twenty counts, one for each $1,000 bond. A forgery charge had not been made, since the exact method of producing the illegal paper had yet to be determined. Minutes after Goodell had received the letter, a deputy sheriff found a deserted scene in Finney's quarters at the Jayhawk Hotel. There was abundant evidence of a hasty departure. Rumors floated that Finney had flown out of Topeka in one of his private planes after receiving a tip that a warrant was out for his arrest. Perhaps he had headed for the hills of Oklahoma or had gone south of the border to Mexico. But, in truth, no one knew, for no one had seen Ronald Finney around Topeka that afternoon.[5]

On Tuesday the total of known forgeries of municipal bonds had risen to $658,000, composed of two duplicate sets of eight issues, each totaling $329,000. One set was being held by Chicago brokers, the other set had been put up as security for public funds in the Finney banks at Emporia and Neosho Falls and the Tucker-owned bank at Eureka. Ironically, this latter set rested in the treasury vault, only a few feet from the original, and genuine, set that was owned by the state School Fund. Preliminary reports from the checking of the School Fund bonds, which Landon had ordered, had thus far turned up no bogus issues among those securities.[6]

Brewster met with some of the officials of the affected municipalities on Tuesday, as well as with worried representatives from the Chicago brokerage houses. In addition to two issues from Kansas City, Kansas, bonds from Johnson, Pratt, Stevens, Riley, and Russell counties and the city of Norton were involved. The forged instruments were pronounced to have been a first-class job of counterfeiting, with excellent printing and clever forging of the signatures. Auditor Will French volunteered that he couldn't be sure whether his signature on the bond certificate was forged or genuine.[7]

Ronald Finney surfaced on Tuesday. Accompanied by his father and O. R. ("Jack") Stites, an Emporia attorney and friend, the self-possessed young man arrived in Topeka early in the afternoon and went directly to the offices of the prominent legal firm of O'Neil and Hamilton. John D. M. Hamilton, a major Kansas political figure who was currently Republican

Ronald Finney at the time of his initial arrest
(Michelle Butler Breihan)

National Committeeman, had been the Finneys' principal attorney for years. Nervously announcing that he had decided not to represent his regular client in this particular case, Hamilton issued a statement, written by Ronald Finney:

> Yesterday afternoon [August 7], at the request of my father, I drove with my wife to Kansas City for a business conference with him and others which was held at the Kansas City club. . . .
>
> At 3 o'clock this morning my father learned of the issuance of the warrant and at that time advised the county authorities that I would be returned to the county attorney's office today, and after driving to Emporia, I voluntarily returned to Topeka for the purpose of allowing the county officers to serve any warrant or other process that may have been issued.
>
> I am not familiar with the charges which have been filed and so have no further statement to make at this time.[8]

After the reading of the statement, father and son, "quite composed but showing evidences of strain," strolled the few blocks to the Shawnee County Courthouse, where Ronald Finney was arraigned on a charge that included only ten of the original twenty counts. The county attorney's office explained that the full secretarial force had not yet been able to type out all the counts in the information. A stenographer in the office observed that it was the longest complaint she had ever typed. Finney pleaded not guilty, and the preliminary hearing was set for September 5. The $25,000 bond was made by the elder Finney, who listed his holdings at a "sound value" of $846,000. While the legalities were being dispensed with, the distraught father was heard to say to acquaintances: "My God—to think that I've raised a son like this." But he did manage to compose himself enough so that he could pridefully explain to reporters that reports of his son's stock-market losses had been greatly exaggerated. Earlier losses of $65,000, he claimed, had been offset by $250,000 in profits since January 1.[9]

An hour after Brewster and Boyd had left the Governor's Office on Monday morning, Landon had received an urgent call from Warren Finney. The alarmed Emporian told the governor that he had only heard about his son's problems a day or two before; that he had a private investigator in Chicago looking into the transactions with the brokerage houses; that he could assure him that there was not a thing wrong in the Treasurer's Office; that neither the state of Kansas nor anyone else would lose a dime, even if it made a pauper of him; and that Landon should take no drastic action until Finney could speak with him in person. Landon listened patiently, then told his good friend that he "would be glad to talk with him the next day."[10]

After the formalities of the arrest had been disposed of in early afternoon, Warren Finney headed toward the Statehouse to keep his appointment with the governor. Landon's aides paced nervously in the outer office as he patiently subjected himself to Finney's considerable persuasive powers. We may be sure that Finney pulled out all the stops in pleading for time to put his financial house in order. He prided himself on always being more than willing to help a friend in need, and of course, he expected reciprocation. But the die had been cast. Alf Landon, the consummate politician, wanted to help a political friend, especially an influential one like Finney, as much as any practical politician could. But this thing had gone too far; it was out in the open now. Topeka was crawling with federal agents. The people had responded with anger, even outrage, at the first disclosures in Tuesday morning's papers. Nothing could be done, not even for an old political workhorse and crony like Warren Finney. After a half hour or so, the dejected banker left the Governor's Office. Shortly thereafter, the governor ordered the bank commissioner to close the three Finney banks. Landon's aides heaved an audible sigh of relief.[11]

Preliminary checking quickly revealed that counterfeit securities abounded in the three Finney-controlled banks. The bank commissioner, H. W. Koeneke, directed that examiners take charge of the banks, accept no deposits, and stay in the banks constantly, sleeping there all night. Commissioner Koeneke and an assistant accompanied Warren Finney back to Emporia to begin checking the records at the Fidelity State and Savings Bank. Before going to the bank for an all-night session, the investigators enjoyed a chicken dinner at the Finney home. No need to eat that horrible restaurant food. You had to hand it to them—the Finneys were hospitable, all right.

Finney resolutely announced late Tuesday that he had the resources to guarantee that none of the depositors would lose a cent and that he expected to have the banks reopened shortly.[12] But after a day of checking in both the Emporia and the Neosho Falls banks, a disillusioned Koeneke announced that "they are in a mess."[13]

That night, on the Topeka radio station WIBW, Senator Arthur Capper and Governor Landon attempted to reassure the anxious public. The bond-forgery case and its implications for the state were discussed at length by the two political leaders. Landon assured his listeners that the alarming turn of events would be thoroughly investigated and that "the case would be sifted to the very bottom, no matter where it may lead or who it may strike."[14] Capper and the public seemed to be satisfied for the moment.

Governor Alf Landon, Senator Arthur Capper, and John D. M. Hamilton (Kansas State Historical Society)

ON MONDAY AFTERNOON a worried Tom Boyd had walked across the hall to the Auditor's Office and let off some steam about the machinations of his erstwhile pal Ronald Finney. Though Boyd and Will French had never been close politically or personally, the treasurer availed himself of the nearest shoulder to cry on.[15] French listened silently but impatiently for a while, and then told the loquacious treasurer that he should follow his lead and "shut your mouth and get an attorney."[16] On Tuesday an even more troubled Boyd had a long, on the record, interview with Clif Stratton of Arthur Capper's *Topeka Capital,* which appeared in Wednesday morning's paper:

> I can't understand it.... I loved and trusted him like a brother. And he lied to me. I used to sit in his office, and watch him talk over three telephones—Kansas City, Chicago and Washington—almost at once. He was such a fast worker. I never have seen his equal. I can't understand what happened. I trusted him and he lied to me.[17]

Boyd not only admitted that Finney had been a frequent and favored visitor to the state treasury, but he also went on to reveal the details of a complicated maneuver that had been engineered by Finney in late June.

The broker had persuaded Boyd to deposit $150,000 in state funds in the Eureka bank. He then had borrowed the funds in order to redeem a like amount of municipal bonds that the National Bank of Topeka had insisted he remove as a result of the examiners' queries. The bonds were then placed in the treasury as security for the $150,000 deposit. A few days later the resourceful Finney told Boyd that he could sell those bonds if Boyd would agree to let Finney take them to Chicago. Boyd not only agreed; he furnished, as protection, a Treasury Department assistant, who toted a gun. Finney promised to pay back the Eureka bank after the sale, and the bank, in turn, would return the state deposit to the accommodating treasurer. But Finney had neither paid the bank nor returned the bonds.[18] "I suppose he put the bonds he took to Chicago back, or part of them, but I am not certain," the confused and frightened Boyd told Stratton; "I don't know any more about those bonds than a year-old baby."[19]

Over his Wednesday-morning cup of coffee, Governor Landon read the Boyd statements in the *Capital* and immediately swung into action. He called the adjutant general, M. R. McLean, who was still with the National Guard at Fort Riley. Landon wanted McLean to come to Topeka at once. McLean protested that a major general was due at any moment to review his troops. Landon then obtained the name of a National Guard officer in Topeka and summoned him to the Statehouse on the double. He informed the officer, Captain Chester Thomas, that he was declaring martial law in the state treasury. He ordered Thomas to station himself at the door of the Treasurer's Office. A noncommissioned officer, whom Landon had called while waiting for Thomas to arrive, took up a post at the entrance to the treasury vault. The guardsmen were not to allow anyone to enter or leave the area without the specific authorization of Landon or his delegate, the state accountant.[20]

The flustered captain, scarcely understanding what it was all about, asked if the guardsmen should go home and put on their uniforms. "No," Landon responded; "go down and strap a couple of guns on your belt." The guardsmen were given to understand that under no circumstances whatsoever were they to leave their posts. But what about food? The governor said that he would have some sent in. And what about answering the calls of nature? the captain queried. He knew that Landon was serious when he crisply responded to the guardsmen: "[You'll have to] piss in your pants until you're relieved."[21]

When the captain showed up in Boyd's office, the treasurer questioned Landon's authority to place his office under martial law, adding that he didn't intend to surrender the office until after he had conferred with the

Martial law at the State Treasury. *Left to right,* the guards are Adjutant General M. R. McClean, state militia; Captain C. L. Thomas, Kansas National Guard; A. R. Jones, state accountant; and D. A. N. Chase, state budget director (*Kansas City Star*)

attorney general. However, he soon reversed that position and acquiesced in the placing of the guardsmen in his office.[22]

Landon then directed the state budget director, D. A. N. Chase, and the state accountant, A. R. Jones, to take their entire staffs of accountants and investigators into the treasury vault and to check every bond and record contained therein. Jones's assistants were recalled from all over the state to aid in the checking of $47 million in bonds deposited by about 250 agencies, public and private. Later that day, when the burglar alarm in the vault was tested to see if it worked, a man in the corridor exclaimed, "Lawdy, lawdy, ain't it a shame that thing didn't go off three or four years ago."[23]

That afternoon, Landon issued an executive order,[24] declaring martial law in the state treasury, and a formal statement explaining the unprecedented actions he had ordered that day:

> Mr. Boyd's statement [in the morning paper], if true, indicates that Mr. Boyd was either a party to permitting $150,000 of state bonds to be taken by Ronald Finney to Chicago for a purely personal transaction, or was a party to sending $150,000 of forged bonds to Chicago in the same transaction. It also appears from his statement that when

the bonds which he says he turned over to Finney to take to Chicago were not returned, he made no report and has not until this time made a report to me of this transaction....

The people of Kansas will not tolerate the action of the state treasurer in granting free access to his vaults [to] Mr. Finney while at the same time denying to representatives of the national government the right to make an investigation.[25]

When the adjutant general returned later that day, regular around-the-clock eight-hour shifts of uniformed and armed guardsmen were set up at the vault and at the door of the Treasurer's Office. The placing of the treasury under martial law, which was of dubious legality and was certainly unprecedented, had a profound effect on the people and on the financial institutions of the state. From that day forward—until only God knew when—the state fiscal agency was to cease payments on bonds and interest coupons of all bond issues made by Kansas' public bodies. Normally, all bonds and coupons of Kansas municipalities were paid through the fiscal agency in the Treasurer's Office. The local municipality then reimbursed the treasurer. Now all the bonds and coupons would be returned unpaid. Many people, especially the elderly, depended on the interest coupons as a major or sole source of their income (Social Security payments did not begin until 1940). A loud clamor to reopen the fiscal agency would soon arise from bankers, financial managers, and the general public.[26]

ON THAT SAME DAY, August 9, Leland C. Caldwell, Ronald Finney's number one assistant, was arrested on the same charges as those against his boss. The handsome Topeka-reared Caldwell, who was Finney's office manager, confidential errand boy, valet, and what have you, couldn't make his bond. A midnight call to Paul Heinz, a prominent Topeka lawyer who had formerly been a Shawnee County attorney, resulted in arrangements for counsel but not for the bond. For a few days after his arrest, Caldwell talked a bit, though not much, to the eager investigators. He told of getting duplicate bonds printed at a local print shop, on the ruse that the mayor had signed on the wrong line, and of taking bond transcripts out of the Auditor's Office at will for Finney. John Schenck, who was Finney's chief counsel and one of the top criminal lawyers in the central-plains area, soon put a stop to Caldwell's wagging tongue. On Friday, Caldwell made bail and was arraigned, pleading not guilty. Paul Heinz, who would subsequently play a prominent part in the affair in a very different role, appeared as counsel for Caldwell.[27]

As the investigators began to piece together the intricate puzzle of the

Finney operations, the finger of public suspicion began to be pointed at others in the Statehouse, in addition to Boyd. A dark cloud covered the public offices, as well as the personal visages, of the auditor, the attorney general, the secretary of state, and the superintendent of public instruction. State representative Matt Guilfoyle, an Abilene Democrat, remarked: "Defense attorneys have claimed that Ronald Finney was smart. I do not believe that. He couldn't have operated if he had not had the assistance of most of the offices on the second floor of the state house."[28]

The total of the forgeries mounted daily. On Wednesday, $41,000 of the issues of Logan and Thomas counties were found to be spurious. The next day an announcement came that $50,000 in Salina and Hutchinson bonds had been duplicated twice, which raised the grand total to $799,000 by Friday.[29]

On August 10, officials from the office of the Shawnee County attorney and the U.S. Justice Department, armed with search warrants, descended on the Jayhawk Hotel. They hauled out of Finney's five-room suite a mountain of checks, letters, telegrams, and financial records. Finney's private office contained huge leather chairs and a desk "massive in proportions and expensive in construction," with three phones, just as Tom Boyd had described them, to the left of the desk.[30] "Dutch" Shultz of the *Topeka State Journal* surmised that there were "sleepless eyes under more than just a few roofs Thursday night when it became known that County Attorney Goodell had gathered a few bushel baskets full of [Ronald] Finney's private correspondence, a few hundred canceled checks and a number of statements rendered by persons on the promoter's payroll. That data is going to be exceedingly disturbing, tho interesting, reading before a federal grand jury or before a jury in the Shawnee county court one of these days."[31]

By the end of the first week, total confusion and consternation reigned among dazed bankers and investors in Kansas municipal bonds. No one could know whether he held genuine or worthless securities or how long it would take for him to find out. Federal investigators were "thick as flies" buzzing around the Statehouse offices and local financial institutions. State Accountant Jones wrote to every depository of state funds, requesting information.[32] "The whole state house financial area," Dutch Shultz sniffed, "[has] the odor of a packing house district just after sundown."[33]

But at this time the worried citizens received the reassuring words of a leading Topeka businessman, Charles L. Mitchell, manager of Topeka's Crane and Company printers. Mitchell, a director of the National Bank of Topeka and a member of the governor's honorary guard, explained in soothing tones that his company had only a few years earlier secured "at a very considerable expense" a special steel plate for bond borders and coupons.

That, coupled with their impeccable office procedures, ensured that "we know exactly just what bonds were printed and we have a thoro record with every safeguard against duplication or forgery or blanks getting into hands of unscrupulous people." To show its total faith, on the next day, Crane and Company voluntarily released a complete list—or so it claimed— of all the bonds that it had printed for Ronald Finney over the previous two years.[34] It was heartwarming to see conscientious citizens like Charley Mitchell doing what they could for their state in this hour of darkness.

The National Bank of Topeka proudly proclaimed that whatever might be the case elsewhere, it certainly did not hold securities of any kind which had been negotiated by Ronald Finney. Coming from Topeka's largest financial institution, that was also most comforting in this hour of stress.[35]

ATTORNEY GENERAL BOYNTON had first learned of Finney's arrest when he picked up a paper in Dodge City on Tuesday on his return from the West Coast. When the train stopped at Emporia, his cousin, Young Bill White, relayed a disconcerting message at the depot from Boynton's financial "advisor." The message: Don't worry. Immediately after arriving in Topeka that evening, the even-more-worried attorney general headed straight for the Governor's Mansion. Landon advised him to put everything on the table regarding his relations with Ronald Finney. Boynton assured him that he had and that he would continue to do so. The next day, Sard Brewster told Boynton that he had proof that Finney had been investing funds for Boynton in the market. Boynton volunteered nothing. The following day, Brewster talked to Boynton again. Boynton then told Brewster about his $400 investment and about the handsome returns it had been yielding. The governor felt strongly that Boynton's position as a prosecutor had been seriously compromised.[36] If that were only arguably so in his general capacity as attorney general, it certainly was valid regarding his potential role as the state's chief investigator and prosecutor in the bond scandal.

On Thursday, Landon announced the appointment of former state senator Fred M. Harris, a respected Ottawa lawyer, as special counsel to the governor for investigation of the bond scandal. In making the announcement the governor declared that the investigation would be conducted entirely independently of the Attorney General's Office.[37] The governor felt that "under these circumstances, it would be sound public policy to have a special counsel, not in any way related to any state offices that might be implicated . . . no matter how ignorantly, with any of the Finney transactions."[38] At this juncture there had not been any public disclosure of the

Fred Harris, chief state investigator (Kansas State Historical Society)

Boynton-Finney transactions or of the other services that the attorney general had performed for the young financial wizard. During the next few days, Harris appointed two capable young assistants: Hugo T. Wedell, a Chanute attorney, and Donald C. Little, an assistant U.S. district attorney under Sard Brewster.[39]

The appointment of Fred Harris, who was currently a member of the state Board of Regents, was an excellent one. Not the fiery criminal courtroom type (Landon later came up with others to fill that role), the thin, sharp-featured Harris had just the mental equipment that the job demanded: thoroughness, doggedness, and even-handedness. He brought his mind to bear on an enormous mass of data and records—documents of every size, shape, and description. From that disorganized and chaotic mountain of paper he fashioned a compact and digested hillock of useful information, organized in a logical and clear-flowing fashion. And he did so under the greatest of time pressures and in the hard glare of the public eye. Thanks to his efforts and those of his able assistants, the investigating committees would be able to assimilate the information quickly and to function smoothly in the weeks and months ahead.

Thursday evening a "heart-broken" Governor Landon addressed the Young Republican Association of Jackson County, Missouri:

> I feel the disgrace of the state's unfaithful servants very, very much.
>
> I propose to pursue the ramifications of those forged bonds wherever they may lead regardless of the public offices held by those involved. The whole story will be laid bare to the people of Kansas if I do nothing else in my administration. . . .
>
> Discovery of the forged bonds has had a depressing effect on Kansas securities but I believe that when this muddle is straightened out Kansas municipal bonds again will be at the top of the municipal securities list where they were a few days ago.[40]

LANDON MADE another bold move on Friday. After a four-hour conference with federal, state, and county officials, the governor announced that he was taking charge of the offices and the records of the attorney general, the auditor, and the state superintendent of public instruction. Files of those officers, particularly those relating to the School Fund, were loaded on a hand truck and carted to an empty office in the Statehouse, where they were studied carefully by investigators. Boynton's files were put in charge of Fred Harris, French's in charge of Lester Goodell, and those of W. T. Markham (the state superintendent of public instruction) were placed under A. S. Foulkes, parole attorney and legal advisor to Landon.[41] As Landon concluded his announcement, he added this ominous note: "We are developing very important new information in this case, which will come to light at the time of the lawsuit or impeachment proceedings."[42] He did not elaborate. The mention of impeachment put up front what had been whispered in the corridors during the past few days and had been publicly called for by Matt Guilfoyle and others as early as Wednesday.[43]

Kansas had had a school fund since its early days of statehood. Monies from the sale of public lands had been the principal source of the fund, which now totaled about $12 million. By statute the fund had to be fully invested in Kansas municipal bonds: in fact, all municipal bonds at original issuance had to be presented first to the School Fund before they could be offered on the private market.[44] Interest from the School Fund was distributed on a per capita basis to the school districts of the state. In 1933 that amounted to a little over $1 per child per year.

Lester Goodell, Shawnee County attorney
(Gerald L. Goodell)

The School Fund Commission, which was made up of the attorney general, the superintendent of public instruction, and the secretary of state, was charged with the trusteeship of the School Fund. The superintendent, as secretary, kept all of the commission's records, files, and correspondence. The full-time clerk of the commission, W. H. Stanley, was on the superintendent's payroll. The attorney general passed on the legality of proceedings that led up to the original issuance of bonds—that is, he reviewed the bond transcript. He also reviewed the soundness of bonds put up to secure state funds that were deposited in banks designated as state depositories, which included the three Finney banks. The state auditor registered all bonds that were issued in Kansas. His signature and seal—the great seal of the state—had to appear on all bonds. Bond transcripts were stored in the auditor's vault.[45]

The worried citizens gained some comfort from the announcement on

Friday by Topeka bond brokers that, in their view, there were few if any forged bonds in private hands. They reasoned that the success of the forgery depended on keeping control of the forged issues. Thus, they were put up as security for state deposits, as collateral for loans, or as margin in stock-market trading. In this way the forger kept control of the interest coupons and kept them from reaching the fiscal agency.[46] The health of some folks around the Statehouse showed marked improvement by Friday, especially those that had been suffering from amnesia of late. Landon reported: "We are very much pleased with the . . . ability of persons connected with the case to show decided improvement in their recollections."[47]

By Saturday the total of known forgeries of bonds and warrants had risen to $1,036,000. The sum included issues that had been deposited in the state treasury as security for the three Finney banks ($371,000), in two Chicago brokerage firms ($429,000), in a Topeka bank ($50,000), in Fidelity Bank as security for Lyon County deposits ($86,000), and $100,000 known to have been printed but not yet located. Investigators worked throughout the weekend, sifting evidence and looking for new leads. Sard Brewster headed for Washington, but no one knew whether to seek or deliver information, and Brewster wasn't talking.[48]

ON MONDAY, August 14, Landon struck once again. After a six-hour conference with federal and state investigators and state lawyers, he directed Lester Goodell to arrest Tom Boyd for embezzlement, charging that he "did feloniously and wilfully convert to his own use and to the use of one Ronald Finney the sum of $150,000 of the moneys of the state of Kansas in his possession as such state treasurer." Landon and Goodell confidently stated that they had plenty of evidence to convict the treasurer on numerous counts but that they wanted to be sure of their ground since no similar complaint had ever been filed in Kansas.[49] In addition, the governor fired off a letter to the treasurer, demanding his resignation: "In view of the revelations of recent days and the development of facts showing too clearly that you, as custodian of the state's funds, have been derelict in your duties, I must ask for your immediate resignation as State Treasurer of Kansas."[50] One of Boyd's lawyers, Leon Lundblade, who had attended the governor's conference earlier in the day, suggested that Boyd might resign if there were to be no criminal prosecution. Landon's letter to Goodell was his answer to this "suggestion."[51] The governor's action represented an abrupt change in his attitude over the weekend. On August 11 he had written to State Senator Claude Bradney: "I do not think we should ask Tom Boyd to resign. If he is guilty he should be impeached and not permitted to resign."⁵²

The next day, Boyd testily responded to Landon, refusing to resign:

> I feel, governor, that in the matter for which you requested my resignation, I have done no wrong and no more than you have requested me to do or acquiesced in on other occasions, and I am unable to understand how similar conduct on my part could be so lawful when requested and acquiesced in by you and so unlawful on another occasion....
>
> Your action in placing the militia in charge of my office, I believe, was unwarranted, without precedent, and I believe, without authority and, as soon as you cease making my office a camping ground and a show ground, I shall return and resume my duties.⁵³

Boyd was arrested on August 15 and was released on a $25,000 bond after pleading not guilty. He was neither photographed nor fingerprinted when he was arrested, assuring the sheriff that he would submit to those indignities "when it could be arranged for privately." He was mugged and fingerprinted the following night at 10 o'clock.⁵⁴ Caldwell had been photographed and fingerprinted, but Finney had not been.

The Kansas Constitution had made it rather difficult for the state to rid itself of a constitutional officer. Boyd continued as state treasurer de jure and de facto, and he would continue in that capacity until he either resigned or had been removed from the office by the Senate, following impeachment by the House. Since he was legally the treasurer, his signature was still necessary on state warrants and other documents; and he, and he alone, could call a meeting of the state Treasury Board, which he served as secretary.⁵⁵

In Boyd's letter to Landon he referred, in an oblique manner, to their joint Treasury Board responsibilities regarding the assignment of excess state cash to banks. The state Treasury Board, composed of the governor, the secretary of state, and the auditor, had been charged by statute with the nearly impossible task of checking all bonds, warrants, vouchers, and the like, in the state treasury on a monthly basis. This assignment hadn't been systematically carried out for decades, if ever.⁵⁶ In the months to come, Landon's enemies would make much of his alleged neglect of duties on the Treasury Board.

THE GOVERNOR decided to enlist the aid of the Legislative Council in the investigation of the bond scandal and its ramifications. The Legislative Council, or "little legislature," was Kansas' "latest experiment in government."[57] It had been established, at Landon's behest, by the 1933 Legislature to act as a fact-gathering and study group, so that the state government would be less obliged to use data that had previously been furnished by the Santa Fe Railroad, the Kansas Association of Manufacturers, and other powerful private interests. The Interim Legislative Committee represents its present-day lineal descendant. The council—a bipartisan group of twenty-five legislators, fifteen from the House and ten from the Senate—had been scheduled to meet on August 15 regarding more mundane matters. Investigation of the bond irregularities represented an unexpectedly early and severe test for the council, but the legislators seemed to relish the opportunity to become involved directly.[58]

On the morning of August 15—in remarks broadcast over WIBW and listened to closely by a shocked, angry, and apprehensive public—Governor Landon delivered his message to the Legislative Council. Two weeks earlier the popular interest would have been focused on his position regarding the legality of 3.2 beer. But not now. The aroused governor passionately detailed the bond-forgery disclosures and the questionable conduct of state officials and called for a full investigation by the council:

> The state has been rocked to its foundation by the exposure of graft, skullduggery, criminal connivance and barefaced disregard of public duty, the like of which Kansas has never before experienced. . . . It is comparable only to the racketeering and depredation of gangsters in our large cities. . . .
>
> Taxpayers of Kansas are entitled to know how their public officials conduct the business of their offices. . . . No one should be permitted to hide behind the cloak of friendship, influence or political prestige. . . .
>
> You men are probably facing the most severe tests as individuals ever placed upon state legislators of Kansas. You will handle matters of far reaching gravity to the state and to the honor of public servants.
>
> Your integrity, your ability and your judgment will be tried to the limit. This is a time for strong men; men of unflinching courage and definite purpose. . . . If you hold the legislative rudder steady, you will unfailingly win the respect and praise of all good citizens, and take your place in that long line of Kansas men who have served the state with distinction to themselves and profit to their fellows.[59]

The "admirably clear and complete message" was enthusiastically received by the council, which promptly and unanimously passed a resolution of approval of the governor's decisive actions during the past week. Lieutenant Governor Charles W. Thompson named a special committee to investigate the conduct of state officials with a view to recommending impeachment where warranted. The seven-man committee, chaired by

Judge S. C. Bloss of Cowley County, was instructed to report its findings, not back to the council, but directly to a special session of the House of Representatives.

Dallas Knapp, a Coffeyville Republican who was president pro tem of the Senate, saved the council from serious error. The original plan had been to include four House and three Senate members on the investigating committee. But Knapp pointed out that it should scrupulously avoid placing a senator on the impeachment committee, so that he would avoid being put in the embarrassing—and illegal—position of being both prosecutor and juror.[60]

STATE AND FEDERAL investigators continued to work at a feverish pace during the latter half of August, frequently remaining in the treasury

Schuyler C. Bloss, chairman of the Board of Managers (Kansas State Historical Society)

vaults inspecting bonds until the wee hours of the morning. They took more than 125 statements from individuals in Topeka, out over the state, or in Chicago, and they followed up on every reasonable clue or suggestion that came to their attention. The state accountant reported, late in the month, that inspection of the over $11 million in municipal bonds in the School Fund had disclosed that all were genuine. Collectively, the state breathed a sigh of relief. The news wasn't so good, however, for the state or for the three counties that had funds tied up in a Finney bank. Preliminary reports indicated that nearly all of the $700,000 deposited by the state in the three Finney banks was unprotected by sound security. The same was true for the approximately $218,000 on deposit by the commissioners of three counties. The total in forged bonds and warrants continued to grow, with a new and somewhat higher estimate every few days.[61]

On August 22 Landon made public a letter that he had written to the federal comptroller of the currency, which was sharply critical of the national bank examiners. Landon noted that since late June the examiners had known that among the assets of the National Bank of Topeka were forged municipal bonds, the originals of which were the property of the state. "The failure of your department to communicate this information to the state authorities permitted continuance of fraudulent transactions for the interim between the time your department became possessed of this knowledge and the time of Mr. Finney's arrest, during which time over $300,000 additional forged bonds were sold to other parties, including the $150,000 which your bank examiner permitted to go out of the bank," Landon charged.[62]

The examiner who had been in charge of the June bank investigation, E. F. Allen, immediately responded to Landon's attack. He denied that the examiners had known that the bonds were forgeries, claiming that, at the time, they thought that the bonds had been stolen from the School Fund. Allen asserted that their report only covered violations of the national banking laws and that they weren't required by law to make any report whatsoever to Governor Landon. But Allen went on to quote W. W. Finney, who, at the time he removed the $150,000 in bonds, had said: "We will have to get the bonds out of the bank, or there'll be the greatest scandal Kansas ever heard of."[63] The following day, in reference to bank president Carl McKeen's statement that the examiners had known that the bonds were forged, Allen replied: "McKeen either has a convenient memory or has been misquoted and I expect him to retract later."[64] The directors of the bank issued a public statement that the bank and its officers were totally innocent of all wrongdoing. They were cooperating fully with the investigators, the directors said, and if they should be found civilly liable as a result of any Finney transactions, they stood ready, willing, and able to pay same in full.[65] The time would come when the bank would exhibit less enthusiasm for that prospect.

AT ABOUT 2 A.M. on August 24, a posse of Shawnee County law officers surrounded the Ronald Finney home in Emporia. A phone call from the local sheriff's office had finally awakened the sleepy inhabitants after vigorous door-pounding and shouting, which disturbed the entire neighborhood, had failed to do so. Accompanied by a group of loyal friends, Finney returned to Topeka with the officers to face new charges, coolly driving up U.S. 75 through the gently rolling eastern Kansas countryside in his mammoth 1932 Pierce-Arrow. The new charges included the uttering and forging of $30,000 in Hutchinson bonds: the two charges on each of the $1,000 bonds totaled sixty counts. Finney failed to make the $50,000 bond, though several relatives and friends had been brought along specifically for that purpose. This time, Finney was mugged and fingerprinted. The higher bond represented a judicial response to recent newspaper editorials that had been critical of the earlier $25,000 bond, which allegedly was lower than that which was sometimes required of less important citizens for less serious offenses.[66]

Young Finney enjoyed his first dinner in jail, consisting of a quart of boiled beans, four slices of bread, a cup of coffee, and a roll. The Finney attorneys promptly appealed to the Kansas Supreme Court for his release on a writ of habeas corpus, alleging that the $50,000 bond was excessive. Leland Caldwell was arrested at about the same hour on identical charges at his Topeka home in the "fashionable Country club residence district." He, too, remained in jail, unable to post the $50,000 bond.[67]

No sooner had Finney settled into his jail cell than a couple of tax assessors of Shawnee County, who had been futilely trying to nail him for months, showed up and started asking questions about the personal property he had acquired in recent months. Ronald said he preferred to have his lawyer present before signing anything. The assessors said that was O.K.; they could wait. They weren't in any big hurry, now that they knew where they could find him.[68]

On August 26 Ronald Finney, Tom Boyd, and Leland Caldwell were arrested on federal warrants. They were charged with using the mails in connection with a scheme to defraud both the state of Kansas and Jackson Brothers, Boesel and Company, a Chicago brokerage firm. A registered letter, mailed by the Chicago firm and containing bogus bonds, had allegedly been delivered to Finney at the Jayhawk on July 28. The complaint charged that the three defendants had tried to obtain $286,000 in cash from the firm in the fraudulent deal. The registered letter contained "[6] falsely forged and counterfeited bonds of Center township, Stevens county, ... and [7] bonds of the city of Towanda, Butler county, ... all of which was contrary to the form of the statute ... and against the peace and dignity of the United States."[69]

Bond was initially set at $50,000 each for Finney and Boyd and at $35,000 for Caldwell, but was reduced the next day to $25,000 for each of them.[70] Boyd attempted to persuade Judge George T. McDermott of the U.S. Circuit Court to reduce the bond still further to $15,000. The judge refused, declaring that, "where a million dollars is involved, there ought to be no chance taken."[71] Boyd's attorney, Tinkham Veale, objected to having his client's name linked with that of Finney in the charge. "Boyd is not in the same class," he protested. "It is irksome to us to have their names linked in this connection at all."[72] Finney and Caldwell remained placidly in custody, but Boyd made every effort to get out. Though he had many friends among Kansas bankers, the treasurer experienced a surprising amount of difficulty in making bond. His potential supporters apparently feared that they would become suspect in the scandal if they signed his bond.[73]

The stunned state received another shock on August 28 when W. W. Finney was arrested on eighteen counts, charging him with the embezzlement of $75,474 from his Fidelity State and Savings Bank. The complaints alleged that Finney did "unlawfully, feloniously, knowingly and wilfully embezzle, abstract, misapply and convert to his ... own use, funds of the ... bank." Lyon County Attorney Clarence V. Beck stated that none of the information in the complaints resulted from the fraudulent bond transactions of the son. He had not yet dug deep enough, he said, to determine if W. W. Finney was involved with forging bonds, though $115,000 of forged securities—both bonds and warrants—had been found in the bank's security for Lyon County deposits. "Most of the manipulations," Beck declared, "were carried on through checks which were floated back and forth between the Finney banks at Emporia and Neosho Falls." Finney pleaded not guilty and was released on a $25,000 bond signed by his mother-in-law, Mrs. Amelia Tucker of Eureka.[74]

Ever since the arrest of Ronald Finney, it had been rumored that additional arrests might be made in Emporia. Since numerous forged securities had been discovered in the bank, many Emporians felt that the elder Finney might possibly be charged on a technicality due to his son's substitution of bad bonds for good ones. His friends and admirers gasped with surprise when they learned that none of the eighteen counts involved bogus bonds generated by the son. Some loyal friends still insisted that he was being blamed for his son's chicanery, steadfastly refusing to believe that he himself was—or could be—guilty of any wrongdoing.[75] But the young county attorney seemed sure of his ground. As the torrid August came to a close, Charley Scott down in Iola seemed to sum up the situation pretty well. "So far as we are concerned . . . ," the veteran editor and former congressman observed, "before it's all through and done with, it's going to be one 'ell of a mess."[76]

3

Gross and Enormous Irregularities

ooooooooooooooooooooooooooooooooooooooooooooooooooo

REVELATION came tumbling after revelation through the months of August and September, disclosing the general outlines of the Finneys' activity and political influence. In late August, Landon told the press: "We are finding something new every day now.... I don't know when we will reach the bottom of this affair." A few days later he reported that "we have about reached the bottom." However, on September 2, Fred Harris declared that the end wasn't in sight. "Every time we think we are near completion, ... something else appears," the chief investigator said. After an "at length" questioning on September 5 of John Knightley, one of Ronald Finney's field men from Wichita, Harris reported that it had been "the most profitable day we have had." The busy investigators hinted broadly at further arrests of prominent people. Sard Brewster, as laconic as ever, returned from a Washington conference with the U.S. attorney general, Homer E. Cummings. Seen carrying two huge rolls of photostats of something or other down a Statehouse corridor, Brewster was queried by reporters about their nature. "Dynamite," he cryptically replied, then quickly moved on.[1]

For the first few weeks after the scandal broke, widespread rumors circulated that what had been revealed might be only part of an extensive clandestine operation that was national in scope. Possibly Ronald Finney was operating as a broker, disposing of bogus securities for an organized Capone-style gang with headquarters in Chicago. Perhaps he was only a small-fry agent, even though his operations ran into the millions. These grandiose speculations and related talk about conspiracy gradually subsided, however, so that by Labor Day, investigators seemed certain that

Finney had been the brains behind the entire scheme. His confederates—and dupes—around Topeka were guilty, it appeared, of enormous "cupidity and stupidity."[2]

The general outlines of the Finney *modus operandi* with respect to school-district bonds and the School Fund Commission began to be revealed. The commission rejected the bond offerings of poverty-stricken school districts, due, their board members were told, to the district's financial "embarrassment" or to the fund's lack of ready cash. Discouraged board members had to go back to the home folks and explain that there just was no market. It was the depths of the Depression, and nobody seemed to be buying, especially from the smaller rural districts. Then, suddenly appeared the affable supersalesman, or one of his associates, who promptly made a contract with the grateful district. The contract called for Finney either to buy the bonds outright at a discount, which he then promptly sold to the School Fund at par, or to market them as the district's agent, for a fat commission, to a "mysterious customer," which also turned out to be the School Fund. When Finney presented the bonds to the School Fund the second time around (in the district's name, unbeknownst to them), somehow they looked a lot better to his friends on the commission.[3]

The Finney commodity-market speculations came under close scrutiny. Initially, investigators and the public assumed that Finney had lost heavily in the market and had frantically counterfeited bonds so as to cover the losses. But brokerage firms in Kansas City and Chicago reported that Finney, who was a heavy trader, especially in wheat, had made huge profits on several occasions. His market moves had been skillfully guided by "confidential advisors" in Chicago, Washington, and New York. Investigators could find no trace of $271,000, which had been loaned to him by a Chicago brokerage firm on July 21 on the strength of his market play and a large batch of Kansas municipal bonds, most of which were bogus. That transaction came just seventeen days before his arrest and at a time when he strongly suspected that the feds were on his trail. "A considerable portion of it [the profit from Finney's various swindles]," opined Jack Harris in the *Hutchinson News,* "is buried in a tin can somewhere or is lying in a still undiscovered bank account in the name, perhaps, of E. Pluvius Mc-Swatt."[4]

RONALD FINNEY had become a fanatic about obtaining information: he simply could not get enough of it. He kept very close tabs on Statehouse visitors through his network of informers in the several state offices. During legislative sessions, Leland Caldwell stationed himself at a strategic point on the third floor of the Statehouse, the better to observe the goings and comings at key state offices. The two Finneys had hired private investigators to check out financial or personal matters in Kansas and on the outside. In early June, Ronald Finney cabled to his sister, who was with the Whites in London, to send him a daily cable summarizing the actions of the international economic conference. He then studied the impact that the deliberations of that august body might have on American financial markets. A 100-word London-to-Topeka cable cost $31 in 1933.[5]

But "inside" information on a regular basis from key areas of the country interested the market speculator the most. From the day of his arrest, stories circulated widely that he had steady informants in the New York area, in Washington, and in Chicago. A check register, which was included in the booty obtained in the raid on the Jayhawk suite, reportedly recorded every check that young Finney had written since January 1. The register showed several checks to writer and publicist David Hinshaw, a native of Emporia who was Finney's brother-in-law.[6] Then living in the Philadelphia area, Hinshaw had known the Finneys most of his life. On his frequent trips back to Kansas he often saw them, father and son. On a recent visit in May, W. W. Finney had hosted a luncheon in Hinshaw's honor.[7] A year earlier, W. A. White had described Hinshaw in the most flattering terms: "Probably no American out of office knows so many prominent people in the Republican party as David Hinshaw and knows them intimately. Moreover he uses this acquaintance as a lever for good. He doesn't use it for himself but to help his friends and to help good causes . . . a hard-working, unselfish, high-visioned man who is contributing his life to the good of his country and making a living incidentally as he goes along."[8]

After reading newspaper reports of the Finney checks, Hinshaw released a bristling statement asserting that "there is a gross inaccuracy somewhere." But he went on to admit that he had done a number of "favors" for Finney and that he had received a total of $1,600 in payments from his brother-in-law within the past year or so. He admitted that he had attempted to secure for Finney the support of the Reconstruction Finance Corporation and of the Federal Reserve Board; that he had been paid $1,000 in the spring of 1933 to investigate the zinc-smelting business in the East for him; and that he had received expense money to interview "business and financial leaders and newspaper men in the East whose judgment and opinion of the trend in business and financial markets he [Finney] desired. It was my custom to grant such favors to him as far as possible without charge or cost owing to the fact that he had married a sister-in-law of mine."[9]

Young Bill White immediately came to the aid of his prominent hometown friend on the editorial page of the *Gazette:*

> Emporia has never turned out a finer, cleaner young man than Dave Hinshaw. He is, of course, keenly intelligent, but it was his obvious honesty and his high ethical standards which have won for him the confidence of those in the high places of government and finance in the east. . . .
>
> Before this mess is over and the culprits stand clearly revealed at the trial the preliminary evidence will bring under suspicion other honorable men, as indeed it already has. But here and now while the clouds of battle still obscure the field, you can bet your last cent that Dave Hinshaw will come out the fine, clean and honorable man that all Emporia knows him to be.[10]

This modest revelation is all that ever surfaced regarding a New York area "contact man." And that is the last that was heard of Hinshaw in the matter. He evidently went back to his profession of being the "fine, clean, and honorable" man that the Whites and all the world knew him to be.

For several years, Finney's regular attorneys had been the firm of O'Neil and Hamilton. Since John Hamilton was prominent in Republican circles and Ralph T. ("Dyke") O'Neil in Democratic ones, they had the Kansas political spectrum pretty well covered between them. Dyke O'Neil was close to Guy Helvering, who was the kingpin of Kansas Democratic politics and currently was the U.S. commissioner of internal revenue, and to former Governor Harry Woodring, who had been rewarded in 1933 for his early and strong support of FDR by being named assistant secretary of war (he would become secretary of war in 1936). By the spring of 1933 Dyke O'Neil, who had been national commander of the American Legion from 1931 to 1933 and who was a member of the Kansas Board of Regents, began to spend more and more time as a lobbyist in Washington, D.C.[11]

That O'Neil was Finney's Washington contact man was generally accepted by those who were investigating the case. An intimate of Finney's and a habitué at the Jayhawk, O'Neil reportedly received $1,000 a month to relay inside information from Washington regarding the impact of New Deal legislation on the financial and commodity markets. One story that made the rounds had it that on days when news was slow (after all, even during the New Deal's Hundred Days, there had to be a few dull ones), O'Neil would pick up the earliest edition of the *New York Times* or *Washington Post* in his quarters at the Mayflower Hotel. Skimming the financial and agricultural sections, he would promptly phone Ronald the most useful items as an "inside tip." Conning the con artist, one might say. Clif

Stratton, who worried a good deal in the *Capital* about the Washington contact man but never came right out and publicly identified him in his columns, was chided in the rival *State Journal* for his reluctance to take the final step to reveal what, by that time, everyone knew.[12] "Our good friend Clif Stratton has kept his public agog over the 'mysterious Washington contact man' .... Clif lives in Washington and his senator-big boss [Arthur Capper] lives at the Mayflower, home of the mystery man. Why doesn't Clif go ahead and solve the mystery? Remember way back when that neighborhood gal in pig tails ran down the street singing, 'I know something I won't tell'?"[13]

Finney's man in Chicago was Harold Trusler, a former Emporia grain and investment broker. After his business had gone bankrupt in 1930, he had been arrested but was later acquitted on charges of embezzlement. Subsequently he took a position in an investment house in Chicago. Trusler was probably the most stylish dresser Emporia ever produced—not unexpectedly, since he bought his expensive, modish clothes in New York City, New York. Trusler and Finney had been boon companions in Emporia and had stayed in close touch after the grain dealer had relocated in Chicago. Finney reportedly paid the dapper Emporian $500 a month in salary and expenses for various useful services in Chicago. Trusler undoubtedly helped Finney to become established with the LaSalle Street brokerage firms in which so many of the fraudulent bonds finally came to reside.[14]

In all fairness it should be stated that there is not a scintilla of evidence that Hinshaw or O'Neil or Trusler knew about the bond-forgery operations. They were Finney's close friends, and they were knowledgeable, intelligent professionals who happened to reside in locales from which Finney needed to obtain useful information for his operations. They helped to alleviate, though not totally to satisfy, his unquenchable thirst for "inside" knowledge of the markets.

A "SULLEN, ill-tempered and somewhat belligerent" Tom Boyd, under guard but without handcuffs, was taken on August 31 from the jailhouse to the Statehouse for a meeting of the state Treasury Board. The law required that the meeting be held in the Treasurer's Office and that he be present as the board's secretary. When the treasurer and his deputy-sheriff guard reached the Statehouse, Boyd snarled at a would-be photographer, "If you put that thing on me, I'll knock the ——— out of you." After that fierce challenge, the photographer retreated, and Boyd strode in high dudgeon on up the steep steps and into the Capitol. The principal business of the meeting was to award contracts to state depositories. Toward the end of the proceedings, Boyd demanded that the Treasury Board pass each month on the validity and value of the entire $50 million in securities that were held in the treasury vault, as the law required. Landon coolly asked if Boyd wanted to make the request a part of the formal record. "No. I don't care what you do," the bitter Boyd replied. "It's up to you. I am just bringing the matter to your attention."[15] Later in the day, after consultation with their attorneys, the board members sat down and actually counted all of the state's cash. The governor made a $10 mistake, which was caught in the recount.[16]

After spending more than a week in jail, Tom Boyd posted his $25,000 bond on the federal charge and was released on September 3. But his freedom was short-lived, because on September 6 the U.S. commissioner disapproved one of his bondsmen and sent him back to jail.[17] Boyd was bound over on September 9, after the preliminary hearing on the state's charge of embezzling—that is, of converting $150,000 to the use of himself and Ronald Finney. After the hearing, he posted acceptable security and was released. At the hearing, the treasury's bond clerk, Miss Bernice Long, who was extremely nervous, sat in the witness chair, directly facing her accused and estimable boss. Her frank and detailed recounting of Boyd and Finney's removal of the Eureka depository bonds to Chicago formed an essential part of the state's case.[18]

The anxious president of the National Bank of Topeka, Carl McKeen, issued a lengthy public statement in mid September, giving in detail the bank's part in the $150,000 transaction. McKeen declared that the federal bank examiners had given their approval to the transaction, and he repeated his earlier statement that the bank had done nothing of an unethical nature. McKeen protested that the bank's "directors are substantial men of this community, whose integrity, in my opinion, cannot be questioned." He then proceeded to question seriously the integrity of one of the bank's former employees, Charles L. Cooke, who had been in charge of its bond department. McKeen claimed that in mid January, Cooke, "without notice to or authority from myself or any other officer of the bank," had allowed his close friend Ronald Finney to buy $60,000 of U.S. Treasury bonds with a like amount of Kansas municipal bonds on a repurchase agreement, rather than for cash as he had been instructed. Fifty thousand dollars worth of these bonds, plus about $100,000 more, were among the assets of the bank when the federal examiners had arrived in late June. Cooke currently headed the newly organized Prudential Investment Trust Company in Topeka, an offshoot from the National Bank of Topeka. Reportedly, some of the money that he used as a down payment to purchase the stock from McKeen came from—guess who—Ronald Finney, of course.[19]

For nearly a month, since his irate letter to comptroller of the currency J. F. T. O'Connor in mid August, an impatient Governor Landon had been trying to obtain an order from the comptroller directing the federal bank examiners to tell all they knew with respect to their inspection of the National Bank of Topeka. Finally, on September 18, after a bristling exchange of telegrams, O'Connor directed examiner E. F. ("Jack") Allen and his assistant examiner, Mark Rooney, to come to Topeka. Landon, assisted by Fred Harris and Lester Goodell, subjected them to an intense seven-hour session of probing questions. Landon reported that the testimony of the examiners hadn't materially changed his perception of the critical transactions. But they had learned that some of the bonds Finney had taken to Chicago in July were genuine. The state had not filed charges of illegal removal against Boyd and Finney, since the investigators had assumed that all the bonds were spurious and that a defense could be readily made that nothing of value had left the treasury.[20] Clif Stratton speculated that if a second complaint were filed and the first one were dropped, it would not be necessary to drag the National Bank of Topeka and Carl McKeen through a district-court trial, as it would be if the initial embezzlement charge were pressed.[21]

On September 5 the original charges against Ronald Finney and Leland Caldwell of uttering forged Kansas City, Kansas, bonds were dropped. In their stead, Shawnee County Attorney Lester Goodell filed an eighty-count charge against each of them, forty counts for forging forty Salina bonds at $500 each and an equal number of counts for selling the bonds to the Citizens State Bank of North Topeka in the fall of 1932. Bonds were set at $50,000 for each; both of them returned to jail after failing to make the bond.[22]

At the preliminary hearing on September 12 in the Court of Topeka, Finney and Caldwell were bound over to Shawnee County District Court for trial on both the Hutchinson bond charges (sixty counts) and the Salina bond charges (eighty counts). Officials from Hutchinson and Salina testified that their signatures on the securities were not genuine and that no such bonds had ever been issued. The cashier of the Citizens State Bank asserted that he had innocently purchased the bonds from Finney at par. There was a "buzz of excitement" at the morning session when the titian-haired would-be movie queen Vivian Tracey—a former Finney employee—appeared at the defense table. She had been questioned earlier by investigators as to her knowledge of the Finney operations. She disappointed the crowd when she failed to return to brighten up the afternoon session.[23]

Fred Harris announced on September 15 that J. C. Shearman, the Wichita handwriting expert, had ascertained that Will French's signature on the registration certificate on the back of each forged bond was a forgery, though so clever that the auditor had for some time believed it to be genuine. Earlier it had been revealed that Boynton's name had been forged on all the attorney general's certificates of approval. The paper and printing of the spurious bonds was of a professional quality that was indistinguishable from the originals. The greatest surprise, though, was Shearman's firm conclusion, after having made intensive comparisons, that the Auditor's Office impression on the bogus issues came from the genuine great seal of the state of Kansas.[24]

ON SEPTEMBER 19, after a several-hour examination by Senator Harris which had left him in a testy mood, Will French decided that he would pay a call on the Shawnee County clerk. He had decided to take a belated look at the 1932 campaign expense accounts of his chief antagonist—Governor Landon—and at the expenses filed by Landon for Clyde Reed in the 1930 primary. One never could tell what might turn up that would prove politically useful; there was no need to be so constantly on the defensive, the auditor reasoned. He politely made his request to the county clerk. The clerk looked high, and looked low, and then looked some more; but lo and behold, the requested reports were missing from the files. Finally, Tom Boyd, Jr., who worked in the office and had overheard the conversation, piped up with the answer: "Dad has them." At his father's request, young Boyd had taken them home for study a week or so earlier. When told of the events, Landon analyzed the situation thoughtfully. "I don't see what defense that would be to a charge of embezzlement against a state treasurer," he said. "And I cannot imagine what those campaign expense accounts might have had to do with the use of the auditor's seal."[25]

The files were quickly returned by the embarrassed young Boyd. He also had taken home the reports that had been filed by the treasurer of the Republican State Committee and the Shawnee County Landon-for-Governor Committee. The statements revealed that W. W. Finney had contributed $500 to the 1932 campaign expenses of Landon. It represented the third-largest contribution—smaller only than those of John Landon, Alf's father ($700), and of Harry Darby, Jr. ($700), the state highway director. The grand total of expenses for the primary were listed as $8,244. (It would have been something of a scandal if a candidate had spent over $10,000.) The Shawnee County clerk was publicly censured by the county commissioners for allowing young Boyd to remove the records from the files. The ruffled governor announced that he intended to ask the legislature for a law prohibiting a private person from removing original public files. A few days later, French called at the office of the Reno County clerk in Hutchinson to examine the financial statement filed by the Reno County chairman for Landon. The chairman expressed surprise at French's interest in the report. French countered that he was only checking, since he had understood that no statement had been filed.[26] Boyd and French were obviously grasping at whatever straws might be available in an abortive attempt to launch a counterattack against their chief tormentor.

ADDITIONAL DIMENSIONS of the enormous Finney influence came to light in late September. Jesse Greenleaf, a Landon appointee to the three-man Kansas Corporation Commission—the state's watchdog over public utilities and the sale of stocks, *inter alia*—admitted that the previous spring he had acted as an agent for the Finneys in a huge cattle-buying operation. Greenleaf's public statement came after intensive questioning by state investigators. A veteran Greensburg cattleman, Greenleaf had been active as a progressive in Kansas politics for years, having headed up the successful Reed-for-Governor Committee in 1928. In 1933 he had been reappointed by his friend Landon to the Corporation Commission, the successor to the Public Service Commission.[27]

After the bank holiday, Greenleaf had made an extensive cattle-buying trip on behalf of young Finney, purchasing nearly twenty thousand head in Texas and New Mexico for a fee of fifty cents per head. Many of the cattle had been sent to the 2,200-acre Munger Ranch near Eureka, which Finney had recently made a Flint Hills showplace. (The *Hamilton Grit* hoped that if Finney put boats on Munger Lake, he would name the first one the *John A. Edwards*. John, it seems, had "gained seven votes in his campaign for [state] representative by assuring an enthusiastic booster for a bigger navy that if 'John A. Edwards is elected it will be my pleasure to use every honorable effort to secure the establishment of a naval training station on Munger Lake.'")[28] Later, Finney completely lost his $43,000 equity in the huge operation. Greenleaf had also bought a prize herd out at Cimarron for W. W. Finney, who, of course, was one of the major utility "powers" in the state. Greenleaf confirmed that Ronald Finney had recently purchased large blocks of stock in the National Old Line Life Insurance Company, of Wichita, of which Greenleaf was president. Finney was the largest stockholder, though he hadn't quite yet acquired a majority of the stock.[29] If there has to be a watchdog, the Finneys reasoned, there's no reason why he shouldn't be a friendly tail-wagging old shaggy dog—no reason at all.

Other evidence testifying to the versatility of young Finney turned up in September. Over the past few years the Fidelity Bank had put up surety bonds totaling about $200,000 for various state deposits, including an Emporia State Teachers College fund. The bonds were written on the regular form of the Fidelity and Casualty Company of New York, a company that Ronald served as agent while he was working in the Neosho Falls bank during the twenties. The company representative, who had come to Topeka from back East to look into the matter, stated unequivocally that it had not written a bond for Fidelity Bank since before 1930. He added that in recent years all its bonds bore an identifying number of at least seven digits. The bond held for the Teachers College fund bore the number 229. The company later filed suit to set aside the bond, claiming that the signature of its authorized agent had been forged.[30]

Kansans began to wonder if Finney had been on his way to buying the entire state when they learned that he had even collected the 1932 premium on Treasurer Boyd's $500,000 surety bond. Reportedly he split the commission on the $1,250 premium with the regular agent, though the state voucher was made out only to "Ronald Finney, agent."[31]

By mid September, Harris and his assistants had identified virtually all the bogus securities that were in public or private hands. None were in private agencies except those held by the two Chicago brokerage houses and the Citizens State Bank. Of the $448,200 in municipal bonds in the three Finney banks that had been put up to protect total state deposits of approximately $700,000, less than $67,000 proved to be of valid issues. (Throughout the period the Tucker-owned Eureka Bank was referred to as one of the "Finney" banks. That was not literally true, though it represented a simple way to categorize the bank and is followed in this book as a convenience. Though the Finneys owned no stock in the bank and were not on its board of directors, Ronald Finney manipulated its security in the state treasury as freely as he did that of the Neosho Falls and Emporia banks.) A total of $426,000 in bogus bonds resided in the state treasury on August 8, $381,000 of which was from the three Finney banks. Lyon County had $127,000 on deposit in the Fidelity Bank; Greenwood County, $54,000 in Eureka; Woodson County, $37,000 in Neosho Falls. Of the $218,000 put up as security for these county deposits—most of which was in the form of warrants—only $5,500 turned out to be genuine. The speculative grand total of forgeries continued to rise as the investigation proceeded, reaching a maximum of about $1.7 million in late August before subsiding somewhat as the cross-checking continued. The final firm total of $1,241,000 comprised all the forged or illegally utilized issues, including a small number that were known to have been printed but were later destroyed or never subsequently located. In most instances the genuine bonds of the seventeen forged municipal issues rested peacefully in the treasury vault, the property of the School Fund Commission.[32]

ON SEPTEMBER 20 Emporia and the state received another jolt when forgery charges, involving a total that exceeded $100,000, were filed against W. W. Finney by the Lyon County prosecutor. The thirteen counts involved five transactions: (1) Three counts of forging, uttering, and possessing a total of $33,000 of Pratt County School District warrants; (2) three counts charging the forging, uttering, and possession of a $3,256 check drawn on the Kansas Home Telephone Company—a company that Finney had sold about 1930; (3) three counts charging Finney with making false entries in the accounts of the Emporia ($6,000), Paola ($4,000), and Sabetha ($2,700) telephone companies at the Fidelity Bank; (4) one count—which linked him to the bond forgeries—charging that in August, 1932, the bank president had sold $50,000 of forged Johnson County School District bonds to Fidelity, with $10,000 of the proceeds going to his son and the remainder to himself; (5) three counts charging the forging of the endorsement, uttering to the bank, and possession of a $4,689.67 Telephone Company check which had been drawn to pay company taxes.[33]

Even the most staunch Finney supporters were at a loss to explain away the last charge. On June 7, 1933, Forrest Haynes, treasurer of Southwestern Bell at Topeka, had mailed the check, which was payable to the treasurer of Lyon County, to Finney to cover company taxes in Lyon County for the last half of 1932. The check had been charged against the phone company account at Fidelity and had been mailed back on June 10 with the rubber-stamp endorsement of the Lyon County treasurer. The county treasurer declared emphatically that the check had never been received by his office, that the endorsement was a rank forgery. County Attorney Beck determined that the rubber stamp had been made for the bank by the J. C. Darling Company of Topeka. The endorsement read:

Pay to the Order of
Fidelity State and Savings Bank

Emporia, Kansas
County Treasurer, Lyon County

Whereas the genuine stamp read:

Pay to the Order of
Fidelity State and Savings Bank
Emporia, Kansas
Ed Benedict
Treasurer of Lyon County[34]

Finney was arraigned and released on $10,000 bond. A few days later, County Attorney Beck asked for an indefinite postponement of the preliminary hearing, due to the illness of Forrest Haynes. The hearing was never held; the case was never tried.[35]

W. W. Finney's troubles continued to mount when the receiver of Fidelity Bank on September 22 filed two civil suits in Lyon County District Court, totaling $130,945. The suits were filed to recover bank funds that he had allegedly converted to his own use and to recover on the $50,000 in forged bonds that he had sold to the bank. A few days later the Fidelity receiver filed a civil suit to recover $89,000 from Ronald Finney. In one complaint the bank sought to recover on $33,000 in worthless securities that had been sold to the bank on August 19, 1932; in the second complaint the bank sought restitution for $56,000 in forged Kansas City, Kansas, condemnation bonds that had been sold to the bank on February 4, 1933.[36]

The disclosures of the criminal activities of the Finneys, father and son, became too much for some of the folks out in Finney County in southwestern Kansas, which in 1883 had been named in honor of Warren's father, Lieutenant Governor David W. Finney. The first proposal to change the county's name came from Garden City residents, who suggested Sugar County, since area farmers devoted a large acreage to sugar beets. Then a clamor arose for Sequoyah, its original name. In mid October a report surfaced that literally "thousands" of Finney Countians demanded a change. The author of that statement happened to be the county chairman of the Democratic Central Committee. Though rumors circulated that a bill to change the name would be introduced at the upcoming special legislative session, in fact, it never was.[37] Shortly after his return from Europe, W. A. White fired an editorial broadside at the movement, claiming that it would be unjust to smear posthumously the good name of one of the leaders of pioneer Kansas. "How cruel the mob can be," he lamented.[38]

PRESSURE to open the fiscal agency continued to mount from financial institutions and the general public. But the obstinate treasurer announced on September 19 that the agency would not reopen in the foreseeable future to process the state's bonds and interest coupons. The bonding company had notified Boyd that it would not be responsible for any improper payments that might be made under its $500,000 bond on him as fiscal agent. And no one else had the authority to make the payments without taking personal responsibility for the action.[39]

Tom Boyd's friends had subjected him to a great deal of pressure to resign after he gained his freedom in mid September. Encouraging him to avoid what appeared to be almost certain impeachment, they pointed out that a good deal of evidence that would not be admissible in a criminal trial could be brought into an impeachment proceeding, to the possible embarrassment of his close personal and political friends. Long before the scandal had broken, shocking stories had been circulating about lively parties attended by Boyd, Finney, and other prominent citizens. But Boyd had been reluctant to take the step urged by his friends, fearing that resignation would be interpreted by the public as an admission of his guilt. But on September 26 his friends prevailed. One of the state's most popular figures—the man who had led the Republican ticket to a smashing victory less than a year earlier—resigned, effective October 1, as treasurer of Kansas.[40]

In his letter of resignation to the governor, Boyd asserted that he didn't see how the fiscal agency could be reopened in the near future with safety and that in the event that mistakes were made, he would likely be criticized more than someone else.

> Please do not construe my resignation as any admission on my part that I am guilty of the charges which have been placed against me, as that is not a fact. I feel, however, that I owe a debt of gratitude to the many people of Kansas who have always been good to me, and that my resignation at this time may help some in unraveling a very regrettable condition in the treasurer's office which was caused on account of the wholesale forgeries.[41]

In an article following the resignation, the publication *Plain Talk* lived up to its name:

> Mr. Boyd, we didn't think you had it in you to resign. We don't know whether some of the "Big Boys" passed you any jack or not but you had more guts than the rest of the dirty skunks. . . .
>
> How would you fellows who attended these parties with Boyd and Finney like to have your names published? Don't kid yourselves —we know whereof we speak. We insist on others resigning from office. French, Boynton and Koeneke must also "hit the trail."[42]

THE RESIGNATION meant an early reopening of the fiscal agency (where about two million dollars had piled up waiting to be paid to bondholders), the quashing of a possible impeachment against Boyd, and, of course, a new state treasurer. The air filled with possible (and impossible) suggestions of who might fill the important post. The names of former governor Ben Paulen, former treasurer Carl White, and former state auditor Seth Wells were among those more prominently mentioned.[43]

Landon determined to make an appointment which would help restore the public's badly shaken confidence in its state government. He decided to go outside the usual group of "pols"—those who might be disposed more to politicking on the job than to cleaning up the office in an efficient, straight-forward fashion and then getting out. On September 28 the Statehouse announced that the position had been offered to Dr. Ernest Pihlbad, president of Bethany College at Lindsborg. He represented precisely the above-reproach "higher type" that the governor had been so earnestly seeking. But it was not to be. After a day of reflection on the burdens of a public official, especially one who would go into office with the hard and suspicious eyes of the state trained directly on him, Pihlbad concluded that the academic serenity that he enjoyed at the small cloistered college would be most difficult to leave.[44]

Pihlbad's refusal placed the governor in a tight spot. He needed a good man, and he needed him immediately. Reports surfaced that the entire treasury might have to be shut down. Landon once again got busy on the phone, calling friends around the state for recommendations. One of these conversations was with Fay Seaton of the *Manhattan Mercury*. Seaton suggested an outstanding Kansan, one who had held several important state and national positions and who happened at this very moment—as Landon's luck would have it—to be unemployed. He recommended William M. Jardine. After serving for several years as director of the Experiment Station and as dean of the Agricultural Department of Kansas State Agricultural College, Jardine had become its president in 1918. After the death of Secretary of Agriculture Henry C. Wallace and after Secretary of Commerce Herbert Hoover had declined the post, President Calvin Coolidge had named Jardine as secretary of agriculture in 1925. Thus Jardine had become the first Kansan to serve as a member of a president's cabinet. (One of his assistants had been twenty-seven-year-old Milton S. Eisenhower.) After Hoover became president in 1929, he named Jardine as minister to Egypt, a position that he had held until he had recently been relieved by a Roosevelt appointee. He had arrived in New York City only the previous week.[45] He agreed to accept the position "until things are cleaned up" and emphatically declared that he would not be a candidate in the election of 1934.[46]

Since Jardine had almost literally been snatched off the boat from Europe, he found it necessary to spend a few days in Washington in order to close out his records. Landon and his brain trust worked out a complicated procedure whereby a stopgap treasurer would be named for the interim. The acting treasurer would have to be selected, sworn in, qualify for a $500,000 surety bond (no easy task), and then resign when Jardine arrived. This unnecessarily complex plan was about to be implemented when a clerk for Senator Harris, Dora Miller, meekly offered an alternative: if Jardine were flown to Topeka and sworn in, he could return to Washington to wind up his affairs, while the office could be functioning normally in charge of the chief assistant. The disconcerted brain trust stared dumfoundedly at Mrs. Miller, and then it proceeded to do just that.[47]

Treasurer Jardine commenced his new duties in a memorable fashion. At high noon of his first day on the job, he called all twenty-one employees of the office together: he had an announcement to make. The staff expected a get-acquainted pep talk from the new boss. Actually he had some bad news and some good news. The bad news was that they were all summarily fired—each and every one of them—as of that moment. The good news was that they would receive their full pay for the rest of that day. Stunned by the sudden news, the dismissed employees dejectedly filed out—many of the women in tears. "Gee, I hated to do this," the new treasurer told reporters. "But I had to start with a clean slate. Talking downtown has to stop." He said that he was going to call on some of his friends to help put the department back on its feet, adding that "this is a time when people owe something to their state."[48] The next day, Jardine attended a function given in his and Senator Capper's honor at the Manhattan ranch of the prominent cattleman Dan Casement. There, at the festive barbecue, just twenty-four hours after firing every employee in the Treasury Department, he casually—and incredibly—remarked that the bond scandal "isn't nearly as bad as it appears." He added: "People on the outside think . . . it a fine joke on Kansas because we've always been so clean out here."[49] It is doubtful that the recently fired employees appreciated either Jardine's sense of proportion or his sense of humor.

The Jardine appointment, however, turned out to be an excellent one and was widely perceived as such. The relieved governor received the congratulations of a grateful public. After the new treasurer had been on the job a month, the *Beloit Gazette* remarked that the public's reaction to the new appointee had been a lot like the little boy who, when asked to spell "dog," proudly spelled out d-o-g. The teacher said that was pretty good. "Pretty good! Hell, that's perfect," the proud student replied. Jardine quickly reorganized the purged department, replacing the Boyd-appointed assistant treasurer with an able accountant from the Budget Department. After receiving a reassuring report from a legal consultant, Jardine reopened the fiscal agency on October 26. Reactivation of the department, which had been unprecedently closed since August 8, was greeted with warm approval by the financial community and the general public, especially its senior citizens. The backlog of bond retirements and coupon payments was quickly worked through, so that Jardine could report to Landon on December 19 that the department was all caught up.[50]

At the end of his first month, Jardine remarked that, in his view, Kansas was lucky to have any money left at all, so slipshod were its fiscal procedures. Over the next several months the treasurer recommended a number of ways to modernize the processing and auditing of bond and coupon payments. The accounting changes sounded good, but where they required additional money, the economy-minded legislature rejected them. The new treasurer kept his word that he wouldn't run for the office at the next election, though it undoubtedly would have been his for the asking. In late January he announced that he planned to resign effective March 1 in order to become president of Municipal University of Wichita.[51]

THE STATE PROSECUTORS had been uneasy about the embezzlement charge against Tom Boyd. On September 28, in Shawnee County District Court, Lester Goodell filed two counts involving $260,600 against Boyd and Ronald Finney. One count charged that $150,600 in bonds had been illegally removed from the treasurer's vault on two separate days in July. The second count charged the illegal removal of $110,000 in bonds that had been deposited to secure state soldiers' bonus funds that were on deposit with the Fidelity Bank. The prosecutors were satisfied that they now had a much stronger case than before. Bond for each defendant was set at only $1,000, since Finney already had $75,000 in bonds on two state and one federal charge, and Boyd had $50,000 on one state and one federal charge. Beginning to be bored with the repeated arrests and arraignments, the lighthearted Finney complained that the $1,000 bond was "petty" and should be raised to a "decent figure." Boyd and Finney were bound over after a preliminary hearing on October 17.[52]

THE GOVERNOR caused a sensation on September 22 when he revealed that there had been a plot to kidnap his daughter Peggy Anne. She was to be held as a hostage to gain the release of six long-term convicts at the State Penitentiary. The original plan, which had failed, called for the kidnapping of the governor himself.[53]

Lightning struck again near the front door of the state's Executive Mansion on September 28, when Landon revealed at a press conference the details of a large financial transaction that Mrs. Landon had had with Ronald Finney. The check register that had been seized at the Jayhawk Hotel had provided the first clue to investigators. Theo Cobb Landon herself had made a full statement to Fred Harris on September 20. She had been left some money by her father, Sam Cobb, former president of the National Bank of Topeka. Charles L. Cooke, head of the bank's Bond Department and an associate of Finney's, handled her investments at the bank. In February, 1932, Cooke had suggested that a loan could be arranged at an attractive interest rate with his—and her—friend. The money, she was told, was to be used by the Hill Packing Company, a Topeka horsemeat firm that had retained Finney to help in sundry financial matters, including the acquisition of capital. Mrs. Landon followed Cooke's advice and made a $3,500 loan, receiving a receipt for Kansas school bonds as collateral. The note was repaid in July, 1932, and a new loan, this time for $10,000, was promptly negotiated by Cooke. Again, Finney put up school bonds as collateral. Whether the collateral had been bogus was never determined. In late March, 1933, Mrs. Landon decided to call in the loan, which was for an undefined length of time. On a Saturday afternoon she received a call from Finney, asking if it was all right to write a check directly to her, since the banks were not open. She agreed, and thus came into existence a check for $10,046.47, payable directly to the governor's wife, from the arrant Ronald Finney.[54]

Landon's political enemies—he had recently picked up quite a few in addition to the normal quota for an aggressive politician—tried to make as much as possible of the check. Copies of the document circulated widely around the state, even popping up among the crowd at the Hutchinson State Fair. Will French was said to have been responsible, though he denied it.[55] After the initial sensation had died away, the check issue caused the governor only minor irritations for the next several months. But it would surface again during the 1934 primary in the capable hands of the only person in the world who could legitimately challenge Ronald Finney's claim to being Kansas' all-time champion confidence man—the goat-gland wizard himself, Dr. John R. Brinkley.

A few days after the check had become public knowledge, two former associates of Finney's—Assistant Auditor Ray Hardin and publicist Lee Meadows—announced that they would make public certain heretofore private information that would also reflect badly on Landon. The threatened disclosures were never made, though both of these august gentlemen would soon have the once-in-a-lifetime experience of testifying under oath before the Kansas Senate sitting as a court of impeachment.[56]

LATER IN THE FALL the legislature appropriated a sum of money for the conduct of the bond-scandal investigations. The introductory clause of that act faithfully captured the Kansas milieu two months after the initial disclosures:

> Whereas, owing to startling and appalling discoveries, publicly made on August 7, 1933, that gross and enormous irregularities existed in the conduct, management and handling of the business and financial affairs of the state; the public thereby greatly shocked; the integrity and credit of the state impaired, and the governor, as chief executive of the state, . . . impelled to take active and decisive steps, and to exercise drastic measures, to the end that normal conditions should be restored . . . .[57]

4

Impeachment

ooooooooooooooooooooooooooooooooooooooooooooooo

THE AROUSED GOVERNOR maintained a high profile during those first several weeks, not only when he took the unprecedented steps of ordering the arrests of prominent citizens and declaring martial law, but also in direct contact with the press and public. "The mess in the statehouse is terrible," he told a reporter from the *Atchison Globe* in a phone message a few days after Black Monday. "The crimes brought to light are a serious offense against the people of Kansas. That alone makes me sore. But another thought that makes me so all fired mad is that after the state legislature and my office tried so hard last winter to put the state's finances on a solid footing . . . , three or four blankety blank blanks do what they shouldn't do, and the effect is a black eye to the state's credit. By thunder, I just can't keep from cussing."[1]

At Labor Day festivities in Salina, Landon asserted: "Kansas people are incensed, and they have a right to be. Our present scandal has attracted nation-wide attention, mainly because such things are not as common in Kansas as in some of our states. However, Kansas and Kansas citizens will set their own house in order without fear or favor, and the Sunflower state will continue to hold the enviable position for civic righteousness it has held in the past."[2] A few days later, Landon told a cheering crowd of three thousand in Shawnee County's Garfield Park that "Kansas has a right to be mad, and I hope Kansas stays mad until this thing is cleaned up."[3] In late September he abruptly digressed from a prepared speech to the WCTU to serve notice that he would "accept the full responsibility of bringing to justice those guilty in the bond forgery scandal and in reporting all the facts to the legislature for its action."[4]

THE POSSIBILITY of impeaching one or more of the constitutional officers was raised immediately after the initial disclosures. On August 8 Landon had hinted broadly at the possibility: "I am going to ask the legislative council, . . . to investigate thoroly the connection of every state official and every state department involved in the issuance and disposal of the forged bonds; also into every phase of the operation of these departments which touches the handling of state funds and the safeguarding of the interests of the citizens of Kansas."[5] A week later, in his address to the Legislative Council, Landon firmly declared that "there should be no hesitancy in laying the ground for impeachment of any individual who has been unfaithful to his trust."[6]

Representative Matt Guilfoyle declared on August 9 that if the facts warranted, the Legislative Council "should prepare . . . the proper impeachment resolutions." "The people of Kansas," he added, "will never tolerate such outrageous proceedings as are indicated."[7]

The need for a special session of the legislature to vote on repeal of prohibition (the Twenty-first Amendment) had been expressed only a few weeks after the end of the regular session. During the late spring, Landon and other state officials saw the necessity of calling a special legislative session to deal with the mounting relief problems, banking legislation, the vexing issue of 3.2 beer, and other problems of a quasi-emergency nature. A call in early autumn had been anticipated. When the bond scandal broke—with the possibility of impeachments deriving therefrom—that issue pushed everything else to the sideline. In mid September, Landon announced that the special session would have to be delayed until the special committee of the Legislative Council had had a chance to study the evidence that was being assiduously assembled by the investigators.[8] It looked as if the upcoming special session would devote most of its time to banks, beer, bonds, Boyd, Boynton, boondoggles, and burst bubbles.

In late September, Senator Harris reported that the mass of evidence had been assembled and was ready for presentation to the special investigating committee of the Legislative Council. It comprised over 2,600 pages of typed manuscript, which included the statements of more than 125 witnesses and over 1,000 photostatic exhibits of bonds, warrants, receipts, checks, and so forth. Making the photostatic reproductions of the relevant documents had kept from three to eight clerks, stenographers, and court reporters busy in the basement of the Statehouse since August 8.[9]

After thoroughly investigating their offices and studying their formal statements, officials announced in late September that no further probe of Secretary of State Frank Ryan and Superintendent of Public Instruction

IMPEACHMENT

W. T. Markham would be made. They were officially "in the clear," though the statements of each were to be included in Harris's report to the special committee.[10]

ABOUT THIS TIME a story was released which involved Markham as the unknowing recipient of the "Finney touch" in the political realm. A nemesis of Finney's on the School Fund Commission—Superintendent of Public Instruction George A. Allen—had been reelected in November, 1932, but had died in an auto accident in early December. A few days later the lame duck Democratic governor, Harry Woodring, who was on a trip to the East which included a visit with FDR at Warm Springs, Georgia, announced from Washington the appointment of the Democrat Markham, who was then superintendent of schools at Yates Center. The Republican secretary of state for Kansas, E. A. Cornell, refused to grant a commission to Markham, claiming that the governor had no legal right to make the appointment while he was outside the state. The Republican lieutenant governor, J. W. Graybill, after a quick conference in Independence with Governor-elect Landon, hurried to Topeka to appoint the Republican assistant superintendent, W. A. Stacey, to the vacant post. Cornell then issued a commission to Stacey. Woodring, who had been detained in the East due to a snowstorm, had Democratic friends in Topeka obtain an injunction to prevent the seating of Stacey pending a court hearing. Markham proceeded to function as the superintendent, and on December 23 the Kansas Supreme Court officially seated Woodring's choice.[11]

Woodring had been alerted to the Republican shenanigans by a timely phone call from Bertha Wetherton, the state accountant. A short while later, Ronald Finney came around to Mrs. Wetherton to thank her for her splendid deed. Finney had fervently desired the appointment of Markham, partly because he felt anyone would be better than George Allen or his understudy, partly because Markham hailed from Yates Center, the seat of Woodson County, which included the old Finney stomping ground, Neosho Falls, and partly because Markham came highly recommended by one of Finney's chief advisors and Jayhawk confidants, Ehret E. Lamb, a Yates Center attorney. Intimating broadly that he had actually pulled the strings to get Markham appointed, Finney offered Mrs. Wetherton $1,000 to show his gratitude for her astute phone call. She declined that, but she did subsequently give him $450 to play the wheat market. After an appropriate interval, Finney returned with a $1,000 check, which, he quite predictably claimed, her investment had yielded.[12]

Actually, up to this point, Ronald Finney had never met W. T. Markham. But that detail was quickly taken care of. Shortly after Markham came to Topeka, Lamb set up a luncheon appointment with the new superintendent, ostensibly to introduce him to an old college chum of his—Dr. Earle Brown, secretary of the State Board of Health. Lamb casually suggested that they have lunch at the Jayhawk Hotel. When the three of them reached the lobby of the hotel, Lamb abruptly proposed that they go upstairs to the fifth floor for just a moment to meet a friend of his. Following the introductions, Finney hauled out an expensive fly-casting rod, which was greatly admired by the avid fishermen Brown and Markham. After a period of good fellowship, the broker called downstairs and ordered lunch to be sent up while the good old boys continued to talk of fish and fishing and the good old days down in Woodson County. It all seemed so easy, so friendly, so natural. Only Finney and Lamb understood what actually was going on. Around the state's school districts over the next several months, in order to demonstrate his political muscle to those interested in school bonds, Finney often referred to his good friend, "the superintendent that I got appointed." That assertion wasn't fully appreciated by Governor Woodring: when he heard about the Jayhawk lunch and Finney's claims, he stammered, "Why, why, the—well, of all the nerve!"[13]

ON OCTOBER 2 Senator Harris addressed the assembled committee of the Legislative Council, which was named the Bloss Committee after its chairman. "It's a most amazing story," Harris exclaimed. For eight solid hours he related the sordid details to the incredulous solons, and he didn't get half-way through.[14] As the story of corruption, forgery, and theft unfolded before them in the days that followed, the astonished committee members learned in detail of the "wretched incompetency" of their state officers.[15] Finney and his associates had been permitted to run wild in the state treasury; to manipulate the School Fund Commission so that it would buy or reject bonds at their bidding; to invent instruments such as the auditor's "Certificate of Destruction," which enabled them to continue to use canceled warrants in the stream of commerce; to wheedle and cajole and lull with soporific small favors. No one in a position of authority, it seemed, had observed anything or suspected anything or even had been roused from his torpor when warned of irregularities directly or when confronted with evidence adduced by others.[16] W. H. Stanley, clerk for the School Fund Commission, admitted that "when Mr. [Ronald] Finney spoke, everybody jumped." When asked why the commission had bought some

Kismet bonds after having rejected them twice, Stanley unblinkingly responded: "I suppose because Mr. Finney wanted them bought." The sanctimonious former minister admitted to having regularly "slaved for Finney, morning, noon, day and night." But, he complained, the pay was irregular and came only in small dribbles—$10 here, $20 there.[17]

Finney's field days with the School Fund had come to an abrupt halt in February, 1933, shortly after Frank J. Ryan had returned as secretary of state. After George Allen's death, Finney had begun to attend the commission sessions on a regular basis. Dutch Shultz surmised that the commission had been opening its meetings with Finney in much the same way as the legislature opened its sessions with prayer. Finney had finally had his monopolistic hold on the commission broken by the vehement objections of the short-fused Ryan. Of course, by that time the inventive broker had discovered other, and much easier, ways to make a dollar.[18]

Of all the state officials, Attorney General Roland Boynton had had the greatest public pressure applied. The *State Journal,* voicing an opinion held by many, stated flatly as early as September 13 that Boynton's "usefulness to the state in an official capacity has ended."[19] Boynton had had his "day in court" before the Bloss Committee on October 5, taking up most of the day. He admitted that Ronald Finney had speculated on the commodities market for him, had made large campaign contributions in his behalf, and had paid him for private legal work since he had become attorney general. But he denied any wrongdoing: he knew nothing of any forgeries; he hadn't realized that Finney had had an interest in many of the bond issues that had come before the commission, though the broker had called him about some of them; and he seemed totally unaware that Finney had been traveling the length and breadth of Kansas boasting of his influence in the Attorney General's Office and elsewhere.[20] When the state's chief prosecutor had been confronted in April with direct evidence of duplicate bonds, he had immediately, he confessed, "dismissed the matter from [my] mind."[21]

Will French appeared before the Bloss Committee on October 6. The charges developing against French centered on the "certificates of destruction"; the use of the auditor's seal on the forged bonds; the close relationship of French's assistants with Finney; and his unprecedented Treasury Board motion in assigning $50,000 to the Fidelity Bank "without additional security." Like Boynton, he also pleaded total innocence, claiming that any assistance that Finney had received from his office had come unknowingly and unwittingly. He had only learned recently, he testified, that his current assistant, Ray Hardin, had been living rent-free for several months in one of Finney's apartments. But he was quite disturbed to learn that Hardin had been writing checks to a bootlegger in southeast Kansas to pay Finney's liquor bills.[22]

On the evening of October 6 the Bloss Committee recessed, to reconvene on October 24, without making a formal decision on recommendations regarding impeachments. Thankful to have such august support in his investigation, Senator Harris turned everything over to the committee with best wishes "and may the Lord bless you."[23] Landon postponed the special session of the legislature until October 30 to allow Harris time to prepare an abstract and to take additional testimony.[24] Before the committee adjourned, its members passed unanimously a formal commendation of the aggressive action taken by Governor Landon since the scandal broke and of the "masterful, concise and comprehensive" presentation by Senator Harris and his assistants.[25]

On October 24 Harris presented the reconvened committee with a 706-page abstract of the evidence. The committee also received a summary of the evidence and of the statements obtained by investigators during their ten-week inquiry.[26]

W. W. FINNEY'S continuing difficulties with the State Banking Board represented the first matter placed before the committee. Perhaps not coincidentally, Finney's criminal trial in Emporia had just begun. The problems, on the record, began in late 1926 and continued without abatement into the summer of 1932. And then, quite suddenly, they improved. The irregular conditions, which had been condemned repeatedly by the board "in no uncertain terms," included check-kiting, excessive overdrafts, shortages in accounts, erasures and changes on the statement sheets of three telephone companies, and numerous bad loans, especially in the Neosho Falls area. At frequent intervals during the period, the State Banking Board had directed the two banks to close the accounts that each had in the other's bank (to stop the check-kiting), had ordered large cash assessments against the Neosho Falls bank, and had demanded the cessation of the improper and illegal practices. Accompanied by his attorneys, Finney had appeared before the board on numerous occasions, contending in a petulant tone that he was the victim of political and personal persecution. He often failed to appear when requested, to answer letters, or to carry out the direct instructions of the board. The Finneys apparently handled the banks' affairs as they pleased, regardless of the instructions and criticisms of the Banking Department.

In January, 1929, at the end of his term as bank commissioner, Roy

Bone, who died ten days after the scandal broke, sent a year-old bank-examiner's report, which gave details of the falsification of the telephone companies' bank statements, to the Lyon County attorney, O. R. Stites. Stites, who was one of W. W.'s defense attorneys in 1933, took no action, stating that he did not have sufficient information for a criminal prosecution and questioning why the report had been so long in coming.

On June 15, 1932, the exasperated board finally read the riot act to Finney. At this time, total irregularities in the two banks, including account shortages and overdrafts by both the bank president and his son, totaled about $175,000. Finney perceived that this time the board meant business, and he responded accordingly. When he reappeared on July 7, reporting marked improvement in the condition of the banks, he presented an appraisal by Charley Cooke of the National Bank of Topeka concerning various Kansas municipal bonds that were owned by the banks. Improvement continued, so that an enthusiastic Finney could report to Commissioner Koeneke a few months later that "wonderful progress" had been achieved. It was now known, Senator Harris caustically told the investigating committee, how this "wonderful progress" could have been achieved and so quickly. The first Finney-forged bonds had gone into the state treasury as security for deposits in the banks on July 19, 1932; many warrants, forged or canceled by refunding, had been placed in the banks for the same purpose during the latter part of 1932; and on June 23, 1932, the Treasury Board, on the motion of Will French, had deposited $50,000 in the Fidelity Bank "without additional security."[27]

ON THE THIRD DAY of their reconvened session the Bloss Committee decided that it had heard enough about Statehouse connivance; it announced on October 26 that it intended to report a resolution recommending impeachment of both Roland Boynton and Will French to the House of Representatives. On behalf of the committee, Matt Guilfoyle—and later Judge Bloss—attempted to persuade Boynton to resign in order to save him further embarrassment and to save the state the trouble and expense of the impeachment proceedings.[28] The incensed attorney general refused to do so. The committee understood that French's response would be similar, so no one went to see him. After refusing to resign, Boynton issued a long, bristling statement, which concluded: "My political enemies have taken advantage of the widespread publicity of this astounding forgery scheme to make me a political sacrifice. I have, therefore, decided to face the issue thus drawn. I have not been guilty of misconduct in office and am confident that when all the facts are known this will become apparent to the people of Kansas."[29]

"THE MOST IMPORTANT special session of the legislature ever held in Kansas" opened in Topeka on October 30.[30] Governor Landon addressed the legislators the following day. Their most important task, he said, was to deal with the results of the bond-forgery scandal which "has shocked the citizens of Kansas by its scope and the personnel involved." The scandal had made it painfully clear, he said, that the current state organization needed modification, since it resembled "a creature without a head." He urged a constitutional amendment which would result in having the people elect only the governor, the lieutenant governor, and the auditor, with the other constitutional officers being appointed by the governor. Several bills that would have made it more difficult to counterfeit bonds and that would have provided for stiff penalties for public officials who neglected their duties or allowed irregularities were promptly tossed into the hopper.[31]

Governor Landon addressing the legislature (Kansas State Historical Society)

The Bloss Committee was specifically asked to recommend new laws that would be useful in minimizing a recurrence of the bond scandal. But Fred Harris told them that the real weakness resided, not in the laws or lack thereof, but in the laxity of observance by the state officials themselves and in the failure to enforce the law. The committee determined that the power to hire and fire employees in the offices of the constitutional officers lay entirely with those officers and that the legislature could not direct the removal of their subordinates.[32]

DISTURBED by the account of the chronic failure of the Banking Department to control the Finney banks, Representative Wilford Riegle, a Republican lawyer from Emporia who was prominent in state American Legion circles, introduced a joint resolution in the House, calling for a committee to investigate the activities of the Banking Department back to 1925. The probe was to include the office of the bank commissioner and the long-term political influence of W. W. Finney in the Statehouse. Reportedly, several governors and attorneys general had received repeated warnings from unhappy bank commissioners about the Finney banks. Evidently, accommodation could always be made.[33]

Asserting that his constituents were demanding action and acknowledging that the purpose of his resolution had largely been achieved by the Harris investigation, Riegle introduced another resolution a few days later, which demanded that Governor Landon ask for the resignation of Bank Commissioner H. W. Koeneke.[34] Landon was asked to appoint a new commissioner "who will not permit flagrant violations of the banking rules and regulations, to the end that the people of this state may feel confident that an impartial and careful supervision will be had of the banking institutions of the state."[35]

Three days later the House rejected the resolution on a 55 to 4 vote, with 7 Democrats joining 48 Republicans to soundly defeat the proposal. Fewer than half of the members of the lower house had voted on the politically charged issue.[36] Many of the abstaining Democrats shrugged it off by saying that it was "a Republican matter."[37] Numerous concerned bankers from over the state had "wired, phoned and called in person upon members of the legislature" to help kill the resolution.[38] Some opponents of the bill charged that it looked like an attempt to whitewash Roland Boynton by directing attention away from him. Landon himself was cool to the measure, which would have forced him to remove one of his major appointees, one in whom he apparently still had confidence.[39] Stoutly defending his resolution on the House floor but fighting what he knew to be a losing battle, Riegle accused the bank commissioner of incompetence and political connivance and went on to reflect on the impact of the bank's closing in his community:

> I have not spoken here for the man who can afford to send telegrams to you, or drive to Topeka, and urge opposition to this resolution. Rather I have been speaking for the child who lost his Christmas savings in the Emporia bank. . . . I have been speaking for the railroad man, the farmer, and the laborer, the business man, whose only earnings went up in smoke in that bank. I am speaking for all my constituents who lost money in that bank, because the bank was allowed to run hog wild . . . you will never change my belief or the belief of most of my people, that for some particular reason and on account of some peculiar influence, in spite of the startling reports of efficient and fearless bank examiners, the Finney banks these many years have been allowed to remain open to the detriment of the entire state.[40]

IMPEACHMENT CHARGES, which were formally introduced in the House by the Bloss Committee on November 2, were promptly referred to the Judiciary Committee, chaired by the omnipresent Judge Bloss.[41] Senator Harris made lengthy statements on the nights of November 7 and 8 to the committee, much as he had done earlier to the Bloss Committee. The full House had been invited to the presentation so as to save time later when the entire body would receive the committee's report. Almost all of the 125 members of the House attended, sitting in rapt attention as Harris systematically unfolded his "amazing story."[42]

Ever since W. A. White had returned from Europe in late October, he had been needling Boynton to assume a more aggressive stance before the howling wolves. White's efforts evidently paid dividends before the Judiciary Committee on November 13, when, in an uncharacteristically bitter and vituperative attack, Boynton charged that the impeachment resolution was "the most unjust document ever presented to a legislature." Earlier in the day, on the House floor, he had been accused of "having been intoxicated"—a highly unlikely event. This scurrilous accusation had been quickly denied by Boynton's friends. From the time that the forged bonds had been discovered, Boynton charged, efforts had been made to get the public mind inflamed by misinterpreting the facts. In an emotional conclusion, he declared that he "would have rather been shot and killed on the battlefield of France than to have my fellow Kansans say that I had been a traitor to my duty."[43]

IMPEACHMENT

The night after Boynton's presentation, Will French made a "clean cut, incisive" statement before the Judiciary Committee that was completely devoid of the acrimony of Boynton's pronouncement. He explained his role in the early stages of the investigation (before Sard Brewster had gone to Landon), his innocence regarding Finney's bond-forgery mischief, and his policy with respect to the infamous "certificates of destruction."[44]

When the House Judiciary Committee, which included seventeen lawyers, failed to produce an impeachment report after two lengthy nighttime executive sessions, the rumor mill began to grind. One report had it that "strong political influence from an unexpected quarter" was being used in order to drop the whole matter in the interest of party harmony. A companion rumor suggested that aspiring candidates for Congress in the Fourth District, who feared the ire of W. A. White, had worked on the committee for the same end. However, on November 20 the committee voted in about a two-to-one ratio—the exact vote was not publicly announced—to accept H.R. 12 (regarding Boynton) and H.R. 13 (French), the impeachment resolutions.[45]

THE FULL HOUSE began debate on the Boynton resolution on November 22. The charges centered around his indifference and unfaithfulness to his trust on the School Fund Commission; his refusal to act on specific complaints that had been called to his attention in the spring of 1933, especially by Thomas County Attorney Leon Roulier and Judge Light of Liberal; and due to his personal and business relations with Ronald Finney, his having been compromised and rendered useless as the prosecutor in the civil and criminal suits that had been brought as a result of the scandal.[46] With regard to the last charge, Matt Guilfoyle compared Ronald Finney with another famous American:

> Today in Kansas Ronald Finney is Public Enemy No. 1. Suppose that when Al Capone, in Chicago, was to be prosecuted, that a personal friend of his, one who had received larger campaign contributions from Capone than he had expended in his own campaign, one who had been given $1,700 winnings on the market without knowing anything about the market transaction, had been public prosecutor. What shape would he have been in to prosecute Al Capone?[47]

On November 23, after two days of debate, the House, in a voice vote, overwhelmingly voted to impeach Roland Boynton. An attempt to pass a substitute resolution, calling on him to resign, had been soundly rejected. On November 25 the House voted—on the record—on the four articles of impeachment: on article 1—yea, 93, no, 13; on article 2—yea, 91, no, 15; on article 3—yea, 87, no, 19; article 4—yea, 90, no, 16. Judge Bloss was named to head the five-member Board of Managers that would prosecute the case before the Senate in early January.[48]

In explaining his vote, George Davidson, a Democrat from Sedgwick County, sarcastically commented that there was really no use in impeaching Boynton, since he had already conclusively been found to be innocent of all charges by the Sedgwick, Wyandotte, and Shawnee County bar associations, the *Kansas City Star,* and the "distinguished editor" of the *Emporia Gazette.* John F. Payton, a Democrat from Sheridan County, concluded—as did many of his colleagues—that if Boynton "were aware of what was going on and made no move to stop it, . . . it gives him the earmarks of a crook, and he should be ousted from his office. On the other hand, if he were not aware of what was going on in his office, relative to the Ronald Finney deals, as he claims, . . . he is too dumb to properly fill the office of attorney-general of the great state of Kansas."[49] Which revived the age-old debate on who was the greater menace to society—a crook or a fool.

The heart of the case against French included the certificates of destruction issued by the Auditor's Office; the ignored letters of complainants, which repeatedly asserted that Finney was misrepresenting the intentions of the Auditor's Office; the connivance with Finney of two different assistants in the office; and the June 23, 1932, Treasury Board motion authorizing deposition of $50,000 in Fidelity Bank without additional security, since no similar board motion had ever been made before. On November 27, after only four hours of debate, the House, in a voice vote, overwhelmingly elected to impeach Will French. A committee was appointed to draw up the articles. The next day the articles were formally adopted as follows: article 1—yea, 95, no, 17; article 2—yea, 96, no, 16; article 3—yea, 96, no, 16; article 4—yea, 94, no, 18. Judge Bloss was again selected to head the Board of Managers prosecuting team.[50]

ALMOST IMMEDIATELY after his return from Europe, William Allen White began to write a series of impassioned editorials in defense of his beleaguered cousin.[51] The editor bemoaned the fact that Boynton was "a frank but somewhat slow-moving young man who showed no dangerous skill at defending his own reputation." In one of these fiery polemics, entitled "His Real Crime," he charged that the defenseless Boynton had been made a goat for political reasons. His real crime, White claimed, was that "coming from Lyon County, he was on friendly personal terms with the Finneys."[52] The Whites had had the editorial mailed to every member of the House. Many of the legislators resented the pressure, contending that House members shouldn't be subjected to such outside influences during their deliberations.[53] Representative Oscar P. May, Republican of Atchison, read a somewhat apologetic statement into the *House Journal* at the conclusion of the proceedings:

> I did criticize the [*Gazette*] editorial, but I would not have done so had it not been mailed on a form printed for the purpose, to each member of the House, sitting in the nature of a grand jury. Under such circumstances it should have been discussed, and criticized if erroneous, as any other evidence before the House on the matter.
>
> I do not wish to be understood as criticizing Mr. White for coming to the defense of his friend and relative, Mr. Boynton. I tried to be fair in performing this unpleasant duty and I had no intention of being unfair to our distinguished Kansan, Mr. White.[54]

WILLIAM ALLEN WHITE fought a lonely battle to try to save Roland Boynton; almost every other paper in the state lined up on the other side. "Overshadowing everything else will be the disastrous, disgraceful and deplorable conditions that have prevailed in the capitol for the past few years," the hard-liner Bill Clugston commented in the *Kansas City Journal Post* on the eve of the special session. "Dominating forces . . . of Kansas in the last few years have left no doubt that they [will] try to produce a masterpiece of 'whitewashing' . . . . They are going to try to protect and shield their puppets."[55] After Senator Harris's revelations to the Bloss Committee, several Kansas dailies, including the *Topeka State Journal,* called for the impeachment of both Boynton and French.[56]

The more cautious *Topeka Daily Capital* editorialized on October 28 that "there are the most convincing reasons why [Boynton] should accept the situation and offer his resignation." A few days later, after the Bloss Committee had reported to the House, the Capper-owned daily declared: "The House will be delinquent in its duty if it does not order the impeachment of these state officials [Boynton and French]."[57] Even the pro-White *Kansas City Star,* though it never openly advocated impeachment, took a solemn view of matters. At the time of the convening of the special session it circumspectly announced: "There are important charges [made by the Bloss Committee] that must be explained. On the basis of these . . . explanations . . . the [House] judiciary committee will be in a position to determine whether impeachment proceedings are warranted."[58]

"Friends of Roland Boynton . . . will be sorry to learn that he is tarred in any way by the Finney stick," Rolla Clymer wrote in the *El Dorado Times* in mid September.[59] Clymer, a former *Gazette* reporter and one of editor White's favorite "boys," often reflected the "party line" coming out of Emporia. Not infrequently, White, in order to test the wind on a given issue, would write a piece and send it down to El Dorado, suggesting that Clymer might want to run it. After Clymer had done so, the *Gazette* would subsequently begin a political editorial with "newspapers around the state are saying . . . ."[60] In October, before the Whites returned from Europe, Clymer commented on the widespread lethargy in the Statehouse:

> But no one ever thought of making the cross-check, or at least was too tired or indifferent to do so. And that seems to have been the main trouble at Topeka. Not many state officers were crooked; the rest merely went thru the routine of office, with the least exertion to themselves. The simplest kind of business vigilance would have made the bond scandal impossible. The crooks who were robbing the state treasury seem to have based their calculations chiefly upon [that].[61]

THE SPECIAL SESSION—the twelfth such—lasted thirty days, the longest and most productive in Kansas' history. Although Landon had urged that only emergency matters be considered, the legislators introduced about 450 bills, of which 130 passed. The governor vetoed four bills, including one that would have permitted capital punishment for murder.[62] The special session did vote to submit the prohibition amendment to the electorate in 1934, but on a close vote, it rejected the decriminalization of 3.2 beer, so that beverage continued to be illegal in Kansas.[63]

Although the legislators were more than anxious to pass bills that would tighten the ship of state and make it less vulnerable to the unscrupulous, the situation, as Senator Harris had told them, didn't really require a batch of new laws. A half-dozen bills relating to the bond scandal were passed, the principal one of which changed the composition of the Board of Treasury Examiners by substituting the bank commissioner and the assistant budget director (the state accountant) for the governor and the secretary of state. One new statute tightened up the procedures to be used in the Auditor's Office for the registration and cancellation of bonds and coupons; another regulated the placement of security in the treasury by depositories of public funds.[64]

Bills that failed included one that would have made any embezzlement or fraud against the state prosecutable within two years of the discovery of the crime, rather than from its commission; two bills that would have given to the state printer the full control and supervision over the printing of bonds; a bill requiring the School Fund Commission to buy bonds directly and in person from municipalities, without using any intermediary agents; and a proposal that would have created a separate fiscal agency for the receiving of bond payments, with a subagency in New York City, New York, of all places![65]

Proposals to eliminate the primary system—which some, through rather distorted logic, blamed for the "mess"—and to replace the regular ballot with a reduced or "short ballot" were also discarded. A few days after the scandal broke, the *Capital* had run a lengthy editorial in support of Landon's proposal for a short ballot, arguing that by electing a governor and then having him appoint the other state officers, the state would have a far more responsible and competent cabinet, thus reducing the chances for a repetition of the current fiasco. The idea was endorsed by a number of papers, though some, notably the *Wichita Eagle,* warned that this might lead to the abolishment of the primary system.[66]

Money concerns, which are always a high priority in the legislative mind and were especially so during the Great Depression, dominated nearly every discussion of every issue. Somewhat begrudgingly, the legislature appropriated $35,000 for the Landon-directed investigations. It appropriated $40,000 for the upcoming Senate impeachment trials and the tag end of the special legislative session (the special session cost a total of $55,000). A bill was killed which would have appropriated $10,000 to Shawnee County and $5,000 to Lyon County to defray the costs of the scandal-related prosecutions in their jurisdictions.[67]

FEDERAL INVESTIGATORS had, of course, been working on the bond cases since late June. The Federal Bureau of Investigation of the Department of Justice had been active in Topeka, Emporia, Kansas City, and Chicago, gathering evidence on Finney transactions. Post-office inspectors had been working on the mail-fraud angle, which in late August had resulted in the only federal arrests to date. Since then the federal agents had been publicly quiet; though just nine days after they had gone public with their revelations, they announced that a full-scale grand-jury investigation would soon be undertaken, implying that many prominent Kansas heads would roll.[68]

Finally, in late October, following by a month the filing of all the state charges, a grand jury reported in Topeka to Judge Richard J. Hopkins to hear evidence in the bond cases. A member in good standing of the progressive faction of the Republican party, Hopkins had received in late 1929 a controversial appointment to the federal bench from President Hoover. Currently the judge found himself embroiled in a nasty divorce in which both sides had filed suit. His wife, the distinguished jurist alleged, had a "violent and nagging disposition." Some observers had been so calloused as to suggest that the newspapers had tried to play up the bond scandal so as to divert the public's attention from the judge's marital problems.[69]

Included among the more than fifty witnesses who were heard by the grand jurors were the federal and state investigators; the bank examiners; school-district officers; executives of the Chicago and Kansas City brokerage firms and the commodities market; Kansas bond brokers; officers of the National Bank of Topeka; employees of the three Finney banks; bond printers; executives of Southwestern Bell; and private detectives. On November 1, as the corridors of the Federal Building "echoed with rumors concerning the case which appears to be including a number of prominent Kansans who are considered to wield much political power," the announcement came that no grand-jury report would be forthcoming at that time. The cautious prosecutors evidently wanted another opinion. The United States attorney general ordered a transcript of the evidence that had been presented to the grand jury. Pending further developments at the nation's highest level of law enforcement, members of the Kansas Grand Jury recessed and trooped back to their homes.[70]

In late November the Department of Justice indicated that it was now ready to proceed. The jurors reported once again to Judge Hopkins in Topeka, and on December 2 the grand jury handed down six indictments against seven defendants:

(1) Ronald Finney, Warren Finney, Tom Boyd, and Leland Caldwell were charged on seventeen counts with using the mails to defraud (these counts had to do with removal of around $400,000 in bonds from the state treasury and disposal of them to brokerage houses in Chicago during the spring and summer of 1933).

(2) Charles L. Cooke and Collis D. Harner were charged with two false entries on the books of the National Bank of Topeka (two bond issues in the account of Ronald Finney were raised $2,500 each to cover what the bank employees believed to be a $5,000 shortage in Finney's account).

(3) Charles L. Cooke was charged with abstracting a $10,000 bond and converting it to the use of Ronald Finney (the bond afterward turned up in a Chicago brokerage house, through Ronald Finney).

(4) Warren Finney was charged in three counts of using the mails to defraud by mailing checks on nonexistent accounts of the Fredonia, Altoona, and Kansas Home telephone companies (the checks were drawn on the Finney banks in Emporia and Neosho Falls).

(5) Warren Finney was charged on thirteen counts of using the mails to defraud by mailing to Southwestern Bell false statements of the Fidelity accounts of the Sabetha, Paola, and Emporia telephone companies.

(6) Carl McKeen, Tom Boyd, Warren Finney, and Ronald Finney were charged in one count of misapplication of funds of the National Bank of Topeka in connection with the removal of forged bonds held by the bank—under a repurchase agreement with Ronald Finney—by Warren Finney and Ronald Finney when they presented the $150,000 state-fund check issued by Boyd for that purpose.[71]

With the federal indictments, all the formal charges had been completed. All the investigative cards, though hardly all the evidence, had been laid on the public table. The roll-call consisted of nine defendants on twenty-one separate and distinct charges. The complete tally of the man-charges came to thirty-three; the sum of the man-counts was 430.

And so, by the onset of winter in that depression year, the people of Kansas had had a smattering of the evidence and all of the charges laid before them. How had they responded to the "startling and appalling discoveries" of the "gross and enormous irregularities" that had occurred under the very dome of the Statehouse of their beloved commonwealth?

5

Homo Sapiens Kansensis

ooooooooooooooooooooooooooooooooooooooooooooooooooooo

THE SUBSPECIES of mankind that occupies the imperfect rectangle on the central plains known as Kansas has always been considered as something of a breed apart—a unique cultural entity—and has so considered itself. Over the years, Mother Kansas developed a distinct personality and character. You either liked the old girl or you didn't. The maternalistic bond of Kansas to her sons and daughters has not been one of unqualified love or unmitigated loyalty, however, but rather a deep-rooted ambivalent condition, not uncommon among offspring, that is best described as filial love-hate. No region of the country has imprinted its citizens with a more profound or more permanent brand. Whatever the precise nature of the personal impress, an indelible impress it is.[1]

Ever since William Allen White wrote his bitingly sarcastic editorial-tirade against the Populists in 1896, the state had become something of an object of mirth and derision for the nation as a whole.[2] Infused with feelings of diffidence and self-effacement, Kansans themselves often authored the most intensely deprecatory anti-Kansas stories and jokes. Sometimes the state has been considered an enigma, like a mysterious woman. "Kansas has always been different from any other state," said Fred Trigg, Kansas correspondent for the *Kansas City Star* in the twenties. "God just dropped Kansas out here on the plains and the next morning it organized a constitutional convention. . . . Even historians don't understand Kansas; I wonder sometimes if anybody except God understands Kansas and sometimes I think Kansas even has Him fooled."[3]

Born of righteousness in the Free State cause in the fierce pre–Civil War days, the territory had been peopled by thrifty, hard-working immigrants, who derived principally from New England and the Old Northwest region of Ohio, Indiana, and Illinois. Though only a minority came from puritanical New England, this intelligent and well-educated group—books could be found among the precious possessions they brought west—influenced the developing culture out of all proportion to their absolute numbers in the population. Many of the business, political, educational, and religious leaders of the late nineteenth and the twentieth century came from their ranks. A "high moral purpose" was as standard a part of the baggage that they brought west as their cows, horses, plows, and newspaper presses. Reflecting the intensity of the place and times, as well as the literacy of the populace, Kansans established nearly forty-five hundred different newspapers over the next several decades—twice the number of the next highest state (New York is a poor second with twenty-three hundred).[4]

The pioneers and their issue had to come to terms with the recurrent hot winds, drought, floods, cyclones, and grasshoppers. Many came, many tried, and many left. The key words became "survival" and "endurance." The hardy and strait-laced souls that did survive and endure proceeded to establish an austere, almost mystic, stronghold that increasingly gained recognition as a prairie island of puritanism in a national sea of license and modernity. In 1880 they approved a constitutional amendment prohibiting the sale and manufacture of intoxicating beverages, the first state in the nation to do so. Encouraged by such as Carry Nation, they perfected their liquor laws so that by the early twentieth century the state could, in truth, be said to be bone-dry. Strong anticigarette and antigambling laws readily passed the state legislature. A tone of moral superiority and cultural righteousness pervaded the prairie-plains realm. Not everyone, of course, gracefully accepted the abstinence that was inherent in Kansas' "peculiar institution" and the mores that it implied. The *Chicago Tribune,* for example, grumbled in the early twenties that if the will of Kansas and its life style were imposed on the rest of the nation, "the greatest architectural monument of the land will be a silo, the greatest work of art a crazy quilt and the greatest thrill in life a snooze in stocking feet by the base burner."[5]

The major prophets of Holy Kansas have almost invariably been associated with moral causes and crusades. The hallowed roll includes the antislavery fanatic "Osawatomie" John Brown, who left his indelible mark one dark night on Pottawatomie Creek; Governor John P. St. John, who, by running for president on the Prohibition ticket in 1884, attracted enough Republican votes to elect the Democrat Grover Cleveland; the fervent Populists of the nineties—"Sockless" Jerry Simpson, Annie Diggs, and Mary Elizabeth ("Yellin' Ellen") Lease; the ax-wielding, saloon-smashing arch prohibitionist Carry Nation; the public-health defender Dr. Samuel J.

Crumbine, an ardent campaigner for disposable paper cups in public places, whose slogans were "swat the fly" and "don't spit on the sidewalk"; Senator Arthur Capper ("the Christ-like statesman"), who stood for everything fine and decent and became one of the nation's leading pacifist-isolationists; the Neo-Populist Dr. John R. Brinkley, who became a multi-millionaire by convincing many good folks in Kansas (and elsewhere) that an implantation of goat testes in just the right spot would cure real or imagined male impotency and who very nearly became governor in the bargain; the proper, progressive word genius William Allen White, whose righteous indignation always boileth over; and the solid, sensible Alf Landon, whose passions included fiscal stability, a balanced budget, and, at the moment, the certitude that the guilty must receive their just due.[6]

For all its puritanical inclinations the characteristic Kansas temperament shares little with that of, say, the flinty, reserved Vermonter, with whom the Kansan shares many cultural values. Rather, Kansans are noted for their friendly, unpretentious manner, as open and candid as their broad, rolling prairies and their wide, uncluttered skies. The Kansas style tends to the simple and direct, marked by unaffected plain-speaking.[7] That such a people would expect straight dealing from their neighbors and irreproachable behavior from their public servants should go without saying.

Its rural milieu had also helped mold the Kansas character. In a state whose largest city had a population of only 120,000, the traditional rural virtues of honesty, decency, and solidity could be expected to predominate, as well as the bucolic foibles of gullibility, provincialism, and priggishness. (As of March 1, 1933, the five largest Kansas towns were Kansas City—120,400; Wichita—101,600; Topeka—65,100; Hutchinson—29,300; Leavenworth—18,900. Emporia, with 12,980, was eleventh.)[8]

Staunch Republicanism had characterized the state from its mid-nineteenth-century "bleeding Kansas" days. The newspapers reflected this proclivity for the GOP. Of the 57 dailies in 1933, only 1 was Democratic; of the 452 weeklies, only 30 were Democratic. Not until the Populist "heresy" reached its zenith in the mid 1890s had Kansas ever swerved to any significant degree from the straight and narrow Republican path. Since that excusable deviance, Kansas had elected only Republicans to any state-wide office below that of governor. In its entire history, no Democrat had ever been elected as lieutenant governor, treasurer, secretary of state, auditor, or superintendent of public instruction. Four Democratic governors had managed to get themselves elected—George Glick in 1882, George Hodges in 1912, Jonathan Davis in 1922, and Harry Woodring in 1930. But one of the basic laws of Kansas nature, William Allen White had astutely observed, was that no Democratic governor could get himself reelected.[9]

THE GREAT KANSAS BOND SCANDAL

WHEN NEWS of the bond scandal broke, *Homo sapiens kansensis* reacted quickly and in no uncertain terms. The initial shock and amazement turned quickly to anger, then to outrage. Many expressed shame and humiliation that such corruption could take place in the Statehouse of their fair state. After all, this was not sin-ridden New York City, New York, with its notorious Tammany Hall, or seamy Chicago, where bootlegger-gangsters like Al Capone ran wild, or even the more staid state of Missouri, where the infamous Pendergast machine controlled "Tom's Town" just across the Kansas state line. Enormities of that sort just couldn't occur within the ascetic bastion of Godly Kansas—or so everyone had thought until August 7, 1933.

Phone calls, telegrams, and letters inundated the Governor's Office immediately following the disclosures, especially after his address to the Legislative Council on August 15. Four former governors—George Hodges, Arthur Capper, Ben Paulen, and Clyde Reed—were among the respondents. On the afternoon following the speech, the Governor's Office overflowed with excited men and women anxious to congratulate Alf personally. Despite the harsh fiscal and meteorological conditions of the day, the bond scandal would remain on the front pages and foremost in the public mind for the next two years.[10]

"Piled high on the governor's desk" were telegrams and letters, most of which lauded his decisive actions of the prior week:

> Bully Alf. Go to 'em.
>
> Every one in our community is singing your praises . . . , not only the Republicans but the Democrats as well.
>
> I have been proud of you for things you have been doing up there many times since January. I have never been prouder of you than now because of what you are doing in this terrible mess.
>
> It is going to involve some of your very closest associates and perhaps some other friends, but you are taking a stand that everyone in Kansas must commend.[11]

Some correspondents saw fit to warn the governor in subtle and sometimes not-so-subtle terms:

> It is a trying place you are in, stay with it and the good people will stay with you.
>
> Clean up and clean out the state house and don't weaken. There will be tremendous pressure on you to ease up. Turn on the heat!
>
> The people have almost lost faith in their Courts and officers, in fact everything pertaining to government. Such conditions breed revolutions. You are getting a lot of praise . . . but the balance of the

statehouse is getting thunder. This may do you more personal good than if it had not happened but it *must* be kept up.

The people are in such a state of mind that they are afraid of almost everyone, but if they know they have a governor who will look after the interests of the whole people, it will go a long ways in building up the confidence of the people of Kansas.

I want to see all the hides on the fence at an early date, and nothing would do this state more good.

Atta boy! We hanged them down here for stealing cayuses [horses]. If you can't manage the thieves up at the state house, send them down here, handcuffed and clogged and there are enough of us old fellows left to push them off in the Neosho river and let them drown like a litter of blind pups.[12]

As the politicians and lawyers would frequently do in the upcoming trials, many disturbed Kansans referred to the tarnished image of the state:

Allow me to congratulate you on the very courageous and firm stand you are taking in the disgraceful bond scandal which has developed in our fair state of Kansas.

As an organization our Sunday School . . . sincerely hope that you as our chief executive shall ever endeavor to preserve the high moral standard of Kansas and protect her citizens from evil enemies that exist within as well as without our border.[13]

On the night of Landon's address, Senator Arthur Capper commented at length on the situation over WIBW in Topeka:

Like most of you, I listened this morning to Governor Landon's message to the legislative council. Like all of you, I have been shocked and pained, aye, humiliated, at the disclosures of the last week in the bond forgery scandals. . . .

But the picture that has been passing before our eyes the last week has been a nightmare. A misguided, and from the long view, very foolish young man, started out to get rich quick. He apparently chose the stock market and the grain market. We keep those two gambling institutions alive in this country, and every year they ruin thousands of men and women.[14]

In the weeks and months that followed, a voluminous and varied correspondence continued to deluge the Governor's Office. It came from the common man and woman in the street as well as from ministers, lawyers, doctors, bankers, and politicians. Letters from out-of-staters sought information on the whereabouts of other bond forgers. A Delaware man, for example, wanted help in locating a "bond crook" who had defrauded his sister of $30,000.[15] Many job seekers, some of whom were from the East Coast, proffered their "unique" services as lawyers, auditors, hand-writing experts, or special investigators ("the Governor needs, at least, one man, experienced in this field . . . whose contacts are State wide, . . . and [who] knows the subject").[16] A hopeful prisoner at the Kansas State Penitentiary offered to check out his underworld contacts in Topeka, Wichita, and Kansas City to gain information about Finney's activities in the bond rackets, if he would just be allowed his freedom in order to do so.[17] Many denunciatory letters remonstrated against Tom Boyd, Roland Boynton, the Tuckers, and the Finneys ("I have known W. W. Finney 46 years and he has been a agent and pastmaster in crooked deals all his life and now he comes to his harvest reaping what he has sown. May he get his just due").[18]

Tips, clues, concerns, and suspicions of every description flowed in. The state had become a huge, unwieldy self-appointed detective agency. Most of the leads represented the overactive imagination of an excited people. For example, a prisoner at Lansing, who had been confined on a blue-sky offense, claimed that the state Insurance Department held $4 million in forged and stolen securities.[19] A few tips did prove to be valuable, such as the one from a Riley County automobile dealer ("when the writer called on Mrs. Andrew [Lucy] Pottorf of Riley yesterday in an effort to sell her a Ford car I find that she holds considerable information").[20] Many anxious citizens suggested methods for preventing future financial scandals by altering printing procedures or effecting other changes in the processing of bonds.[21] From the nervous public came frequent demands to launch local investigations of this and that—to look into everything from finance companies and brokerage houses to U.S. Liberty bonds.[22] Apprehensive bondholders pressed for additional information on specific fraudulent issues and importuned for the early reopening of the fiscal agency.[23] The more religiously inclined commended sundry biblical passages to Landon for his spiritual sustenance.[24] The entire membership of Topeka's Kansas Avenue Methodist Church sent a message lauding the governor for his actions.[25]

A FEW IRRITATIONS did appear to knit the gubernatorial brow. A Howard man was reported in September to have said that Landon had gone the bond for one of the Finneys. "You have been misinformed," Alf acidly wrote to the unfortunate soul, "I hope you will be good enough to see the gentlemen you have misinformed . . . and correct the information."[26] A worried Finney County banker wrote the governor that the Democrats out there had been spreading a not-very-favorable "gospel" regarding the inception of the investigation. "Our Democratic chairman claims that U.S.

Attorney Brewster made a presentation to yourself and further demanded certain detailed action . . . and further DEMANDED that such action be accomplished within a limited period of time, namely thirty minutes, 'or else,' he, Mr. Brewster, would immediately take his report to Washington for Federal intervention."[27] At Landon's suggestion, Brewster immediately wrote to the businessman: "There is absolutely nothing to the story that I made any demand on the Governor for action. I simply told him what I had discovered and asked his assistance in getting in the Treasurer's vault. . . . In fact before I hardly finished my story the Governor had commenced his investigation."[28]

In early November an employee of an Emporia milling firm, George Bordenkircher, wrote Landon, protesting against the "unconscionable expenses" of the Banking Department in liquidating the Finney banks. Landon huffily responded that he found "it somewhat difficult to understand your attitude in regard to the Bank Commissioners' office in view of the fact that you appeared in the Emporia trial as a character witness for Warren Finney." Bordenkircher was not willing to let that remark lie even if it did come from the governor:

> My dear Governor, I am perfectly willing to let bygones be bygones, but it should be no more difficult to understand that I was a character witness than to understand why the governor's picture should appear in the Gazette of August 3d, in connection with a big news story telling us that the Governor had been a guest at the W. W. Finney home that day. I testified to what I thought was Mr. Finney's general reputation in these parts prior to August 8th.[29]

THOUGH FLOATING in a sea of troubles, Kansans did not lose their sense of humor or proportion. A veterinarian wryly observed that an odor, thought to have come from cats at a Topeka residence, was now believed to have been emanating from the Statehouse all the time. Nearly everyone quipped that a check should be made to see whether the state or Ronald Finney had title to the Statehouse.[30] When a news story appeared in late September that the original cornerstone of the Statehouse couldn't be located, many papers around the state came back with some version of "Great Scott! Did Finney get away with that, too?"[31] As the legislators gathered for the special session, some exhibited mock surprise that the dome on the Capitol was still there. Matt Guilfoyle suggested that what Kansas had wasn't so much a political as an engineering problem—that is, the dome of the Statehouse needed to be jacked up and the second floor removed.[32] Lynn Broderick's *Marysville Advocate-Democrat* discovered that new standards had been developed for bond quality—flimsy, phoney, and Finney. It also observed that things had gotten so rotten in Topeka that Doc Brinkley's goats had refused to graze on the Statehouse lawn.[33]

A "prominent Kansan" (Clyde Reed?), visiting Topeka in November, said that he had looked in vain for a Thanskgiving proclamation from the president of the Kansas Bar Association. "The lawyers of Kansas," he remarked, "should unite in an offering of thanks to the Finney family. Nothing thruout the depression has done more for the attorneys than the Finney case.... Nearly every section of Kansas has profited.... And there are many, many months yet of pay dirt."[34] Charley Trapp suggested in the *Pink Rag* that Sally Rand, Doc Brinkley, and Ronald Finney were the champion skin-game artists in the country. "Sallie cashed in on her cuticle, Doc sold goat epidermis at fabulous charges but Ronald took the hides of suckers." "I'm proud of Kansas," he had written earlier, "always she's at the forefront. Any other state would have been content with one set of forged bonds."[35]

Emporia and Emporians came in for their share of the jibes. The *Fort Scott Tribune* thought that Alf might suggest to William Jardine that since he'd been in Egypt and hadn't followed things in Kansas too closely, maybe he should "go a little easy on whom we fall in with down around Emporia."[36] The *State Journal* described Emporia as the "home of progressive thought, new moral codes and advanced standards of living. It is the home of William Allen White, "Young Bill," and the Finneys and the late Mit Wilhite [who] made it possible to enter the town from four directions without getting in the mud."[37] The "Athens of Kansas" received a shot from Chet Shore, the editor of the *Augusta Gazette:* "Emporia is the home of mean, bad boys who throw gravel in the faces of unsuspecting motorists as they drive through town. Last night the Shore car was bombarded with gravel causing much excitement for a short time. Emporia is fast becoming the crime center of the United States."[38] Mr. White would surely have a lot of interesting things to tell his neighbors about his trip to Europe when he returned in October, noted the *Abilene Reflector;* of course, "the neighbors will want to tell him about a lot of things that happened in Emporia while he was away."[39] And then there was the unnerved Wichita man who swore to Emporia friends that he would never again touch a drop of "Jake leg" whiskey[40] after seeing such a lifelike apparition just outside Eureka—five elephants placidly grazing in a Flint Hills pasture.[41]

Some six hundred Kansans attended the American Legion Convention in Chicago in early October.[42] The *Gazette* reported on some of the goings-on:

A Song at Twilight

Here is a little ditty which the Emporia boys brought back from the Legion convention in Chicago,—a parody of an old French gospel hymn.

> O Kansans are a finney race
> Parley-Vous!
> O Kansans are a finney race
> Parley-Vous!
> O Kansans are a finney race,
> They impeach their friends—
> To save their face!
> Hinkey,
> Dinkey
> Par-
> ley-
> Vous

The boys say that the Democratic Legionnaires started singing it and presently it spread like a virulent case of contagious wildfire to the entire delegation.[43]

Emporians themselves didn't view the dramatic events entirely with a sour face. Instructors at the Teachers College had been denied some books and equipment, since the college had $20,000 in badly needed funds tied up in Fidelity. To help relieve the fiscal situation, some enterprising students got together and proposed an all-school revue dubbed the "Finney Follies."[44] A half-page ad in Arthur Capper's *Kansas Farmer,* extolling the virtues of a marvelous new thief catcher, recommended especially for farmers, caught Young Bill White's eye. He thought that, with proper modification, it could be put to good use in Topeka:

> Let the Senator install his "Bloodhound Thief Catcher" in the state treasury, properly wired with electricity. Then when any phony bonds went into the treasury vault, automatically a gong would ring, a signal gun would go off, payment on all uncashed salary checks to members of state boards and commissions would be stopped, a buzzer would sound in the office of Federal District Attorney Sardius M. Brewster, telegrams, previously prepared, would be dispatched calling the legislature into extraordinary special session, and a knitting machine would start weaving a laurel crown for the brow of Cliff Stratton—all of this happening instantaneously, automatically and untouched by human hands.[45]

THE SCANDAL even attracted attention outside the confines of Kansas.

Newsweek carried a full-column story on August 19. On August 21, under a caption of "Forgery Deluxe," *Time* led off its summary article with: "There is no greater state than Kansas. No mountains distort its surface.... Its citizens lead lives of regularity. Last week Kansans had as great a shock as if the Rocky Mountains had suddenly risen from their harvest fields."[46]

Jay House, who had formerly been a Kansas journalist and mayor of Topeka and was now a Philadelphia and New York City columnist, deplored the fact that Kansas had become the "burrowing ground and the broadcasting station of innumerable reformers, do-gooders, forward-lookers and other public pests." He wrote to an old Topeka friend, lampooning the current Kansas scene:

> As one who has had and retains a sentimental interest in Kansas and its people, I wish to speak a good word for [Boynton] who ... is not being properly appreciated for his virtues.... At a time when he is the subject of innuendo from White Cloud to Liberal, Mr. Boynton continues to go fearlessly ahead suspending county officials who fail to enforce the prohibitionary law or who are suspected of taking a little nip now and then.... That is the true Kansas spirit and I hold Mr. Boynton should be commended for showing it.... Boynton's ousting of these public servants, his violent opposition to 3.2 beer and his preoccupation with slot machines will be remembered in Kansas long after the bond scandals are forgotten. And they should be.[47]

A letter to the editor of the *Topeka State Journal* from a former Kansan who was living in Chicago complained that the scandal should have been investigated more sanely and calmly to avoid the "front page advertisement of our state's disgrace.... The Kansas people have become a flock of vultures. They have been done wrong and they are demanding payment in blood."[48]

Ned Beck, who was the editor of the *Chicago Tribune* and the son of the well-known pioneer Kansas newspaperman Moses Beck, took a sardonic editorial view of the recent troubles in his native state:

Kansas Tribulations

> The misfortunes of the truly good and the really just do not move other people to mirth. Even the most cynical would refrain from taking delight in the unmerited confusion come upon the worthy person or community out of an adversity when that person's or community's life and acts have been guided by the model patterns of a noble mind....
>
> These highly moral reflections ... are evoked by the plight of Kansas and will explain why there is a mite of satisfaction elsewhere when this highly self-esteemed state discovers itself in an embarrassment of counterfeited bonds....

Probably if Kansas had been less militantly and assertively virtuous, less the national censor and less the common scold, less the state self-appointed to set the moral standard for the whole country and stamp its priceless idea upon the common thought, there would be more generosity in the feeling for it when a first rate scandal rocks the dome of government. It appears that Kansas would have done well to pay less attention to other people's business and more to its own. Experience often proves that to be a good policy.[49]

Beck's sister, Martha, who was coeditor of the *Holton Recorder*,[50] responded in kind:

> Perhaps our state has been a trifle smug and self-righteous and deserves to have the finger of scorn pointed at it. But we'd like to call the esteemed Tribune's attention to the fact that three of our public enemies have been arrested and in jail, while . . . a lot of Chicago's . . . crooks have never been inside prison walls. At least we try to punish our faithless public servants.[51]

KANSAS has always enjoyed a noisy and multitudinous press, which has fed the fires of her righteousness. The journalistic response to the bond scandal came quickly from all sections of the state, floating in on gallons of printer's ink:

Newton Kansan: [The scandal] has arisen to carry its stench upon the heated atmosphere of a Kansas summer.
Leavenworth Times: It is hard to understand how the state could have been duped to the extent it has been . . . without the connivance of some of the state officials.[52]
El Dorado Times: The state is robbed blind, a scandal rears its ugly head, banks are closed, more misery is added to the common lot.
Garden City Telegram: Governor Landon has pledged himself to "sift the whole thing to the bottom" and "let the chips fall where they may." Certainly the state of Kansas will be satisfied with nothing less.
Fredonia Herald: Ronald Finney . . . has plunged the state of Kansas into a scandal it will take years to live down.
Kiowa News-Review: It is the old, old story of the small-town boy who thinks to buck the game in a big city and stoops to criminal methods to accomplish his ends, losing sight of the fact that pay day always comes at last.[53]
Leoti Standard: During the past few years while Mr. and Mrs. Kansas Citizen have been working their fingers to the bone trying not to get too far back with their taxes, it seems there has been a fairly

numerous gang of their trusted officials and appointees who have lived like princes at their expense. To these hard-pressed citizens who have been robbed—the legislature owes a complete unmasking of official Topeka.[54]

While most of the state's newspapers gave free vent to their feelings regarding the sensations that were so unaccustomedly breaking around them, that wasn't true for all of them. Out of a sense of shame or pressure from the Finneys, or both, the *Neosho Falls Post* ("the only paper that's interested in Neosho Falls") carried almost no news that fall of the bank's closing or of the scandal.[55] No anger, no table pounding, no vituperation—no news.[56]

Down in Eureka, where Mabel Finney's brother-in-law George G. Wood owned and edited the *Herald,* only the most meager reports were printed during the sensational revelations and their aftermath. It all might have been occurring in New York City, New York, or on the moon, so far as you could tell from the *Herald.* But Eureka's other weekly, the *Democratic Messenger,* printed a good deal of news about the scandal and reprinted every anti-Republican, anti-Finney, or anti-White story it could lay its feverish hands on.[57]

At the other site of major transgressions, Emporia, the *Gazette* carried the wire-service stories on the breaking news from Topeka and many local news items on W. W. Finney's trials and tribulations. But it maintained a very tight editorial lip on the broader ramifications of the story, especially considering the inherent interest of the revelations to Emporians. On August 9 the *Gazette* published a lengthy editorial, which was virtually identical to a *Capital* editorial that had appeared that morning. Three days later, Young Bill wrote a short editorial praising Landon, which concluded with "no friend who is criminally involved need expect one single drop of mercy from him." The Finneys, father and son, got on him a good bit about that. Through the rest of the fall, rigorous statements of support for Boynton appeared with regularity, but the Whites' typewriter fell silent insofar as the Finneys were concerned.[58]

Statements of a personal nature interrupted that silence twice. Shortly after Ronald Finney's early-morning arousal in late August by the gendarmes, the phone rang at the Whites'. A sleep-groggy Young Bill picked up the receiver. He heard a familiar and demanding voice—it was Mabel Finney's. Then came the pleadings from the insistent old friend: Would he go to Topeka and help on the bond for Ronald now? At least three distinct and conflicting emotions must have rushed through Bill's mind: the demands of friendship; the ethics of the journalistic profession; and the public's expectations of a politician, for he had been giving serious thought to running for public office again, possibly for the U.S. Senate. After only a moment's reflection, Bill dressed and drove to Topeka to help in trying to keep his friend out of jail.⁵⁹ (The next morning he lamented the fact that any hopes for political office had gone up in smoke as a result of this act, which bound him irretrievably to the Finneys in the public mind. But his wife saw a silver lining. "Yes, but now you have a book," she said. And so, *What People Said* was first conceived in their minds.)⁶⁰

After White had returned from that exhausting and futile trip, he felt that he owed the community an explanation for his unorthodox—for a newspaperman—action. Years later, he still fondly recalled the quality of the piece: "Sometimes before you sat down to write something, you knew it would be good."⁶¹

A Friendship

The undersigned knowingly and deliberately violated an old unwritten law of the newspaper world yesterday when he announced his willingness to sign an appearance bond for Ronald Finney. . . .

As against this is the close personal friendship between the Finney family and that of the editor of this paper, for more than two decades. . . .

But the editor . . . and his family are grateful to the Finneys for countless thoughtful acts and kindnesses through the years and for their steadfast loyalty and comfort during a dark period of sadness and bereavement.

This deep obligation will be paid in kind, outside the columns of this newspaper, by the editors of this paper, in any personal comfort they may give to the Finneys in this time of their great anguish and distress, and the writer's only regret is that the distress is so great, and the opportunities to repay this obligation of friendship so limited. . . .

Under ordinary circumstances the social relations and personal friendships of a newspaper man are matters in which the public has no concern. But yesterday morning the junior editor of this paper, in the dingy basement courtroom of the Shawnee county courthouse, signified his willingness to obligate his worldly goods so that his boyhood friend, Ronald Finney, accused of a major crime, might remain at liberty at least until a court has heard his defense. The readers of this paper have a right to know just what this obligation of friendship is and how far it extends. It should not influence either the editorial policy of the paper or color the news, as these duties of a newspaperman take precedence over any obligation of friendship he may have.⁶²

Two weeks later, White took another unprecedented step when he closed the letters-to-the-editor column, called "The Wailing Place," as regards the Finney case, until further notice:

Public discussion of the [Finney] case at this time when only a part of the facts are known would be valueless and a waste of good white newsprint. So The Gazette bars from the wailing place, as it has already barred from its editorial page, all opinion and argument as to the innocence or guilt of the Finneys, until all the facts are known.

Any opinion rendered today might be ridiculous in the light of tomorrow's developments. But when all the evidence is in then the wailers may romp, snort and tear up the gravel to their heart's content.[63]

Contrary to the promise in the editorial, the Wailing Place—even after William Allen White's return—did not reopen on the Finney case to give the frustrated wailers a chance to "romp, snort and tear up the gravel."

While the small-town and country papers manifested intense interest in the scandal, the big-city dailies spilled the most blood, sweat, tears, and ink. In direct contrast to press coverage of the national Watergate of the 1970s, the most conservative papers took the hardest line against the transgressors, while the more liberal press stammered and stuttered, hoping against hope that the whole embarrassing affair would go back to wherever it had come from.

The *Wichita Beacon,* which was published by the Levand brothers, held a conservative, Neo-Populist viewpoint. After it had been purchased from former governor Henry Allen, the paper had espoused pro-Brinkley and anti-Progressive sentiments—vibrating on the same pro–Henry Doherty wavelength as the *Kansas City Journal Post.* Mr. White once remarked that the *Beacon* "has about as much influence in Kansas as it has in Greenland's icy mountains." Be that as it may, it took a hard line toward the establishment wrongdoers who usually wore the Progressive cloak. "Let the chips fall where they may, tho the inquiry rock the statehouse to its foundations," the paper blared on August 9. Four days later they demanded that "every department of state government be subject to a searching inquiry, conducted without fear or favor, regardless of whom it may affect or bring to justice."[64]

Victor Murdock, a former congressman and a Progressive ally of White's, published the *Wichita Eagle.* Not unexpectedly, the *Eagle* took a less strident and more generous view of the unpleasantness. At the outset, it concentrated on minutiae, being careful to avoid saying anything that might increase the public fervor, which was already building to an alarmingly high pitch. In concluding a soft editorial on August 10, the *Eagle* worried that the bond-forgery racket "may be far more extensive than the public imagines. . . . It bears the earmarks of an organized criminal industry, nation-wide in its ramifications."[65] It may have borne those earmarks initially, but the bonds had been printed in Topeka and sold in Chicago not vice versa.

By far the most extensive and intensive coverage came from the two Topeka and the two Kansas City, Missouri, dailies. Each paper had a full-time Kansas correspondent assigned to the Capitol. For over six months, most of the time, talents, and energy of these political reporters were devoted to the bond scandal and its many ramifications. Though all four papers were nominally Republican, they nonetheless held quite different political philosophies and sensitivities.

The hardest line, and the most excited reaction to the scandal, came from the *Kansas City Journal Post* and its Kansas correspondent, William G. Clugston. The conservative Henry Doherty, who was head of the Cities Service Gas Company, controlled the paper and its policies. Doherty and Cities Service had been involved in what seemed like interminable litigation in Kansas over gas rates, which had resulted in their becoming the favorite Black Beast of the white-hatted Progressives. A long-standing feud between the *Journal Post* and its crosstown rival, the *Star,* had culminated in a $12 million lawsuit which Doherty had unsuccessfully brought against the rival paper. Clugston—a curious mixture of equal parts of idealism, conservatism, and irascibility—felt that Kansas had been controlled for years by the same establishment crowd, whether Republican or Democratic. In 1932, for example, he saw little difference between Woodring and Landon; so he had supported Brinkley, blindly hoping that the good doctor would prove to be more a Populist than a promoter. "With all his honesty, charm and cultural erudition," W. A. White once observed, "Clug never has been nearer to the game in Kansas than to look through a knot hole at the changing outfielders. He has never even seen the home plate."[66]

The *Journal Post* loved to rail against the "holier-than-thou, *Star*-White clique," so when the bomb went off in the front ranks of the Progressive faction, it went after its favorite targets with relish:

> The Finney case, better than anything else, shows what sort of government Kansas has been getting in the last decade—a decade in which the Kansas City Star has dominated the officials of the state. . . .
> The Finneys . . . occupied places high in the civic, political and business life of the state. . . . [This] was possible because they were integral parts of the political cabal that ran the state with the aid . . . of the . . . Star.[67]

In September, Clugston wrote an eight-part series, reviewing in colorful terms what he claimed had been "whitewashings" (to be taken two ways) of Kansas political scandals over the past several years. He had harsh words for the whole Progressive camp, including William Allen White, Warren Finney, Clyde Reed, William Smith, Richard Hopkins, and Charles Griffith. The iconoclastic reporter fumed about the Anti-Saloon League frauds, the state fire-insurance settlement, and the abortive investigations of the Textbook Commission, the State Printing Office, the Highway Department, and the Banking Department.[68]

Attorney General Boynton was singled out as a special target of the *Journal Post*. From Clugston's vantage point, Boynton was a total loss. In addition to prosecuting the gas cases against Clugston's bosses' company and becoming the darling of the hated WCTU and antigambling crusaders, Boynton had the misfortune to be the cousin of William Allen White. To Clugston, Boynton represented the quintessence of a no-good Kansas do-gooding Progressive.[69] Clugston claimed that the *Star*-White crowd had maintained a rigid control over the Office of the Attorney General ever since 1918, when they had gotten Dick Hopkins elected.[70] The usual route for the Progressive attorneys general—a high road that Boynton had been traveling until he had been sidetracked—was from that office to the Supreme Court.[71]

Marion Ellet represented another potent weapon in the *Journal Post*'s arsenal. Her "Mugwump" column contained some of the most biting political satire to be read in those parts. A brilliant young Concordia woman who had returned to Kansas after completing an eastern education, she had only recently joined the *Journal Post* staff after a short stint on the *Star*, which had ended unhappily. During that fall and winter, Marion—who was referred to as "the ring-tailed hell-cat" by Young Bill White—turned her considerable talents on the accused, most especially on poor Rolie, with telling effect.[72]

For years the *Kansas City Star*, which had been founded by the philanthropist William Rockhill Nelson, had been a leading voice for progressivism in Kansas. Though not as all-powerful as Clugston would have it, the Missouri paper had long enjoyed an enviable influence on the political landscape of its neighboring state due to its crusading editorials and the personal contacts of its Kansas correspondents and editors. In addition to the bitter battles with its intown rival, the *Star* had mounted in the late twenties an all-out attack on Dr. Brinkley, which resulted in his losing his state medical license and his radio station (KFKB—"Kansas First, Kansas Best"). The irate doctor sued the *Star* for millions, an action that turned out to be as unsuccessful as the Doherty suit.[73]

The *Star* (and its morning edition, the *Times*) reported the technical facts in the Finney cases, often in considerable and accurate detail, as they were supplied chiefly by its Topeka correspondent, Cecil Howes. His stories were augmented by articles emanating from the Kansas City, Kansas, office of Lacy Haynes, who was W. A. White's brother-in-law (Haynes had married a younger sister of Sallie Lindsey White) and a political confidant of numerous Kansas governors.[74] The *Star*'s editorials on the scandal were cautious, carefully considered, and tightly reasoned. No irate clamoring or righteous posturing could be found here. Like Mr. White, with whom they had long been closely allied, they devoutly wished that the whole sordid affair would just go away.

> The people of Kansas have felt keenly the humiliation of the disgraceful Finney bond scandal, touching as it does so many public officials. But the honor of the state is redeemed by the thoroughness of the house cleaning now in progress. . . .
>
> But the investigators, . . . are going to the bottom of the whole wretched mess. The Star believes they will have the aggressive backing of the whole state in any proceedings that the facts seem to warrant.[75]

The most influential daily published in Kansas was the prim, proper, and Progressive Capper-owned *Topeka Capital*. Though the paper was moderately liberal in outlook, the paper's publisher and its star reporter had been outraged by the scandal, resulting in its carrying far more column inches on the affair than did any other newspaper. The author of most of this prodigious outpouring was the studious Clif Stratton, its ace political reporter and Senator Capper's chief aide. The prolific Stratton later estimated that he wrote about 250 columns on the bond scandal, totaling around 250,000 words. For a considerable period, well-researched lengthy feature articles—which were studied reflections on the fast-breaking news—appeared several times a week. These essays enticed his readership with tantalizing titles such as "How Did He Do It?" "Big Fish Only for Ronald Finney," "Taking Care of Folks, Ronald Finney Style," "Routine and Organization Were Ronald Finney Allies," "Fifteen-cent Mistake Costly to Ronald Finney," and "Get-Rich-Quick Wallingford." Stratton not only wrote about the events; to a limited degree he helped to shape them. His revealing interview with Tom Boyd had led directly to Landon's declaration of martial law at the treasury the following morning. Stratton later testified before the federal grand jury and at Boyd's trial. The governor considered Stratton's testimony for the latter to be critical enough that in January he directed Brewster to call Stratton back from Washington.[76]

Without question the consistently tough, somewhat preachy line taken by the *Capital* had a significant impact on events as the accused, one by one, were marched before the bar of justice. Since the paper had long been in the Progressive camp, it might have been expected to take a somewhat dispassionate and aseptic view of the mischief, as did the *Star,* or even mount an open counteroffensive, as the *Gazette* did for Boynton. But it did not; and this only added to its effectiveness. No one could legitimately claim that its reporting tilted in favor of the accused or that it encouraged, even to the slightest degree, a political whitewashing. So when the paper condemned a person or a process, people listened. Again and again the *Capital* dwelt on the affront that had been dealt to the fair name of Kansas—the lamentable reduction of its image as a sound, sensible, and stable community:

> The state particularly suffers from this man's [Ronald Finney's] dealings which have become a national sensation. Much of the prestige gained by Kansas last winter in handling the problems which grew out of depression, bankruptcies, mortgage foreclosures, with so much good sense and conservatism . . . is smeared by these staggering revelations. This is the major loss. Time will be required to recover from it. When the investigations and audits and prosecutions are finished , . . , it will appear that Kansas has been damaged by a few persons, some guilty of criminal acts and others of negligence in performance of duties. But Kansas will suffer as a whole, as a state and a community, because of the acts of a few individuals. The valuable work of last winter will be forgotten.[77]

The conservative *Topeka State Journal,* which was managed by the respected publisher Frank P. MacLennon and editor Arthur J. Carruth, Jr., went after the Progressive transgressors with enthusiasm. The paper's chief political reporter was the free-swinging, flamboyant veteran A. L. ("Dutch") Shultz, who had proven to be a significant factor in many state elections, especially gubernatorial ones. His weekly column, "Kansas Political Gossip," was one of the state's most influential.[78] White once labeled Shultz the "tin horn herald of Kansas conservatism." Alf Landon complained in 1938 that Shultz was the "most unreliable newspaperman in Kansas," though Shultz had been a warm supporter of the governor's decisive actions during the scandal period.[79]

The *State Journal's* position had been succinctly stated on August 9—"Let the probe be pitiless." The emotional Shultz had a field day with the sensational developments:

> Kansas has had her thrills and sensations. . . . She has battled thru all the hardships of frontier life and won struggles against drouth and hot winds and grasshoppers. She has gone merrily on her sprees of frenzied reform and has surprised the nation with sanity and unerring judgement. . . .
> But until just the other day, Kansas really never had a Ronald

Finney. She had read about Ponzi and a score of comets that flashed and crashed after flights thru spectacular spaces around the stock and grain pits. Now that Ronald Finney came to provide a performance which Kansas never dreamed would appear on her own stage, the state is dizzy and dazed and trying very awkwardly to understand it all. . . .

Finney was an almost perfect showman. His benevolent kindness won applause while back stage the mad plunger was grabbing for high stakes in the . . . market.[80]

Shultz opened a long column at the end of August with: "This Finney matter holds possibilities beyond anything previously hinted." In conclusion he expressed a deep desire to get away from it all:

Next week the Kansas Legion holds its annual state convention in Salina. What a relief. It will be genuine joy to get away from [this] sordid scandal for a couple days . . . after more than three weeks around the slime of the worst mess Kansas has known. . . . It will . . . get the cobwebs and dust and accumulations of corruption gossip out of the attic.[81]

If it was too much for Dutch Shultz, who loved political gossip like a cat loves catnip, that indeed was saying something.

A few days after Ronald Finney's arrest, Fred Brinkerhoff's *Pittsburg Sun* took time out from the swift pace of events to reflect on the impact on the Finney family:

There is a tragedy in the scandal.
The family of the man arrested . . . has been one of the most prominent in the state. His family's name long has been well known in Kansas. . . .
Today this foremost citizen and his wife [Warren and Mabel Finney] have seen their names dragged into what promises to be the state's greatest scandal with their son as its leading figure. . . . They have noted the pitiless tales about their son and his spectacular financial operations. They can see nothing but darkness ahead.
Tragedy of the most depressing kind has come swiftly to a Kansas family that thousands of warm personal friends will swear by no means deserved it.[82]

What of this talented, energetic family that had risen to political, economic, and social prominence through three Kansas generations and now faced such a bleak future of shame, humiliation, and despair?

6

The Blood Line

ooooooooooooooooooooooooooooooooooooo ooooooooooooooooooooo

WHEN twenty-six-year-old David Wesley Finney—the father of Warren—left his native Indiana and headed west to the Kansas country in a team and wagon in the summer of 1866, he could scarcely have dreamed of the spectacular events that would swirl with cyclonic velocity around the vortex of the Finney name sixty-seven years later. David was a descendant of one branch of the Finney clan, which had made at least three separate American colonizations in the seventeenth and early eighteenth centuries from England and from Scotland via Ireland. The tribe could count many more than its share of ministers and physicians, but also an innkeeper here and there. Foremost among the clerics was that outstanding "harvester of souls," the renowned Reverend Charles Grandison Finney, a prominent mid-nineteenth-century Congregational minister and cofounder of Oberlin College.[1]

David was a sixth-generation descendant of Robert Finney, a Scotch-Irishman who had fought under the banner of William of Orange in the Battle of the Boyne and had been left for dead on the battlefield in that famous 1690 encounter. But he survived and subsequently removed to America, where in 1733 he purchased nine hundred acres in Chester County, Pennsylvania, near the Maryland border. David's father, another Robert, had migrated from North Carolina to Indiana in the early nineteenth century. There, on a farm in Parke County on August 22, 1839, David Wesley came into the world.[2]

David's early education in a log schoolhouse became restricted to three months a year as soon as he was old enough "to chop wood, split rails, cut saw logs and clear the land for cultivation." He later asserted that "the boys of those days endured all the privations of pioneer life, which resulted in the development of strong, brainy, self-reliant manhood."[3] The gaunt six-foot-two-inch son of a farmer enlisted in 1862 as a private in the 85th Indiana Volunteer Infantry; he was discharged three years later as a first sergeant. Captured with the rest of his brigade at Thompson's Station, Tennessee, in 1863, he spent the next two months in an involuntary survival exercise in Richmond's infamous Libby Prison. After being released, he rejoined his old outfit and accompanied General Sherman on his famous march through Georgia to the sea.[4]

After being discharged in June, 1865, the blue-eyed, taciturn young farmer returned to Parke County and, "feeling the need of more education," enrolled in the nearby Waveland Collegiate Institute. At the close of the term the next June, heeding the call of the western opportunity, the veteran, in company with three recently discharged young friends, headed for Kansas with a fine span of mules and a custom-made wagon. The cocky Union veterans had a large American flag painted on the side of their wagon. They were warned that there might be trouble if they did not cover up the offensive symbol when they crossed into Missouri. "But having fought three years to maintain the honor of the flag," the emigrants declared, "we did not propose to do anything of the kind." They arrived without undue incident in August at Neosho Falls in Woodson County.[5]

LOCATED in a region that had originally been reserved for the New York Indians, Neosho Falls had almost no history and not much of a present, but it entertained large hopes for a bustling future. It was just the right place for an unattached, ambitious young man to grow up and prosper with the country. Only three years before Finney's arrival, most of the Seminole Indian nation had spent over a year at Neosho Falls as Civil War refugees, supervised by Union soldiers. That throng of a few thousand, encamped in a pecan grove on the bank of the river, had presented an arresting social spectacle: while the white soldiers watched the Indians, the emaciated Indians, in turn, guarded their black slaves, who were camped only "a few rods away."[6]

Although Neosho Falls didn't prosper as its early settlers had hoped it would, David Finney did. He opened a general store soon after his arrival, later specializing in hardware. Still later he ran a milling business. He did well—investing prudently in farmland—and in the mid 1870s he built one of the most substantial houses in the town. When the village was formally incorporated in 1870, Finney became one of its trustees. A Mason and an officer in the Grand Army of the Republic, the pious young businessman helped to found the Congregational Church, which he served for years as a trustee. He also served a term as the town's justice of the peace.[7]

From his first months in his adopted state, Finney had taken a keen interest in politics. Described as "aggressively Republican," he was elected to represent Woodson County in the Kansas House in 1867, a year after he had come west. He did not seek office again until 1874, when he was elected to the Kansas Senate to represent a district that embraced Woodson and Coffey counties. A recurrent delegate to the Republican State Conventions in the sixties and seventies, he was reelected to a four-year Senate term in the centennial year of 1876. During his Senate tenure his most noteworthy accomplishment came when he chaired a joint committee that extensively revised the school laws of the state.[8]

DAVID FINNEY reached his political pinnacle after the conclusion of his second Senate term in 1880. That year, in late summer, the Republican Convention assembled in Representatives Hall in Topeka on "one of the most outrageously hot days that ever struck the melting heavens and the perspiring earth." "Every inch of space to the last spittoon," reported the *Atchison Champion,* "was occupied by a sticky and dissolving patriot, and thousands kept pressing to the door after not another person could have been driven in with a maul and wedge." Incumbent Governor John P. St. John and most of the other state officers were assured of renomination in that GAR-dominated conclave, leaving attention centered on the offices of lieutenant governor and attorney general. In those preprimary days, the convention nominee ran in the general election, and in heavily Republican Kansas that meant almost certain victory.[9]

Former congressman Sidney Clarke led off the speeches, of course. "No meteorological conditions have yet been found which could prevent him," wailed the *Champion.* "He would speak with equal facility if he were transfixed on the North Pole or straddling the burning equator." At the conclusion of his extended remarks, the voluble Clarke placed the name of Charles H. Langston, a black man, who later became the maternal grandfather of the noted Kansas author Langston Hughes,[10] in nomination for lieutenant governor.[11]

Langston "was called for loudly," but since he was not present, the Reverend T. W. Henderson, a black delegate, spoke for him, suggesting that it might be politically wise to put one Negro on the state ticket. While he was speaking, someone in the back of the hall raucously yelled, "Put him out!" or, perhaps, something even more discourteous. The malefactor was promptly ejected "amid much excitement." After a modicum of order had been reestablished, the "terror and scourge" of western Missouri and eastern Kansas during the late war—the Old Jayhawker himself, Colonel Charles R. Jennison—rose and gave vent to his considerable feelings. He stormed that while Henderson had been speaking, "a remaining vein of rebellion" had entered the room and tried to shout him down. The old warhorse thundered that he felt like crying, "For God Almighty's sake, give me a musket!" In conclusion, and to loud applause, he sternly cautioned that the "people not be deceived by demagogues or by Democrats."[12]

On the first ballot for lieutenant governor, T. T. Taylor received 118 votes; D. W. Finney, 67; C. H. Langston, 51; others, 88. The next morning—after a night of intense politicking—on the second and final ballot, the results were: Finney, 166; Taylor, 158; Langston, 2. This nominated David Finney and "ended the liveliest fight of the Convention." The nominee for attorney general became young William A. Johnston, a Senate colleague of David Finney's and at that time an assistant U.S. district attorney for Kansas.[13] More than fifty years later, the paths of Johnston, the then venerable chief justice of the Kansas Supreme Court, and of the scions of David Finney would cross in a much different setting.

After his easy two-to-one victory in the fall, Finney had the "satisfaction" in early 1881, as lieutenant governor and president of the Senate, of signing the first prohibition law. A prohibition leader, he had cast his senatorial vote in 1879 for the submission of the constitutional amendment to the electorate. As the Senate's presiding officer, he "proved himself a courteous gentleman as well as an able parliamentarian."[14] He was readily reelected in 1882, a year that saw St. John's bid for an unprecedented third term as governor dashed by the Democratic challenger, George Washington Glick. Kansas had its first Democratic governor and its first—and only—Negro state officer in auditor Edward P. McCabe, a Millbrook Republican.[15]

A bill passed the 1883 Legislature which would permanently affix the Finney name to the map of Kansas. Some of the counties in the western part of the state had been organized and then had become "unorganized" through loss of population. In the southwest section an unorganized county named Sequoyah, changed somewhat in configuration, was renamed Finney in honor of the incumbent lieutenant governor. It was the second largest county in Kansas in area, and it took Garden City as its county seat. Fifty years later some of the residents had cause, or so they thought, to reconsider that decision.[16]

At the conclusion of his second term in 1885 Lieutenant Governor Finney retired from the active political arena and did not again seek elective office. In his later years he became a sometime employee of the Santa Fe Railroad, as a right-of-way and town-site agent, perhaps as a modest reward for his support of the railroad during his legislative days. Though a staunch Republican throughout most of his life, he became disaffected by the 1912 "theft of the Chicago convention" and thereafter identified himself with the Bull Moose Progressives.[17]

During his politically active period, David Finney was widely respected as a quiet man of ability and acumen. He was variously described as "a gentleman of high character and conceded abilities," "a solid, sensible business man . . . , quiet in his manners and reliable in his convictions," and a man of "notably modest and retiring disposition, [whose] honesty and sincerity of purpose, . . . fine intellect and sterling worth have won him honors in Kansas which he well deserves."[18] In business he drove hard bargains as he rose to a materially comfortable station in life, but no shadow of public scandal fell on his career or life.[19]

In 1869 David Finney had married Hellen Hester McConnell, an attractive, twenty-four-year-old brunette ("the best woman that ever lived"). A native of Indiana, Hellen had come to Neosho Falls in 1857 with her family. Her father, Hiram, "one of the early and influential" settlers of Kansas, had been the first elected sheriff of Woodson County.[20] After having

Hellen and David Finney, about 1900

been a widow for fifteen years and in declining health, Hellen spent her last years in the home of her older son and his family in Emporia. Mercifully, she died in 1931, almost two years before the family's disgrace.[21]

TO THE UNION of David and Hellen a son was born five years after the marriage—Warren Wesley Finney—on April 3, 1874 (in later years he often gave his birthdate as 1873, perhaps to make himself more acceptable as an extremely young candidate for the legislature). Little is known of his early childhood; he apparently went through the Neosho Falls public schools in normal, though somewhat precocious, fashion. In 1890, as a sixteen-year-old, he enrolled in the prep class at Washburn Academy, a Congregational institution, at Topeka. The following year the brown-eyed, aggressive youngster was admitted to Washburn College, where he became a full-time liberal-arts student for the next three years. Tall, slim, and handsome, Finney was socially popular and was active in extracurricular activities. Elected president of Gamma Sigma, a literary society, he gave an "oration" in the college chapel in December, 1893. He frequently hosted fishing and boating parties down on the Neosho for his college friends during the summer vacation periods. Ironically, one of his Washburn classmates was an aspiring lawyer-to-be, Sard Brewster. Finney's last work at Washburn was in the spring of 1894. Though he apparently had enough credits to graduate and was so listed in subsequent college catalogues, curiously his transcript fails to show that he did, in fact, graduate.[22]

After completing his studies at Washburn, Finney joined his father in the milling business in Neosho Falls. Shortly thereafter he became fascinated with the embryonic, though rapidly developing, telephone business. A natural for the intelligent and curious young Warren, it enabled him to utilize his mechanical aptitude along with his sound head for business. In 1895 the budding entrepreneur organized the Neosho Falls Telephone Company and devoted most of his energies to that emerging business until he moved to Emporia ten years later.[23]

WARREN FINNEY had another idea of the sort that bright, ambitious young men fresh out of college entertain from time to time but rarely act upon. He decided, as a twenty-two-year-old, to run for the state legislature. The times were not the most propitious for a Kansas Republican in that year of 1896, for even in that rock-ribbed G.O.P. stronghold, the Populist "heresy" was at flood tide. The Populists had swept the state offices in 1892, including the governor's chair, had taken control of the Senate, and had

Warren W. Finney as a twenty-two-year-old legislator (Kansas State Historical Society)

just failed to organize the House in the infamous Statehouse melee that became known as the "legislative war of 1893." At eighteen, Finney had been one of the sergeants at arms pressed into service at the height of those pushing, shoving, and battering festivities. Given his eager and self-confident competitiveness, we can be sure that the youthful Finney thoroughly relished his "official" duties on that historic occasion. The "Pops," or "Popocrats," had received a setback in the elections of 1894, but all the signs looked favorable in 1896 for them to make another strong showing on a ticket headed, at the national level, by William Jennings Bryan.[24]

Nevertheless, Finney ran and was elected to the same House seat that his father had held thirty years earlier. Like other Republican candidates running in that year when the economic misfortunes of men received a thorough airing in Kansas and elsewhere, he was helped a good deal by

Will White's editorial "What's the Matter with Kansas?" from up river in Emporia. (At the succeeding legislative session, Warren Finney and William Allen White met for the first time.) Finney had won, but not many other Republicans had. For the first and last time in Kansas history, they had been pushed out of all the major Statehouse offices and had lost control of both houses of the legislature as well. Their defeat was total; their shame profound.[25]

On January 29, 1892—Kansas Day—four Republican "young turks" (Harry W. Frost, Charles M. Harger, Ewing Herbert, and William Allen White) had organized a rump political meeting, the purpose of which was to give the young bulls a chance to rip and snort about the Populist threat without the inhibiting presence of their party elders. (The affair still continues, in a somewhat different format, as an annual event, having become the traditional day on which Republican hopefuls announce their candidacy.) Speaking at the annual affair quickly became a highly regarded prize for the politically hopeful. Those fortunates who were selected were asked to give one of several inspirational political talks or "toasts," the most prestigious being the "toast to Kansas." On January 29, 1897, that honor went to Warren Wesley Finney, the boy representative from Woodson County.[26]

Drawing on his Washburn oratorical experience and evidently having frequently consulted an unabridged dictionary, Finney gave a polished, if somewhat stilted, speech:

> I assure you that I am not insensible to the honor which belongs to this occasion and this position. Cognizant at all times of my deficiencies in public address, that sensibility is intensified tonight when I reflect that this is a natal day; that I have been called upon to speak of Kansas, the memory of whose hallowed past, thrills with delight every patriotic heart, whose present grandeur, eclipsed by the cloud of Democracy, awaits only its dissipation for her future glory, as the effulgent rays of God's own sunlight, to fill all the earth.[27]

Finney followed that lead-in with a high-flown philippic against the Populists and their bankrupt philosophy, and then came dramatically—and ironically, considering subsequent events—to his grand conclusion:

> Young men of the Kansas Day Club, our duty to Kansas and to the world is to repeat with pitiless reiteration, not in words only, but in deeds, the bitter lesson we have learned—the eternal lesson—that it is not silver or paper money that brings success, but that it is honesty, integrity and fidelity. As an old abbe once said, "It is on the virtues of mankind that the future of mankind is to be built."[28]

LATER THAT SAME YEAR, Warren Finney married Mabel Tucker, the eldest and very proper daughter of a prominent Eureka rancher and businessman. They met at Washburn, which she had entered in 1891 after graduating from the Southern Kansas Academy, a Congregational prep school that had been founded by her father. A part-time student in 1892 and 1893, the young matron completed her last formal work at Washburn in 1894, but did not graduate.[29]

Her father, Edwin, a native of Vermont, had come to Kansas in 1857 as a nineteen-year-old, herding twenty-five head of cattle behind an ox wagon driven by his aged father. Discovering a spring in the Flint Hills country, they cried "Eureka!" and thus founded the seat of Greenwood County. Edwin subsequently served in both houses of the Kansas Legislature—sometimes in the same body as did David Finney—and as a regent of the State Normal School. He served as a deacon of the Congregational Church and taught in its Sunday School for over fifty years. Subsequently, his oldest son, Howard, took over operation of the bank that Edwin had founded—the Eureka Bank. Later, Howard's older son, Edwin Sparr ("Ted") Tucker, who was born in 1895, joined his father as a cashier at the bank.[30]

Warren Finney quickly became a leading citizen of Neosho Falls, serving terms as mayor and as Sunday School superintendent of the Congregational Church. Then, in 1905, an attractive business opportunity dictated a significant move: he sold the Neosho Falls Telephone Company (which he later bought back) and purchased the Independent Telephone Company at Emporia. His purchase of the somewhat dilapidated company forced the Bell Telephone Company, which also served the area, to adjust their rates, the first in a long series of unhappy encounters between Finney and Bell.[31]

JUST A FEW YEARS after Finney's arrival in Emporia, a heated disagreement arose between him and the town over telephone service and rates, a dispute that would not be fully resolved for five years. The controversy sheds some fascinating light on Finney's character and his early *modus operandi,* on the developing friendship between Finney and White, and on the relationship of each of them to the townspeople.

The difficulties surfaced initially in January, 1909, when agitated farmers in the Emporia trade area demanded "up-to-date" service and a new switchboard. At this time the Emporia City Council had under consideration an ordinance granting a new franchise for the phone company, which included a basic rate increase (from $1.00 to $1.25 per month) but required Finney to make a number of expensive improvements before it would go into effect. The council seemed inclined to pass it, and White loudly proclaimed up and down the length of Commercial Street that he favored the new ordinance, the first of six distinct positions that he was to take on the issue over the next several months. The editor then ambiguously led a vigorous and successful campaign to allow the town to vote on the proposal in a nonbinding referendum ("I stood for the referendum because I believed it right").[32]

Despite the almost daily exhortations in the *Gazette* to support the new franchise, the people overwhelmingly rejected the proposition in mid March (847 to 188). "This town does not want Mr. Finney to have a new telephone franchise on any terms," White commented after the election. "The Gazette feels that dislike for Mr. Finney was the overbearing issue, and that the real issue was lost sight of. But if the people desire to sacrifice their phone service to their emotions that also is their royal American privilege. This is a free country." Editor White hadn't quite made up his mind about businessman Finney at this juncture, but he did take the time to pen a heartening note to the disappointed phone-company owner: "You should cheer up. This town is not so bad as you think it. . . . You have let a lot of people have it [with] both barrels . . . and [they] laid for you. They have quarreled with you, and that makes it impossible for most men to see another man's case. . . . They do not realize that they have skated so close to real trouble for you. They think you are made of money. The big house and the automobile fooled them."[33]

Despite the clearly expressed preference of the town, the council proceeded to pass the ordinance, making it effective when and if the specified improvements in the plant had been completed. By the close of 1910 all the requirements had been complied with—or at least so Finney claimed. But in January, 1911, the council voted unanimously not to activate the ordinance with its included rate increase since Finney, they said, had failed to make all the specified changes in the metallic circuits. Asserting that he had spent $70,000 for a new building, a new switchboard, and new lines, the incensed Finney fired back: "I regret very much the action the commissioners have taken. It probably will throw matters into court at a great expense to the losing side. The rates, beginning with December 1, 1910, will be raised, and to insure collection, the supreme court will be appealed to."[34]

Phone-company collectors then proceeded to bill subscribers at the higher though totally unauthorized rates, threatening to cut off their service if they didn't comply. Ten days later a citizens' Telephone User's Protective Association was formed, which "practically lines up citizens and telephone users of Emporia against the Emporia Telephone Company."[35] Petitions were circulated around town to gain support for the citizens' committee. White, who at this point was drifting with the crowd, carried the petition in his Fourth Ward. The phone company stubbornly affirmed its publicly proclaimed—but very illegal—position and warned that it would cut off service to any subscribers who failed to pay up by January 20. The citizens' committee countered bravely with the threat that if anyone's phone were cut off, all would ask to have their phones removed. On January 20 Warren Finney triumphantly declared that the phone company now operated only under a charter from the state of Kansas, not under a franchise of any kind from the city of Emporia.[36]

The phone office bustled with activity as people flocked in, albeit reluctantly, to pay up at the higher rates. One hesitant soul, admitting that he did not fully comprehend the situation, was promptly ushered into Finney's private office, and the door was firmly shut. Blessed with the received word when he emerged a few minutes later, the newly enlightened subscriber cheerfully paid the new rate and left. "The town buzzed with telephone talk today," the *Gazette* reported in late January. "The path of W. W. Finney along the street was marked by conglomerations of citizens on foot each half block . . . a gesticulating knot below Fifth Avenue, of which Mr. Finney was the center, attracted all the loafers for blocks, and when they arrived breathless in anticipation of slaughter, all they found was a merry josh between Mr. Finney and Dr. Hunt."[37]

In a front-page editorial on January 20, White took a new approach, making an "unauthorized suggestion in the interests of honorable peace." He proposed that the question be submitted to an impartial arbitration board to avoid "a shameful wrangle." Such a settlement would avert a nasty lawsuit, an action that would be indicative of "a combatative spirit on both sides, unbecoming a thoroughly decent town like Emporia." Finney quickly agreed to the proposal; but the City Commission did not.[38] Suddenly recalling his Progressive philosophy and credentials, the mercurial White struck out abruptly in a wholly new direction three days later. He wondered editorially if it wouldn't "pay Emporia to buy the telephone plant, hook up the farmers and give people good service—even at a small annual loss?"[39] That advanced proposal was promptly forgotten by everyone.

Irate citizens put intense pressure on the City Commission not to compromise its position. Needled into action ("Isn't this town big enough to tackle Finney?") and flatly refusing the White-Finney offer to arbitrate, the commission announced that it would file suit to enjoin the phone company from raising its rates.[40] The city proceeded to file suit in late January and obtained a temporary restraining order preventing the company from charging the higher rates.[41]

Suddenly, on the day set for the hearing, the city withdrew its request for a restraining order, which allowed the phone company "to do as it pleases." Members of the citizens' committee agreed to pay at the advanced rate, though "under protest," until the suit was settled. Three years and two Kansas Supreme Court decisions later, Warren Finney had his rate increase and a clean-cut victory.[42]

As he was wont to do, White got in the last word in this little municipal melodrama, coming down squarely in Finney's corner: "Since the construction . . . and the installation . . . , Emporia has a telephone system which is second to none in the state. Mr. Finney has struggled under discouraging conditions and the people of Emporia should be willing to give him the credit and to support his enterprise."[43] And from that time on, White, who was most impressed by Finney's gumption and bravado under fire, became his "close and intimate" friend.

WHILE MANY FARMERS had been frustrated by their inability to get hooked up to the Emporia Telephone Company, others encountered W. W. Finney through his electric company. Finney held an interest in a company that brought electricity during the pre–World War I period to several small communities, including Hartford, a small town fifteen miles southeast of Emporia. In lieu of payment for a right-of-way easement, Finney had orally agreed to run a spur line a quarter of a mile up to the house of a farmer, Tom Evans. Several years passed; Hartford, but not Evans, had its lights. Finally, after World War I, the soft-spoken Evans decided that he had had enough of Finney's excuses and temporizing. Accompanied by his teen-age daughter Mary, he marched determinedly to the phone-company office. The shabbily dressed farmer confronted the natty Finney, whose shoes were so polished, the daughter remembered, that "I could see my reflection in them." "Mr. Finney, it is time you lived up to your word," Evans began. "Why, I . . . ," stammered Finney. "You agreed to put an electric line to my door," Evans continued. "I-I-I . . . ," from Finney. One word led to another, more heated word. Finney's initial "palavering" expression changed abruptly to a "fiendish" one. "You're a damn liar," was Evans's parting shot, as he and his daughter rushed angrily down the rickety wooden stairs and out onto Merchant Street. "Mary," the older and wiser farmer counseled on the way home, "sometimes you have to pay a price to find someone out."[44]

A FEW YEARS after he had moved to Emporia, Warren Finney, borrowing heavily and buying on thin margins, began to acquire an extensive series of small phone companies in eastern Kansas—at Yates Center, Burlington, Sabetha, Paola, Fredonia, Altoona, and other towns—over twenty in all by the early 1920s. By World War I the aggressive entrepreneur, always "quick on his feet in a trade," had become the largest independent telephone owner and operator in Kansas. In the mid 1920s, Finney organized a number of these properties as the Kansas Home Telephone Company. When that company was sold to a Salina group in 1930 for about $500,000, the now-affluent Finney publicly stated: "I feel badly of course to lose the intimate and pleasant relations enjoyed with the friends and subscribers in these localities, but my other interests . . . demand so much of my time." The purchasers later went bankrupt.[45]

Finney had begun to have an impact on the Bell Telephone Company shortly after his arrival in Emporia because of his company's lower rate structure. In 1917 he consolidated the Sabetha exchange with Bell, and in the early twenties there began a series of bitterly negotiated contracts with the developing utilities giant, which involved, principally, Emporia, Sabetha, and Paola. In 1926 an understanding was reached whereby Bell would purchase the controlling shares, and Finney would stay on as president and general manager for the remainder of his active career.[46]

The agreement threatened to come undone in February, 1927, when Bell, which was upset at Finney's fiscal policies and procedures, proposed that it would sell its Burlington exchange back to Finney if he would agree to get out of Emporia, Sabetha, and Paola altogether. Finney told his troubles to his friend Mr. White, who by now had become quite convinced that Finney was the best thing to happen to Emporia since the Santa Fe had located its divisional shops there. White, who was anxious to promote both Finney and what he saw as Emporia's best interests, wrote to their mutual friend Attorney General William A. Smith ("My dear Captain Bill"), outlining the problem and enlisting his help:

> There is a marked divergence of policy between Mr. Finney and [Bell]. I have been through this thing now for the last four or five months. . . . Mr. Finney believes in low rates and fairly competent service and the Bell believes in high rates and a service, which it seems to me is more than the average customer in a town like Emporia can afford to pay

for. . . . Please talk with Mr. Finney and go over with him the whole situation, particularly the points I have outlined. Of course, you know that he is my very good friend but even if he were not, I would be interested in this, as a citizen. . . . If you can[,] insist that this is a matter of public interest and that the divorce is contrary to public policy.[47]

White and U.S. Circuit Judge George McDermott, a friend of both Finney and White, were asked to act as arbitrators in the controversy for Finney and Bell, respectively. On July 1, 1927, a new agreement, witnessed by White and McDermott and approved by Attorney General Smith, was signed. It gave Finney the right to stay on as president and general manager at Emporia through 1932 at a salary of $500 per month. The contract was later extended to 1936, providing a comfortable pension for the president and a continuation of his substantial salary.[48] It appeared that Finney had gained a considerable victory over the corporate giant. Bell had evidently decided to exercise patience and to wait the irascible Finney out rather than to force an ugly and embarrassing public battle with him. But Warren Finney still harbored rage—from old wrongs, real or imagined—in the dark recesses of his heart. How else can we explain why one so affluent would habitually manipulate Bell's accounts in order to gain but a few thousand dollars? Or why he would forge an endorsement on Bell's $4,689.67 tax check for a possible six-month gain at 5 percent interest of $117.24? He hated not wisely, but too well.

AFTER BECOMING well established as one of the state's leading utilities powers, Finney decided to go into banking. It would prove to be a fateful decision, one that would lead directly to his downfall. He bought controlling interest in the Farmers State Bank at Neosho Falls about 1920 and soon consolidated it with the rival Neosho Falls State Bank. That proved to be a very costly acquisition, since the latter was essentially failing at the time of the purchase. The ill-fated bank reported resources of $318,000 in 1924, but these had slumped to only $117,000 by 1932. Finney purchased and reorganized the Fidelity State and Savings Bank at Emporia in 1924. The bank then had total resources of $350,000, which grew to $935,000 by 1933. Though he was manifestly a success in the utilities field, somehow Finney didn't seem to have the temperament for banking. He didn't like the tedium of it, and he made a lot of bad loans, especially in Neosho Falls. This had led to his running six-year feud with the state Banking Department—and, his son would later claim, to the subsequent massive forging of municipal bonds.[49]

THE GREGARIOUS Warren and Mabel Finney plunged headlong into the civic, social, and religious life of Emporia soon after their arrival from Neosho Falls. They joined a host of civic organizations, becoming charter members of the Emporia Country Club and the Good Road Boosters and official welcomers to sundry visiting caravans and dignitaries. The annual picnic for employees of the far-flung Finney phone network, which was held at the family cabin east of town, regularly drew about two hundred and fifty lively guests. Each June, Finney hosted an elaborate breakfast for fifty Santa Fe luminaries, including the company's president and the heads of the operating unions. After the Finneys moved into the pretentious twenty-five-room mansion on Twelfth Street, elaborate teas at their home became regular and featured attractions at the most prestigious social events held in the town. As many as two hundred out-of-town conventioneers who were attending meetings hosted by organizations such as the Congregational Church (Finney was a featured speaker on the convention program) and the Kansas Federation of Women's Clubs ("one of the loveliest social events of the convention") had an opportunity to partake of the gracious Finney hospitality. More strictly local events included bridge parties to benefit the unemployed, at which many of the town's leading women poured tea.[50]

A state leader in the YMCA, Mr. Finney immensely enjoyed employing his masterful, almost lordly, persuasive powers at "inspirational" luncheon talks held for solicitors at the outset of the annual fund-raising drive. The

The W. W. Finneys' Twelfth Street home (Walter M. Andersen)

Finneys and the Whites often headed the "special committee," which meant that they contacted the town's potentially largest givers—a group that included a disproportionate percentage of the more difficult ones. Finney served his alma mater, Washburn, on its Board of Trustees from 1917 until his abrupt resignation in the fall of 1933. He also became a lay leader in the Congregational Church, whose board of trustees he headed up for several years. A member in good standing of the WCTU, he had the honor of introducing the out-of-town speaker at the October, 1932, meeting, who was none other than the attorney general of the state of Kansas, the honorable Roland Boynton. The banker was in frequent demand as a speaker to local current-interest clubs on economic topics dealing with the business outlook, taxes, and such. On one occasion, Finney read a paper that had been prepared by the scheduled speaker, his son, who was ill and therefore unable to attend. The topic of the paper was Kansas municipal bonds.[51] On that evening the group certainly heard from the world's two leading authorities on that subject.

From the time that automobiles first became available to the public, Finney possessed the largest, most conspicuous cars in Emporia. The current model was often pressed into service when celebrities came visiting. "Emporia owes a debt to W. W. Finney," the ever-appreciative *Gazette* reported, "because Mr. Finney owns one of the few seven-passenger touring cars in Emporia. . . . It has become a recognized and expected fixture in all parades for visiting dignitaries." The occasion for that public statement was the visit of Vice-President Charles Curtis, a Kansan, in 1930. Finney also was conspicuous on the Emporia streets due to his sartorial splendor. His penchant for being well turned out didn't end with his shoeshine. One of the reasons the Whites invited the Finneys to formal dinners when important personages passed through town, they said, was that W. W. always looked so sharp in his formal attire. "He had the only dinner jacket in town," they quipped, which probably wasn't so very far from the truth. In 1930 he strode jauntily down Commercial Street wearing a perfectly fitting "snappy gray suit with a full-length, matching swallow-tail coat," which he had had made in 1913. "I'm proud of this suit," the vainglorious wearer proclaimed, "because it is absolute evidence that I have retained my girlish figure."[52]

ALTHOUGH HE never again ran for political office after his term as the "boy representative," Warren Finney maintained a lively interest in politics throughout his life. A staunch Republican, he became increasingly a liberal one, following the tutelage and example of his mentor, Mr. White, so that by the early twenties he had become one of the major behind-the-scenes political forces in the state. Aspiring Progressive candidates greatly prized his support as well as that of White. In 1924 he helped the *Gazette* editor in his mad-dash gubernatorial campaign, being credited with its "White Is Right" slogan. Judge Richard Hopkins received his support in his lengthy and controversial bid for a federal position. Governor Clyde Reed and Finney developed a "warm personal friendship" as the Emporian helped to organize the Reed-for-Governor boom in the late twenties. It was rumored that the one favor that he had asked of his newly elected gubernatorial friend in 1928 was that he replace Roy Bone, the state banking commissioner who had been making Finney's life miserable because of his banking practices.[53]

By the late twenties, Finney, who by now owned several farms stocked with prize cattle, had become increasingly disturbed by what he felt was an unfair tax burden being borne by the Kansas farmers. He became a vigorous proponent of the Progressive-sponsored, graduated-state-income-tax amendment. In 1930, at his own expense and after months of preparation with the aid of some Teachers College students, he published a well-received, thirty-two-page pamphlet, "The Farmer's Unjust Tax Burden." Presenting a well-reasoned attack on the current system of taxation, the pamphlet argued cogently that farmers were paying as much as twenty-three times the tax being paid by their comparable neighbors in town.[54]

A laudatory introduction to the pamphlet, which was entitled "Shake Hands with Warren Finney," had been contributed by the admiring editor of the *Gazette*:

> This is a business man's inquiry, written in a straightforward style by a man who has no political ambitions, no desire for political power or control, by a man whom I have known for a quarter of a century and have admired for his quenchless zeal for the common good. . . . He is a public-spirited citizen who gives of his time, his energy and his material substance much more than his share to the public welfare. I commend his book to all serious minded Kansans as an example of clear thinking, lucid writing and fair treatment of one of America's major economic problems.[55]

Finney read a lengthy paper on the problem to the venerable Emporia Current Club, and in late October he presented a radio talk over WIBW. At election time the *Topeka Capital* published an extensive editorial entitled "What Made W. W. Finney Go for the Income Tax." The *Gazette* mailed to every legislator in Topeka a copy of its edition containing an article by Finney on the tax question. Federal Judge Dick Hopkins praised Finney for his vigorous efforts in the righteous cause. "I think you are doing a splendid job," he said.[56]

The effort had to be repeated two years later, this time successfully, since the income-tax amendment went down to defeat in the 1930 election. Once again leading the fight for the proposal, Finney served as chairman of the finance committee of the statewide citizens' Income Tax Association.[57] After a "fighting speech" by Finney that was delivered over WIBW a few days before the election, White once again held up this public-spirited citizen to the admiring gaze of all:

> The time and money that other men would spend on golf, or bridge, or poker, or duck hunting or motoring, Mr. Finney has spent for the public good in this patriotic service.
> What does he get out of it?

Warren W. Finney, about 1930

No one can say just what—except satisfaction as a good citizen of seeing justice done in his state. . . .

But he has no nest to feather, no interest to further, no axe to grind. He is just a good citizen doing his best to make his state more livable.[58]

WARREN FINNEY first became acquainted with Alf Landon in the twenties through the Whites and through the Finneys' oil-well interests in the Flint Hills. Finney had been an active supporter of Reed; and Landon had been Reed's campaign manager.[59] By the late twenties their relationship had ripened into warm friendship, as is shown by this July, 1929, letter from Alf, responding to an earlier money-raising proposal from Finney:

> My dear Warren:
> Always you are thoughtful and considerate of your friends. You have saved my life, that is, my financial life at least, with the discovery which you have so fortunately made [at a] psychological moment. One half of everything I make out of this shall be yours. Don't refuse because I will not take no for an answer, and you will just simply save a postage stamp.
> I feel so grateful for what you have done that I am going to give one-half of my one-half to establish a home for aged politicians. There are all kinds of homes now-a-days, even the dogs and cats have homes, but nobody ever thinks of the politicians except to damn them.
> Hope Mrs. Finney is getting along fine. Give her my love.
> Your friend[60]

Landon became a regular visitor at the Finney home, and the two men frequently consulted on patronage matters. In July of 1932, as a gubernatorial aspirant in the Republican primary, Alf gave one of his standard prosaic campaign talks at Emporia's Broadview Hotel. Warren Finney introduced the would-be governor to the partisan crowd. After the speech, Finney, along with Young Bill White and lawyer O. R. Stites, accompanied Landon on a hot, dusty tour of the Lyon County country towns. A month later, Landon's sixteen-year-old daughter, Peggy Anne, spent a few days in Emporia as a houseguest of Warren Finney's eighteen-year-old daughter, Mary Jane.[61] In August, 1932, Finney solicited John Landon, Alf's father, for a contribution to the state YMCA. The senior Landon responded that he was backing Alf "to my very limit," since "I am very anxious that he should be elected." Regretably, he could only send a small check for the YMCA and "this is on account of the warm friendship between you and Alfred."[62]

After Landon's narrow victory over incumbent Harry Woodring, Finney elatedly wired: "Congratulations and love from Finneys to the whole damm Landon family."[63] A few days after the election, Landon's campaign manager, Frank Carlson, wrote to Finney, stating that Landon had suggested that Finney might be able to raise some additional funds to help eliminate the campaign deficit. Finney, who had been a major contributor to the gubernatorial campaign, as Tom Boyd and Will French later discovered, promptly sent $185 to Landon (including an additional $100 from himself and $50 from his son).[64] The grateful governor-elect responded on December 8:

> Your very valuable letter of the 3rd received. I would not have had the nerve to ask you to do any more, knowing what you did in the campaign.
>
> The trouble with you is you are always so glad to help your friends that I am afraid of working a willing Hoss to death.[65]

In an angry public protest meeting held in March, 1933—which was attended by about forty Emporians—Landon, Finney, and White were all accused of collusion, connivance, or worse with respect to utility rates. W. S. Kretsinger, a lawyer who, ironically, had been a Finney supporter in the 1911 telephone-company fight, spoke with some fervor about the dark linkage between the governor's Public Service Commission, the Emporia Telephone Company, and the local newspaper:

> Governor Reed's board [the Public Service Commission] did nothing for the people. During and after the campaign, the manager of the Emporia Telephone company was Reed's advisor. It was a valid assumption that his utilities board would be friendly to the Emporia Telephone company. . . .
>
> Now we have Governor Landon. Every time he comes to Emporia he parks his car in front of the Emporia Telephone company. . . .
>
> We could get lower rates in this town if The Emporia Gazette would make a fight for these things. It seems to me that there is a wonderful opportunity for a newspaper to do something in this town, but because of the relation between The Gazette and the Emporia Telephone company, the people are not getting the service to which they are entitled.[66]

PERHAPS the most fully satisfying day of Warren Finney's life came on February 29, 1932. In an attempt to get badly needed currency out of backyard tin cans and the family sugar bowl and into circulation, President

Hoover had launched a national antihoarding campaign in early 1932.⁶⁷ The national campaign director, Chicagoan Frank Knox (Landon's 1936 vice-presidential running mate), announced that he sought as state chairmen "aggressive individuals who have the confidence of the people."⁶⁸ Mr. White, of course, was asked to recommend someone to head up the Kansas campaign. He wired three recommendations to Knox, stating (though many bankers held misgivings about the project) that "my first choice and by far [the] most emphatic would be Warren W. Finney."⁶⁹

Taking White's suggestion, Knox asked Finney to lead the Kansas campaign, and he readily accepted. Flying into the task with his characteristic gusto, Finney utilized his administrative skills to perfect an organization that included a chairman in every Kansas town with a population of twenty-five hundred or more. He addressed Rotary Clubs, Lions Clubs, YMCAs, Cooperative Clubs, Chambers of Commerce, a high-school assembly, church groups, acquaintances—even total strangers on the street. He managed to show a specially prepared film at the local theater. He and his message were everywhere. The citizens of Emporia and across the state responded, not without some apprehension, by bringing their long-hidden cash, including some ancient, outsized bills, into their friendly neighborhood bank in exchange for interest-bearing treasury certificates.⁷⁰ At the conclusion of the successful campaign, Mr. White wrote Frank Knox that the indefatigable Finney had been "a double distilled daisy. He made the bankers come to it and like it whether they wanted to or not."⁷¹

A festive dinner, held on February 29 at Topeka's Jayhawk Hotel for the thirty-eight "advisory council" members, represented the culmination of this frenzied activity. The Finney-invited list (thirty-two of the thirty-eight showed up) read like a Kansas Who's Who of the 1930s. More ceremonial than functional as regards President Hoover's project, the advisory group represented one of the most talented, powerful, and diversified groups ever assembled under one Kansas roof at one time.⁷² And on the dais sat a serene and charming Warren Wesley Finney, benignly surveying the sea of Kansas notables who had responded to his patriotic call. Flanked by Governor Woodring on the one side and by his very best friend and Kansas' most eminent citizen on the other, he indeed beheld a prospect that pleaseth. After the repast, Chairman Finney "took his guests into his confidence and explained the plan in great detail." Governor Woodring gave his unqualified endorsement, remarking that it was "a fine thing," just as important now in peace time as the bond drives had been during the late war. After some of the other worthies had chimed in with their warm approvals, Mr. White rose to offer a resolution, extending a vote of confidence in Mr. Finney and his plan. To no one's surprise, it carried unanimously.[73] As he motored back to Emporia with Mr. White on that late winter night, Warren Finney would certainly have been most pleased with the evening's festivities. Yes, it had been a glorious and memorable night—and right there in the Jayhawk Hotel, whose fifth floor son Ronald would make notorious within eighteen months.

7

His Father's Son

ooooooooooooooooooooooooooooooooooooooooooooooooooooo

THE *SINE QUA NON* of the scandal, Ronald Tucker Finney, was born on September 18, 1898, in Neosho Falls. He moved up river to Emporia with his family at the age of seven. So far as the limited evidence goes, he had a reasonably normal childhood. Raised as an only child—his sister didn't come along until he was nearly sixteen—Ronald was hugely indulged by doting parents. Possessed of probing brown eyes, he was filled with an enormous nervous energy, which often spilled over into boyish pranks and devilment, but nothing so very serious or beyond the peccadilloes to be expected from a high-spirited youngster. He evidently managed to find socially acceptable releases for this high-voltage energy up into adulthood.

Ronald developed a fondness for animals at an early age, keeping an exotic menagerie in his backyard that included such unlikely creatures as foxes, monkeys, and alligators. As a teen-ager he attracted a good deal of attention from downtown shoppers by displaying two pet coons and a 'possum in a store window. An avid fisherman both as a teen-ager and as an adult, young Finney liked nothing better than to wet a hopeful line in the catfish-filled Neosho or the trout-laden streams of Colorado. A tendency toward obesity, which remained a distressing and long-term problem, first manifested itself in boyhood. The tall (six feet) and plump extrovert loved to eat and, like his father, became one of the great trenchermen of eastern Kansas. He attended the Congregational Church, as dictated by his pious parents, where once he had the daughter of U.S. Senator Preston Plumb as his Sunday School teacher. As an adult, he attended church sporadically at best.[1]

Ronald absorbed the family preoccupation with money at an early age.

Long before he was in a position to do much about it, he confidently bragged to chums that he intended to become a millionaire as a young man, probably before his thirtieth birthday. The first faint but definite signs of a tendency toward duplicity and a scornfulness of the rules—which later served him so badly—manifested itself when he was but a youngster. He often kept undersized fish, telling his companions that it didn't make any difference—no one would ever know anyway. His father once assigned the delivery of new telephone books to his teen-aged son, for a liberal stipend. The enterprising young man then proceeded to subcontract with his buddies, who performed the actual work for a very modest wage. He pocketed the considerable difference, unbeknownst to the family. Years later, Ronald would employ that same technique as a broker between local school boards and the state School Fund Commission.

Possessed of a well-developed, rowdyish sense of humor, the popular and free-spending teen-ager became a leader of Emporia's affluent Twelfth Street crowd. His high-school peers included the sons and daughters of the business and professional community—the indulged, socially active "in" crowd found at the top of the pecking order in every high school in the land. His many extracurricular activities included membership in the Christian Boys Club ("The Club stands for clean speech, clean sport, clean living") and the presidencies of the student senate and the senior class. Enrolling in school a year later than most of his contemporaries, he graduated from Emporia High School with a reasonably good academic record a month after America entered World War I and just three months before his nineteenth birthday.[2]

That fall, Ronald entered Washburn College, following in the footsteps of his parents and numerous other relatives. He was promptly elected president of the freshman class, played guard on the football team, and pledged the Phi Delta Theta social fraternity. Nicknamed "Fin" by his fraternity brothers, the likable young man became a popular figure on campus, both because of his outgoing personality and because he always seemed to have ready cash which he was more than willing to lavish on his fawning friends. Ronald had firmly established an essential part of the Finney mystique—a lifelong pattern of excessive generosity to his friends and acquaintances.[3]

Deciding that an eastern education would be more prestigious than that offered at a small midwestern institution like Washburn, the doting Finneys sent their beloved son to Cornell University in Ithaca, New York, in 1919. Ronald majored in liberal arts and graduated in 1921.[4]

HIS FATHER'S SON

SHORTLY AFTER he had returned from the East and at the urging of his father, the new graduate took charge of the bank at Neosho Falls. Rapidly gaining a reputation as a "stern custodian" of its funds, he thoroughly absorbed the ways and wiles of business and banking à la Warren Finney. In urging the position on Ronald, the anxious father had more in mind than an attractive business opportunity for his promising and pliant son. Father Finney's banking practices required an understanding cashier in the Neosho Falls end of the business. So, in addition to the usual procedures, Ronald learned the fine art of check-kiting, the routine deceiving of the hard-eyed bank examiners, the systematic stalling of the relentless state Banking Department, and other fraudulent practices designed to help keep a shaky country bank solvent. In those impressionable days, Ronald felt that he and his father "had a little secret between them." After public revelation of the scandal, the relationship of the father and the son—who had led whom down the primrose path—became a favorite Kansas living-room topic. Insofar as the world could see, the filial relationship was a reasonably normal one, with the son eager enough to please the father. As in any father-son pairing, the role of the teacher is both potent and predetermined.[5] And sometimes the student learns his lessons better than the teacher intended.

Farmers State Bank, Neosho Falls, now the town's post office
(Joan Larson Bader)

A year or so after Ronald went to Neosho Falls, the elder Finney bought the other bank in town and consolidated it with the Farmers State. The former was in a failing condition at the time of the purchase, but the father either failed to perceive this discouraging reality or, seeing it, refused to acknowledge it. This unpleasant fact—plus a number of bad loans to farmers, who were being regularly devastated by floods, and to cattlemen, who were just as persistently being wiped out by drouth and low prices—resulted in a continual scramble by father and son to keep the economic noses of the Emporia and the Neosho Falls banks, especially the latter, above the water line. Bad notes were often "hidden" with correspondent banks, marked "paid" when they had not been, or otherwise removed from sight by whatever means were available to prevent them from being discovered by the ever-present examiners. When some progress could be shown, the examiners relaxed their pressure a bit, and the Finneys breathed more easily for a spell.[6]

The Neosho Falls Bank turned more and more to cattle loans. Young Ronald helped out by falsely increasing the age and weight of the cattle on the notes, enabling them to carry a larger loan and permitting him to work a part of the bank loss into the loan. "This I did," he wrote years later. "I know now and I knew at the time it was not right. But by making a yearling a short two year old, and taking the average weight at 800 instead of 500, it enabled the loan to 'stand' several thousand dollars of the customer's bad paper. It was always the hope that the cattle would make money, and when sold, be able to retire the full note."[7] The normally cheerful Ronald became discouraged at times, because of the persistent floods on the Neosho River and the constant juggling of the books to keep the bank afloat. "I know now," he later said, "that it was not only bad, but very foolish to try to keep a failed bank, or several failed banks[,] from closing."[8]

HIS LIFE brightened considerably, though, when on April 21, 1923, in a Methodist Church ceremony in Emporia, he married the very attractive Winifred Wiggam, his childhood sweetheart. Her father, John H. Wiggam, a well-known stockman and respected officer with the Warren Mortgage Company, one of the largest land-mortgage firms in the Midwest, had been active in Republican politics for years. Her mother, Jennie, the daughter of a chief justice of the Indiana Supreme Court, was a leading clubwoman in Kansas. A former high-school principal, she had organized the Women's City Club in Emporia (which boasted no less than thirteen hundred members) and later served as president (1927–29) of the Kansas State Federation of Women's Clubs. In 1911/12 she and a feminist friend visited every one of the 116 country school districts in Lyon County, stumping for an upcoming vote on woman suffrage. A pillar of the Methodist Church, she had taught the women's Bible class for years. A rather stern puritanical type—like Mabel Finney—she had been a leader in the opposition to the screening of movies on Sunday. When Winifred showed a serious interest in a high-school classmate whose father was "only a horse trader," the well-educated, aristocratic Mrs. Wiggam would have none of it, urging instead young Finney, the scion of one of the town's leading families.[9]

The slim, brown-haired bride, one of the best-looking young women in her class, had run in the same high-school crowd as Ronald Finney. They became engaged after a somewhat stormy and lengthy courtship. Two years younger than the bridegroom, she had been sent by her parents after high school to a very proper finishing school for girls (Ward-Belmont in Nashville, Tennessee), perhaps to break up the romance with the horse trader's son. After she had spent a year in exile there, her parents relented, and she entered Washburn in 1918—thus overlapping for one year Ronald's stay at the Topeka campus. After Ronald went on to Cornell, she transferred to the University of Wisconsin, from which she had just graduated at the time of the nuptials. Like her husband, Winifred was gregarious, spent money freely, and loved parties and the good life. But she became a good wife and mother under trying circumstances and apparently had little inkling of what Ronald and his father were up to until the fateful summer of '33.[10]

The newlyweds moved into a comfortable, modern clapboard bungalow in Neosho Falls that he had just had built. They did their best to fit into the staid life of the small agricultural community. They frequently entertained the town's "better people," as a prudent banker should, and sincerely tried to help those who needed help, often preparing sumptuous food baskets for the needy. Poker parties, occasionally lasting all night, and big, rowdy fish fries for Emporia friends became frequent events. After banking hours, Ronald often went fishing with old reprobate cronies like "Chigger" Boner, the town ne'er-do-well and sometime bootlegger. Squatting under the willows on the Neosho's muddy banks, lazily watching the cottonwood leaves float by, old "Chig" must have listened in awe as Ronald convincingly explained how he was going to be a millionaire with this "plunge" or that before he reached his thirtieth birthday.[11]

THE YOUNG BANKER became increasingly frustrated running his father's small business, so after a half dozen years, he decided to branch out a bit. Improbably, he went into the newspaper business. In the summer of 1927 he launched the *Four Counties Paper,* so-called because Neosho Falls was situated near the common corner of Anderson, Allen, Coffey, and Woodson counties.

In the long, hallowed annals of Kansas journalism, a more peculiar specimen than the short-lived *Four Counties Paper* has rarely been seen. Full of advertisements (one of the largest of which trumpeted the virtues of the Emporia Telephone Company), the weekly boasted that it went into every one of the fourteen thousand homes in the four counties. It offered its readership humility ("The Four Counties Paper is a power . . . unique in the annals of publication"); circumspection ("The moment this first issue was placed in the mail, a power began to be exerted that would prove dangerous without proper direction"); positive thinking ("The paper . . . feels that an apology is due its readers for presenting such incidents as the Lebo tornado"); and an enhanced sense of community ("LeRoy [population 650] is a good little town. The visitor to LeRoy is struck with the 'swing' of the place"). The publication's statement of policy asserted that it posed no threat to the region's established papers (which was true enough) and that it fervently supported "whatever will draw our people together in social or civic effort." With Ronald Finney at the helm, one could only conclude that more of the ship remained below the water line than above it. In the fall the editor mysteriously declared that "the primary purpose . . . of the paper never has been revealed outside of the organization that produces it." Unfortunately, the world never learned that deep, dark secret; the weekly abruptly ceased publication in the summer of 1928.[12]

Though not formally connected with the quixotic enterprise as an officer, Ronald Finney conceived and controlled the operation from start to finish. Through political pull, he wheedled a charter from the state charter board to sell up to $100,000 worth of stock without any permanent investment by the incorporators or himself. The formal incorporators included several area newspapermen, among whom was Lee R. Hettic, a former secretary of the state Democratic Central Committee. "We would not ever let anybody know on the outside that Ronald Finney was connected with the paper," an employee said after the debacle had ended. Why not? "They all thought he was crooked."[13] Ronald's check-kiting reputation had begun to catch up with him.

Finney persuaded F. G. Bodley, a salesman whom he had met in a Kansas City hotel, to come down to Neosho Falls and sell "blue-sky" stock in the new paper.¹⁴ The attorney general, Charles Griffith, recommended Ronald Finney and his father to the salesman "in the very highest terms, and said they was very fine men for me to be connected with."¹⁵ One of the purchasers of stock in the fledgling enterprise offered a promissory note to the salesman in lieu of cash. Bodley managed to interest young George Berry at the nearby Aliceville Bank in exchanging the note for a certificate of deposit, with the explicit understanding that the CD would not be cashed until the note had been paid.¹⁶

With this transaction as the opening wedge, the Finneys proceeded to unload a number of worthless notes, which the state Banking Department had been complaining about, on the Finney-inexperienced Berry. Ronald and his father agreed that the CDs received in exchange wouldn't be cashed until the notes had been paid. One of the notes had allegedly been signed by a Topeka grocer named George Rockhill (he said his name had been forged). Another note, signed "H. B. Hogeboode," couldn't be traced to anyone, living or dead, in the entire area. A few months after these shady transactions, an affable, debonair W. W. Finney appeared in the Aliceville Bank with $13,000 in CDs in his briefcase, which he said he would please like to have cashed. Berry reminded him of their agreement. Finney said he didn't know a thing about that: he was "an innocent purchaser" and demanded his money forthwith. Berry held his ground, and the Finneys eventually took him to district court, where the judge found for the plaintiffs. The Aliceville Bank appealed to the Kansas Supreme Court. Justice Richard J. Hopkins wrote the high court's opinion in late 1929—one of his last acts on the court before assuming the federal bench. Hopkins's opinion sustained the lower court's decision on the narrow ground that insufficient evidence had been adduced to clearly demonstrate that the Hogeboode note—the one on which the suit was brought—had been covered by the agreement. Ironically, Clarence Beck of Emporia and Sard M. Brewster of Topeka served as the Finneys' lawyers in these proceedings.¹⁷

In 1927 Finney recruited a Kansas State journalism student, G. McDill ("Huck") Boyd (no relation to Tom), for the summer to help get the paper out.¹⁸ The banker-turned-newspaperman bragged a good deal to his young apprentice about his great accomplishments and his even greater plans. He offered to make the college student an officer in one of his grandiose enterprises, assuring him that if any trouble developed, he "could not be held responsible," since he wasn't of age.¹⁹ Wisely declining the proferred opportunity, Boyd went on to become a prominent Kansas journalist at Phillipsburg.

AT ABOUT THIS TIME, Ronald began to phase himself out of the bank "by stages." He received considerable encouragement in that direction from the banking commissioner, Roy Bone. The commissioner, who was upset at the recurrent examiner's reports of check-kiting and other nefarious practices, reportedly had threatened to remove Ronald from the bank and to bar him from working in any other bank in the state.[20] Taking the "hint," Ronald decided to expand his heretofore limited insurance work.

If God ever created a natural salesman, it was Ronald Finney. "Finney is a dynamic salesman," reported one acquaintance who had an opportunity to watch up close. "He had ability far beyond that of us ordinary mortals, and used along legitimate lines, could have been outstanding in financial circles in the state within a few years."[21] An old Neosho Falls farmer recalled that "Ronald sure was a talker. He sure could make a believer out of you."[22]

In 1927 the young banker sold over half a million dollars worth of life insurance for the Kansas Life Insurance Company. He also negotiated the sale of two life insurance companies, receiving $25,000 on one transaction and $10,000 on the other, but only after he had had to file a recovery suit against the receiver company. Finney had negotiated the deal in the law offices of O'Neil and Hamilton. But since they had been called as witnesses in the case, he had gone to the law firm of Wheeler, Brewster and Hunt— Kansas' oldest and most distinguished. One day Finney created quite a stir in their staid Topeka office when, after having been told that they would not hand over his recovery check until he paid their $1,750 legal fee, he sullenly slammed the money—in bills of very small denominations— down on the counter.[23]

By the late twenties, Ronald and Winifred had become increasingly restless and had determined to leave Neosho Falls. Ronald was beginning to make some money, but he had to go out of town an awful lot to do it. There just wasn't that much money to be made in the Falls, no matter how many angles a creative young schemer tried, because there just wasn't that much money there to begin with. Besides, the ambitious young promoter had passed his thirtieth birthday in 1928, and still he wasn't a millionaire—or even close to being one. A daughter had been born to the couple in 1926; a son in 1929.[24] "Win" raised more than a few eyebrows one morning by pushing the baby buggy down the main street while on roller skates. The disapproving biddies got another chance to cackle one afternoon when she was seen returning from a swim down at the gravel bar. They glowered disapprovingly as she, daringly dressed in an "advanced" bathing suit, hung gaily on the running board of a car as it raced wildly up Main Street, with her roguish husband at the wheel. Yes, Ronald and Winifred were definitely "ideas whose time had not yet come to Neosho Falls."[25]

WHEN THE YOUNG FINNEYS finally shook the dust of Neosho Falls from their shoes and moved up river to Emporia, they displaced the obliging Wiggams in their large, comfortable two-story house at 929 West Street. For a time, Ronald dabbled indifferently in this and that: he bid unsuccessfully on an Arkansas City office building ("its only skyscraper"), peddled slot machines, and tried to market buffalo steaks. By 1930 his incipient bond-brokerage business, which overlapped the insurance work, began to capture the major share of his time and interest. This activity, which was initially legitimate, grew rapidly and soon became his principal source of income. He began to do well financially, and his prospects, in spite of the deepening depression, brightened considerably.[26]

To further his bond business, his attention turned more and more to Topeka and the Statehouse. In the winter of 1931 he lobbied a bond-exchange bill through the legislature to passage ("I got a bill through the legislature," is the way he put it).[27] Finney hired Leland Caldwell as his general factotum about this time. Caldwell, who had spent a year in Tom Boyd's Treasury Office, knew the ropes. Finney set Caldwell to work making a complete list of all the bond issues that would be eligible for exchange under the proposed law. Even though the bill was amended in an attempt to thwart him, Finney estimated that he cleared about $30,000 from the legislation. By this juncture the Finney repertory of skills, both legitimate and illegitimate, had fully matured and had begun to be finely honed—though the forging of bonds and warrants was still to be invented. In his "novel" *What People Said*, Bill White has Finney (as Lee Norssex) crassly crowing at this period that he would size up an adversary and "then I'd either tell him to go to hell or buy him off, 'cording to whichever seemed cheaper."[28]

In addition to the business brought on by the new exchange law, a significant increase in bond refunding had resulted from the general economic depression. Bonds of public bodies frequently had to be refunded for longer periods of time at different, often lower, interest rates. This required the services of an experienced person, a bond broker. In the 1930-33 period, Ronald Finney and his associates drove and flew the length and breadth of Kansas negotiating contracts with local governmental units.[29] And if the unit happened to be a small town or a rural school district, where the folks had never been enlightened on such esoteric subjects as warrant cancellation or the fiscal agency, so much the better. It gave a sharp, enterprising fellow a little more room to maneuver.

In the beginning, the municipal bond business had been "squarely handled and profitable." Legitimate profits from his refunding operations came to over $100,000. The ambitious Emporian had begun to make a serious move toward the one-million-dollar mark. Not counting the later forgeries, he sold about $6 million in securities to Kansas banks, eastern insurance companies, and, later, to the state School Fund Commission. He outlined his practices with respect to the School Fund in a remorseful statement written ten years later in prison:

> I found it was more profitable to handle bonds through or sell to the State School fund Commission. These sales, in some part, were not above board. The bonds were good, but the fact that the commission bought my bonds, and did not buy bonds from other dealers, caused other dealers to say that I was "paying off." It was not handled that way but the practice was not clean. Also, in order to get these bond refundings for myself, rather than having them go to other dealers, I paid public officials. This was not honest.[30]

THE NEWLY PROSPEROUS bond broker didn't limit himself to the securities business. Carl J. Peterson, a former state bank commissioner, had organized a building and loan association whose assets included several apartment buildings and an addition to the city of Topeka. In early 1930 Finney bought the assets of the then defunct company and organized the Home Finance and Realty Company. Directors of the company included the prominent Topeka realtor David Neiswanger; John Kirk and Charles Cooke of the National Bank of Topeka; and Dyke O'Neil. The company decided to build some houses in the Topeka addition. To finance the deal the new organization sold a $110,000 mortgage to a Wichita life-insurance company. That company attempted to substitute the mortgage for some securities that it had deposited with the state Insurance Department. The insurance commissioner, Charles Hobbs, and his young assistant, George Brewster—Sard Brewster's son—gave an emphatic no to the deal. The furious Finney demanded that they reconsider. The commissioner's office responded by sending out their own appraisers, whose evaluation of the properties was less than half that furnished by the insurance company (one of whose appraisers had been Leland Caldwell). The commissioner's final answer was an even more emphatic no. Finney was enraged. "I'll cram that mortgage down your throat before I'm through," he screamed. He threatened a $1.5 million damage suit against Hobbs and Brewster. A much reduced suit, filed in federal court, never came to trial.[31]

Finney became a major creditor and financial consultant to the Hill Packing Company, a Topeka horse-meat packing firm. At Finney's invitation, Attorney General Boynton became the company's legal advisor. In the spring of 1932 a Topeka city commissioner introduced a bill—aimed at the Hill operation—to outlaw the processing of dead animals within the city limits. Disturbed at this development, Ronald went to a lawyer friend —who happened to know the mayor quite well—to see what could be done to get the bill killed. On the day that it was killed, Leland Caldwell appeared at the lawyer's home bearing an envelope that bulged with a good-sized fee from the grateful and generous broker.[32]

LIKE MANY KANSANS of some means, the Finney family had been spending summer vacations in Colorado for years. Around 1930, Ronald "discovered" Hinsdale County, a lovely, isolated Alps-like region in the southwestern part of the state. The county had about $110,000 in bonds outstanding for bridges and road construction and was experiencing a great deal of trouble in retiring the issues as they came due. Enter our master salesman in 1931. His passage through Hinsdale County "caused more excitement than the late World War." Waxing eloquent about the beauties of the area and its potential for the tourist trade, Finney promised to buy up $94,000 of the outstanding bonds—at less than forty cents on the dollar—if the county commissioners would agree to refund the bonds and levy a new tax to pay for them. Ronald proceeded to try to line up the Colorado equivalent of the Kansas School Fund Commission to buy the bonds. That had been his purpose in persuading the attorney general to accompany him to Denver in 1931. If the deal had gone through as planned, Finney would have cleared over $50,000. There was only one small fly in the ointment. A local taxpayer brought civil suit to prevent the commissioners from levying the tax. Postponed several times, the suit was scheduled to be heard in Denver on August 14, just a week after the much larger explosion in Kansas. Finney had been named as a codefendant in the action. Eventually a permanent injunction against the deal was obtained, and Finney's bond investment in Colorado became a total loss.[33]

As a result of his interest in Hinsdale County and to show the locals how things should be done in a big-league fashion, Finney bought a run-down ranch resort southwest of Lake City, the only town in the county.

He rehabilitated the place, building a group of "luxurious" cabins in an old mining area. As another manifestation of his generous—and scheming—nature, he invited carloads of his influential Kansas friends to come out at his expense to share the magnificent scenery and the clean, sparkling air. In the summers of 1932 and 1933 a steady stream of free-loading intimates and acquaintances—chiefly from Emporia and Topeka—made the long trek to the rustic mountain retreat. Lester Goodell, the chief Shawnee County prosecutor, had been extended a "hearty invitation" by the prescient Finney just a few weeks before August 7. Fortunately for everyone except Finney, Goodell declined.[34]

After the crash, the editor of the *Lake City Times* wrote an appreciative and incisive editorial, "Giving the Devil His Due":

> ... Even to the many friends he made in this part of Colorado his present position is not a terrible surprise. Ronald Finney was a plunger; he lived on plunging—it was his very life. He plunged in every direction. He plunged for investment, ... in art, sports, pastime, pleasure and for his friends. He asked for the dinner check, the wine check and the picnic check—was insistent that he be permitted to pay all bills for his own and his friends' entertainment. There was none of the piker, or squeezer, about Ronald Finney....
>
> In his dealings [here] Ronald Finney shot fair and square. He loved this place and loved most of its people. His intentions concerning the development and building up of this territory were bona fide and without guile and had he not been interrupted many of his planned improvements would be concretely in evidence here today.[35]

ALL WORK and no play would make Ronald a dull boy, and Ronald was never a dull boy. Continuing his boyhood interest in animals, he bought a pony-drawn fire-engine wagon for his two young children. They attracted a great deal of Sunday morning attention as they gaily drove through the streets picking up neighborhood kids for an exciting ride. In 1932 he purchased a magnificent pair of matched Arabian horses (Nemo and Pedro) for Win and himself, paying the unheard-of sum of $7,000 for them. George Godfrey Moore, a well-known Topeka insurance executive and civic leader, helped him train the sensitive animals. Finney had a barn built at the rear of his property to house them, and he hired a young man, full time, to care for them.[36]

In the spring of 1933 the "ungovernably hospitable" young Finneys installed a lighted tennis court at the rear of their Emporia home. A steady stream of their "high society" friends—if there be such in Kansas—dropped by for a swift set of tennis, a cool drink by the swimming pool, and warm conviviality. There were lobster and champagne dinners and wild weekend "bashes." About two o'clock one memorable Sunday morning, Ronald, a couple of sheets to the wind, saddled up Pedro, rode him into a houseful of startled guests, and good-naturedly chased them back and forth from one room to another, the ladies screaming in mock terror all the while. A similar incident occurred later at a Topeka restaurant, when he rode Pedro into the main dining room during a birthday celebration for Winifred. The "almost numberless" motor cars included his "flagship"—an expensive and powerful 1932 Pierce-Arrow. The well-groomed Winifred made frequent 100-mile trips to Kansas City with her affluent friends to shop or just to get her hair done. Fifty spenders like Ronald Finney, someone quipped, could end the depression.[37] If money was pouring in like water, it was flowing out like wine.

Finney's most elaborate and expensive plaything was the 101 Ranch Real Wild West Show. As part of their extensive 101,000-acre operation around Ponca City, Oklahoma, the eminent Miller family had developed a celebrated "real" Wild West show—a circus complete with stagecoach, covered wagons, trained horses, buffalo, cowboys, and cowgirls. In an earlier, more affluent day the show had played in the East and before the crowned heads of Europe. The colorful Zack Miller had had the popular Tom Mix and a number of other early cowboy film stars under contract. After the 1929 market collapse the 101 Ranch operation fell on hard times, and the show passed into receivership.[38]

Ronald Finney heard about the show and its financial problems. With two friends, he flew to Ponca City in early May, 1933, and negotiated for the property with Lew H. Wentz, a prominent oil man, who held the mortgage. Wentz had a firm $25,000 price tag on the show—take it or leave it. Finney suggested that they flip a coin—$20,000 or $30,000. Wentz blinked at that but would have none of it. Finney finally paid the $25,000 in cash, thus acquiring a Wild West show with over 200 head of animals (including five elephants) and 125 people (including several Indians) on the payroll.[39]

The show entrained immediately for the Midway at the Chicago World's Fair. Red and green roadside billboards over the Midwest loudly proclaimed: "When you go to Chicago to see the great 101 Ranch Wild West Show[,] also don't fail to see the World's Fair." Finney persuaded Zack Miller to come along to front for the show. (Later the flamboyant Miller reportedly offered to hide Finney out in the northern Oklahoma hills.) Whether due to its peripheral location—perhaps it was too far from where Sally Rand seductively manipulated her fans—or to more intrinsic shortcomings, the show lost a good deal of money in Chicago, reputedly at a rate of $500 per day. When Finney made his infamous July bond trips to Chicago, with armed protection by courtesy of the Kansas state treasurer, he and his guests enjoyed the sights at the Midway, including, of course, the 101 Ranch Wild West Show.[40]

In late July, Finney abruptly terminated the performances at the "Century of Progress" and returned the show to Eureka, where it became the central attraction at the Greenwood County Fair. When the bubble burst, the stranded circus—including its principal attraction, the five elephants—was quartered at the nearby Finney-owned Munger Ranch and at the Eureka fairgrounds. The elephants earned their keep by giving performances at the fairgrounds and rides (for a nickel) to excited children. The schoolchildren of the area made organized contributions to the pachyderms' welfare. The show was sold to a circus in early 1934, and the elephants were shipped to South Carolina.[41]

ALTHOUGH SOME of Ronald Finney's generosity was apparent to his friends and acquaintances, much of it was not. His almost frantic magnanimity by late 1932 resulted from the fusion of a naturally generous spirit with a very guilty conscience. Ronald had always been an easy mark for a solicitor—he gave to church groups, welfare associations, prohibition societies, children's homes, you-name-it. Emporia's black population swore by him for his benevolence. During the winter of 1932/33 he spent several thousand dollars footing the entire free-milk bill for the children of Emporia's unemployed. That same winter, when his young daughter was stricken with pneumonia and needed an oxygen tent, he bought it outright and presented it as a gift to the hospital. At that same time, when he discovered that children of two families whom he did not know were seriously ill and in need of special medical care that the families could not possibly afford, he hired two private nurses and paid all the expenses for both youngsters. In another project—which by its nature could not remain wholly anonymous—Finney rented a plot of garden ground near Emporia and set up a bank account for the unemployed to draw on for seeds and gardening tools. All this and more was done with a strict insistence that he remain nameless to the recipients of his largess. White pleaded with this philanthropic young man with a "fine social conscience" to allow him to publicize at least some of his good deeds in the pages of the *Gazette*.

But the good Samaritan, keeping his own counsel, would have none of it. The editor remained puzzled at this total rejection of favorable publicity—this was a strange and idealistic young man, indeed, he thought.[42]

WHEN FINNEY first began to turn his attention to the Statehouse, he became a frequent overnight visitor at the Jayhawk Hotel, which was located just one block north of the capitol. Initially his quarters were modest enough. "Nothing uncommon," remarked Will French, who visited there in 1931.[43] But as Finney's activities expanded, his needs for additional and more elaborate space grew. Soon he had a suite of five rooms, including sleeping quarters. The general office contained an elaborate telephone switchboard, with direct lines to Chicago, Washington, and Emporia as well as several "blind" phone connections with which he often fooled a visitor when he simulated a "conversation" with an important personage. There was a stock-market ticker and a Dictaphone system, which allowed interoffice communication. Three well-used phones sat to the left of his large, cluttered desk. He often had all three in use at once, as he simultaneously transacted business in, say, Kansas City, Chicago, and Washington. This spectacle, remarked upon by numerous witnesses, had dazzled his intimate friend Tom Boyd. Through endless calls he kept in constant touch with the stock and commodities markets, farm and cattle conditions, selected mining and smelting operations, and business conditions generally. His monthly phone bill was astronomical; his telegraph bill for June, 1933, reportedly was $3,300.[44]

Finney found no difficulty in staffing his operations, since it had been said—with only slight exaggeration—that everyone in the state "either worked for him or wanted to." Known as the "Kingfish" (like Huey Long) around the suite, Ronald was an easy employer, usually allowing a good deal of room in which his subordinates could operate. "Ronald liked to hatch things out," an associate said, "but he wouldn't give two hoops for any detail. . . . He would just say; 'Don't ask me; do anything you want.'" His fifteen regular employees included a lawyer, a publicist-journalist, a switchboard operator, an auditor, a commodities specialist, secretaries, and sundry others—all of whom were presided over by his number one man, Leland Caldwell.[45]

Immediately after the scandal broke, Vivian Tracey, who was variously described as a "titian beauty" and "exciting redhead," became the most publicized of the Finney employees. Tracey had come to work for Finney in 1932 after spending two months as an apprentice in treasurer Boyd's office. She had recently passed a screen test for Paramount Pictures (allegedly arranged for by Finney), but her screen career "had hit a snag since her funds were tied up with those of Finney." In her formal statement to investigators, she flatly denied that she knew anything about the forgeries. The newspapers tried to make more of the sex angle than the facts warranted but that potential sensation never developed.[46]

Rumors abounded—probably greatly exaggerated—regarding "wild" parties in the Jayhawk suite, where female hostesses allegedly helped the ambitious broker wheedle important political and business favors. But without question, Finney did use his quarters to entertain and impress those from whom he wanted something. Numerous state and county officers, legislators, bank officials, and other significant folk were common sights around the suite. In the evenings the crowded offices often buzzed with happy revelers partaking of the Finney hospitality. At other times, Finney quietly focused on a solitary key individual, such as Superintendent of Public Instruction W. T. Markham, the Thomas County attorney, Leon Roulier, or a visiting out-state school-board member.[47]

ALL THIS INDUSTRY reached a grand crescendo at the time of the bank holiday in March, 1933, making Finney the most talked-about young man in the state of Kansas. For all his frenzied activity and occasionally erratic behavior, Finney approached financial matters basically in a rational way. He had a plan. The plan was based on the reasonable assumption that with the country going off the gold standard and cheaper Roosevelt money coming in, with prices at unprecedented lows, and with the national administration trying desperately to increase the people's purchasing power, prices would almost certainly rise in the weeks and months ahead. The concept, which was hardly original with him, was frequently and avidly discussed with numerous friends and associates during the late winter. Then, with the arrival of the week-long bank moratorium, he almost literally went crazy.[48]

With a bundle of hard cash protected by a "giant revolver" and so large that it "resembled the Southeast corner of the federal reserve vault," he bought everything that wasn't nailed down and much that was.[49] Eggs, peaches, cotton, beef, bacon, hams, sugar, milk of magnesia, copper, lead—commodities of every description, many in carload lots, were bought up by the frenzied financier, on the thinnest margin possible. Finney had two rented planes in the air most of the time during this hectic period. He sent Jesse Greenleaf on his cattle-buying spree into the Southwest; by May, he had purchased twenty thousand head. He dispatched agents loaded with cash into the field all over the cash-starved Midwest, who feverishly bought land options in the town and in the country. One potential agent, rousted out of a warm bed at midnight by the jangling phone, heard an urgent voice beseeching him to drive the seventy-five miles to the Jayhawk immediately to pick up his instructions and his bundle of cash.[50] "All his Kansas world wondered, marveled, and a lot of it worshipped, at the Ronald Finney shrine," the *Capital* wryly observed.[51]

SPECULATION on the commodities market occupied the lion's share of Finney's time, attention, and money from the fall of 1932 till the time of his arrest. He invested to a limited extent in corn, oats, and cotton, but as befitted a loyal son of the wheat state, his heaviest "plunges" were in the wheat pit. He dealt principally with Mensendieck Grain Company of Kansas City, Missouri; Mitchell-Hutchins Company of Chicago; and most especially, the venerable and respected La Salle Street firm of Jackson Brothers, Boesel and Company.[52]

Finney had played the market to some extent since 1931. He stepped up his speculations markedly in the winter of 1932/33, and he began to deal in such a huge volume after the bank holiday that he had become something of a legend around Kansas City. He bought and sold in lots of 10,000 or even 100,000 bushels, usually sending in his orders just after the opening bell or just before closing. Some brokers at the Board of Trade didn't know him by name but had heard of the reputation of the high-rolling, "big-shot" speculator from Topeka, the "Kingfish" who dealt in huge lots and made a lot of money.[53]

Finney's grand plan consisted of cleaning up on the commodities market and then "retiring" the forged bonds, which rested threateningly in such great volume in the state treasury vault. By late winter, he was channeling all available capital into the market. During the spring he did extremely well in a "long" position on the futures market as wheat went from fifty to eighty-five cents. When he sold out, he reportedly took down a few hundred thousand in profits. With advice from his confidential Washington advisor that the government wouldn't let the price rise over eighty-five cents, he went back into the market, but with only part of his winnings, in a "short" position. He took moderate losses as the market continued to rise to nearly a dollar. He then returned to the long position just before the market broke abruptly in mid July (down thirty cents in a few days) while still under $1.25. Reportedly, his Washington contact insisted, again erroneously, that wheat would go to $1.40. The sharp downturn resulted in an urgent margin call from Chicago and necessitated his putting up additional thousands of municipal bonds, most of which were forged.[54]

On balance, Finney made a good deal of money in the market; exactly how much cannot be precisely determined. By his own estimate, made years later and without the records before him, he lost about $50,000 in 1932 but netted about $200,000 in 1933. In a statement taken after the crash, his auditor put his 1933 net winnings at about $230,000. Finney never claimed, nor is there a scintilla of evidence, that he began to forge bonds to cover market losses. He claimed that it was done to cover "bad paper" in the two Finney banks.[55] High living and pure greed would seem to have been major contributing factors.

THE FINNEY DIKE sprung several serious leaks in the spring of 1933. Some shaky Casper, Wyoming, bonds that he had sold to the Farmers State Bank in West Wichita had been questioned by the receiver of the failed bank. The receiver went directly to Finney, and to avoid trouble, the prudent broker bought them back. An ambitious district attorney from western Kansas had caused near panic at the Jayhawk in April when he appeared with four duplicate interest coupons. About the same time the city treasurer of Hutchinson became upset when she discovered that the city had been charged by the state fiscal agency for two different sets of identical $3,000 bonds.[56] Though he handled each of these threats with consummate skill, such events could shake even the most able and confident of young men.

Some well-calculated efforts to obtain additional credit and standing with the banks hadn't come off as well as he had hoped either. Tom Boyd had introduced him at a Topeka bank and had vouched for him. Finney obtained a small loan with good security, and he promptly paid it off. Then he brought in large amounts of cash, which he exchanged for sight drafts that were in turn promptly deposited in another Topeka bank. He figured that this would help his standing in both banks. When he tried to negotiate a more substantial loan by offering Kansas municipal bonds as security, the first bank balked. That was the last they saw of the incensed Mr. Finney. On another occasion he obtained a sight draft for several thousand at one bank and then walked across the street to cash it at another bank. The second bank, puzzled, called the first one. "Do you think I'm a crook?" Finney indignantly asked. The bank responded that they really didn't care to handle any more of his business.[57]

The threats to his now-substantial empire, the frantic daily market transactions, and his hectic social life began to wear on young Finney and on his wife by the spring of 1933. Somehow life didn't seem to be as much fun as it used to be. Ronald had changed from his normal extrovertish, life-of-the-party behavior. He snapped at his wife and at Caldwell over nothing at all. He worried about his health. He trusted no one. Trailing a stream of cigarette ashes on the carpet, he often nervously paced the floor. He became enormously preoccupied and even, on occasion, downright morose. A tense, haggard Winifred sensed that all was not well, although she didn't fully realize what was going on. Like her mother-in-law, she especially disliked the two banks, feeling that they should have been sold or closed long before. Drawing liberally on the supply of sleeping pills, she channeled her energies into busily redecorating the house and anxiously replacing the old locks with stronger ones. She still felt vaguely threatened, but by what? Perhaps there were medical solutions. In an attempt to find one, the advanced hypochondriacs went to Kansas City on May 31 and both had their tonsils removed.[58] A year later, to the day, Ronald would take a very different and much longer trip.

THOUGH NO LONGER his normal self and though suffering acutely from feelings of guilt, Ronald continued his feverish pace right up until his arrest. When the 101 Ranch Show returned in late July, he and Winifred led gay parties down to special performances put on by the troupe for the boss man and his guests. In addition to making numerous trips to Kansas City and Chicago, he frantically shifted the security of the three banks in the treasury vault in an attempt to stay one step ahead of the federal investigators. The demand by the National Bank of Topeka—his favorite financial institution, which was filled with his friends—that all his securities be removed forthwith had alarmed him and his father. It was a new game now. The end could not be far off.[59]

In the final few days before Ronald's arrest, the troubled Finneys held intense conferences to try to prevent, or at least to stall, the inevitable. On Sunday evening, August 6, Warren and Ronald conferred in Emporia. The ever-optimistic father suggested that they travel to Kansas City the next day to try to negotiate a loan to cover Fidelity-held municipal bonds about which "some question" had recently been raised. Ronald called his accommodating Eureka cousin, Edwin Tucker, and made arrangements for him to be flown to Topeka the following day for some last-minute switching of securities in the treasury vault. The next day an iota of hope flickered when father and son did successfully negotiate a $31,000 bank loan at the Kansas City Club. When the weary father returned on the last train from Kansas City, arriving in Emporia at 3 A.M., his distraught wife met him at the door with the crushing news that a warrant had been issued—by the governor of all people—for the arrest of their only begotten son.[60] Warren Finney's lonely walk in the garden of Gethsemane had begun.

8

The Sins of the Father

○○

IN THOSE FINAL HECTIC DAYS before his son's arrest the desperate Warren Finney grasped at every available straw. He assigned a Kansas City private detective—whom he had used off and on for years—to the task of trying to discover what the federal agents had uncovered about Ronald's activities. At the bank he held what would prove to be the final meeting with his by-now apprehensive cashiers on Sunday afternoon, August 6. The young assistant cashier, Robert Needels, due to increased misunderstandings and mounting tensions with Finney, had asked the chief cashier, Fred Baird, also to be present as they all went over the books that afternoon. And Finney had his ace in the hole—a 10 A.M. appointment on August 8 with his very good friend the governor of the state, at which time he intended to press for time so that he could privately straighten out the family affairs in order to avoid public disclosure.[1]

Although "suffering from severe nervous shock," Warren Finney insisted on accompanying his son to Topeka on the morning of August 8. They did not depart until the father had held a hurried conference at home with Fred Baird. The swift-moving events had caught Finney with several loose accounts showing, so he attempted to make some last-minute changes in the records at the bank through his head cashier. Later, at the trial, Baird and Finney would manifest radically different memories of what had transpired between them on that hectic morning as close friends dropped by to offer their sympathies and the two attempted to conduct a bit of business in the living room.

On Tuesday afternoon, a short time after the unsuccessful conference with Landon, the dejected banker headed back for Emporia, accompanied by the bank commissioner and an assistant attorney general. Before leaving the capitol he phoned a *Gazette* reporter, assuring him that the necessary collateral to replace any forged bonds that might be discovered among the Fidelity's assets would be "promptly forthcoming and the bank [re]opened without delay."[2] After enjoying one of Mrs. Finney's delicious dinners, the two examiners, without Finney, went to the bank, where they scrutinized records far into the night.[3]

The next morning, Finney announced that the bank would not be reopened in the immediate future. He had offered Bank Commissioner Koeneke $367,000 in personal assets, outside the bank, as security to replace any forged bonds. Initially that had appeared to be a satisfactory solution, but as the discovery of forged bonds continued, Koeneke reluctantly had to refuse the offer. At this juncture, Governor Landon learned that Warren Finney did "not have in excess of Fifty Thousand Dollars worth of clear property." He had always bought on narrow margins, spreading his assets over a maximum of holdings. Nevertheless, Finney resolutely announced on Wednesday that "every cent that I've got will be used to take care of the home folks first."[4]

INDEED, THE HOME FOLKS and other Finney admirers took the startling revelations involving Ronald and the bank closing remarkably well. Former governor Clyde Reed commented in his *Parsons Sun* on August 9 that "the *Sun* doesn't know anything about the alleged bond forgeries. . . . But it does know Warren Finney, and loves him and respects and admires him. And knows him for what he is, one of the finest and most useful citizens of Kansas." The Emporia air had been thick with "I told you so's" after highflier Ronald's arrest, but the natives' faith in the solid and substantial Warren Finney remained unshaken. The bank's depositors demonstrated no undue excitement, no pounding on the doors, no profane exclamations; rather, they expressed every confidence that they would soon get every cent that they had coming.[5]

During the next several days the citizens of Emporia and of Lyon County received several severe tests of their deeply rooted confidence as County Attorney Clarence Beck revealed the extent of the bad paper among the bank's assets. Of the bank's $871,000 in total resources, $422,500 had been put into bonds, of which $336,000—most of it forged—was on deposit in the state treasury as security for public funds. On August 11 Beck announced that $86,000 in forged or otherwise worthless bonds and warrants, which had been put up to secure Lyon County deposits, had been discovered. A week later the final total came to $113,300 of the $116,000 which the bank had put up to secure $127,700 in Lyon County deposits.⁶

These startling disclosures brought an abrupt change in the town's attitude toward Warren Finney and his bank. In mid August he wrote a doleful letter of resignation to the president of the Rotary Club:

> The terrible events of the last few days has convinced me that it is best for me to sever my connection with Rotary. As my friends bring me reports of the expressions on the street[,] the stories of criticism and condemnation—many from members of the club—[it] makes it impossible for me [any] longer [to] associate myself where I find I am not wanted[,] happy as I have been in the association and much as I have drawn in inspiration and friendship from my long association.⁷

ON AUGUST 24 Koeneke placed the Emporia and Neosho Falls banks under general state receivership and appointed Charles W. Johnson as receiver of the two banks. Koeneke estimated that the two banks contained not less than $400,000 in forged bonds and warrants. Liens were filed on the property of the banks' stockholders to the extent of their double liability.⁸

As soon as the banks were closed, Warren Finney began to dispose of personal property and to pay off certain favored depositors, taking in return the assignment of their deposits. Finney paid off literally thousands of dollars of bank obligations in this fashion, but he had to cease this practice in late August, when the Banking Department placed liens against his

Commercial Street, Emporia, 1932 (Walter M. Andersen)

property.⁹ In a public statement on August 26 he tried to explain the situation to the home folks and to fix the blame elsewhere:

> I pledged the home folks who were depositors that I would exert every effort to see that they were paid in full.
>
> As evidence of my good faith in this matter, both Mrs. Finney and myself proceeded to use what means we had at our ready command to relieve those depositors who were in greatest distress. . . .
>
> I have labored unceasingly and to the limit of my strength and endurance to turn some of my investments into cash. . . .
>
> I regret this situation exceedingly, as I feel sure that if I had been permitted to proceed in my own way, I could have taken care of all the home folks in a very short time.¹⁰

Finney's friends continued to hope against hope that eventually everything would be righted, that he was just an innocent purchaser of bad paper, that he had been victimized by his malevolent son, that there was indeed another, untold side to the sordid affair. But when on August 28 he was arrested on eighteen counts of embezzlement of Fidelity funds—none of which charges were directly related to the forgery counts against his son—public sympathy all but disappeared along Commercial Street and in private homes around Emporia.¹¹ Henceforth his defenders included only his immediate family and a small nucleus of faithful friends.

ON SEPTEMBER 2 the Bell-controlled Emporia, Sabetha, and Paola telephone companies filed a civil suit against Warren Finney to recover on $40,500 in deposits that were locked up in the closed Emporia bank. The suit charged that Finney had deceived the phone companies as to what the company ledgers in the bank had actually shown and that he had made unauthorized charges against phone-company accounts.¹²

On September 11 Finney filed a counter suit against Southwestern Bell. The judge granted him a restraining order against Bell, enjoining it from holding meetings and attempting to remove him as president and general manager of the three companies. In late November, after the criminal trial, Bell filed a motion to vacate the restraining order. A week later, on December 2, Finney dismissed his counter suit against Bell, and on December 11 he resigned as president and general manager of the three companies.¹³

The phone-company suits represented the first flakes in what would become, during the succeeding months, a veritable snowstorm of civil suits. In early September, six suits were brought in district court, asking for mechanic liens on materials and labor that had been contracted for by

Finney to remodel a property on Commercial Street. Clarence Beck filed on behalf of the Lyon County Board of Commissioners for recovery of the $127,700 in county deposits in Fidelity. The bank receiver filed two major suits against Finney, seeking recovery of a total of $131,000. Receiver Johnson filed to recover on several Finney promissory notes. In mid December the Attorney General's Office presented the receiver with a state claim for losses of nearly $600,000 (a total that would later be raised) in the three closed Finney banks.[14] The snowstorm continued unabated until, by year's end, it had become a full-scale legal blizzard.

Of all the civil lawsuits, the one that caused the greatest pain and embarrassment to the Finneys' concerned their home on West Twelfth. The home, the largest and most ostentatious in Emporia, had been built in 1921 by Selleck Warren, one of the "old rich" families of the town, at a reported cost of over $100,000. The huge English Tudor structure had twenty-five rooms and five bathrooms, as well as a large garage with servant quarters above. The Finneys bought the house in 1931 for $25,000, assuming a $10,000 mortgage with an insurance company. In early September they moved back to their former residence on State Street, in order to reduce upkeep costs and because homesteads were exempt from liens and bankruptcy claims (even so, a foreclosure suit against the State Street home was filed in February). In late December the insurance company filed a foreclosure suit on the Twelfth Street property. In the petition they alleged that during their exodus, the Finneys had removed eight electric fixtures from the walls and ceilings, an electric thermostat, a gas burner from the furnace, and a bathtub from the maid's room.[15] Thus came the sad demise of what had been the center of the upper-stratum social life in the city of Emporia.

THE DATE OF THE EMBEZZLEMENT TRIAL had been set for October 9, though the defense attorneys announced that they would seek a continuance. They alleged that they had been unable to gain access to the relevant bank records either in Emporia or in Neosho Falls. The state contended that the defense was deliberately stalling, for no such request had been made since the arrest on August 28. In an October 5 hearing on the defense motion, the judge denied the request for access. Two days later the judge heard a defense motion for a continuance based on the absence of a key witness—William Allen White. Several of the state's counts turned on the degree of financial freedom that Finney had had in his contract with Bell Telephone. Finney contended that as president and general manager, he was authorized to handle the funds of the three companies as he saw fit. Attempting to use the most respected man in the state as his shield, Finney argued that White was very familiar with his telephone contracts and banking operations. If Mr. White were only here, this dreadful nightmare would be straightened out in no time at all. The judge didn't quite see it that way and again denied the motion for a continuance.[16]

The trial opened on October 9, but it aborted a few hours later after a hectic morning of legal wrangling and technical maneuvering. The large crowd of subpoenaed witnesses, prospective jurors, and the just-plain-curious scarcely understood what was happening as the lawyers argued back and forth. The defense presented several affidavits from witnesses who were absent from the state. One of these was a deposition written by the defense in the first person as to what White would testify to regarding the phone company's finances if he were there. "The state is not asking for a continuance," the impatient prosecution asserted, "but we will not admit these affidavits as depositions of absent witnesses. We want Mr. White in court where we can cross-examine him. . . . The statement in the affidavit . . . , is so broad and unbelievable that I do not believe Mr. White would make it."[17]

With great reluctance the judge agreed to a continuance to October 23. White, who had been named as a material witness, was due to dock in New York in mid October. Finney scored a victory on October 10, when the Kansas Supreme Court ruled that he should indeed be allowed to examine the "bank books, records, papers and documents from a date one year previous to the earliest charge in the information to the closing of the bank." The writ, they warned, was not to be used by the defense to cause a further delay of the trial. On a more prosaic note at this hour, Mrs. Finney reported to police that several cans of fruit and some lard had been stolen from the basement of their home.[18] Evidently someone had felt that turnabout was fair play.

ON JUNE 1 Mr. and Mrs. White had sailed for London, where he covered the International Economic Conference for the North American Newspaper Alliance. They sailed with Henry Haskell—the editor of the *Kansas City Star*—and Mrs. Haskell and were accompanied by Mary Jane Finney.[19] Their original plans called for them to be back by late summer or early fall. But they subsequently decided to include Russia in their itinerary, as well as France and Italy. They spent the month of September in Italy, and they docked in New York City on October 19, in company with White's old pal, former governor Henry J. Allen, whom they had met in Moscow. They arrived back in Emporia on October 22, the day before the trial was to begin.[20]

Although Bill White had kept his parents abreast of the events in Kansas by cable and letter, they had decided not to tell Mary Jane until after they had returned. In letters awaiting them when they arrived in Rome about September 1 the senior Whites had read full particulars of the scandal, including the recent arrest of Warren Finney.[21] In late August, Bill had written to "Uncle" Lacy Haynes, asking him to use his potent persuasive powers to help keep his parents in Europe:

> Now I think that under no circumstances should they come home, although I believe the Finneys have changed from their original attitude and now want them back because the[y] think father would help them more than I would.
>
> Now they are apt to ask all kinds of god damned crazy, unreasonable and embarrassing things, and I can turn them down where Father might impulsively get himself into trouble by trying to help them. You know him as well as I do. He is very fond of the Finney's personally, and I don't want to put him to the mental strain which all the necessary refusals of help would mean. . . .
>
> Of course, if you think he should return on Rol's [Boynton's] account, that's another matter. But my notion is that he couldn't help there. Whatever is done has already been done. Alf and Fred Harris are good friends, and they would do no more than their duty.
>
> I had a little jangle[22] today with the Finneys about keeping something out of the papers,—nothing important, but if father were here he would probably have done it.[23]

As soon as he arrived in New York City, White wired Bill that he would like to attend a Roosevelt Association executive meeting and that he wanted to "see [Harold] Ickes and [Cordell] Hull in Washington but shall return if desired as any kind of witness." He also reported that he was sending a second telegram "at Mrs. Finney's telephone suggestion to mother," which "you may or may not present to Judge McCarty as your judgment dictates."[24] One of the Finney lawyers had been dispatched to New York City to brief White on the developments from the Finney perspective and to prepare him for his testimony at the trial. But the cagey editor was cautious: he was polite enough to the envoy, but he made no commitments. To New York press inquiries about the big scandal out in Kansas, he gave a very uncharacteristic "no comment." In an attempt to ensure that his father would receive a balanced picture of the affair, Bill met the White party in Kansas City and thoroughly briefed his distressed parents on the heartbreaking events. It had been the longest continuous absence of the Whites since they had come to Emporia in 1895. "[We] had a swell trip," they commented brightly when they arrived in Emporia, "and the best part of it was that [we] paid [our] way as [we] went."²⁵

The return of the Whites and the newspaperman's reaction to the storm that found his closest friends and his cousin-protégé at its eye were awaited by the public nearly as eagerly as they awaited the impending trial itself. One group of White's friends expected—or at least profoundly hoped—that he would tell Finney "where to go," while others felt that he would smooth things over as best he could, because the political involvements were so deep that an open break would be nearly impossible. The *Kansas City Journal Post* gleefully observed that Finney and White were "as sticky-thick as cold molasses in winter" and that their friendship had become "as firm and more lasting" than the affinity between Henry Allen and White.²⁶

> William Allen White is due home from Europe shortly. What a different Kansas he will find! What a different Emporia! . . .
>
> Perhaps . . . it is a good thing Old Bill wasn't at home. For what the Kansas City Star couldn't do—save the crooks—Old Bill couldn't have done, even if he had been moved to try. . . . We think he probably would have found business outside Kansas, possibly making prohibition speeches. . . .
>
> Kansas—and the nation—will watch with interest to see whether he joins in the crusade to clean up the state . . . or whether the self-righteousness which he has capitalized in the past becomes a pose when those involved belong to his own crowd.²⁷

Out in western Kansas the *Leoti Standard,* a Democratic weekly, had some even harsher advice for the returning celebrity and his family:

> Kansas has done much for the William Allen Whites; made them rich, stood for their political gymnastics, and has honored them in the past. . . .
>
> If Old Man White and his son have any decency about them, they would line up on the side of the state of Kansas and not get out to protect a grafter like Finney. Young White, it should be remembered, signed one of Finney's jail bonds. It might be highly interesting to know just what other transactions the Finneys and the Whites had between themselves. . . .
>
> Perhaps the proper way to spell whitewash in Kansas is White Wash.²⁸

White's dominant emotion on returning was one of sadness, as he wrote to Erwin Canham of the *Christian Science Monitor* on October 27:

> Our homecoming was one of the saddest of my life. For twenty

years and more . . . I have enjoyed the friendship of a man named Finney in this town. . . . I know him as a fine, public-spirited, generous, intelligent, courageous and sometimes cantankerous man. But like all bankers he was leading some kind of double life. What, I don't know. . . . There are two theories of the crash and the disgrace that followed. I can subscribe to either. One is that the son is trying to protect the father; the other is that the father is trying to protect the son. . . . It is a hard life. When you get along in your sixties you like to feel the stability of your friends. . . . It is all sad and breaks my heart.[29]

The traumatic events that had transpired during their separation permanently changed the relationship between the two families. Things could never be the same again. The frantic Finneys pushed hard, attempting by every imaginable device to use the White name as a screen against the dreadful onslaught. White resented their attempt to draw him directly into the conflict ("I was deeply hurt . . . that he would use my name in a false affidavit to delay the courts"). Finney and White "did not see things eye to eye" after the Whites' return, and thereafter they did not engage in any serious discussions.[30] The two old friends, who had been cochampions for decades of a better Emporia and a better Kansas, went their separate and very different ways.

Direct testimony regarding the 1927 Bell-Finney agreement was not permitted at the trial. Thus, White did not appear as a material witness, even though the trial had been specifically postponed for his return. The editor told Finney's attorneys that he preferred that they not summon him, since "I know very little, probably nothing material. I shall go to the stand and testify as to the little I do know and tell the truth. Possibly it will help Mr. Finney, possibly it will hurt him." White did appear as one of Finney's character witnesses. He testified that the families were close and had worked together on numerous civic and church matters and that he had been "a very close friend" of Finney's. When queried about a possible business relationship, he bristled and emphatically asserted that he had "not the slightest" financial interest in the Fidelity Bank.[31] Immediately after his return, White had begun to focus his enormous talents and prodigious energy on an all-out effort to save his esteemed cousin. Prospects for success in that enterprise seemed somewhat brighter, though dim enough, to the heartsick Sage.

SINCE MR. FINNEY had been impressed for years by the importance of competent counsel, he assembled an intimidating array of legal talent.

Headed by two former justices of the Kansas Supreme Court—William D. Jochems of Wichita and Edward R. Sloan of Holton—the team also included Topekan John Schenck, a master courtroom tactician who was widely recognized as one of the top criminal lawyers in the Midwest.[32] Schenck's son Clyde and two former Lyon County attorneys—Owen Samuel and O. R. ("Jack") Stites, who were close friends of the Finneys'—rounded out the potent legal corps.[33]

Aligned against this awesome crew we find, for the state, Lyon County Attorney Clarence V. ("Prunes") Beck and the special assistant attorney general, Hugo T. ("Dutch") Wedell. The thirty-seven-year-old Beck had been reared in Americus, a village in Lyon County, by Swedish-born parents. After graduating from the University of Kansas Law School, he had served as assistant county attorney under one of his present adversaries, Jack Stites. Beck was now in his second term as county attorney, and this trial would

Clarence V. Beck, Lyon County attorney (Kansas State Historical Society)

represent his most severe test by far. Wedell, a native of Hillsboro, was the youngest of twelve children born to first-generation German parents. In his college days he had become well known around Emporia as an educational and athletic leader. He played professional baseball in the Philadelphia Phillies organization for one year, then attended the University of Kansas Law School. After a few years in private practice, he served two terms as Neosho County attorney. He had made an unsuccessful bid for Congress in 1930 and had then settled down to a small-town practice in Chanute when Landon tapped him to serve as a special assistant to Fred Harris a few days after the scandal broke.[34] Wedell, at forty-three, had attained a local reputation as a vigorous, even fiery prosecutor. That reputation would not be diminished in the Finney trial.

In announcing the assignment of Wedell to the case on October 3, Landon asserted that the entire weight of state support would be thrown

Hugo Wedell, assistant state investigator (Kansas State Historical Society)

behind the Lyon County attorney in his prosecution of the case. "I am glad to say that the state is ready for trial in the case against Warren W. Finney," the governor confidently announced.[35]

On the bench of the Lyon County District Court sat his honor Alonzo C. McCarty. McCarty had handled his duties in the past competently enough, but he now faced the trial of his life. He and the prosecution well knew that the appeal-oriented defense would be searching for judicial errors as a red-tailed hawk looks for chickens. Judge McCarty did manage to make it through the trial, but with little enough to spare.

At the very outset of the trial on October 23, the defense moved to disqualify the judge, based on what they asserted were his prejudicial comments and decisions at the earlier hearing. They complained both of his fumbling treatment of the issue of access to the records (the intricacies of which frequently had to be carefully and slowly repeated for him) and of his audible grumbling with respect to the hearing itself ("I don't like to spend Lyon County's money in this way").[36] The judge himself, however, provided the simple and unassailable answer to the question of whether or not he was biased against the defendant: "I am not biased or prejudiced against the defendant. . . . I, myself, would know whether or not I was biased or prejudiced in any way." And that was the end of that. Motion denied.[37]

The trial—one of the longest and most hard-fought legal battles in Kansas court history—attracted huge and boisterous crowds. Each day the eager spectators pressed into the courtroom, quickly taking all the available seats and lining the walls three deep. On several occasions they had to be forcibly shoved back to allow adequate passage for the defendant, the attorneys, and the jurors. They stood on tables and chairs in offices that adjoined the courtroom, craning their necks for an occasional peek at the proceedings. The curious—mostly men—filled the corridor outside the courtroom, spilling over down the steps and out into the courtyard, where clusters of animated townspeople and farmers avidly discussed each new and exciting event. People brought their lunches so as not to lose their precious seats during the noon-hour recess. Business in downtown Emporia virtually came to a standstill.[38] One conscientious onlooker announced that he would have to leave at 4 P.M. "I'm following the NRA," he quipped, "and I can't stay here such long hours and run the risk of losing my Blue Eagle."[39]

The crowds seemed to enjoy themselves, creating something of a Roman-holiday atmosphere. The judge frequently admonished them—usually after first excusing the jury—for "commotion, giggling and laughter." On one occasion he threatened to shut the door and lock them out. Though generally good-natured, the spectators often displayed open hostility toward the defendant. The audience included many furious bank depositors who were thirsty for revenge. Mr. Finney hardly occupied the position of influence and respect that he had held only a few months before. Times were hard, bitter hard, and the Finneys had been conspicuous in their considerable consumption, which was not at all in keeping with the low-profile life style that was traditional among Kansans of means. And now the mighty were falling, and the people smelled blood. The defense charged that Judge McCarty seemed to be more anxious to maintain a friendly rapport with the crowd than to give the defendant a fair hearing. ("Now, folks, nobody on earth appreciates friends more than I do, and no one on earth would feel worse than I to lose a friend.")[40]

Clarence Beck gave the opening statement for the state, covering each of the complex counts in some detail. Of the twelve counts that went to the jury, all were for alleged acts within ten months of the bank's closing, all but two having occurred since the spring of 1933. Several of the charges entailed relatively small amounts of money, such as $439.54, $611.92, $1,700, and $1,325.23. The last was the amount of overdraft in Finney's personal account when the bank was suddenly closed at the governor's direction. For that and each of the other offenses with which he stood charged, the defendant was liable for up to fifty years in the Kansas State Penitentiary. The total in the twelve charges came to $57,774.[41]

Several of the counts involved transactions in which Finney had received credit from the bank in his personal checking account, which was frequently overdrawn by several thousand dollars, or in which he received personal credit for taking up cash items (bank assets for which the bank has paid money but has not yet received payment). The difficulties arose when the president had failed to repay the bank after he received a credit, although he had intended—or said that he had intended—to do so. For example, he was charged with having received $5,800 to cover an overdraft at his last Sunday meeting with Robert Needels. Finney told Needels that he planned to be in Topeka on Tuesday for his appointment with Governor Landon and that he would credit the Fidelity account in the National Bank of Topeka with $5,800 at that time. Finney failed to do so, arguing that in his distraught condition on that day he had simply forgotten to do what he had had every intention of doing. In a similar charge, Finney had received credit for $7,000 in December, 1932, to help cover an overdraft of nearly $8,000 in his personal account. He told Needels that son Ronald would credit the Fidelity account in Topeka with the $7,000. That had not been done, though it had been called to Warren Finney's attention on numerous subsequent occasions. Finney's lawyers implied that that was the son's fault, not the father's. In another similar charge, Finney had received credit for $10,000 in cash items—his personal obligations—and had told the cashier that Ronald was selling to the bank $10,000 in bonds which had previously only been on loan. Although a memorandum had been carried in the cash-items drawer for months (in fact, there were several such memoranda, carrying progressively more recent dates for the edification of the bank examiners), the bonds had in fact never been turned over to Fidelity. Keeping track of Finney's maneuvers had become so difficult that the disquieted Robert Needels had taken to keeping a secret "reconciliation book," a ledger that showed the differences between the Fidelity's account in the National Bank of Topeka as shown by Fidelity and as shown by the Topeka institution. "This book is a record of what wasn't in the bank," Needels testified.[42]

Another series of charges involved checks written on long-defunct telephone companies that had once been owned by Finney. For example, on August 3 Finney had sent to Topeka a check for $611.92, written on the Altoona Telephone Company account in Fidelity, for credit to his personal account. The phone company in question, which had been sold in 1930, had no account in the Emporia bank. In defense, Finney claimed that these and similar checks had been written to make a record of certain collections that were still being made as a part of the liquidation of said companies. He had had no intention that the bank would be left "holding the sack." Similar checks, he claimed, had always been paid by him and would have been in this case had not the banks been arbitrarily closed. Other charges involved similar checks written on nonexistent accounts of the Kansas Home and the Neosho Falls telephone companies. The checks had been signed by Finney with the name of his secretary, Nell Roach, who had served as treasurer of the defunct companies.[43]

The most difficult charges for Finney to defend against involved his ancient and implacable enemy, the Southwestern Bell Telephone Company. One count concerned some bonds of the Emporia Telephone Company that had come due on May 15, 1933. Finney asked the company's treasurer in Topeka to send a check for $6,000 to cover the bonds; in the meantime Finney drew a $6,000 check on the phone company's Fidelity account. The treasurer's check promptly came in, and the bonds were paid; but Finney still held $6,000 in company funds. He proceeded to invest the funds in "some very good bonds"—school-district securities that his son had recommended and of issues that Ronald had duplicated. On the day the bank closed, the Emporia Phone Company finally received credit for their $6,000 when Fidelity bought the bonds.[44]

In a similar transaction, Finney had drawn a $4,000 check on the Paola Telephone Company account in Fidelity in April. The check ostensibly was to be used as earnest money in a phone-company deal in Paola, which later fell through. Rather than crediting the phone company's account, Finney kept the money, and so as "to have [it] available at any time," he deposited it in his personal account at a Kansas City, Missouri, bank. In May he invested the money, he admitted, in a Chase County farm mortgage. Finally deciding "to let the bank make the profit . . . on this mortgage," he sold it to Fidelity, he claimed, on August 1. He said that Fred Baird just hadn't gotten around to crediting the phone company's account until August 8. A similar charge involved $2,700 and the Sabetha Telephone Company.[45]

The bank's bookkeeper testified that Finney had asked her to prepare a monthly statement for Bell Telephone which showed balances that were $6,000 (Emporia), $4,000 (Paola), and $2,700 (Sabetha) more than they actually were. He also ordered that the canceled checks for those amounts not be included with the monthly statement. She then delivered the statement to Finney at his office in the phone company's building. Fred Baird testified that early on the morning of August 8 Finney had asked him to "have the girls fix the [phone company] statement like they had been fixing it" and had ordered him to make the appropriate credits on the statement. Baird had protested, he testified, that he couldn't do that, but the record showed that the Finney-ordered credits had in fact been made on that day. In their sworn testimony, both Mr. Finney and Mrs. Finney vehemently denied that any such conversation had ever taken place. Baird also testified that Ronald Finney had once told him that he could make a lot of money for Baird on the wheat market. A few days later, Baird received a $600 check, which Ronald said represented the profit on his speculation. Baird returned the check. Later Ronald sent a $100 check, which Baird was still holding, uncashed, at the time of the trial.[46]

The state rested its case on the evening of October 30. The prosecution's position appeared strong and well developed by Beck and Wedell. But the Finneys were fighters, and it was a battle every step of the way. Nearly all the counts involved intricate financial transactions and had to be developed slowly and painstakingly for the jury and for the judge. At one point a lengthy and heated discussion concerned a $14 bank note. Cross-examination by the six defense counsels had been fierce. Hugo Wedell complained that the defense seemed to be trying to make its case by cross-examination of the state witnesses.[47]

Before making its opening statement, the defense moved that the related counts be combined into one, since they constituted but a single offense "like stealing three hogs." The motion was denied. As the major thrust of his defense, Finney's attorneys attempted to show that what he had done with the bank and phone-company funds under his control was germane to the question of intent. The bank and the phone company had lost nothing in the transactions, they repeatedly argued. The prosecution vigorously objected, usually successfully, to the introduction of such evidence, claiming that it was irrelevant after the crime had been committed. Restitution is no defense, they argued. The defense attempted to identify as one the bank and its president: "You never heard of a man stealing from himself," they contended. And in every transaction on every count, the defense admitted nothing—absolutely nothing. Not even bad judgment or imprudence. Anything and everything that the upstanding Mr. Finney had done had had a sound, proper, and ethical purpose, they claimed. Any problems that might have arisen had been due to the shortcomings of others, including his son. Mr. Finney was simply the victim of political persecution by the county attorney and the Governor's Office.[48]

The defense attempted to show that Finney had been victimized by Bell Telephone. In an offer of evidence that was ultimately denied by the judge, the obstinate Finney claimed that shortly after his initial arrest, C. A. Ullfers, general manager of Southwestern Bell at Kansas City, had come to Emporia. He had demanded that the $50,000 that would be due to Finney in January, 1934, from the sale of the phone company be applied to the $40,000 in deposits that Bell had in Fidelity. He also demanded that Finney resign immediately, thus forfeiting his handsome pension, which was to begin in 1936. In return for this, Finney claimed, Ullfers promised that Bell "would use their influence to prevent any criminal prosecution against [Finney] growing out of the failure of Fidelity . . . , or any matter . . . in connection with the . . . 'bond scandal.'" Mr. Finney promptly told Mr. Ullfers "to go to hell."[49] An hour later the sheriff of Lyon County appeared, accompanied by a Bell lawyer, to serve a summons for three separate suits. The defense further charged that a high-ranking Bell official, H. O. McBride, had come all the way from St. Louis, Missouri, to do what he could to get Finney convicted so that the company could rid itself of a troublemaker and thus save his salary and pension.[50]

Finney's faithful secretary, Nell Roach, accompanied by a nurse, left a hospital bed to testify for the defense. In a voice that was barely audible, she murmured that she knew Mr. Finney had been signing her name to the checks of the nonexistent phone companies and that whatever he wanted to do was perfectly all right with her.[51] "I have worked for Mr. Finney 25 years," she whispered, "and he never has asked me to do a dishonorable thing." For the first time in the trial, the defendant showed some reaction to the testimony, being visibly affected by this public expression of loyalty from his girl Friday.[52]

THE TRIAL'S MOST DRAMATIC moments occurred when Finney took the stand on November 1. With no visible signs of displeasure the defendant had remained poised as he listened to a steady parade of prosecution witnesses state or imply that he was a liar, a cheat, or worse. He had remained aloof from the spectators, engaging in no backslapping or recognition-seeking unless he was approached directly. Each day he carried to the courtroom a bulging portfolio, filled with neatly banded envelopes. Frequently conferring with his attorneys, he played an active role in his own defense, contributing facts and figures in profusion from the briefcase.[53]

In the direct examination the defendant coolly recited a mini biography of his professional and business life. Then, looking squarely at the jury and with his eyes flashing, he stated defiantly that never for a minute had he possessed "one cent of the Emporia Telephone Company's money or one cent of the Fidelity Bank's money." When the bank closed, he said sorrowfully, "My heart was broken."[54] He flatly contradicted the testimony of the bank's cashiers and bookkeeper. He had, he said, never asked anyone at any time to falsify records or change accounts. He asserted that the bank's bookkeeper had never been to his phone-company office to deliver the phone company's bank statements (he was supported in this by the subsequent testimony of three phone-company clerks). He claimed that he had removed thousands of dollars of worthless or slow-paying cash items that were not his obligations in order to help the bank. During the direct examination, Hugo Wedell frequently jumped to his feet to object, but the witness often answered before the objection could be fully voiced, to which Wedell made frequent and caustic complaints to the judge.[55]

Spirited combat, which was marked by bitter debate between able counsel for the two sides, characterized the trial from its inception. When Hugo Wedell cross-examined Warren Finney, the enthralled spectators were treated to a direct confrontation between two masters of their own styles. A torrent of malevolent, adversarial questions poured from the febrile prosecutor in a voice that brimmed with hostility. As if fired from a machine gun, the unyielding responses shot back, short, bristling, defiant. Wedell tried to get Finney to admit that no Altoona or Neosho Falls Telephone Company existed. But Finney stubbornly stuck to his story of how checks of the long-defunct companies could legitimately be out in the stream of commerce. In one interchange, Finney even scornfully denied that the introduced bank statements included what Wedell said they did, even though Finney was holding the documents in his hand, which trembled in anger.[56]

After two full days and one night on the stand, Finney began to show, for the first time, signs of emotional exhaustion. Answers to Wedell's loaded questions came more deliberately, as Finney struggled to control his temper. He chose his responses carefully, knowing more fully than anyone in the courtroom could know that he was literally fighting for his life. For an instant his voice would "ring out in wrath," after which he would quickly regain his composure, returning to his characteristic outer calm and preparing to ward off yet another blow from the unrelenting Wedell.[57]

The state claimed that in July, 1933, the bank had withdrawn its remaining sound bonds from the state treasury and had substituted forged securities. Finney heatedly denied that he had any knowledge that any Fidelity security was forged or worthless. Later in that day of grueling cross-examination, Clarence Beck—who had held his former client in high regard until the recent revelations—suddenly wheeled and asked Finney point-blank if that was his forged endorsement on the phone company's tax check. The aghast defense attorneys jumped up in unison to object, as if they were six puppets on a single string. Surprisingly, after the question had been slightly rephrased, even though it was totally out-of-order with respect to these charges, the judge ruled that it could be put to the startled witness. Finney shifted uncomfortably in the witness chair, stared angrily at Beck, and answered in a voice "made loud by emotion": "No, it is not. I never forged an indorsement on any check."[58] And that took care of that. The emotionally drained bank president left the stand on November 6. In all, he had been in the witness chair a total of four days and one night, the longest in Lyon County history.[59]

CLARENCE BECK LED OFF the closing arguments, pointing out that "the entire state is watching this case and waiting for your verdict." The public was especially interested, he said, due to Finney's power and influence in Kansas. "If you sympathize with the Finney's," the county attorney warned, "you should also sympathize with widows who lost money in this bank, many of whom must be taken care of by charitable institutions."[60]

For the defense, E. R. Sloan stressed intent, reminding the jurors that they must believe that the hand that wrote the checks was guided "by a wicked design intent upon defrauding the Fidelity bank." Finney was moved to tears as Sloan recited the hardships that the criminal action had brought on the Finney family. "No man, rich or poor, had ever been denied the hospitality that the Finneys had always been [so] free to give," he irrelevantly noted.[61] Closing for the defense, John Schenck complained: "This is a political lawsuit starting from the statehouse. Governor Landon sent Wedell here and the attorney general sent an assistant here to aid in the prosecution of this man. The Southwestern Bell Telephone Company is responsible for this prosecution and the principal charges are the so-called telephone company counts."[62]

The fiery Hugo Wedell made the final closing argument for the state, in which he launched at the case of the defense "a dynamic 90 minute broadside[,] cruel and terrible." Nearly one thousand eager listeners, who were jammed into every available square inch in the courtroom and the adjacent corridors, heard an impassioned philippic from the governor's special assistant:

> If the defense . . . thought we wouldn't fight, they grabbed the wrong sow by the ear . . . if Governor Landon's action in sending aid to help clean up this dirty mess was a political move, it is the greatest bit of politics the state of Kansas has ever known. . . .
>
> And then they talk to you about character witnesses. In the name of God, what are we coming to? . . . I am sure Benedict Arnold could have had all the character witnesses in the world. . . .
>
> W. W. Finney is guilty to the core. He was the master mind of this big swindle. . . .
>
> The fact that this man held himself up as a civic leader, violated the trust of persons who had confidence in him, makes him ten times worse than a thief who sticks a gun in your ribs.[63]

IT TOOK TWO HOURS for Judge McCarty to read seventy-eight written instructions to the jury. After dinner, he recited another half-hour of oral instructions, which were frequently objected to by the defense, and then released the jury in care of the bailiff. Thus, on November 7 at 8:45 P.M., "one of the greatest court battles ever staged in Kansas" went into the capable hands of twelve good and true citizens of Lyon County. Speculation ran rife along Commercial Street as to how long the jury would deliberate. Football-pool operators sold numbers on the length of time that the jury would be out. After two hours of deliberation the panel retired for the night.[64]

After the lunch break the next day, one of the jurors, the studious and eccentric Harold Bixler, abruptly rose in open court and—to everyone's astonishment—addressed the judge:

> Your Honor, being a tyro in the courtroom, I would like to know what aid I—we are entitled to when we come to an impasse. For instance, I stand charged with insincerity because I am unable to write the word "guilty" without connotation of wicked design. The difficulty lies on the distinction between bad judgment and wickedness.[65]

The judge looked startled, as did the spectators and the other jurors.

After a few soothing remarks, the magistrate sent the jury back to chambers, while the spectators scrambled for the nearest dictionary. At about 3 P.M. members of the jury returned to the courtroom and announced that they had been unable to reach a verdict. The perspiring judge told them to try again—and harder this time.[66]

That evening—about twenty-four hours after the jury had begun its deliberations—the foreman indicated that it had indeed reached a verdict. The defendant had been found guilty on each and every count. To the question "Is this your verdict?" the jury members responded in chorus for each count with a resounding "It is." Whereupon the wily John Schenck jumped up and requested that the judge ask each individual juror: "Is this your verdict and are you satisfied therewith?" The country judge asked the city lawyer if that wasn't a bit out of the ordinary, and then proceeded to do exactly as he had been requested to do. The first juror queried was Harold Bixler. The conscientious citizen responded with a determined "no." As the courtroom buzzed with amazement, the disgusted and weary jury members filed back to their chambers.[67]

The next morning Hugo Wedell wrote to his chief in Topeka, implying that there might have been Finney skullduggery with the jury: "You may rest assured the defendant did not make any capital on the statement of his attorneys that this was a political fight directed from the governor's office. . . . I have my own ideas as to why Bixler is taking the present position."[68]

Wedell had briefed the governor a few days earlier about the way things had been going: "Alf this has been two weeks of grueling battle—Day and night. Beck and I have of course faced terrific odds with six lawyers on the other side. The going has not been easy but we have fought them every inch of the road. If the jury has not been fixed, I believe we will score a victory."[69]

The day after the false start, at the morning recess, Bixler, who was an engineer in the power plant at Emporia Teachers College, attempted to pass a note to Judge McCarty regarding "further procedure." The alarmed judge declared that it would be "the rankest kind of error" to receive a private communication from a juror. Bixler persisted, declaring that the jurors were "babes in the woods, legally," and badly needed counsel. He especially needed guidance, he pleaded, on "how to act on a basis of good sportsmanship." "Sportsmanship does not enter into it at all," snapped the exasperated judge.[70] Bixler then arcanely asserted that his greatest concern was to protect the commonwealth. "I know no man [who] has more respect for the commonwealth than I." He declared that he could not "apply the word 'felon' to a citizen who I consider caught in a fortuitous concourse of circumstances over which he had no control." He added, not quite so cryptically, that he had hoped that this impasse might be closed "to the benefit of all concerned by making a concession in the shadow of the Supreme Court."[71] The distraught judge stared hard at his maverick juror. "May it please Your Honor. I ask questions which in the eyes of the Court are childish," the quixotic Bixler concluded. "No," replied Judge McCarty, biting hard into his stiff upper lip.[72]

Finally, at about 5 P.M. on November 9, a verdict of guilty on all counts was rendered. Schenck raised a strenuous objection when the jurors weren't individually polled, as before, as to their satisfaction with the verdict. The judge had a ready answer for that. "I took a chance last night," he cheerfully declared; but he had decided that "that is not a proper question & that it would not be a proper polling." Inside the witness rail a few close friends gathered around Mr. Finney to express sympathy and consolation; outside the rail there was raw hostility. It did indeed appear, as Mr. White later said, that "the chickens of his revenge" rather than "the doves of his kindness" had come home to roost.[73]

The defense immediately announced that it would file a motion for a new trial, and if this were denied, it would take an appeal to the Kansas Supreme Court. The appreciative county commissioners (whose chairman, ironically, had been a character witness for Finney) passed resolutions of gratitude to the governor and to the attorney general in behalf of the people of Lyon County for the substantial assistance that had been lent by their offices.[74]

Elated citizens from all over the state shared with the governor a great sense of satisfaction and relief at the outcome of the trial. A month after the verdict, Fred Harris wrote to Landon that it had been "common talk that the prosecution would not [get] a conviction. That seemed to be generally accepted but when they did secure the conviction there was the most general approbation of that, that I have ever seen. I think that a very large proportion of the members of the legislature talked to me concerning that, and expressed their most sincere gratification over the result of the case."[75]

The *Gazette* had been under considerable pressure to publish extensive accounts of the trial, since rumors persisted that the Finney-White bond would force Emporia readers to buy out-of-town papers if they wanted a complete and unbiased account of the trial. The Whites exploded that concern by providing a thorough reporting (often verbatim) of the proceedings, publishing upwards of twenty columns on the trial on some days. An extra edition came out on the evening of the verdict. No editorial comment appeared, however, and the letters-to-the-editor column remained closed on the subject. "In the Finney case," the famous daily declared in self-congratulation, "The Gazette tried earnestly to present the news—all the news and nothing but the news. It has been no easy task. Yet public interest demanded all of those interminable columns of testimony."[76]

ON NOVEMBER 15 the defense filed a motion for a new trial; it was heard on December 1. Three of the ten affidavits that were offered sought to disqualify one of the jurors, Jake Matile. According to two of his neighbors, Matile, a farmer in northern Lyon County, had asserted before the trial that "the old ——— is guilty as hell" and "I want to get on that jury and stick that old ———." Those who signed the affidavits had themselves been arrested on various criminal charges. One was a tenant on a farm owned by Finney.[77] A furious Landon wrote Beck in mid December, urging him to make "a thorough investigation" of the men who had signed the affidavits. "It seems to me to be a clear case of tampering with the jury," Landon fumed.[78]

Finney's lawyers advanced eleven causes for setting aside the judgment and ordering a new trial. They included the denial of a fair and impartial trial due to "outbursts of display of passion and prejudice" by the courtroom spectators; misconduct of the state's attorney (Wedell) in appealing "to the passion and prejudice" of the jury; erroneous rulings by the court on offers of evidence; erroneous instructions given by the court to the jury; disqualification of the judge; failure of the court to properly poll the jury; and so forth. These causes later became the foundation for their appeal to the Kansas Supreme Court.[79]

On December 2 Judge McCarty rejected the defense causes, denying their motion for a new trial. He believed that the suspect juror, Jake Matile, was an honest man and that the statements made against him were untrue. He then sentenced Warren Finney to three to fifty years in the Kansas State Penitentiary on each of the twelve embezzlement counts, yielding a grand total of 36 to 600 years, to run consecutively. A stoical Finney received the staggering sentence with no show of emotion. Many in the crowded courtroom expressed surprise that McCarty had pronounced the maximum sentence. Released on a $25,000 bond, the down-but-not-out banker filed an appeal on January 3 with the Kansas Supreme Court, where the battle would be vigorously continued. Two of his lawyers—John Schenck and Clyde Schenck—immediately began to prepare themselves for the upcoming trial of Ronald Finney, which had been scheduled in Topeka for early December.[80]

9

Crime and Punishment

WHILE LANGUISHING in the Shawnee County Jail that fall, Ronald Finney had ample time to reflect on his deceitful practices and fraudulent activities of the past several years—had he been so inclined. His ultimate deed of counterfeiting bonds and warrants represented the culmination of a four-step evolutionary sequence, which entailed progressively greater daring and duplicity. The first overt manifestations appeared in the middle twenties as shady practices in the operation of his father's bank and in the funding of the short-lived newspaper. After this incipient Neosho Falls stage, a more aggressive Topeka phase in 1930/31 featured his questionable behavior in hustling numerous communities under the bond-exchange law and his finagling the compliant School Fund Commission into buying the first of many municipal bond issues. Up to that point he had operated in an ethical-legal twilight zone. Emboldened by these unmitigated successes, he took an ethical quantum jump in late 1931, when he began to employ canceled school-district warrants for his own purposes. For the first time, illegal paper for which he alone was responsible floated in the stream of commerce. He had moved progressively—or degeneratively—from a good way to a better way and then, finally, to the best way of all—the outright counterfeiting of wholesale lots of municipal bonds.

How could Ronald Finney have repeatedly committed these unscrupulous acts, these ineffable crimes, we are moved to ask—traveling steadily and deliberately down the primrose path to shame, humiliation, and oblivion? How could the gifted son of a puritanical family, reared in a puritanical church in a puritanical town in a puritanical state, have so woefully disregarded the most elementary lessons from his Sunday School?[1]

An unhappy meeting of the talent, the inclination, and the opportunity is perhaps the most that can be said, given the imperfections of his early record and the primitive state of the behavioral sciences. And what of the genesis of the moral sensitivities of the father? It is perhaps easier to derive the son from the father than the father from the grandfather.

Some apologists spoke vacuously of "relentless outside pressures" on the son (from the father) and of "circumstances beyond his control" (presumably the father). Governor Landon attributed the downfall to "that early training at Neosho Falls and the fact that he was able to get away with that unchecked." For his part, Ronald emphasized opportunity, attributing the inclination to the disastrous state of his father's Neosho Falls bank in the twenties. "I think it was natural," he wrote in his so-called confession, "when turning to this crooked way of raising money to meet the demands coming in from bad paper [in the banks] and other debts, to have duplicate issues printed on school districts and cities where I had handled previously legitimate transactions. Anyway that is what I did."[2]

In working with funding districts from all over the state, Kansas' "public enemy number one" had familiarized himself with the minutiae of the bond-issuance procedure in the field and at the Statehouse. He knew what would go and what would not—what people looked for and what passed by even the most experienced and eagle-eyed. The puzzled federal and state investigators took quite a while to figure out exactly how he had done it. Conventional wisdom among investment brokers, bankers, and printers held that such massive duplications were impossible. He must have stolen the bonds or borrowed them or invented some new technique which cranked them out in the dead of night. But he had pioneered no new technological breakthrough, no innovative process that duplicated the special bond paper, the ornate marginal scrolls, or the elegant script. What he relied upon chiefly was his innate reading of the human mind and its motivations. Why worry about technology when you can press anxious-to-please friends into service to produce the real stuff, and in broad daylight too.

A bond transcript comprises a detailed history of the legal actions leading up to the issuance of the bonds—the ordinances, the votes, the official authorizations. It bears much the same relationship to a bond as an abstract bears to a piece of land. Finney and his associates spent a good deal of time in the auditor's vault, and they had no difficulty in checking the transcripts out. It then became a simple matter to ask a friendly printer to reprint an issue on one pretext or another—that the bonds were to be exchanged at a lower interest rate, that the interest rate needed to be raised to make them more marketable, or that the mayor had inadvertently signed on the wrong line, thus invalidating the original issue. The gullible printers cheerfully indulged their best customer. All that needed to be done was to change the dates of maturity and the interest rate, and there they were in all their pristine beauty—a crisp new series of, say, twenty-five bonds of $1,000 denomination. And at a cost of, say, $35—a pretty favorable exchange rate in anybody's league.[3]

Finney always worked with a compelling sense of urgency that his business had to be done, and now. This calculated habit did not allow much time for thinking by those in the printing firms or the Statehouse offices. The personable Ronald could be traced from office to office by the trail of candy and flowers that he left in his wake for the ladies, ladies who were in a strategic position to do him or his a certain favor. And for the very special big shots—such as Boynton, Boyd, Stanley, Hardin, Voorhees, Baird, and Wetherton—Ronald always had at the ready his foolproof wheat-market investment plan. When necessary, he might even go a step further and add an especially deserving soul to the regular payroll or put him up rent-free in an apartment.[4]

The duplicate bonds appeared to be indistinguishable from the genuine article. "When you bit them, they tasted the same," someone observed. When the bonds came from the printer, Leland Caldwell did his thing. He forged the signatures of the officials of the issuing municipalities and the names of the attorney general and the auditor on the registration and approval forms. The forged signatures were done freehand—that is, no attempt was made to produce a spurious signature by tracing with a pencil or stylus, as usually occurs in counterfeit penmanship. And very good facsimiles they were, too. The forgers tried to use inks that would simulate those used on the originals, though the differences could always be detected on close scrutiny. A bond normally bore two seals—one from the local district or county and the other the Great Seal of the State of Kansas. The latter was kept in the Auditor's Office and was affixed when the bonds were registered. The fake local seals were bought in Topeka and were partially mutilated in order to yield an impression that would be difficult to read. Who reads seals anyway? Ronald had observed. To everyone's amazement and to the auditor's acute embarrassment, the impression of the large state seal on all the forgeries passed every stringent test when compared with ones made by the authentic seal. It was the real McCoy.[5]

Even with an excellent product, one had to have control of the duplicate issues so as to keep them out of the usual commercial channels. And those troublesome interest coupons, which came in regularly every six months, had to be controlled. The bond broker had been dealing with the School

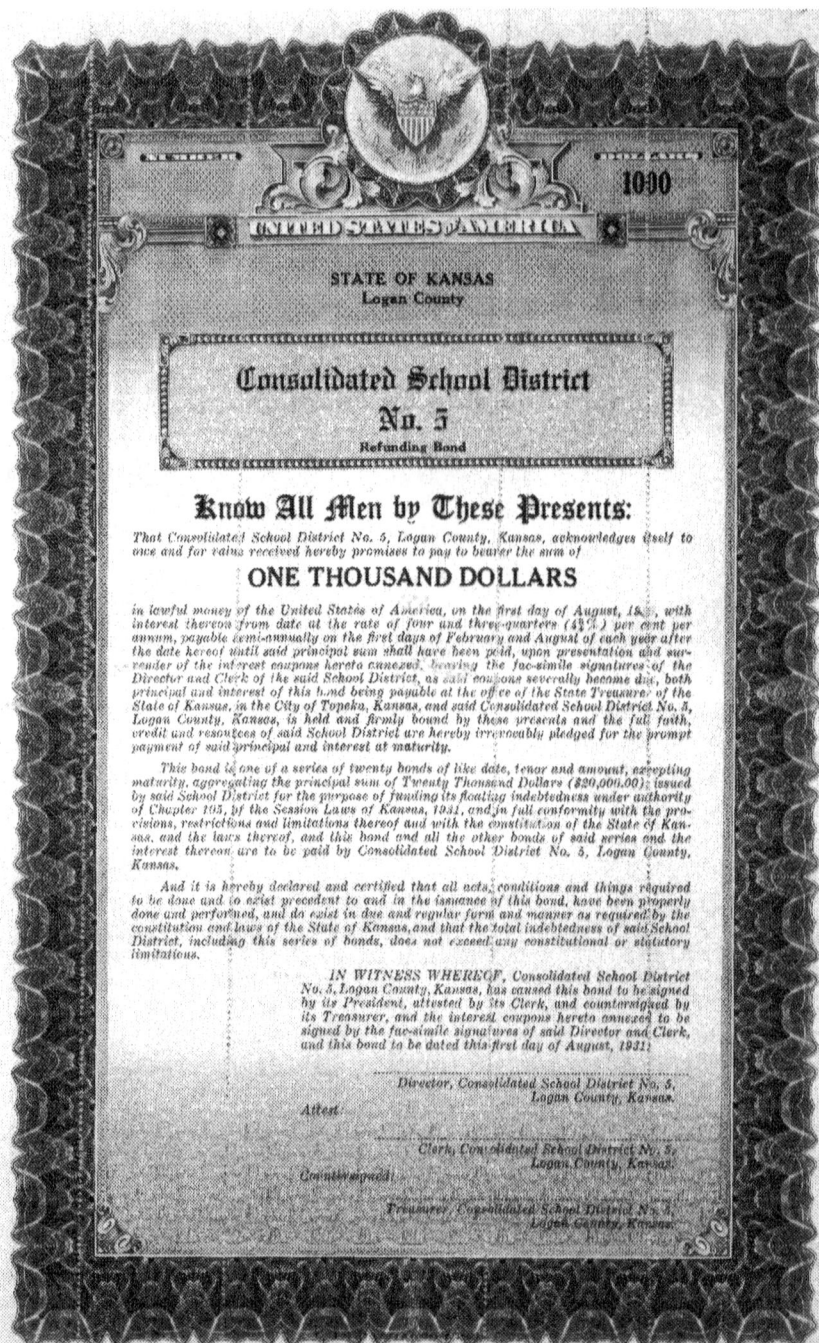

A Forged Logan County Bond

Fund since 1931. He knew that a large red-ink stamp marked the face of its purchases and that its bonds never entered the commercial market. Therefore, duplicates of bonds held by the School Fund seemed attractive. The bonds needed to be kept out of circulation and yet perform an antisocially useful purpose. The duplicates could be substituted in the state treasury for genuine securities, whose "work" consisted of securing deposits of public funds in the three Finney banks. Ironically, many of the bogus bonds did that work without being detected only a few feet from the original issues, which were also held in the treasury vault for the School Fund.[6]

After it became clear that the substitute bonds in the treasury were working without a hitch, Ronald decided to raise additional cash by a more direct method—the repurchase agreement. He sold large blocks of previously duplicated bogus municipal bonds to financial institutions, usually the National Bank of Topeka or Chicago brokerage firms, with the oral understanding that if they wanted to unload the bonds at any time for any reason, they would come back to him for first refusal. Rubber bonds with a rubber band attached, you might say. He paid interest on his "loan"; but as a part of the arrangement always insisted upon, he retained the right to clip the coupons.[7] The interest on the loan often exceeded the return on the bonds, but Ronald was getting his money's worth.

By July of 1932, the will, the wiles, and the way had met in young Finney, and the first fraudulent bonds (from a Johnson County school district) entered the state treasury. Building slowly at first, the output from the Finney machine had become a veritable flood a year later. So menacing had it become that federal investigators requested his arrest before their case had been perfected, for fear that Kansas bonds would soon find their principal use in the dining room as wallpaper, or in the outhouse. Altogether, seventeen different issues were duplicated—several, more than once—for a total value of approximately $1 million. Over one thousand individual bogus bonds—usually in the $1,000 denomination—eventually were identified. When one adds nearly $225,000 in forged and worthless warrants and $94,000 in worthless Colorado bonds, the grand total of bad Finney paper is approximately $1,335,000.[8]

WHEN RONALD FINNEY was arrested on the Hutchinson charges on August 24, he went to jail to stay. Although he exerted half-hearted efforts to make bond, secretly he must have felt a great deal of relief at finally having been apprehended, given the hectic, tension-filled life that he had led through the previous spring and summer. He found the Shawnee County Jail a safe, serene haven from creditors and hatemongers alike.

Outside, the storm raged; the pure Kansas air was filled with epithets and vituperations against the fallen entrepreneur. His fellow Kansans called him everything in the book—the "Ponzi of Kansas," the "Krueger of Kansas," a get-rich-quick Wallingford, the prince of Kansas crooks, Judas Iscariot, Houdini, a super slicker, a snake in the grass, an archfiend, and more.[9] The last gay party had been held at 929 West in Emporia; the new tennis courts were darkened now; the magnificent Pierce-Arrow had been signed over to the attorneys; the 101 Ranch Show struggled to make enough to feed the elephants; the once-bustling Jayhawk suite stood empty and silent. The fair-weather friends—the sycophants always found fawning near the rich and successful—had long since dropped away, often adding their own toady voices to the righteous chorus of scorn and vilification.[10]

As the state and federal charges piled one on another in a seemingly endless series, Kansas' most cussed and discussed citizen faced his mounting adversities calmly, even jovially. After his arrest on the Salina charge, Finney remarked that "maybe there will have to be an inflation [for me] to get bond."[11] When he and Boyd were charged in late September with having illegally removed treasury funds, he quipped: "They must be weakening a little. This only charges me with aiding and abetting [and] is only equivalent to petit larceny. They're slipping." He told avid newsmen, who greedily hung on every Finney syllable, that "September is a dull month [for news], so, in order to provide the reporters with copy they file a new charge every few days." His attorney, John Schenck, complained: "The only reason that they haven't charged Ronald with the attempt to kidnap the governor's daughter is that he was in jail at the time. At that, they may charge him with planning the whole affair."[12]

For the first few months at least, the impenitent Finney seemed to genuinely enjoy his jail life, as he spent his time conducting sundry business affairs, talking to visiting friends and relatives, and enthusiastically entering into the organized life of the jail. He admitted that his disposition had improved considerably since his incarceration. Tom Boyd had been declared a model prisoner: he occupied the jail's "parlor cell" and was shaved every morning by an inmate who was a barber. Finney was elected judge of the kangaroo court.[13] After making his noncommittal statement on the day of his arrest, the garrulous Finney had remained officially silent, on the advice of his lawyers. Time and again, federal and state investigators tried to get a statement from him which would "tell all." He readily conversed and joked with everyone that came around, but to questions about the scandal he played deaf and dumb. "I don't know anything about that at all, I tell you," he repeatedly insisted.[14]

Somehow he did manage to maintain his official silence regarding the scandal, rarely breaking it in the months and years ahead. To a close friend he confided that he had been offered immunity in exchange for information but had decided to remain mute, adding that if he did talk, "a lot of important people would be in big trouble."[15] In mid November, when he granted an interview to a *Topeka Capital* reporter, he refused to discuss the bond scandal but held forth on almost everything else. A lot of words, bottled up for months, just had to come out. He wore his favorite jail "uniform": a clean, well-pressed white shirt, seersucker pants, silk hose, and polished white-and-tan sports shoes. Add a straw hat and a cigar, and you would have had the debonair bond broker of 1930–33. Sitting on the edge of his iron cot and reaching for a cigarette, Finney, now weighing 240 pounds, shared a few thoughts with the reporter. He guessed that jail life wasn't so bad; in fact, he admitted to getting quite a kick out of it:

> A year ago the thought of going to jail would have been dismaying. If I were outside now I would prefer to spend two days in jail to making a two-day trip to Kansas City. It is just as entertaining here as a trip to Kansas City and I can get much more rest. The only objection to jail life is the disgrace—if it is a disgrace, and I think it will take time to decide that.[16]

Finney would come to have a somewhat different attitude regarding the joys of confinement in the years ahead. There would subsequently be ample opportunity to ponder the question of disgrace and to calculate the price of peculation. He had a good deal to say about the business trends of the day, which gives some direct insight into the financial philosophy which he had translated into such spectacular action the previous spring.[17] He related his "naked man" economic theory that he was so fond of:

> In past depressions things that come from the soil have recovered quickest. Probably the soil itself will be the first to come back. Farm equities ought to be a great investment. Then come grain, livestock and all things that come from the soil. . . .
>
> It is my belief that if you take a naked man out in the rain he will have the same impulses and the same desires that all other men have. First he will want shelter. Then he will want food and clothing. These are fundamental desires and the first to be satisfied when a man has money. This eventually will bring commodity prices back up.[18]

While life may have been pleasant enough in the jail, news on his personal financial front was more discouraging. In early December the federal government filed a $90,105 tax lien against his property, which represented unpaid taxes on his estimated income for 1933. Guy T. Helvering, commissioner of internal revenue, announced that they had closed the 1933 tax year on Finney in anticipation of the dissipation of his assets and had rather arbitrarily assessed the $90,000 tax. A few days later the State Tax Commission levied a $14,270 income-tax lien on his property, based on an estimated net income of $360,000 for 1933.[19] The tax assessment and the filing of the liens prevented the transfer of property and would help in the location of property. Perhaps the Finneys began to have second thoughts about the social usefulness of the state income tax which they had worked so diligently to get passed.

THE TRIAL OF RONALD FINNEY for forging (thirty counts) and uttering (thirty counts) to the Citizens State Bank of North Topeka $30,000 in bonds of the city of Hutchinson began in the second division of the Shawnee County District Court on December 11. The prosecution was confident that it had chosen an especially strong case to bring to trial. Finney and Caldwell had each been charged with a total of 140 counts in the Hutchinson and Salina cases. Caldwell had received a separation from the Finney case and was to be tried in January on the Salina charges.[20]

Lester Goodell, the Shawnee County attorney, and his able assistant, Paul Harvey, headed the prosecution team. Goodell, who was the same age as Finney and was a graduate of Washburn Law School, had served a term as assistant county attorney before being elected county attorney in 1932. Assisting the Shawnee County prosecutors was Hugo Wedell, who had also been assigned by the governor to assist in the upcoming Caldwell and Boyd cases. Fresh from his triumph at Emporia, Wedell basked in the sunshine of public acclaim for his vigorous efforts against the father as he prepared to prosecute the son. "I have no hesitation in saying that in my judgment the successful termination of [that] prosecution resulted from Mr. Wedell's efforts," Fred Harris told Landon just before the Topeka trial. "It is the general feeling that he was the outstanding figure among the entire bunch of lawyers." As the governor's representative, Wedell expected to play the same lusty role that he had played in the first trial. Finney's lawyers—a mere remnant of Warren Finney's powerful array at Emporia—included only John Schenck and his son, Clyde.[21]

The honorable Paul H. Heinz occupied the bench. A graduate of Washburn Law School, the Topeka native had practiced law since 1912.

After serving in various judicial capacities in Topeka, including that of Shawnee County attorney, the forty-three-year-old judge had gone into private practice with Judge Otis E. Hungate. Heinz had represented Leland Caldwell in his arraignment on the original charges in August. He had had to sever that relationship in early September when he had received an appointment from Governor Landon to fill a vacancy on the district-court bench.[22]

As the date of the trial approached, public interest in the case became intense. The state made plans to subpoena fifty witnesses, including Governor Landon. The defense kept its plans to itself. It was feared that the trial might cost as much as $10,000; the handwriting expert alone would cost $450.[23] Horrendous figures these for the poverty-stricken public to read.

The defendant was joined at the defense table by his wife, his mother, and his mother-in-law. His father remained in Emporia. Finney—chainsmoking and with his black hair neatly trimmed, brushed flat, and "parted at the equator"—wore a stylish brown suit, a light gray hat, and an air of unconcern.[24] Throughout the trial he busily occupied himself by wisecracking with reporters, scrawling notes to sundry people, and drawing caricatures of the leading courtroom figures. Peggy of the Flint Hills[25] observed that anyone who came to the trial expecting to see Ronald Finney dragging a ball and chain would be very disappointed. He "wandered casually in," she observed, "as if he had just come from lunching at his club and had had some amusing conversation with a few bank presidents and state officials."[26]

During most of the first week the crafty John Schenck, who was stalling for time, questioned the prospective jurors in exasperating detail. Introducing the political dimension as often as possible, he extracted a pledge from each accepted juror that he would not be influenced by the fact that the governor had sent special assistant Wedell to aid in the prosecution. Had any member of their family ever accepted or applied for a job from the Landon administration? Once, in reference to Landon's role in the prosecution, he used the phrase "butted in," but then, realizing that that was perhaps going a bit far, he quickly corrected himself. Another Schenck test presented a more difficult hurdle for the prospective jurors. He sought to eliminate all those who had read newspaper accounts or had formed any opinion whatsoever, regardless of how tentative or faint, on any aspect of the bond scandal. That, of course, pretty much eliminated the entire literate population of Shawnee County and the state of Kansas.[27] One hopeful, when asked if he had formed an opinion, summarized the problem for all: "It was hard not to have had one."[28] Nevertheless, on Friday,

Zula Bennington Greene—"Peggy of the Flint Hills"—columnist for the *Topeka Capital* (Zula Bennington Greene)

December 15, twelve Shawnee Countians (four women and eight men, five of whom were farmers) were finally accepted, of the some fifty-five called, and the trial proceeded.[29]

At the outset the state agreed to reduce the uttering counts from thirty to one, since the bonds had been sold in one transaction. A motion by Schenck, which was denied a few days later, would have reduced the forging counts from thirty to ten on the theory that since the bonds matured in groups of three, only ten offenses had been committed rather than thirty (the "stealing three hogs" theory again). Each count of forgery bore a penalty of one to twenty-one years in the Kansas State Penitentiary.[30]

In his opening statement, Lester Goodell chose not to limit himself to the narrow ground of the Hutchinson charge; instead, he attempted to place the entire range of the Finney-Caldwell operations into perspective for the jury. Goodell's thorough presentation seemed to convince even the most skeptical. When Fred Harris ambled over from the Statehouse at the beginning of the second week, rumors flew that the defendant would plead guilty to one count of forgery in exchange for a ten-year sentence.[31]

An accountant with the Chicago brokerage firm of Jackson Brothers, Boesel and Company testified that nearly $400,000 in counterfeit bonds had been turned over to that company, most of them by Finney personally. The accountant refused to answer detailed questions regarding Finney's market activity, though he acknowledged that the Emporian, who had opened an account in April, 1933, now owed the firm over $285,000. Each time that Finney placed bonds with the firm, he drew down some money, either as a loan or as profit on his trading. The firm had always deposited the bonds in a bank, after an appraisal to determine how much Finney could be allowed on them. Altogether the firm had advanced $352,761 to the swindler.[32]

Russell Reed of the Superior Printing Company, Topeka, testified that Caldwell gave him a trial order on September 1, 1932, "to see whether [we] could print satisfactory bonds."[33] Having found their work acceptable, Caldwell returned on October 22 and delivered to Reed a transcript for printing thirty $1,000 bonds of the city of Hutchinson and forty $500 bonds of the Board of Education of Salina. A few days later, Caldwell placed an order with the Darling Stamp Company, Topeka, for a seal bearing on its face the words "City of Hutchinson, City Wheat Board, Reno County, Kansas" and a comparable one for Salina. Finney and Harry Betzer, cashier of the Citizens State Bank, had worked out a trade early in October, whereby Finney would turn over to Betzer the Hutchinson and Salina bonds in exchange for $50,000 in earlier-maturing issues that the bank was holding in the state treasury as security on deposits. On October 28 Finney delivered to Betzer a receipt from the state treasurer for the Hutchinson and Salina bonds and a treasury withdrawal sheet that listed the bonds that were coming from Betzer. Thus Betzer never actually saw the forged securities as the accommodating broker merely substituted them in the treasury for the good bonds that he withdrew.[34]

For some unknown, perhaps purely capricious, reason the unpredictable Finney made the switch with the bank without a repurchase agreement and its explicit control of the maturing bonds. That had led to problems which Hutchinson officials brought out at the trial. Early in the spring the city treasurer, May D. Harsha, received three $1,000 park bonds that had matured, and she dutifully remitted $3,000 to the state treasury. A month later a set of identical bonds came from the treasury, with a request to remit another $3,000, the amount that the treasury had already paid for the bonds. The city complained to Treasurer Tom Boyd. Then, early in

May, a heavyset stranger in his early thirties landed at Hutchinson in a private plane. One of his part-time employees met him at the flying field and drove him to city hall. The stranger solemnly informed Miss Harsha that he had come from the state treasury and wanted to straighten out the error that had evidently been made in their bond accounts.

Miss Harsha, of course, was delighted to see a response to her complaint to the state treasury. The tall, dark stranger removed some very official-looking papers from his briefcase and asked to see her records. As he poured over the documents, his brow knit in studied concern. He requested some additional records which the obliging treasurer had to retrieve from an adjacent room. After doing some figuring on an adding machine that he had called for (perhaps multiplying by pi or dividing by the square root of two), his heretofore-concerned face brightened considerably. Eureka! He had found the error. And wouldn't you know it, the mistake had been made by those bureaucrats in Topeka. It certainly wasn't the fault of the efficient city treasurer. He promised to correct it as soon as he returned to the capital city. The "auditor" handed the records back to Miss Harsha, thanked her profusely for her patience, stepped into his waiting car, and was whisked back to the airport.[35] On the way he told the driver that the treasurer sure was "a nice lady." So they stopped and bought a box of candy for her before returning to the flying field.[36]

A few days later Treasurer Boyd notified Treasurer Harsha that "we are crediting your account $3,000 to take care of bonds paid in error."[37] The state's assistant treasurer testified that Finney had given him $3,000 in currency, explaining that it was to correct an error in the Hutchinson account, and that Finney himself had dictated the treasury letter that corrected the "error." After the stranger had departed, Miss Harsha noticed that her records, which had previously listed bonds received from Topeka at a total of $30,474.29, now, with an obvious erasure, totaled only $27,474.29. And from that day to this, the second set of those park bonds has never been seen by Miss Harsha or by any other living soul.[38]

The state was developing what appeared to be an airtight case, and it opted not to call the governor as a material witness. When a lengthy conference took place in the judge's chambers on December 21, after a series of delays marked by legal wrangling, the rumor mill again began to crank out reports that Finney would soon plead guilty. The big crowds waited expectantly for counselor Schenck to spring his "big surprise." But Schenck was ostensibly looking for a reversible judicial error, and the trial continued apace.[39]

Even the most serious of endeavors will manifest lighter moments.

The clerk of a Russell County school district, who had been asked by Schenck to write his name, apologized for his shaky hand, pleading nervousness. When the attorney asked why, he replied that he was nervous because there were "so many dignitaries present." In a night session, Finney and the courtroom had a good laugh when Schenck queried a school-board member about his signature on some interest coupons. "Tell me which are the genuine bonds," the cautious farmer replied, "before I answer that question." In the concluding session before the state rested its case, the sole business consisted of Schenck's asking the handwriting expert, J. C. Shearman, how much he was being paid. He replied "$100," which was exactly what he received (as his per diem fee) for that answer.[40]

A GOOD DEAL OF SPECULATION centered on the defensive tactics of John Schenck when the state concluded its case on Saturday, December 23. From the beginning of the selection of the jury, Schenck had been publicly stalling while privately trying to work out a reduced sentence for his client in return for a guilty plea. Rejecting an original offer of ten years, the prosecution insisted on at least fifteen, though the judge seemed to find considerable merit in the defense's offer. On Saturday morning, John Schenck and Paul Harvey fell into prolonged bargaining. Harvey argued that since the state had completed its case, the defendant should plead guilty to all thirty-one counts. Judge Heinz entered the room—the meeting was being held in his chambers—as the two attorneys negotiated. He remarked that fifteen counts should be "amply sufficient," since it would carry a maximum sentence of over three hundred years. Soon Goodell joined the conference and agreed that if the defendant would plead guilty to all thirty-one counts, Goodell would accept fifteen consecutive counts along with sixteen which would run concurrently, for a total minimum of fifteen years. Judge Heinz readily concurred.[41]

After the noon break, Schenck sprang his "surprise." He asked the judge to immediately appoint a "sanity commission" to examine Finney. If found insane, Finney would be committed to the ward for the insane at the Kansas State Penitentiary. If found sane, he would plead guilty to the thirty-one counts with the clear stipulation that sixteen counts would run concurrently with the other fifteen. This arrangement seemed to be agreeable to all.[42]

The judge immediately convened in his chambers a commission composed of three physicians to examine Ronald Finney. Schenck handed the panel a list of Finney's behaviors that he considered eccentric. After questioning Finney for an hour, the doctors reported that the defendant was "not insane, not an imbecile, and not an idiot and was able to comprehend his position."[43] When the subject heard their conclusions, he was moved to remark, "I'm damn glad of that."[44]

A few minutes later, at 5:03 P.M., in the dimly lit room on the gray wintry afternoon, the old legal warhorse John Schenck rose slowly and addressed the open court. "After consultation with the defendant . . . , and his wife," he said in tired and measured tones, "I desire to enter a plea of guilty."[45] The courtroom buzzed at the sudden turn of events, though the plea scarcely came as a total surprise to the public. Sentencing was set for December 30. When the court was formally adjourned, the unpredictable defendant rose immediately and addressed the crowd, particularly the judge: "Now, there's just one more thing. . . . Judge, I have been collecting a Christmas fund for prisoners in the county jail. I started to ask you for a dollar the other day, but you scared me to death by telling me you didn't care to talk to me. If wonder if now it would be all right for me to ask for a contribution to my fund?"[46]

One paper reported that the startled judge dug in his pocket for a dollar, but that evidently was incorrect. The "thoughtful and conscientious" judge felt compelled to issue a public statement on the matter on Christmas Day: "I don't believe in a bonus for evil doers when law abiding men and women of my acquaintance need food and clothing. The little money I can give will go to them. Men in the county jail are well fed and sleep in a warm place. I know people who never violated a law who are hungry."[47]

Ronald Finney would be the recipient of the judge's ire for a much longer period than he could have imagined on that Christmas Eve. He lightheartedly went off with his bodyguard, as he called the deputy sheriff, after trying to cheer up his tearful wife, who struggled to manage a small, brave smile. In spite of his failure with the judge, "Santa Claus" had managed to collect $37 for Christmas gifts for his fellow prisoners. It came mostly from newspapermen who particularly owed him something, he said, since he had made so much news for the papers. The headline in the *Gazette* following the guilty plea ran "Ronald Finney in Santa Claus Role."[48]

IN THE WEEK FOLLOWING the trial a great deal of conjecture regarding the probable sentence occurred both in public and in private—what the sentence should be and what it would be. Representing a clear consensus, the *State Journal* quickly made its views known on December 26:

> The people will await eagerly the announcement of the sentence

imposed upon Ronald Finney. . . . The public would view with alarm any evidence of a tendency toward leniency at this time.

Finney's punishment should be in keeping with the enormity of his offense, if the recommendations to the court are to be based on public interest instead of sentimentalism. . . .

A sentence in keeping with Finney's deserts would arouse the hope that the bond scandal, instead of destroying confidence in Kansas institutions as it threatened to do, might be made the agency thru which confidence is revived and restored.[49]

The *Ottawa Herald* reflected the attitude of small-town Kansas:

He had dragged the credit and honor of the state of Kansas in the dust.

The court has the choice of letting him off easy . . . , or of sending him to the . . . Penitentiary for many times the years of his life span. The people will not countenance maudlin sympathy for the man. . . . The people will stand for nothing short of a penalty that will keep Finney behind the bars for a lifetime. A man who dared to dishonor his state as did Finney, deserves no less.[50]

Much of the public felt like the St. Paul man who wrote to Landon, worried that the wealthy Finney would escape his due punishment: "We are watching with a keen interest the development and outcome of all of this, as every one seems to be vitally interested in this terrible scandal. . . . I notice in the papers that young Finney has confessed, and that he and his lawyers want to fix the penalty, haven't we got the law and the penalty fixed for such as that, it would be if it was a common every day man, and which they would socket to hard, so give him the same dose."[51]

On December 30 Judge Heinz abruptly announced in open court that he had discovered in the past few days (or, perhaps, had had discovered for him) a recent Kansas Supreme Court decision which in his view seemed to preclude concurrent sentencing in the state. He could not, therefore, be bound by the earlier agreement of a fifteen-year minimum sentence in return for the guilty plea. A startled and angry defense counsel asked for a delay in the sentencing to January 2, which was promptly granted.[52]

The *State Journal* immediately came forth with a New Year's Day editorial that was calculated to bolster the resolve of the judge.

An Inadequate Sentence

A fifteen-year term in prison would be an inadequate sentence . . . , whatever the promise of the county attorney.

A sentence of fifteen years would be a victory . . . for the political clique, which has boasted of the power it possesses in this county. It sincerely is to be hoped that Judge Heinz stands firm. . . .

It is the almost universal opinion, as expressed in Kansas in spoken and written words, that Ronald Finney should go to prison for a long term of years, if not for the remainder of his life. . . .

The public feeling will be that justice has been outraged if this prince of Kansas crooks is put away for anything less than a minimum period of 30 years.[53]

The jammed courtroom on the cold winter afternoon of January 2 was to witness one of the rarest of spectacles in Kansas legal history. Judge Heinz declared firmly that he had made up his mind and was ready to pronounce sentence. He felt that the recent Supreme Court decision (137 Kansas) was binding. In that case a defendant had been sentenced on one offense and had appealed. While the appeal was pending, he was arrested, tried, and convicted on a second and totally separate charge. The Supreme Court had ruled that where there were two separate offenses, trials, and convictions, the two sentences resulting therefrom could not run concurrently.[54] These conditions patently did not pertain in the Finney case, except in the all-important mind of Judge Heinz.

Winifred and Ronald Finney at the time of his sentencing
(Kansas City Star)

John Schenck vainly attempted to enlighten the judge, arguing that "the court seems to stumble on this 137 Kansas; I don't think it applies to this case at all."[55] Schenck also made reference to the harsh *State Journal* editorial of January 1, "complimenting this court and denouncing the county attorney . . . for consenting to this."[56]

When Schenck had finished, a very disturbed Lester Goodell addressed the court. He said that ordinarily the county attorney should make his recommendations when called upon, and let it go at that. But this was no ordinary case. He intimated that others on the prosecution team were seeking personal publicity rather than legal justice. He noted that a lot had been written in the papers since the plea had been entered. A good deal of it that related to the agreement was in error: someone had been giving out distorted information. He felt that, in the interests of the truth, he should make a public statement regarding the extended bargaining that had occurred in the judge's chambers—with his honor's complete blessing—prior to the plea.[57]

When Goodell had finished his lengthy remarks, the court was treated to that rarest of legal rarities—the astonishing spectacle of members of the same legal team quarreling in open court. Hugo Wedell, whose role had been much diminished compared to the Emporia trial, had taken exception to some of Goodell's candid remarks. Wedell attempted to keep his composure as he rose to speak.

> I happen to be here . . . in a capacity that is a trifle different than representing Shawnee County, and in a sense [have] a responsibility to the state at large. . . . I do thank the county attorney for stating absolutely correctly the last and only definite agreement that I ever participated in, and that was the agreement . . . that we would entertain no plea of any kind, based upon any consideration of leniency of this defendant. . . . Considering the magnitude of what was shown . . . , it would be an outrage to permit the withdrawal of any plea in this lawsuit.[58]

At the conclusion of Wedell's remarks, the assistant prosecutor, Paul Harvey, white-faced with anger,[59] jumped to his feet.

> If Your Honor please, I want to say that Mr. Wedell . . . started out to assist. . . . Of course, he has departed from that entirely and has gone back to the thing that has troubled us from time to time, the great publicity features of this case. We are here, Your Honor, trying to get our word kept, that was given in conjunction with the court. . . . He says it would be an outrage to withdraw this plea. I wanted the record to show that we consent to the withdrawal of this plea and the county attorney's office is running this case.[60]

The still-agitated Goodell had more to unburden on the court:

> I am somewhat worked up about this, but I am not mad, except I am mad with the thought . . . of double-crossing anybody. If a man was as low as a snake's belly in a wagonrut, I would not double-cross him . . . it may be the last official act I ever perform, but I will have the satisfaction of keeping my self-respect . . . and [I] feel very deeply, that we are honor-bound to make the recommendation that Your Honor, inasmuch as he was in the room and participated in the making of the final arrangements, couldn't do anything but carry out.[61]

All the histrionics notwithstanding, Judge Heinz had come to the courtroom with his mind made up. Who helped him in that cannot be asserted with finality. Certainly he knew of the great public displeasure at the prospect of the fifteen-year sentence, and he knew that he would be running for election for the first time in the fall. What interaction did he have with the executive branch of government? There were those who thought that the shots were being called from there. Years later, in a letter to Young Bill White, Ronald Finney claimed that during the period between the guilty plea and the sentencing, "this judge was with Landon three times (we had him followed)."[62] We are left with no smoking gun, no taped conversations, no footprints on the grounds at the gubernatorial mansion. Nevertheless, there is the distinct possibility that there was a major transgression of the executive into a judicial decision. But we shall never know. . . .

Judge Heinz denied the defense motion—even though it was unprecedentedly supported by both the prosecution and the defense—that the guilty plea be allowed to be withdrawn.[63] He then asked Finney if he knew of any reason why the sentence should not be pronounced. "No reason in the world except the agreement in Your Honor's chambers that the minimum sentence should not be more than fifteen years, and that that was the reason I consented to plead guilty."[64] The defendant was then sentenced to be confined in the State Penitentiary at Lansing, Kansas, "at hard labor," for a period of from 31 to 635 years with the sentences to run consecutively. The outraged defense immediately announced that it would take an appeal to the Kansas Supreme Court.[65]

IN A PREACHY EDITORIAL about the evils of crime and the stockmarket, the *Capital* congratulated Judge Heinz and made a prediction:

> Judge Heinz, whose sentence of Ronald Finney . . . to a minimum of 31 years . . . will be generally approved as a just penalty. The judge

conducted his first important criminal trial with admirable judgment. . . .

The Finney case . . . affected so many people in every part of Kansas and it became so notorious, that there need be little doubt that the man will serve out the long term of his sentence. No governor will desire to defend before the people the pardon of a criminal who systematically swindled all the people of the state. The penalty in this case will fit the crime.[66]

Down in Emporia, White and Son took a markedly different view of the proceedings and also made a prediction:

Editorials and aroused public opinion clamored that the reported 15 year sentence was not enough. And by a coincidence the judge, when he came to pass sentence a week later, also decided that it wasn't enough. . . .

This should answer those . . . who believe judges should perch on ivory towers, . . . detached from public clamor and beyond private influence.

But now enters the spotlight young Lester Goodell . . . . He knew, of course, that the agreement which he had consented to had become unpopular. . . . He and the judge undoubtedly read the same newspapers.

But he held his own pledged word as something more sacred than popular opinion. In one bold speech before that court protesting an injustice was being done to his opponent, he sacrificed his reputation as a relentless prosecutor of criminals, preferring to keep intact his honor as a gentleman.

But we predict that a statesman with so distorted a sense of values will not last long in Shawnee county politics.[67]

While Finney's appeal was pending before the High Court, the state prosecutors considered their next move. On February 2 Hugo Wedell wrote to Alfred Landon that in his view

the [second] Finney case [Salina] should be tried at once. In the light of the position taken by the County Attorney . . . in the Ronald Finney case, I do not believe it wise to permit the Salina . . . case to be continued. . . . It is entirely probable that if the Salina case is tried promptly . . . and Ronald faces the possibility of an additional sentence of forty-one years . . . , that he might be glad to withdraw his appeal . . . and begin serving his sentence.[68]

In early March, Fred Harris wrote to the governor that Goodell seemed to feel that "he would not care to put the county to the expense of another trial, unless the supreme court should modify the sentence in the appeal." But, Harris added, "it might be the best plan to push the trial of this other case promptly. . . . I think that everything should be done to absolutely insure the confinement of Finney in the penitentiary for a long, long time."[69]

On May 5, 1934, the Kansas Supreme Court, in an opinion delivered by Justice William A. Smith, found no merit in any of the defense contentions of error except one. They held—to no one's surprise—that Judge Heinz had indeed misinterpreted the decision in 137 Kansas. Sentences could run concurrently in Kansas if they were based on different counts in the same information and at the same trial.[70] The case was remanded to the district court with instructions to resentence the defendant "providing that the term of imprisonment on each count shall run concurrently or consecutively as in the judgment of that tribunal the circumstances of the case and the ends of justice require."[71]

Some of the justices recognized that remanding was a futile gesture, as indeed proved to be the case. After the Supreme Court's opinion had been delivered, Judge Heinz dutifully reconvened the district court and, despite his enlightenment from the High Tribunal as regards 137 Kansas, resentenced Ronald Finney to precisely the same term as before. The defendant entered the State Penitentiary on May 31, 1934.[72]

THE RIFT among the prosecutors did not end when the trial terminated. The day after the sentencing, an incensed Lester Goodell called on the governor and curtly informed him that he doubted that he could continue as the chief prosecutor if Wedell continued to serve as the governor's representative.[73] Goodell indignantly told the press that "when one lawyer of the prosecution double-crosses the others, it is natural that his invitation to participate be withdrawn."[74] Caught in the cross fire on the eve of the upcoming key trials, Landon attempted to patch things up between the proud and intractable prosecutors. He assured the restless public that, regardless of the outcome, he would "tolerate no let-down in the prosecution of the cases."[75] All attempts at reconciliation ended on January 5, when Goodell wrote to Landon that "because of differences which have arisen between myself and your representative . . . , I respectfully request that if you desire a representative in these [Boyd and Caldwell] trials . . . that some different arrangement be made."[76]

With Goodell's letter, Hugo Wedell's role in the bond scandal cases, except for some minor mopping up, came to an end. Landon hated to lose the impassioned prosecutor, who had distinguished himself so admirably at the Emporia trial and whom Alf had come to respect, even to admire. His sterling deeds were not soon forgotten by the grateful governor. At Landon's earliest opportunity—the resignation in June, 1935, of the grand old man of the Kansas judiciary, Chief Justice William A. Johnston—he appointed Wedell to the Kansas Supreme Court, where he served with honor for the next twenty years. (After World War II, in recognition of his distinguished service on the bench, Wedell received, but declined, an invitation to serve as a judge on the war-crimes tribunal in Nuremberg, Germany. In 1945 Landon recommended to Branch Rickey that Wedell be named the next commissioner of organized baseball, citing Wedell's brief career in professional baseball and his continuing intense interest in the game.)[77]

On January 6 the governor responded to Goodell, maintaining the fiction that Wedell had voluntarily resigned.

> It is a matter of much regret to me that Mr. Hugo Wedell, who has assisted you in the trial of the Finney case, does not care to continue in the case of the State vs. Boyd. . . .
>
> I am today naming Mr. S. M. Brewster of Topeka to assist your office in the trial of the case of State vs. Boyd.[78]

While Goodell scored a victory with the substitution of Brewster for Wedell, he was taking his lumps from the aroused public.[79] Many would have agreed with a Topeka doctor who shared his feelings with the governor: "Hugo Wedell for special prosecutor in the Boyd-Finney scandal. Goodell for cheerleader of the sob squad. Let him keep his word, also his oath. After the disgusting spectacle in the Finney case, the people of Kans. can have no confidence either in his ability or his sincerity as a prosecutor."[80]

The *State Journal,* in a caustic editorial entitled "Eyes on Shawnee County," raised a number of questions (and eyebrows) about Goodell's behavior at the trial and about the alleged favoritism shown to the defendant. "The public is going to satisfy itself as to whether an outside influence enters into the prosecution of those accused in the bond scandal."[81] And then there was the barely legible scrawled message from an anonymous letter writer to the harassed county attorney: "Unless Finney is given full punishment and returns the money, we will take the law into our own hands," signed the KKK.[82] While Lester Goodell pondered his public relations, he and Sard Brewster—indeed, all of Kansas—next turned their attention to the trial of Tom Boyd, the erstwhile state treasurer.

10

A Brother's Trust

DURING THE TWENTIES, Treasurer Tom B. Boyd rose to become one of the most effective politicians that Shawnee County and the state of Kansas had ever known. Born in 1877, the now graying and balding Boyd had spent his entire life in Shawnee County. After high school, he briefly attended a Topeka business college, then went to work in the central offices of the Santa Fe Railroad. For the next twenty-five years the popular, fun-loving Topekan held progressively more responsible positions in the railroad's passenger and accounting departments. With the Santa Fe's encouragement and support, the six-foot, brown-eyed Boyd belatedly decided, in his mid forties, to translate his personal popularity into political success. The erstwhile accountant was then elected to three successive terms as Shawnee County treasurer before successfully running for the statewide office in 1928. Serving his third term as state treasurer in 1933, the late bloomer had only some minor blots, plus a few innuendos, on his record.[1] The hard-earned tax money of the people of Kansas appeared to be in safe hands. As a 1932 political announcement crowed, "During these years hundreds of millions of dollars have passed through his hands without loss of a single penny."[2]

Boyd established a solid and progressive political base throughout the state, with his Shawnee County "machine" as its core. His Topeka organization regularly did battle with the Republican conservatives, who were led by the powerful David Mulvane and his successor, John Hamilton. Of late, clubs had begun to be formed by Boyd's friends to promote his prospects for governor. The treasurer possessed in abundance all the basic in-

Tom Boyd, state treasurer (Kansas State Penitentiary)

stincts and required behaviors of the professional politician, though, on occasion, he could become a bit testy, even grumpy, with his public when he was in a bad mood. He and his wife, Helen, who were Presbyterians, had five grown sons and a daughter, several of whom worked in state and local political offices around Topeka. Appreciated by the man in the street and well connected with influential citizens, the personable Boyd led the Republican ticket in its state sweep in 1932. Even after the bond scandal had exploded, with its consequent troubles for the treasurer, you could get an even-money bet on Kansas Avenue that a Shawnee County jury could not be found that would convict Tom Boyd.[3]

TOM BOYD AND RONALD FINNEY had met in the late twenties, when the latter was beginning to establish Topeka as his base of operations. A strong attraction had quickly developed between the sociable treasurer and the ambitious bond broker, who was young enough to be his son. Boyd, like Finney, had a well-developed sense of humor. Both loved to live the good life, and live the good life they did: fun and games at the Jayhawk; lively dinners and parties with influential people; exhilarating plane trips to Kansas towns and to Chicago, combining business and pleasure; hunting, fishing, and poker—all the high-spirited conviviality that only "good old boys" can fully know and savor. Tom Boyd did indeed come to "love and trust him like a brother."[4]

But their social relationship represented only the patina of a much more profound and useful symbiosis between the two. "Ronald Finney had an entree into the office of the State Treasurer," Fred Harris said, "which is hardly possible for one to conceive." A janitor recalled that the first time he had seen Finney in the treasury, he was "going backwards and forwards through the office." In gradual steps, Boyd permitted Finney to utilize the state treasury as an adjunct personal office. The treasury's employees were instructed to give Finney every consideration—type his letters, take his calls, make appointments for him, and help with his constant shuffling of bonds in the vault. Sometimes, to liven things up, Finney would slip in with sacks of camouflaged scotch or champagne, and beer as a chaser, for an impromptu party in the Treasurer's Office with Boyd and their friends.[5]

Finney had a private phone in Boyd's office, from which he made long-distance calls, though Finney, not the state, paid for them. Boyd provided a private safety-deposit box for his favorite private citizen. Checks ranging from a few dollars to twenty thousand dollars were routinely cashed, the clerks frequently having to run out to a local bank to obtain the necessary cash. The fiscal agency often carried large Finney checks uncashed for considerable periods of time, which amounted to a loan from the state to him, which was unsecured and without interest. Copies of the daily balance sheet, indicating what state funds were on deposit and where, were regularly given to the broker. The sheets were even mailed to him when he was out of town.[6] The relationship between Boyd and Finney, which was well known to the Kansas financial community, was used to full advantage by the latter in his transactions around the state. Boyd wrote highly laudatory letters of recommendation to municipalities and banks in Finney's behalf. Many of these organizations came to rue the day that they had done business with the man who came so highly recommended.

In certain transactions the public treasurer and the private broker worked together smoothly as a team. In 1931, for example, Finney sold $50,000 in Hinsdale County bonds to the Peoples National Bank of Kansas City, Kansas, and he received $40,000 in cash on a repurchase agreement. As part of the consideration, Finney promised that the bank would receive a $40,000 deposit of state funds. The day the deal was consummated, Finney took with him a check from the state treasury for $40,000. In the summer of 1932 the bank began to get a little nervous about the bonds, and it asked Finney to live up to his agreement to buy them back. A short time later, Finney, accompanied by Boyd, visited the bank to smooth things over. Boyd carried a satchel containing three issues of Kansas school-district bonds totaling $47,250. The bonds either had been forged or had been illegally removed from the state treasury. The two cronies said they wanted to place the securities in escrow to guarantee Finney's good faith to buy back the Hinsdale bonds at a later date. The bonds were left in a safety-deposit box, and Boyd pocketed one of the two keys to the box.

In the early fall an officer of the bank visited Colorado, where he heard some disturbing things about the current value of Hinsdale County bonds. After his return, the bank insisted that Finney carry out the terms of the agreement and buy back the bonds. Finney flatly refused to do so. A few days later a lawyer, representing the bank, visited Finney and John D. M. Hamilton, his attorney, and threatened to bring suit against Finney and Boyd for defrauding the bank. When they pointed out that the bank had the school bonds as security, the lawyer retorted that they didn't have sole custody since Boyd had one of the keys. That prompted Hamilton to go to Boyd, obtain the key, and return it to the bank's attorney. The bank remained unplacated, however, and threatened to cause further trouble. Since it was the eve of the election, "the boys" had a change of heart. On November 2, 1932, Leland Caldwell delivered a check for $41,708 to the bank and retrieved the bonds.[7]

In addition to these benefits from his association with the state treasurer, Finney had gained ready access to the fiscal agency that made payments on all municipal bonds and coupons. Any embarrassing errors in Finney's "bond department" could be quickly corrected in that friendly office. And it didn't hurt to be able to drop the name of the state treasurer casually when he was in a grain firm in Kansas City or a brokerage house in Chicago as they evaluated the collateral for a loan or a margin call.

On the Boyd side of the interpersonal equation, the satisfaction that he derived from socializing with the fascinating young plunger was augmented by the excitement of the Jayhawk scene, where the treasurer watched in awe as Finney handled his endless business transactions in his wheeler-dealer, big-shot way.[8] Boyd loved the free vacations that were provided for him and his top aides at Finney's Colorado retreat; sometimes he was even permitted to drive out to the mountains in one of Finney's cars.[9] And, of course, Boyd was a frequent recipient of generous Finney gifts. "Mr. Finney is the nicest man," Boyd's daughter purred. "He stocked my father's farm with the finest cattle. And he gave my mother the most beautiful chair."[10]

Pleasant as these social advantages were, they didn't get at the heart of Boyd's most serious and persistent problem—money. The cost of high living and the rearing of a large family had strained every resource of the hard-pressed treasurer. And hopelessly beyond his financial reach lay his fondest heart's desire—a 250-acre farm in Shawnee County. If Tom had a problem, Ronald had a solution. Finney's middle name wasn't really Tucker—it was Money. On an annual salary of $3,600, Boyd had managed to "save" upwards of $9,000 a year, and he had also deposited more than $7,000 in an account in his daughter's name. These deposits had usually been made in currency; they came straight from Finney checks that had been cashed at the Treasurer's Office and were often carried to the bank by one of Boyd's employees, which included his own sons. Ronald Finney later acknowledged that he had paid Boyd a total of about $25,000 during the 1930–33 period.[11] A friend in need is a friend indeed.

FOR SOME TIME, both of the principals prospered, though the fraternal equation teetered in a delicate balance, one that could be easily and profoundly disturbed by suddenly adverse conditions. Over the years, Finney had asked many favors from Boyd and had always kept his end of the bargain. Toward the end of June, 1933, Finney asked his "brother" for the biggest favor of all. For the first time, Finney failed to keep his end of the bargain, leaving his friend holding an empty bag. A visit by the bank examiners to the National Bank of Topeka would set off a chain reaction that would lead directly to Finney's and Boyd's subsequent downfalls.

The National Bank of Topeka, one of Kansas' most substantial and venerable institutions, had been incorporated in 1868, during the early, heady days of statehood. Its incorporators included Colonel Cyrus K. Holliday, the "father" of Topeka and one of the founders of the Atchison, Topeka and Santa Fe Railroad. The bank had grown into one of the largest financial institutions in the West under the prudent leadership of John R. Mulvane and his successor, Sam Cobb. Cobb had been succeeded as president by forty-one-year-old Carl W. McKeen, who was said to have been the youngest president of a major bank in the Southwest.[12] Named vice-president of the Bank of Topeka in 1923, he assumed the presidency of the reorganized National Bank of Topeka in 1925.[13] A Congregationalist, the president was said to have had "ambition, wide and intelligent vision, ceaseless energy and sterling personal character." He also had a motto: ". . . Bite off more than you can chew, then chew it. Plan for more than you can do, then do it. Hitch your wagon to a star, keep your seat, and there you are."[14] An appropriate enough motto for a young, ambitious Kansan on his way to the stars, through difficulties.

The vice-president and trust officer of the bank was John E. Kirk, a political activist who was a strong Landon supporter. Charles L. Cooke headed the Bond Department, where he did sundry favors for his chum Ronald Finney, in return for which Finney let Charley hang around the Jayhawk. David W. Mulvane, who had been Kansas' Republican National Committeeman for twenty-five years and a leader of the conservative standpatters, chaired the institution's board of directors. In 1932 the bank had proudly moved into modern quarters, a new fourteen-story building at the corner of Sixth and Kansas avenues.[15]

Carl McKeen was a warm friend of Warren Finney's down in Emporia, where the McKeens occasionally enjoyed one of Mabel Finney's fine chicken

The National Bank of Topeka
(Builders of Topeka)

dinners. Finney's Emporia bank kept an active account in the Topeka institution, which it used as its depository for bonds securing Lyon County's deposits. Ronald Finney had tried a number of banks, but he found the prosperous Topeka institution to be by far the most congenial. Doing a voluminous business in bonds and warrants, Ronald Finney had become since 1930 one of the bank's largest and most favored customers.[16]

In January, 1933, Ronald Finney told Carl McKeen that he would like to buy $100,000 in U.S. Treasury Bonds. McKeen, saying he thought that this could readily be arranged, turned him over to Cooke.[17] Instead of receiving cash for the U.S. bonds, Cooke took several issues of Kansas municipal bonds on a repurchase arrangement. By June the bonds that were so held by the bank had increased to $150,600, and Finney had a loan of $145,500. In addition to young Finney, the Fidelity and Neosho Falls banks assumed ownership of some of the bonds. The Finneys, father and son, paid 5 percent interest on the loan. While this rate was greater than the interest paid by the bonds, the all-important coupons thus remained under tight Finney control.[18]

Enter now the national bank examiners on a routine examination on June 21. Ten of them, headed by E. F. ("Jack") Allen and his principal assistant, Mark Rooney, spread out like a plague of grasshoppers into the several departments of the bank. In Cooke's Bond Department on June 24, they discovered that the clerk, Collis D. Harner, had written the fateful word "Finney" in pencil in the lower right-hand corner of the ledger sheets for each of the nine bond issues that secured the Finney loan. Their interest piqued, the examiners asked what that meant. The nervous Harner stammered that he really didn't know, except that it indicated the source of the bonds. But, the curious inspectors pointed out, the source had not been so indicated on the other bond ledgers. Why had he entered it only on Finney's? Obviously terrified, the bookkeeper froze, and they could not pry anything further from him. The examiners then found a credit memorandum for $3,000, which represented interest on the loan for the five months since the first of the year. They discovered that $25,000 of the same $150,000 set of bonds was simultaneously being carried in escrow by Finney to secure his trading account with Jackson Brothers, Boesel. Further investigation disclosed that there had been a fraudulent increase of $2,500 in the Finney account for each of two bond issues in order to cover what the bookkeepers believed to be a $5,000 shortage in the Finney account.[19]

Suddenly what had begun as a routine examination had taken an abrupt turn for the worse. The troubled examiners began to ask a host of questions, and they weren't too happy with the often devious answers. An anxious Charley Cooke explained that Harner was due to get married that very weekend, which naturally accounted for his high state of nervousness. During the following week the examiners recalled the frightened bridegroom from his Colorado honeymoon so that he could answer some additional questions.[20] Reporters asked him if he had spent any time at the Finney ranch. "I consider that personal," young Harner responded.[21]

Convinced that the repurchase agreement with the Finneys was in fact a camouflaged loan arrangement to avoid the upper loan limit, the examiners recommended to the bank officers that the bonds be removed from the bank. The bank contacted Byron Gourley, a trusted Topeka bond broker, and asked him to pay a quiet visit to the Statehouse. On June 27 the circumspect Gourley, armed with a bank-supplied list of the serial numbers and descriptions of the questionable issues, headed straight for the Auditor's Office. There he determined from the bond transcripts that the state School Fund owned identical issues; in one instance the interest rates differed by a quarter of a percent, though everything else was identical. Puzzled, Gourley returned to report his findings to the bank officials and to the examiners. Still incredulous, he returned to the auditor's vault the following day to confirm his discovery.[22]

The examiners sought entry into Boyd's treasury vaults to make the direct comparison. Mark Rooney visited the treasury four times during the examination period. On the first visit, Rooney gave a treasury assistant a list of the Finney bonds and requested information on who was receiving credit for the coupons. The next day, Boyd told Rooney that he had had to stop the investigation: it would be illegal, he said, for him to release that information without the written approval of the attorney general. A few days later, Boyd told the frustrated examiner that he had written to Boynton, but apparently the letter had gotten lost. He would try again soon. The last trip was on July 3, Rooney's final day in town. An apologetic Boyd said that the staff had been awfully busy; perhaps they would get to the coupon business in a week or two, provided that the attorney general gave his permission. Boyd said that he would write to the examiner at his Kansas City office if anything turned up.[23] Let's hope that Rooney didn't hold his breath while waiting.

After hearing Gourley's alarming news, the bank's officers became more anxious than ever to rid themselves of the offending securities. Though they had received a very clear indication that the bonds were either stolen or forged, no serious consideration was given to calling the situation to the attention of the proper authorities. Their responsibility, they would argue later, was to the bank—first, last, and always. They simply did what they had to do to remove the highly questionable bonds from the bank, callously pushing them out to muddy the stream of commerce. Both the state of Kansas and two major investment firms would pay the price for the irresponsible folly of the bank officers' narrow-minded decision.

Carl McKeen would never admit that he had contacted his friend Warren Finney about removing the bonds. Somehow, miraculously it would seem, Finney just happened to drop by the bank on the afternoon of June 30 and told the officers that he guessed he would take those bonds off the bank's hands if that was all right with them. Son Ronald had paved the way for the final transaction the day before: first a word with Tom Boyd; then an urgent evening phone call to his cousin in Eureka, Edwin ("Ted") Tucker, vice-president of the Eureka Bank. Ronald insisted that Tucker come up to Topeka early the next morning—said that he would send a plane down for him and explain later. The next morning, Ronald told his perplexed cousin that a check was waiting for him at the state treasury. Tucker walked over to the Statehouse and picked it up from the assistant treasurer. Without giving it a close look, he shoved it into his pocket and returned to the Jayhawk. Up in the fifth-floor suite, Tucker did a double take when he had his first good look at the check, for it was made payable to his country bank for the staggering sum of $150,000. Ronald was starting to explain things to his bewildered cousin when Warren Finney arrived on the scene. The senior Finney was anxious to talk to Ronald alone, so Tucker was dismissed to cool his heels in the lobby for what turned out to be a five-hour wait.[24]

Ronald Finney had arranged with Boyd for a $150,000 deposit of state funds in the Eureka Bank, which the bank had neither solicited nor secured. Ronald then "borrowed" the money from the bank so that he could retrieve the vexatious bonds. The Finneys then used a rubber-stamp endorsement of the Eureka Bank, which they had obtained in some fashion, below which was added a rubber-stamp endorsement of Fidelity Bank. When Warren Finney arrived at the National Bank of Topeka with the state check in hand, the apprehensive Carl McKeen asked him to add his handwritten signature to the endorsements. The triply endorsed check was then deposited to the credit of the Fidelity Bank in its account at the National Bank of Topeka. Since the state deposit that was being tapped was also in that same Topeka bank, the transaction amounted to moving state funds from one account to another in the National Bank of Topeka. Finney then wrote a check on Fidelity Bank for the $150,000 in bonds and left with the nine issues wrapped insecurely in an old newspaper. As soon as Finney was out of sight, the bank examiners, who were lurking expectantly in the background, pounced on the check and had it photostated. They had already made photostatic copies of the bonds, which would prove useful in the subsequent federal investigation.[25]

In late afternoon the Finneys called the long-suffering Tucker up from the lobby and explained the deal to him. He protested that that sure was a lot of money for a small bank to be borrowing and that he didn't know if he could handle it.[26] Ronald assured his uneasy cousin that all was well, that the whole matter would be "cleaned up in four or five days."[27] Since the Finneys planned to put the recovered bonds in the treasury as security for the deposit in the Eureka Bank, this meant that cousin-nephew Ted owed them $150,000. He obligingly wrote a check to Fidelity for that amount. Thus the Finneys had offsetting entries in their books—a Eureka Bank loan and Tucker's check for the same amount—and no risk. The next day the bonds were duly credited to the Eureka Bank to secure the state deposit.[28]

From Boyd to Tucker to R. Finney to W. W. Finney to McKeen. The transaction resembled a Tinkers to Evers to Chance double play in the early days of baseball. The overwhelmed Tucker had gained an unsolicited $150,000 debt, which he owed the state of Kansas; the opportunity to write a $150,000 check to his uncle and cousin; title to $150,000 in very questionable bonds; and oh yes, a free round-trip plane ride between Eureka and Topeka. The poor man hadn't even gotten a scraggly little receipt for his trouble. And as subsequent events would reveal, all but $34,700 of the $150,000 in bonds were of the funny-Finney variety.[29]

AFTER A FEW DAYS of studious contemplation, Finney, the Younger, again swung into action. He had another good idea, he told his friend at the treasury. If he could get those bonds to Chicago, he had reason to believe that they could be sold without any difficulty. With the proceeds, his loan at the Eureka Bank could be repaid, and the bank could then return the state's deposit. That seemed like a pretty good idea to Boyd, who had begun to worry just a bit about the whole audacious maneuver. So the ever-accommodating treasurer gave his blessing to this new venture by permitting a private citizen to withdraw thousands of dollars in securities that were jointly owned by the state and the depository banks.[30]

On July 10 Boyd asked the young lady who worked in the treasury vault, Bernice Long, to bring all the Eureka Bank bonds into his office. Finney sorted through them and picked out $32,000, which he sold the next day to the Mitchell-Hutchins brokerage firm in Chicago. On July 20 a much more spectacular transaction occurred: Finney took to Chicago the bonds remaining from the "$150,000 caper"—that is, $118,600—plus $181,000 that Fidelity had used to secure two state accounts, thus leaving those accounts virtually unsecured. The grand total that was illegally removed on these two days came to a staggering $331,600. Of this amount, only $39,000 represented valid issues. One brokerage house returned a few bonds, including genuine issues that Finney had salted in among the bogus securities, because their advisors declared that the municipalities that backed the bonds were on too-shaky financial ground for their taste. All the remainder passed the scrutiny of the eagle-eyed LaSalle Street experts.[31]

The huge bundle of bonds that Finney took on July 20 called for some special precautionary measures. Finney asked Boyd to lend him an assistant to come along to supply protection. Boyd sent, as Finney's traveling companion, a treasury employee, Coryell Gove, who carried a gun in a concealed shoulder holster. The bonds were all sold as planned, most of them to Jackson Brothers, Boesel and Company. Finney used the bonds to secure his trading accounts and to obtain substantial loans from the brokerage firms. He received $271,000 in cash as a result of his July trips to Chicago, an amount that was never satisfactorily accounted for. Only a relatively small amount ever found its way back to the Eureka Bank to relieve the anxiety of Tom Boyd and Ted Tucker. The uninsured Jackson Brothers, Boesel and Company ended up going bankrupt. Its senior partner, sixty-three-year-old Arthur S. Jackson, who was a widely respected LaSalle Street leader, died "after a short illness" in New York City on September 28, immediately after his return from a trip to Europe. The possibility of suicide was rumored, though the official death certificate listed natural causes.[32]

BOYD'S TRIAL on state charges on two counts of illegal removal of $260,600 in bonds on July 10 and July 20 began on January 15, 1934, in Division Three of the Shawnee County District Court. The first count concerned $32,000 in bonds of the Eureka Bank that were taken to Chicago for sale by Ronald Finney on July 11; the second count included $118,600 of Eureka Bank's bonds and $110,000 of Fidelity's bonds that were taken on July 21. The defendant faced the possibility, if convicted on both counts, of serving four to ten years in the Kansas State Penitentiary.[33]

The prosecution team of Lester Goodell and Paul Harvey were joined by Sard Brewster, Landon's substitute for Hugo Wedell. In the shrewd and able Brewster, Landon had made the best possible choice. Brewster, now sixty-three years old, had grown up in Doniphan County and had served there as county attorney for ten years (1899–1909). After serving in both houses of the legislature, he completed two terms as attorney general (1915–19). He had been cofounder of the prestigious Topeka law firm of Wheeler, Brewster and Hunt, the oldest firm in Kansas. Appointed as the U.S. district attorney for Kansas in 1930, Brewster had gained an enviable reputation as one of the most vigorous prosecutors the state had ever had, especially in the field of liquor control. He had once prosecuted forty-four liquor violators in one fell swoop, obtaining convictions of over half of them at a single trial. Unkempt in appearance, the leonine-maned prosecutor could recite extensive chunks of Shakespeare verbatim as well as read the ancients in the original Greek and Latin.[34] Since Brewster was a man of "rather aggressive" demeanor in the courtroom, some observers felt that Landon had unleashed a monster when he had chosen him. "Eating breakfast with a grizzly bear is a joy," Dutch Shultz warned, "as compared with being on the opposite side of a rough and tumble lawsuit with Brewster."[35]

Tinkham Veale, an able and well-known Topeka lawyer, with Leon Lundblade as his assistant, defended Tom Boyd. Both had previously served as county attorneys. On the bench of division three sat the veteran highly regarded jurist Otis E. Hungate. To him, the dean of Shawnee County judges, a hard-fought, highly publicized case was nothing new. In 1925, on the day before he left office, Governor Jonathan Davis and his son had been charged with selling prison pardons. Hungate had heard the case, his first on the Shawnee County bench.[36]

At the hearing on preliminary motions on January 8—in a major victory for the prosecution—the judge ruled that the testimony given in September by treasury employee Bernice Long relative to the Boyd embezzlement charge was admissible, even though it had been given in response to a different charge. Miss Long had died shortly after the preliminary hearing on the charge of embezzlement. The prosecution announced that Boyd would be tried on the embezzlement charges at the conclusion of the trial regarding illegal removal, but that case never came to trial. The U.S. District Attorney's Office said that it preferred to try Boyd first on its mail-fraud charge, but that case was not tried either.[37]

Two days before the trial began, Ronald Finney broke his lengthy silence to give a public answer to a letter from his old friend Tom Boyd:

> I beg to acknowledge your letter of recent date suggesting that, due to the fact that there has been so much publicity given in the newspapers ... to the so-called bond scandal, which has more or less associated you with the same, that you think it would be fair to you that I make a

public statement regarding my knowledge of your participation, if any, in the same.

In reply, will say that I know of no way you could have learned of the existence of any forged bonds until about the time of the investigation when it was published in the newspapers.[38]

Kansas leaned forward expectantly to await the anticipated sensational disclosures during the trial. The state announced that it expected to go deeply into the social as well as the financial activities of Boyd and Finney. Their witness list comprised 178 names from all parts of the state. Since Boynton's impeachment trial had commenced the week before, the reading public, which was already nearly satiated after months of news about the scandal, almost had more than it could digest for the next couple of weeks.

On the opening day, attorney Veale filed for a continuance (which was denied), on the ground that newspaper articles had so inflamed the public mind that it was impossible to hold a fair trial. The articles had "worked people up to a frenzy," counsel claimed. Following John Schenck's example, Veale and Lundblade questioned each venireman closely with regard to his political interest in the case. Each prospect was asked if the fact that the governor-prosecutor had asked for an appropriation for the case had impressed them; if they had been influenced by the appointment of Brewster; or if they expected to get a job from the governor. After two days of this, the jury of nine men and three women was selected from among the twenty-two persons who had been questioned.[39]

Sard Brewster summarized the state's case in the opening statement: "We expect to show that this whole thing is the most sordid mess in which a state officer has ever been involved." Then followed a parade of witnesses detailing the "$150,000 caper"—Edwin Tucker, examiner Rooney, bank vice-president John Kirk, assistant treasurer Austin Logan, and several employees of Chicago brokerage firms. Because the maze of credits and debits arising from the intricate manipulation confused the court and the jury, it frequently had to be retraced. A broker at Mitchell-Hutchins testified that Finney often mixed business and pleasure in Chicago. In late June a Finney party had been together from early morning to late at night, "seeing the sights" and attending a rehearsal of the 101 Wild West Show on the Midway. In addition to Finney and Boyd, who had flown up together, the party included the Finney informants Harold Trusler and Dyke O'Neil as well as Colonel Zack Miller of the 101 Ranch.[40]

The payments of money by Finney to Boyd played a key part in the prosecution's case. The state traced $7,200 from Finney to Boyd during the May-August period, including $1,200 that was wired by Chicago brokers to Boyd, even though he had never been a customer of theirs. A guard at the state treasury had given an unequivocal statement to investigators in August that he had made a cash deposit of $3,500 (which he received directly from Finney) for Boyd in a Topeka bank; that he had watched the teller count out the money in $20 bills and make out a deposit slip to Boyd's daughter, Helen. On the stand the nervous witness had second thoughts, testifying that the envelope had actually been sealed, so he had had no way of knowing how much it had contained or whose account had been credited. The more he was examined and cross-examined, the more confused the loyal employee became. After that session a furious Lester Goodell summoned the reluctant witness to his office for a conference. The county attorney subsequently announced that he was contemplating arresting the guard for perjury. He didn't.[41]

The mayor and city clerk of Kismet—the brothers Prater—testified that in December, 1932, they had visited the Jayhawk Hotel, where they had been introduced to fifteen or twenty citizens who were socializing there, including the cigar-smoking Boyd. They had also been introduced to a tall, slim man, who had been palmed off as Roland Boynton, the attorney general. In cross-examination, Veale asked sarcastically if perhaps they were mistaken, if it might have been the Shawnee County attorney that they had met in that den of iniquity. Goodell, taking sharp exception to that shot, immediately took the stand to testify heatedly that in 1932 he had not even known Ronald Finney.[42]

The state rested its case on Saturday of the first week. Due to a state law regulating the activities of jurors on Sunday, Judge Hungate cautioned the bailiff to allow no card-playing. So the resourceful jurors resorted to a popular and still legal game in Puritanland—dominoes.[43]

SEVERAL DIFFERENT PLANKS made up the defense's platform for Boyd. Counsel argued that Boyd had been duped by Finney; that the state laws didn't specifically direct the treasurer about how to handle state funds; and that—above all—Boyd had never harbored a single evil thought of defrauding the state of one thin dime. The defense pointed out that other prominent Kansans had gone to Chicago, had run around with Ronald Finney, and had escaped with their substantial reputations still intact.[44] The twelve character witnesses for Boyd included several Santa Fe employees, members of boards of education and county commissions, and the president of the Chamber of Commerce. "We are trying to show," Tinkham Veale asserted, "that Mr. Boyd received no aid from the governor and the treasury board in depositing this state money." For example, one day during the summer of 1933 the treasurer had met the governor in the corridor and had complained that he had millions to deposit and no satisfactory place to put it. Landon, putting his arm around Boyd's shoulder in a fraternal manner, replied: "I haven't time to take care of that matter, Tom, I'll leave it to your judgment."[45]

The chief clerk in the treasury vault, Ruth Pennick, testified that Finney spent several days in the vault in mid July, listing bonds, and that he had left a "satchel full of bonds" on July 20 when he went to Chicago. The defense claimed that the contents of the satchel—which were never disclosed and probably were known only to Finney—secured the bonds that he took to Chicago. Finney often sent candy and flowers to the girls at the treasury, Pennick said. She stated that Garnet Stiers, another treasury clerk, was "sick and tired" of seeing Finney in the vault so much. But the broker usually got what he wanted. On one occasion Finney had wanted to use the desk of Pennick's assistant in the vault and had imperiously instructed the assistant to move. He did.[46]

Mrs. Boyd took the stand to express her complete faith and confidence in her husband. They had, she said, put up $1,200 with Finney as a market speculation in February, 1933. The profit had grown to $6,000 by May, when she had asked Finney for $3,500 so they could make a down payment on their Shawnee County farm. Later they bought a second farm with a down payment of $2,500, which also came from market profits. Mrs. Boyd admitted that she knew nothing about the details of the speculation—what Finney bought, how much, or when. But she did trust him implicitly and felt that he was "very competent and successful."[47]

THE CLOSING ARGUMENTS began on January 25 in a jammed courtroom. The eager spectators filled the aisles, pushing up next to the counsel's tables and the judge's dais. The evidence, which was often involved and highly technical, included 110 exhibits offered by the state and 112 by the defense. The judge repeatedly had to urge the attorneys to clarify their presentations for his and the jury's benefit.[48]

Veale attempted to put as much daylight as possible between his client and the "arch fiend" Finney. "Down at the Jayhawk," he summarized, "[Ronald Finney] was a high-pressure man dealing in millions of dollars, with a reputation for being wealthy, a reputation for making immense amounts of money. A man who impressed state officers, big business men, bankers, with his magnetism. He had a way of making people believe in him. . . . Tom Boyd is just as innocent of any wrongdoing, as if [Finney] had robbed the vault while Tom was home asleep." Veale added that the governor and the others on the Treasury Board, in addition to his client, had a basic responsibility with respect to state deposits. "But the governor isn't on trial here. . . . And I don't think Tom Boyd should be either."[49]

But it was Sard Brewster—the rough-and-tumble veteran "who walked like a bear"—who held the packed throng enraptured in a dramatic hour of masterful summing up. All signs of levity disappeared as the hushed crowd hung on every word in tense silence.[50]

Referring to Veale's charge that the death of treasury employee Bernice Long had been caused by the hounding of the prosecution, Brewster responded in kind: "Her murderers sit in the county jail and in this courtroom. She rises from her grave to tell you that Tom Boyd told her to bring [him] the Eureka bonds . . . while Ronald Finney was in his office last July."[51] The defense, Brewster contended, had changed its strategy and had decided to make a scapegoat of Ronald Finney. "When Finney is caught . . . short in the . . . market," Brewster roared, "he turns to his friend Boyd, the man who fenced for him all thru the years. . . . [Finney] returns [from Chicago] sans money, sans bonds, sans everything. Then does Tom Boyd ask the governor to arrest him?"[52]

Brewster declared that he had much sympathy for the Boyd family, mother and children. He really couldn't blame Mrs. Boyd for defending her husband by telling the tale of money that came from alleged market speculation. Then, "transfixing the defendant with a piercing gaze," he stalked close to his prey. Shaking his finger almost in the face of the accused, he insinuated that while Boyd was willing enough to defend himself by putting his wife and children on the witness stand, he wasn't man enough to take the stand himself. "The wife and boy were put on the stand to testify to these"—and then Brewster hesitated. Boyd, who was beside himself with rage, suddenly rose and started to move toward his tormentor. He had to be physically restrained by counsel and by one of his burly sons.[53]

After deliberating seven hours on January 26, the jury retired for the night. Shortly after they had convened, they asked to have the testimony of Bernice Long, and then that of Edwin Tucker, reread. They still appeared to be confused by the mass of bewildering financial evidence. But on the next morning, they returned a verdict of guilty on both counts. Surrounded by his family, Boyd heard the verdict "without visible emotion." Members of the jury reported that a decision on one count had been quickly reached, but that a decision on the second count had required five ballots before a verdict had been reached.[54]

THE PRESS'S RESPONSE to the conviction reflected the prevailing Kansas mood. The *Capital* felt the verdict was proper and just:

> The State Treasurer was out to put money in his pocket. He conspired with his crony, Finney, . . . loaned him state money without security, gave him privileged access to his office, . . .
> Finney's plea of guilty and Boyd's conviction are reassuring to the state, following the greatest public scandal in Kansas history. The success of the state . . . will have a wholesome effect, proving that neither social position and connections nor the popularity of politicians who reach high office will protect them in wrong doing.[55]

The *Wichita Beacon* seconded the motion at a higher pitch:

> Once in the net of illegality Boyd found . . . it simpler to pursue the easy way than to extricate himself from a situation that could only lead to disclosure and disgrace. Yet even so, it is difficult to see how he could have been dragged into the worst political mess in the history of Kansas by the addle-pated, egotistic, slippery, crooked Finney, except thru his own desire for the fleshpots that his limited legitimate income did not permit him to enjoy.[56]

BEFORE THE SENTENCING on February 17 Judge Hungate heard a spirited argument for a new trial. Tinkham Veale presented eleven points on which, he claimed, the court had erred: it had given improper instructions to the jury; it had permitted misconduct of counsel (Brewster); and it had especially erred when it had permitted in evidence the testimony of Bernice Long that had been given at the preliminary hearing in the embezzlement case.[57]

Challenging the state "to show that Tom Boyd had one bit of fraudulent intent," Veale complained that the people were in a "convicting mood." He indicted the press, declaring that "it was an impossibility to get a fair trial because the newspaper boys kept the public aroused." He characterized the law under which Boyd was prosecuted as a "highly technical, vicious, vindictive statute. The matter of right and wrong has nothing to do with it. [We have] asked the state to prosecute under the embezzlement charge where moral turpitude is involved. But they were afraid to try that case altho they knew we wanted them to." Lester Goodell quickly responded that if Veale were so anxious to have his client tried on that charge, he would accommodate him by moving that case to the head of the list of suits going to trial the following Monday morning.⁵⁸

After denying the motion for a new trial, Judge Hungate sentenced Tom Boyd to the Kansas State Penitentiary for two to five years on each of the two counts, a total of four to ten years. The defense attorneys immediately filed notice that they would appeal to the Kansas Supreme Court. Boyd remained at liberty on a $28,000 bond on the two state charges.⁵⁹

In the spring, Boyd received a continuance on his appeal to the October term of the Supreme Court so that the legal abstract could be prepared. In their December 8, 1934, opinion the Kansas Supreme Court found no merit in any of the defense's contentions. On December 27 the defendant filed for a rehearing; the motion was denied on February 2, 1935. Boyd seriously considered taking an appeal to the United States Supreme Court, on the ground that the court had erred in allowing Bernice Long's testimony. Defense counsel felt that admission of her testimony had violated the constitutional protection given to those who have been charged with a crime to have witnesses face them in court so that they can be subjected to cross-examination. Boyd—after two postponements so that he could decide whether to make an appeal to the highest court in the land and after consulting with Topeka lawyer Harry Colmery, who advised on the futility of that course—decided against taking any further legal action with its attendant heavy expense. A bitter and truculent Tom Boyd entered the State Penitentiary on March 11, 1935, thirteen months after he had been sentenced.⁶⁰

THE SIX INDICTMENTS made by the federal grand jury in December, 1933—most especially that of Carl McKeen, president of the National Bank of Topeka—had dealt the dazed financial community a severe shock. Friends of McKeen's had put up a brave front, claiming that the indictment gave the accused the opportunity "to substitute truth for whispered rumors and insinuations." The bank's board of directors stood loyally behind McKeen, fully convinced that he was "absolutely innocent of any wrong or violation of any statute."⁶¹

Carl McKeen stood charged with the misapplication of $146,172.71 of monies of the National Bank of Topeka and with intent to injure and defraud the bank and the state of Kansas as a result of the "$150,000 caper." McKeen was charged as the principal; Tom Boyd and the two Finneys were accused of aiding and abetting. The criminal count charged that

McKeen knew, or should have known, that the $150,000 check was issued for the "private and personal use" of Boyd and Finney; that the check was not used "for the benefit of the payee, the Eureka Bank"; that the Finneys were using state funds to discharge Ronald Finney's personal debt to the bank; and that McKeen knew that the Finney indebtedness was collateralized "by certain forged or stolen Kansas municipal bonds."[62]

McKeen's demurrer to the indictment was filed on March 2, 1934. The demurrer charged that the government's indictment was "so general, vague, indefinite and uncertain" that the defendant could not properly "prepare his defense thereto."[63] A few months later the newly appointed U.S. district attorney, S. S. Alexander, would publicly accuse his predecessor, Sard Brewster, of imperfectly drawing up the document.[64] Oral arguments were heard in Topeka before Judge Richard J. Hopkins on March 9. Dan Cowie, Brewster's assistant, argued for the government. "Why," asked Charlie Trapp in the *Pink Rag,* "was Cowie, not Brewster, at the hearing? . . . Here was a $150,000 case and pulling down one of the highest positions in state financial circles. Just why was the roaring oratory of the high muck-a-muck stilled?"[65]

On March 25 Judge Hopkins announced "indictment insufficient; demurrer sustained." In his written opinion, Hopkins held that McKeen couldn't be held responsible for Boyd's action or the Finneys' duplicity.[66] "I am of the opinion that the facts set out tend to show a transaction in the regular course of banking business, rather than a wrongful conversion," the judge wrote. "It may be that the mere fact that defendant's bank was having business relations with Ronald Finney put the defendant under suspicion of wrong-doing."[67]

In March, Governor Landon asked both Boynton and Harris to investigate the prospects of bringing successful state criminal action against McKeen, but eventually the matter was dropped. After McKeen's success, the other federal defendants—both of the Finneys, Boyd, Caldwell, Cooke, and Harner—filed demurrers. On December 3, 1934, a year and a day after they had been drawn, the indictments of all the defendants were dismissed, except for those involving fraudulent use of the mails. These, too, were dismissed in October, 1935.[68] Though the federal investigators had uncovered the case, their prosecutions had come to naught.

Pleased with the outcome of the Boyd case, the hard-working prosecution began to do their homework for the upcoming trial of Leland Caldwell, the first lieutenant in the Finney army.

11

The First Lieutenant

ooooooooooooooooooooooooooooooooo ooooooooooooooooooo

LELAND C. ("LEE") CALDWELL, Ronald Finney's jack-of-all trades, was born in 1902 in rural Shawnee County of Scotch-Irish parents. Reared in Topeka, he had lived in the capital city most of his adult life. Dropping out of high school after a year, the slim, sandy-haired youth had gone to work as a messenger boy at the Santa Fe Shops around 1916. From then until 1929, he had knocked around Topeka in various dead-end jobs, including short clerical stints in two banks. After being laid off from a white-collar position with the Santa Fe in 1929, he went to work as a clerk in the treasury vault, where he first met Finney. After a year in Boyd's office, Caldwell decided to seek his fortune in Oklahoma, where he found gainful employment with a marriage mart in Oklahoma City. After a short tenure with that agency, he returned to Topeka and went to work for Finney in November, 1930.[1]

Caldwell possessed a number of traits that might have caught his future employer's scrutinizing eye. Perhaps it was Caldwell's resolute determination to get ahead in this world (he loved money and the things that it bought), his tractable willingness to take orders (he asked the boss no embarrassing questions), his clean-cut presentability to clients and prospects (he was handsome, so the ladies said), or his taciturn discreteness on matters of sensitivity (he tended to be secretive and a loner). Perhaps his unusual avocation—which during his treasury tenure had become almost an obsession—attracted Finney. Caldwell, it seemed, loved nothing more than to copy the signatures of authorities that he found on official documents that were lying around the Treasurer's Office. Hour after painstaking hour he would sit at his desk and practice copying the signatures of Alfred Landon, Roland Boynton, Will

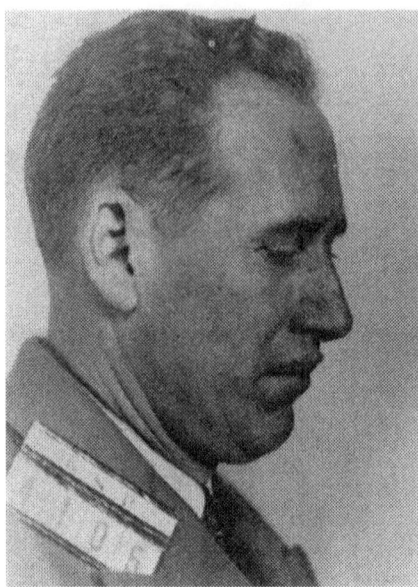

Leland C. Caldwell (Kansas State Penitentiary)

French, Tom Boyd, Frank Ryan, and Charles Hobbs. He showed a lot of pride in his penmanship; he got really good at it too. After a while you could scarcely tell his handiwork from the originals. But he may have gotten too wrapped up in it at times. Boyd's not-very-understanding secretary complained that too often Caldwell spent his time laboriously practicing his penmanship instead of doing his assigned work.[2]

When Ronald Finney began to do a volume business in municipal bonds in early 1931, Caldwell was given a new assignment. Since Caldwell was familiar with the bond business from his year in the state treasury, Finney asked his new employee to compile a master list of all Kansas municipal bonds with interest of five percent or greater. Using this list, Finney approached numerous municipalities with his fat-commission bond-exchange deal. As the brokerage business expanded, Finney sent his trusted assistant into every part of the state by car and by plane. Usually Finney himself made the initial contact and agreed on the specific terms with the local governmental unit. Caldwell then came in for the mop-up—delivering checks and bonds for local signatures, ironing out minor problems, and in general expediting the consummation of the deal, legitimate or otherwise. He often spent hours at a time—occasionally as many as three or four days in a row—inspecting transcripts in the auditor's vault, or exchanging bonds in the treasury vault. The financial community soon came to understand that the low-key Caldwell spoke and acted for the boisterous Finney with the full authority of the big bossman. In addition to the more usual business-related duties, the thirty-one-year-old Caldwell assumed the hybrid role of valet, chauffeur, factotum, or what have you. One of his duties entailed rousing the boss out of bed every morning at the Jayhawk and setting out his clothes for the day.[3]

Caldwell often dealt with the Topeka printing firms that handled the Finney business. It was he who gave the printers the contrived stories of why a second (or third) issue had to be printed. Following the boss's lead, he typically presented the work hurriedly as a rush order for which he cheerfully paid a premium, leaving little or no time for questions or deliberation. For an especially skeptical printer the first lieutenant could render an academy-award-winning performance. Assuming an indignant attitude toward his boss, the talented assistant would verbally abuse Finney for his carelessness in handling the bond details. Unfortunately, he complained to his gullible listener, another printing would be required in order to correct the error.[4]

On June 18, 1932, Caldwell walked into the J. C. Darling Stamp Company and ordered a seal for the nonexistent Wheat Board of Pratt County. The phrase "Wheat Board" was to be placed in the center, with the name of the locality at the periphery. Later the center would be mutilated by a coin so as to render an illegible impression. Caldwell wrote the name of J. L. Thompson on the order sheet. As bad luck would have it, the saleslady had known Caldwell by sight for years, though they had not been formally introduced: she had frequently seen him singing in the Methodist Church choir. During the following weeks, Caldwell returned to order several additional "Wheat Board" seals, paying in cash and always signing the order with the name of J. L. Thompson. The clerk kept her own counsel and never confronted him about the fabricated name, apparently deciding that that was his own business. He paid his last visit to the Kansas Avenue shop on November 8, 1932.[5] Evidently by that time Finney and Caldwell had acquired all the tools of their trade that they needed.

THE CALDWELL TRIAL began in Topeka on February 5, 1934, a week after the Boyd verdict and while the French trial was still in progress a few blocks away in the Statehouse. The cast of principals remained essentially unchanged from the Boyd trial except for the defendant and his attorneys. Goodell, Brewster, and Harvey led the prosecution; Judge Hungate occupied the bench. Roy Angle of Wichita, assisted by F. J. Rost of Topeka, represented the defendant. Caldwell's original attorney, it should be remembered, had been Judge Paul H. Heinz, before he had been called by Landon for higher duty. Caldwell was to be tried on the Salina School District charges. On motion of the prosecution at the outset, all but one of the uttering charges was dropped. Since the $20,000 Salina issue had been in the $500 denomination, forty bonds had been printed. Thus, Caldwell faced a charge of forty counts of forgery and a single count of uttering.[6]

Flint Hills Peggy remarked that going to the numerous trials had become something like drinking whisky; "You can't stop." Juries tend to be like frogs, she said; "You can't tell . . . how far they will jump." The witty correspondent added that perhaps the chief value of the trials had been the opportunity it afforded those from "remote parts to journey to [Topeka] to testify, thereby broadening themselves a bit. It was the only way that farmers could get any traveling done, except riding to Kansas City or Wichita . . . with a load of hogs."[7]

Dressed in a dark-blue suit, the debonair Caldwell watched the selection of the jury with intense interest. He was surrounded by his close relatives, including his petite bride of a year. It was his second marital experience; he had two children from a previous marriage. Prominent among the 142 witnesses who were subpoenaed was the first Mrs. Caldwell. Evidently it hadn't been a completely amicable parting, for she volunteered to furnish samples of Lee's handwriting. The public-spirited former wife attended all the sessions, avidly following the proceedings and cheerfully supplying useful information to the state.[8]

In Lester Goodell's opening statement, he confidently told the jury that the evidence would show that Caldwell had obtained transcripts from the Auditor's Office, had ordered the bogus bonds printed, had bought the fake seals under an assumed name, and then had forged the names of the appropriate officials on the bonds. And, indeed, the evidence did just that.[9]

Many of the witnesses had appeared at Ronald Finney's or at Boyd's trial, or at both.[10] A key witness for the prosecution, J. C. Shearman, the handwriting expert, testified for more than two days. Shearman declared that the same person who had written the script on samples of writing that had been admitted by both sides to be that of Caldwell had also written the signatures of the Salina and Hutchinson officials. The defense, in cross-examination, tried futilely to shake Shearman's credibility as a witness. They questioned him in minute detail regarding pens and inks and the forger's ability to duplicate so closely the signatures of the four Salina officials on the forty individual bonds. The veteran Shearman admitted that the man who had done it possessed extraordinary skill. Though they cross-examined the Wichita expert for more than a full day, the defense hadn't begun to exhaust its detailed questions (though it had begun to exhaust the audience), when the weary judge stepped in and called a halt. In the record, the attorneys filed 290 additional questions that they had prepared but had been prevented from asking by the long-suffering judge.[11]

IN ITS OPENING STATEMENT on February 13 the nearly desperate defense asserted that it hoped to prove that the first lieutenant was really only a know-nothing errand boy; that he had only been dutifully following instructions; that he didn't fully appreciate the depths of Finney's duplicity; that he hadn't enjoyed the boss's confidence—when Finney had really big blockbusting business to discuss, he usually sent the "errand boy" to the Jayhawk's lobby to cool his heels. Hoping to exonerate his client by a vivid demonstration of the all-pervasiveness of the Finney contacts, attorney Angle read off a lengthy list of regular and sometime visitors to the Jayhawk suite. It sounded like "the Kansas social register."[12]

At the beginning of the second week, to a packed house, Caldwell took the stand as a witness in his own behalf. He admitted that he had frequently taken transcripts out of the Auditor's Office and that he had ordered bond issues to be printed on the basis of data contained therein. But he flatly and categorically denied the forgeries. He gave the eager throng a glimpse of his role as valet. He went to work at 7 A.M., sent Finney's clothes downstairs to the tailor to be pressed, got them back, laid them out, and then called the chief. While Finney was dressing, Caldwell ordered breakfast. Finney customarily took all of his meals in his rooms. Though Caldwell ordered the meals, he never ate with the "Kingfish." Always following Finney's instructions unquestioningly and to the letter, the loyal assistant never imagined that his employer might be up to some dirty tricks.[13] "Did you ever have any suspicion of Mr. Finney?" he was asked on direct examination. "Not once," came the straightfaced reply.[14]

Though the prosecution hurled "blasts of incredulity" at him, Caldwell stubbornly stuck to his story that he was only a poor, ignorant hired hand. He did admit having placed the orders for the seals—a changed stance, since he had denied it when originally questioned in August.[15] Finney had told Caldwell that he and "J. L. Thompson" were organizing wheat-control boards by which they hoped to control the markets and force the price up. So far as Caldwell knew, Thompson was a real person, though, he admitted, he had never met him. "Isn't it a fact that there isn't any such person?" Goodell asked. "I don't know," Caldwell responded; "I believed there was when Mr. Finney told me." "Do you believe everything he tells you?" "Not any more," the rueful assistant replied.[16]

Goodell bored in on other discrepancies between Caldwell's current testimony and statements that he had made following his arrest. The "errand boy" answered guardedly, declaring that as a Finney employee, he hadn't wanted to get his boss into any trouble when he was initially questioned by the authorities. Goodell did force Caldwell to admit that even though his salary was only $1,800 a year, he had been able to make a $2,400 down payment on a fashionable home and that he owned two automobiles and an airplane. Caldwell unconvincingly explained that since he drove seventy thousand miles a year on Finney business, he had been able to make the luxurious purchases from savings on the gas money—at two cents a mile.[17]

Caldwell, like his boss, admitted to having a "blind" telephone number. Why the unlisted number? He didn't want girls "calling him or bothering his wife after they were married." Caldwell named several long-term employees on the monthly Finney payroll, including lawyers Dyke O'Neil and John Hamilton. The pliant assistant's response to a Goodell query near the conclusion of his testimony seemed to sum it all up. Would he have "jumped off a bridge" if instructed to do so by Finney? "If he'd paid me, I would have," the young man unflinchingly replied.[18]

IN A PITILESS HOUR of summation, the prosecution drew a contemptuous picture of Caldwell's activities and protestations. Declaring that he was much more than an innocent errand boy, Goodell observed that if Caldwell hadn't known about the forgeries, "he must have been deaf, dumb and blind."[19] The county attorney went on to compliment Finney's factotum on his penmanship. "A fine job of forging," he said admiringly, "one of the cleverest forgeries [I] ever heard of."[20] Caldwell's mother, becoming ill from the harsh words that were being hurled at her son by the county attorney, made a dramatic exit from the courtroom while the damning summation continued in full force. At the conclusion of Goodell's remarks, the defense—in a surprise move—waived its right to make closing arguments. That maneuver denied the expectant crowd a chance to hear Sard Brewster give his patented "fiery summary," which he had been primed to do.[21]

On February 15, after four hours of deliberation and five ballots, the jury returned a verdict of guilty of first-degree forgery on all forty counts. They found him not guilty on the single count of uttering the bonds. The harsh verdict caught many by surprise. Speculation along Kansas Avenue had run that Caldwell would only be found guilty on from one to ten counts. This verdict opened up the possibility that the accomplice would receive a longer sentence than the chief perpetrator.[22]

ON MARCH 2 Judge Hungate sentenced Caldwell to the maximum term allowable—one to twenty-one years on each of the forty counts, an ungrand total of 40 to 840 years. The sentence of confinement "at hard labor" represented the longest one stemming from the bond scandal. In fact, it was the longest sentence in Kansas criminal history. It took the judge fifteen minutes to read the entire sentence, count by count, and he had to do it twice. After Caldwell had been returned to jail following the initial pronouncement of the sentence, a defense attorney called the court's attention to the fact that the judge had failed to rule on a defense motion to stay the judgment. So, poor Caldwell had to be hauled out of jail and returned to the courthouse, where the judge perfunctorily overruled the motion and then read the entire sentence once again.[23] Perhaps for a sentence of that magnitude, it was appropriate to have two readings.

After the sentencing, Caldwell, who had been almost as officially silent as his boss had been since his arrest, released a lengthy formal statement to the people of Kansas through the press:

> I worked for Ronald Finney as any man would have worked for an employer. . . . I signed no bonds, neither did I intentionally do anything else to defraud the state of Kansas. . . . I don't consider the fact that I have been made the victim of circumstances and have been convicted by powerful political factors in Kansas, a disgrace to either myself or my family. . . .
>
> I am asking you to demand that this bond scandal have a thoro and non-political investigation because only thru such an investigation will the true facts come out. Those facts . . . will convince you beyond any doubt that what I say now is true. . . . My only hope is in the investigations themselves because . . . I haven't the money or political influence to fight for myself . . . [and] without those two, no man, no matter how innocent he is, has a chance in this case.[24]

Lester Goodell scoffed at the statement, pointing out that Caldwell had had numerous opportunities to tell everything he knew. Caldwell, he said, had never told them anything that they hadn't already known.[25] The *State Journal*, however, thought that Caldwell should be encouraged to tell all:

> All through the weary months the . . . authorities were seeking the facts, Caldwell remained silent. If his lips were sealed by the hope that his former employer and powerful political associates would help him, [he] must have been disillusioned by . . . [the] recent sentence. . . . The public wants the Caldwell story, if he will tell it, even this late. . . .
>
> If Caldwell or anyone else . . . has any information . . . about the gigantic fraud, it is his duty to come forward with it now, . . . before the heat of a political campaign arouses prejudice and causes the

selection of unfit persons for offices, or does an injustice to those innocent. Let's silence the whispering by shouting the truth.[26]

On March 7 an aggravated Lester Goodell had Caldwell brought to his office to give the suddenly talkative young man a last chance to tell whatever it was that he had to tell. "What I meant in the statement was that I'm innocent of any crime," Caldwell told the county attorney, "therefore, there must be others involved." "Can't you tell us names of anyone you suspect?" "No, I wasn't in any position to know," responded Caldwell. "But, I know one thing—I didn't forge a single one of those bonds. . . . I'm going to Lansing and work hard and try to make friends, and get out as soon as possible." He added: "Naturally, I don't bear [Ronald Finney] such a friendly feeling. He got me into all this trouble, then refused to help me out."[27]

In their infinite wisdom and humanitarian mercy the 1903 legislature had sought to salvage those prisoners that were salvagable by passing the indeterminate-sentence law. The statute provided for a minimum and maximum term for all offenses except the two most heinous crimes that one could commit in Kansas: murder in the first degree and violation of the state liquor laws. Caldwell went to Lansing on March 9 to begin serving his 40-to-840-year sentence. Only Methuselah could have looked forward to much of a life after doing that much time.[28] Since Caldwell could anticipate a life somewhat shorter then Methuselah's, his future didn't appear to be particularly bright.

ABOUT THE TIME Caldwell left for Lansing, some public resentment at his exorbitant sentence began to surface. A petition that was circulated by his friends and relatives called for a full and complete pardon. They naïvely believed that if public opinion opposed to the lengthy sentence were focused and forcefully brought to the governor's attention, Caldwell would be pardoned forthwith.[29] Many conscientious people did feel that Caldwell had been made a goat of for the "big boys'" benefit. One irate citizen wrote to Landon that at a town he had recently visited, "they said if things did not go right for him [Caldwell] they were coming 6,000 strong with ropes."[30]

A Topeka man made a poignant connection for the governor between the just-completed trial and the next election:

> I am one of many, many people who are dissatisfied with the treatment Caldwell . . . received during his recent trial. I attended that trial and I wish to tell you that it was a disgrace to our state. The young

man was convicted before he went to trial by powerful political interests of this state....

That trial lost you the votes of the working class of people of our state, Mr. Landon, because to them it proved that in our courts of so-called "justice" the poor man hasn't a chance! ...

That young man has been, shall we call it "framed," by both Ronald Finney and those in Kansas and Washington connected with him, and his character and future have been sacrificed upon the altar of political corruption. Yes, but the people have not been fooled.[31]

A Muscotah man wrote to tell Landon that folks thereabouts weren't very happy with the way things had been going:

> The people of this end of the state are watching the progress of the bond trials, and are not very well pleased with the results, so far.
> Hundreds of dollars expended and not one of them in the pen, where they belong.
> Poor Mr. Caldwell is made the goat because his money ran out. The whole thing is a disgrace to our fair state.[32]

To which Landon immediately responded:

> I thoroughly agree with you that if Leland Caldwell were to be the only one to suffer because of the bond troubles, it would be a great disgrace to the state of Kansas.... Both ... Goodell and ... Brewster gave him every opportunity to come clean and tell the story but he still persisted in covering up the bigger criminals.[33]

THE THEORY that perhaps all had not been told and that a forgery ring might still be at work received a decided boost late that winter. From Dodge City came the alarming report that a duplicate coupon had been paid at the state treasury on a Ford County bond. Roland Boynton sprang into action with energy that you wouldn't believe. He wired the county attorney to bring the coupons to Topeka at once so that he could launch a thorough investigation. Immediately after that hurried conference the newly galvanized attorney general left for Dodge City, the better to direct the investigation himself.

In this instance the truth wore a prosaic dress. After accidentally spoiling a sheet of coupons, the printer of the bonds had carelessly tossed it into the nearest wastebasket. Subsequently the sheet had blown out of a trash wagon, and a mill employee had picked it up on the street and presented one of the $29 coupons at a local bank. They sent it to Topeka, where it was promptly paid by the still-muddled state treasury. But the sheepish finder made good the loss, and the state sat back and breathed a giant sigh of relief. The treasury promised to do better, and it used the scare to renew its perennial plea for additional help, the better to make a thorough check on incoming coupons and bonds.[34] And Rolie Boynton—the intrepid investigator—wore a self-congratulatory smile for weeks.

12

Honest, But...

THE SCANDAL'S most tragic figure was Roland Boynton, the attorney general. Fundamentally he was honest, decent, and able, but as in all tragedy, he had a fatal flaw. Cursed with devastating naïveté and gullibility as regards his friend Ronald Finney, he paid a tremendous price for a large friendship and a tiny profit.

Born on May 29, 1891, in Manitou, Colorado, Boynton was William Allen White's first cousin, once removed. White's mother, Mary Anne Hatten, was the older sister of Boynton's grandmother, "Aunt Kate." Boynton's mother, Catharine, who was born in Kansas, had migrated to Colorado shortly before Roland was born. She talked so much of "Kansas and its glories" to her impressionable young son that upon graduating from high school in 1910, he decided to attend the University of Kansas. He pledged Phi Delta Theta—the fraternity that both White and Ronald Finney belonged to—and graduated with an A.B. (in liberal arts) in 1914 and a law degree in 1916. After he came to Kansas as a student, the cherubic-looking Boynton established a second home in Emporia, frequently spending weekends and vacations at the W. A. White home.[1]

Boynton enlisted as a private in the army in June, 1917. He served two years, including a year and a half in France as an officer in the Rainbow Division. After a short postwar period in California, when he lived with his mother, the jowly, heavy-set former serviceman returned to Emporia and a law partnership. Elected as Lyon County attorney in 1920, he was reelected in 1922. In 1926 he received an appointment as assistant attorney general. His major assignments included gambling and liquor control, *inter alia*. As the successful candidate for attorney general in 1930 and in 1932, he

Roland Boynton, attorney general *(Kansas City Star)*

succeeded his boss, William A. Smith, who moved up to the Supreme Court bench.[2]

A Mason and a member of the Congregational Church, Boynton served as vice-president of the University of Kansas Alumni Association in 1931/32 and became its president in 1932/33. He married Mary Elizabeth ("Betty") Coley, a native of Oklahoma who was a Phi Beta Kappa graduate of the University of Oklahoma. Betty and Roland had met in Emporia on one of her frequent trips there to visit an aunt.[3]

Mr. White always claimed that the serious and introvertish Boynton "grew up under my wing." The patronage-minded editor denied that he had used his influence with Attorney General Griffith to help Boynton gain the state appointment ("Griffith, rather against my judgment and absolutely without my suggestion, appointed him Assistant Attorney General"). According to White, the young lawyer was "absolutely incorruptible," with a "tremendous lot of quiet courage." "The only trouble," the editor wrote Alf Landon in 1929, "is that he can't talk loud and bang his fists on the desk, and is not much of an advertisor." Roland was definitely the low-key, easygoing type. "He took life as he found it," a friend observed, "and didn't much care to disturb it at all."⁴ It was a disconcerting trait to be found in the state's chief law-enforcement officer.

As late as 1929, Boynton was still a political unknown outside Lyon County. In that year, White had had to correct Landon's spelling of the name ("he does not spell his name Boyington") as he gave his friend and political ally a detailed rundown on his cousin's developing political ambition ("when you come [down] we will talk more definitely about it"). White offered all the advice he could to Boynton since he had become genuinely fond of his young protégé—Rolie had become almost an adopted son—and since he had long ago developed a special interest in the attorney generalship. "In the last ten or dozen years," he proudly wrote in 1931, "I have been rather specializing in attorney-generals because they have more power and not patronage. I have so far got a 100% record."⁵

AS A MEMBER in full standing of the White family, the friendly Boynton had soon become well acquainted with the Finney family. During his student years, he had come to know and admire Warren Finney—Ronald Finney was scarcely a teenager when Boynton first came to Emporia. But as time passed, Boynton's association with the junior Finney developed and matured. After Boynton went to Topeka, Ronald Finney came for dinner or dropped in at the office with increasing frequency. Boynton retained only a vague recollection of Ronald's difficulties during his days at the Neosho Falls Bank—and had given no thought whatsoever to the dark implications with regard to Ronald's character.⁶ Boynton looked on the Finneys, father and son, as basically honest but "sharp dealers," men who could look after their own interests to the best of their ability so that "you would have a hard time taking advantage of [them]." But that didn't mean that he thought that they would cheat people or anything like that. He felt "absolutely sure" that Ronald "would not do anything of a criminal nature."⁷

Finney had gone to his friend the attorney general in the summer of 1931 and asked him to accompany him to Colorado and give him the benefit of his legal expertise—for a fee, of course. So they passed a pleasant day in Denver, visiting various state offices and meeting the attorney general, a justice of the Colorado Supreme Court, and the venerable secretary of state, who just happened to watch over the blue-sky bond department. Boynton didn't render any legal opinions or give any specific advice. In fact, he seemed to be genuinely puzzled that Finney had asked him to go and had paid him $100 plus expenses.⁸ "Did it ever occur to you," Boynton was asked at the impeachment trial, "that Finney might have taken you along to Denver for the purpose of adding the prestige of your high office to the purposes of his private enterprises?" "No, sir, that didn't," came his frank and naïve reply.[9]

Finney had been Boynton's biggest booster for reelection in 1932. He printed a number of fliers which he and his friends tacked up all over eastern Kansas. Finney's mother-in-law, Mrs. Wiggam, sent out hundreds of Boynton cards to her influential women's-club contacts around the state. Finney paid out a total of about $1,100 in the campaign, which made him Boynton's largest contributor. Since the attorney general listed his total expenses at only $700, Ronald apparently had a refund coming.[10]

SHORTLY BEFORE the start of the national bank moratorium on March 4, Finney invited the Boyntons down to the Jayhawk for dinner. Ronald was just beginning his buying spree in anticipation of inflation. He told the gullible attorney general that he "had $10,000 he was saving for [an] emergency. He thought the emergency was there." The $10,000 had turned over so fast that he couldn't keep track of it, he boasted to his wide-eyed friends. Finney said that he was making money—lots and lots and lots of money. When Ronald came out to the Boyntons' house a few days later, he again started excitedly to tell about how much he was cleaning up—he even suggested that he might be able to cut the Boyntons in on the bonanza. "He was just full of it," Boynton recalled. "All he could talk about [was] what was happening. Talked to Mrs. Boynton and me."[11]

The Boyntons talked it over, but they were inexperienced in such matters and told Finney so. "If I was going to buy wheat, I would probably go to the grain store; if I was going to buy meat, I would go to the butcher shop," Boynton protested. Friend Ronald said that while he really didn't like to do it, if they did have a little money, he could spread it in with his transactions. A few days later, trusting to Finney's sound financial judgment, the Boyntons turned over $400 to Finney.[12]

Later in the spring, Finney told his friend that he had made a tidy $1,100 profit. Still later, Finney reported that the account had grown to $2,800, including the $400 investment. Boynton then drew down the original $400 plus a $1,000 profit. Finney came around to the Statehouse on July 25, the day before Boynton was to leave for California to visit his mother, and gave the grateful Boynton another $700. From time to time, Boynton had pressed Finney about the details of the financial transactions, wondering somewhat uneasily where and for what his money was going. "But," Boynton admitted, "he never said what deals they were."[13] Except for a few U.S. steel stocks, no evidence was ever adduced that Ronald invested the

Boyntons' money in anything at all except the twenty-four-carat Finney "fool proof" investment plan.

THE KANSAS CONSTITUTION provided for a perpetual School Fund, which arose primarily from the proceeds of the federal lands that had been granted to the state. The fund could not be diminished and had to be fully invested in U.S. or Kansas municipal bonds. The interest derived therefrom had to be "inviolably appropriated to the support of common schools." The $12 million fund generated about $500,000 per year that went toward the support of 550,000 school children.[14]

The constitution further provided that a board of School Fund commissioners—composed of the secretary of state, the superintendent of public instruction, and the attorney general—had the responsibility, as trustees, for the management, investment, and general oversight of the school funds. According to statute, all newly issued municipal bonds in the state had first to be offered to the School Fund Commission before being sold on the commercial market. Furthermore, the law provided that the commissioners "shall not pay for any such bonds or warrants any greater sum than par, nor more than the actual market price thereof at the time of purchasing the same, [at] less than par."[15]

The day-to-day administrative detail of the commission was handled by a bond clerk, who was a commission employee on the payroll of the state superintendent of public instruction. Since the three commissioners occupied themselves with numerous other duties, the clerk, though he had no formal vote, represented a most significant factor in the School Fund equation. He set the agenda, he kept the records, and he knew the precise amount that was available for investing at any given time. Since 1927 this important post had been held by William Herbert Stanley. Before filling the public position, Stanley had been a "frontier" missionary in southwestern Kansas—that is, he had been a preacher in the Methodist Episcopal Church.[16]

In addition to his state salary, which he felt was overly modest, Stanley had ingratiated himself onto Ronald Finney's payroll—as a sort of paid consultant, you might say. Finney paid him on a piece basis for favors rendered in the handling of issues of interest before the commission. When the Finney business was especially brisk, Stanley told the impeachment court, he would stop by the Jayhawk to "get my instructions for the day. . . . That is, I think everybody here will understand what I mean if I put it that way." When the curtain rang down on this symbiotic relationship in August, the money-hungry clerk had a beef—his patron was in arrears on a couple deals, and the erstwhile minister of the gospel feared that the "statute of limitations" might run out on him.[17] The ever-trusting Boynton didn't doubt the unscrupulous Stanley's integrity, even after having worked cheek by jowl with him for years. Representative Matt Guilfoyle said that Stanley suffered from "Statehouse-itis"—a disease that afflicts persons on the public payroll who are so busy working for outside interests that they have no time left for the thing that they are being paid to do. "The Almighty must have had his arm around us," Guilfoyle sighed, "to have had anything left with that man in charge."[18]

Ronald Finney's first sizable business before the School Fund Commission (SFC) resulted from the 1931 bond-exchange bill (Chapter 256, Session Laws, 1931). The statute provided that the SFC could exchange bonds in their possession that carried an interest rate of 5 percent or greater for their equivalents at no less than 4.25 percent. The legislators intended to save money for the hard-pressed municipalities that were caught in the grips of the Depression, many of which were months or years in default on their outstanding obligations. Even before the bill had passed the legislature, Finney had made a number of contracts with municipalities—totaling over $50,000—by working from the list compiled by Caldwell. Finney lobbied the bill through the legislature, even though it had been amended to permit only legal fees and to prohibit brokers' commissions. The undaunted Finney, working with a business associate of his father's, the Emporia lawyer W. W. Parker, had the contracts redrawn, substituting a "legal fee" for the previously ascribed broker's commission.[19]

Finney had charged $2,000 as a "legal fee" for an exchange of Dodge City bonds. The actual work entailed filling out a form that any normal twelve-year-old could have completed in about five minutes. Finney charged a $700 fee on a Kinsley bond exchange and similar amounts in other contracts. Generally, as prescribed in these contracts, the school district would realize only about 50 percent of the savings that had been effected from the bond exchange, and Finney would pocket the other half. The exorbitant charges had been provisionally approved at an SFC meeting on June 6, though a disturbed George Allen voted against it.[20] "It looked to me like robbing the school children," he charged. Recognizing that some additional pressure needed to be brought on Boynton and on E. A. Cornell, the secretary of state, Allen went to Clif Stratton at the *Capital* and related the particulars of Finney's scheme. Disturbed by this intelligence, Stratton ran six lengthy exposé feature stories between mid June and early July, giving details of the "slick scheme" that had been worked out by "a smart young man," though he avoided mentioning Finney by name.[21]

Due to the Allen-Stratton pressure and the public indignation generated therefrom, the SFC reconsidered and permitted only greatly reduced fees

Clif Stratton, reporter for the *Topeka Capital*
(Mrs. Clif Stratton)

on the contracts. The commission on the Dodge City contract was reduced from $2,000 to $450; that on Kinsley, from $700 to $350; and those on ten others ranged from $250 down to $50. "Consider the time we spent getting the bill passed," the frustrated Finney protested to the commission; "we ought to be allowed something for that, oughtn't we?" Even though it hadn't panned out quite as well as he had originally planned, Finney managed to collect "legal fees" on the exchange of $413,000 worth of bonds under the terms of the act.[22]

Boynton adopted the attitude that the SFC had discharged its legal function by simply making sure that the boards of education paid nothing except legal fees, that is, no brokers' commissions. Exactly what they paid for legal services was up to them. He did acknowledge that he knew that Finney "was interested in these exchanges" and that he thought the proposed fees were "too high." But this 1931 incident did nothing whatsoever to arouse the suspicions of the somnolent attorney general regarding the greatest bond swindler in Kansas history. "I undoubtedly talked to him," Boynton hazily recalled, "but don't remember the conversation about this matter."[23]

RONALD FINNEY'S first large-scale adventure into bond refunding came in April, 1931. He developed a *modus operandi* that would be perfected and used again and again over the next two years. Arma, a little mining town of about nineteen hundred down in the Kansas "Balkans," had a large indebtedness in spite of having one of the state's highest tax rates. For the past several years the school district had developed the lamentable fiscal habit of spending more than it took in. Its financial condition could best be described as unfortunate. In the winter of 1931 a number of "unpaid for want of funds" warrants floated through the town, being passed around the community like cash. When the Arma bank rather abruptly declared that it wouldn't cash any more of the warrants, the school board decided to take up the warrants with a bond issue. When the bonds were offered to the SFC in mid April, the 5 percent refunding bonds were promptly rejected.[24]

A few days later, Tom Boyd called the school board to say that "he had a man in his office . . . that was interested in buying [the] bonds." Shortly thereafter, enter our villain, Ronald Finney. As usual, he was in a big hurry to close the deal. He thought he knew where he could place them if he could get hold of them right away, he told his anxious audience. They haggled over price. Finney told them that bonds of Crawford County school districts were considered very poor property (which was true) and that the bonds would be like white elephants on his hands (which was false). They finally agreed on a price of ninety-six (par would be one hundred), and they agreed that if Finney could sell them at an interest rate below 5 percent, he—not they—would realize the savings.[25]

The next morning, Finney abruptly and paradoxically told the board members that he needed someone "that was very much interested in the welfare of Arma that could go to Topeka and help him dispose of the bonds." M. D. Frazier volunteered and rode up with Finney that afternoon. Finney confided to Frazier that he believed "he could sell the . . . bonds to the State School Commission." Frazier's special assignment was "to convince . . . Mr. [George] Allen that they were a good buy for the state of Kansas." "It seemed that Mr. Allen had a special dislike for Mr. Finney," Frazier said. Finney told Frazier that he "would try to convince the other two members of the . . . Commission." Cornell would go for the deal, Finney said, since he was "dumb and crooked, and didn't know a bond from a street car ticket." "If we could get the other two . . . to buy the bonds while

Mr. Boynton was out of town, it would be just as well," Finney told his unwitting accomplice, adding that Boynton was "straight and smart."[26] Boynton's defense counsel would make much of that remark.

Finney then escorted Frazier to the Statehouse, warning him that "under no circumstances around the Capitol Building was I to show any recognition of him, especially in the presence of Allen." Finney wanted the commission to believe that the bonds were being offered directly by the school board. Though the conscientious Frazier did the best job of selling that he knew how to do, Allen remained evasive and noncommittal. After a few days, they were joined by another Arma man, James Barnes. "Finney allowed," Frazier testified, "that possibly an additional board member or . . . citizen from Arma might guarantee the performance of the school commission a little more."[27]

Whatever the board members said, it finally did the job. On May 5 the SFC bought the bonds at par and at the reduced interest rate of 4.5 percent. Stanley presented the bonds to the commissioners in the name of the school district; the check was made payable to the school district's president. And Ronald Finney made $3,161.25 in public money on the deal. At Boynton's trial, Senator Harris testified that the bonds were not worth over ninety—that the actual market price was $45,900 rather than the $51,000 that the SFC had paid.[28]

Emboldened by this initial success with the SFC, Finney pulled a number of similar deals from 1931 to 1933, brazenly pocketing public funds that rightfully and lawfully should have gone to the poverty-stricken local districts. His moves became bolder as he began fraudulently to alter the documents that were presented to the SFC and to grossly misrepresent himself to the communities. A prime example involved the small southwestern Kansas community of Satanta (population 508). Its issue of $15,000 in sewer bonds had been rejected by the SFC in October, 1931. After almost a year on the open market with no takers at eighty-five, Robert Booth, a Finney field man from Wichita, entered into a $2,250 (15 percent) contract with the city, as their agent to sell the bonds.

In early September, Booth asked for two city representatives to go with him to Topeka to help make the sale. Two dutifully went, though they later wondered why. While in Topeka they took a tour of the Hill Packing Company, visited the Jayhawk suite, and ogled other fascinating sights of the capital city under Finney's aegis. While the paperwork was being prepared, Booth carefully explained that the funds for purchase of the bonds had been left by an estate to a couple of schools and that they had been bequeathed in such a manner that, as a formality, they had to pass through the hands of the School Fund. On September 7, at a meeting that Stanley called specifically for the purpose, the SFC bought the bonds at par. The offer to the SFC had purportedly been signed by councilman Herbert Foster, and the city's financial statement purportedly had been signed by "President" Coyle Branam. The financial statement had been erased and rewritten—falsely lowering the city's indebtedness by $30,000, which conveniently placed it just below the 15 percent legal requirement. Both Foster and Branam denied having signed the documents.[29]

Until sometime after the deal had been consummated, the good small-town folks out at Satanta believed that they had sold the bonds to Booth, as "fiscal agent," at eighty-five. Admittedly, they didn't fully appreciate what was going on or understand exactly what "fiscal agent" implied. "Bless their hearts," Senator Harris said, "they didn't know what 'fiscal' meant. You haven't got one west of the sixth principal meridian." Enraged when they finally did comprehend how fully they had been taken, they employed a lawyer to try to get their "commission" back.[30]

The mayor of Kismet (population 195), out near Satanta, proudly claimed that his newly developed town was the "smallest incorporated city in the world." Be that as it may, though it was tiny, it had big, modern ideas—it fervently wanted a "waterworks." The central feature of the waterworks consisted of a large tank, set on four posts and filled with water bought from the Rock Island Railroad. The contractor, it was claimed, had paid $100 for the water tank down in Texas, had had it hauled up to Kismet for another $100, and had charged the city the sum of $2,500. But that is another story. To pay for their brand-new waterworks the city had issued $7,000 in 5 percent bonds in the fall of 1931. After the bonds had been rejected twice by the SFC in 1932, Kismetans cheered up considerably when the "fix-it-up chappies," Finney and his associate John Knightley, visited their fair city in late September and announced that the town's troubles were over. For "a some [sic] of $1,350" they agreed to find a purchaser for the vexatious bonds.

On December 21 Finney phoned the mayor, F. A. Prater, and his brother, W. R. Prater, the city clerk, and asked them to come up to Topeka to clean up the bond sale. With no inkling as to the identity of the mysterious purchaser, they paid the $1,350 and picked up the freshly printed bonds and Finney's cashier's check for $7,000 at the Jayhawk. While in that bustling den of iniquity, they were introduced to the "attorney general," a man about six feet tall, "kind of slim, pretty good-looking."[31] It definitely wasn't Rolie Boynton, but the description seemed to fit Leland Caldwell quite well.

The School Fund bought the bonds at par on December 27 at 4.5 percent interest on an offer that had allegedly been made by the city. The original offer blank of March 12, 1932, had been reused, with appropriate changes in the date and the interest rate. The bonds' true value, Senator Harris stated, was about eighty; that is, the School Fund paid $7,000 in public funds to buy $5,600 worth of bonds from another public body, with the difference going to Finney.[32]

The Kismet deal had been called to Finney's attention by W. H. Stanley. Finney had told Stanley that if he would call profitable issues to his attention, he, Finney, would split the profits with Stanley fifty-fifty. One day, Stanley looked up from his desk, winked, and said, "Mr. Finney, you might try Kismet. They have been trying for a long time to get a little waterworks plant down there for their little burg."[33]

The check for the Kismet bonds had been made payable to the city clerk. In January, Finney appeared in the "little burg" with the state check clutched in his hand. Giving the clerk his patented rush act, Finney hurriedly explained that he had resold the bonds and it was necessary that the check be made to the city. Puzzled by the lame excuse, Prater nevertheless endorsed the check. When he and his brother mulled over this latest maneuver, they came to the belated conclusion that the School Fund had indeed been the mysterious purchaser.[34]

Early in 1933 Finney decided that since the SFC was becoming increasingly difficult, he would make one big killing and call it a day. W. T. Markham had replaced George Allen on the commission after the latter's death in early December. Markham, "Finney's appointment," could perhaps be chalked up in the plus column. But the outspoken Frank J. Ryan had recently been elected as secretary of state; and in the hot-tempered Ryan, Finney had been dealt an even tougher customer than George Allen.[35]

After Allen's death, Finney had started attending the SFC meetings in person. Ryan attended his first commission meeting in mid January, prepared to kick up a fuss—having heard the common gossip around Topeka that Finney had a virtual monopoly on presenting issues to the School Fund Commission. Ryan encountered the broker in the corridor as they walked together into the meeting. The secretary of state loudly objected to the presence of the outsider, and the ruffled Finney had to retire from the field. The other two commissioners patiently explained to Ryan that Finney had been attending their meetings, "giving us some advice."[36]

During January, Finney picked up a number of bonds at prices ranging between eighty and ninety. On February 3 he presented $113,000 worth of these municipal issues to the commission. Stanley's "orders of the day" were to have $64,500 accepted at par and the remainder rejected. The latter group consisted of top-quality, easily marketed issues. The rejections would make Ryan feel good, and they could readily be sold later on the open

Frank J. Ryan, secretary of state (Kansas State Historical Society)

market. Finney mentioned to his pal Boynton that he would be making the big offer in the name of Fidelity Bank. Boynton said that that was fine with him ("I had a friendly feeling for the home institution").[37]

At the February 3 meeting, Ryan strenuously objected to having the commission buy bonds directly from brokers—especially this particular broker. He indignantly declared that the bonds "didn't smell good," and furthermore he "didn't like the man offering the bonds." The secretary of state then became embroiled in a vociferous argument with both Markham and Boynton. Boynton admitted that he personally wouldn't buy the bonds but that the bank "really needed money."[38] At that, Ryan exploded—he didn't care about the bank; he wasn't there to help any bank. The obtuse attorney general remained puzzled by the eruptions emanating from the volatile secretary of state. "I never could get in my mind what he was talking about," Boynton said. "He had something in mind, but I never got it."[39]

Someone, possibly Markham, suggested that the purchase of the bonds should be delayed until additional information could be obtained. Stanley was appointed to obtain data on the indebtedness of the municipalities. When the commissioners reconvened a couple of days later, Stanley spread telegrams on the table from five of the municipalities—all of which spoke in the most glowing terms of the soundness of their finances. The telegrams bore the name of the mayor, the city treasurer, or another responsible official. On close inspection, which the commissioners failed to make, the messages bore a disturbing similarity to one another. Each began with the phrase "Reply to yours," which was followed by the valuation of the city, the indebtedness, and, in conclusion, a short, cheery message ("affairs of city in excellent shape"), in exactly that order. Stanley later admitted that there was no "yours" to reply to: that is, he had sent no telegrams to which these wires purported to be answers. Evidently Ronald Finney had only to pass the word to his trusty legions in the field (allegedly he had a contact in every town in Kansas), and then perverse nature took its crooked course.[40]

But the obstinate Frank Ryan remained unconvinced; additional meetings were held concerning the issue. On February 6, Ryan finally conceded defeat and voted with the other two to make the $64,500 purchase. The actual market value of the bonds was $56,700, which meant a tidy profit of $7,800 that day for the Finneys.[41] As charged in Article 1 of the articles of impeachment, on eight transactions before the SFC from May 1931 through February 1933, Finney realized a profit of $21,026.[42]

After the February 6 SFC meeting, E. E. Lamb—Finney's handyman who had introduced Finney to Markham—stuck his head into Stanley's office and coolly announced: "Mr. Markham said for me to tell you to drop everything and proceed to transcribe for us all of the bond purchases during Mr. Ryan's previous terms as president of the commission . . . state specific details . . . where you think it would be of interest to us."[43] Stanley gave the data, which listed in detail Ryan's votes on bond purchases and rejections over the years, to Finney and also to commissioners Boynton and Markham in the expectation that they could use it against Ryan if he continued to object to Finney's offerings. A little later, Stanley asked Finney (with another wink, we may suppose), "What do you think Frank Ryan is thinking now?" "He has been in politics a long time," Finney cogently responded, "and if he knows anything about it, he knows he is framed."[44]

IF THE EVIDENCE recorded by their five senses wasn't enough to shake the Statehouse officials from their lethargy, some others who came into contact with Finney's operations saw clearly enough and became sufficiently alarmed to notify the proper authorities. Two of these instances, in which Finney's misdeeds were directly and forcefully called to Boynton's attention, formed the basis for impeachment charges against Boynton which he and his attorneys found the most difficult to explain away.

When the Satanta folks realized in mid October that they had been taken for $2,250, they retained the good offices of a Liberal attorney, Judge G. L. Light. In late October he visited the Statehouse and called at the offices of the attorney general, the superintendent of public instruction, and the secretary of state. The attorney general was out of town, so Light described the problem to W. C. Ralston, an assistant attorney general. Ralston took Light to see Stanley, which was rather like taking a chicken to see the fox. Stanley assured the judge that the Satanta deal had been a perfectly legal transaction (untrue), that there had been no irregularities (untrue) or falsifications (untrue) or forgeries (untrue), and that the Satanta officials themselves had been present when the issue came before the SFC (untrue).[45] One thing you could say about Stanley—he was consistent.

Undaunted, Light returned to Liberal and wrote a four-page letter to Boynton on November 10 about the matter: "I think it is a certainty . . . that Ronald Finney was directly connected with Booth in this deal. . . . It is quite evident that a fast one has been put over to the detriment of the taxpayers in this little deal . . . and that both the city of Satanta and the School Fund Commission have been defrauded." Boynton responded two weeks later that the deal "went through in the regular way so far as the School Fund Commission is concerned." But he added that "there was nothing to challenge my attention to any peculiar situation except, perhaps, the telephone call just mentioned [from Ronald Finney]. As I look back on it I can see that perhaps that should have aroused some suspicion but it did not at the time." That statement was as close as Boynton ever came during the entire course of the scandal to making an admission that he had been less than diligent in following up leads regarding the notorious activities of Finney.[46]

Nothing significant transpired for several months, due to a quarrel among the Satanta city commissioners. For a few months, Light became "un-retained." He was "re-retained" in mid April—having heard nothing further from the attorney general regarding possible prosecution, as he had been promised. After an exchange of letters with Governor Landon, Light came to Topeka on April 24 with a legal petition drawn up to file against Finney and Booth. He stopped at the Statehouse first and accidentally bumped into Boynton in the elevator. Boynton told the surprised Light that he was making a thorough investigation of the Satanta business. Light told Boynton that he intended to file that day. Alarmed at the prospect of negative publicity for the SFC, Boynton asked for "a reasonable time" to try to get the matter settled. "It would just mean a couple of days," Boynton pleaded. Light agreed to that, adding firmly that he did intend to file if a settlement wasn't reached and quickly.[47]

Boynton immediately met with Finney and relayed to him Light's intent. "I told Ronald . . . they better go and see if they could fix that thing up," Boynton said. "Why?" he was asked. "Just to keep from being sued. Also, I wasn't anxious to have a suit brought here in Topeka, there had been so much talk." How had there been so much talk? "I had talked to the governor about it—I didn't want to have a suit filed—that has a comeback." "But you learned in the fall there was another thing in which Finney had engaged that . . . was wrong?" and "Not a very ethical transaction?" Fred Harris asked him. "Well, I don't know what ethics of bond men are," Boynton replied.[48]

When Judge Light returned the four hundred miles to Liberal the day after his meeting with Boynton, he found a long-distance-call message for him. Robert Booth and his lawyer came on down from Satanta to see him that evening. On May 1 Satanta officials signed a statement whereby the city would receive $2,000 in exchange for its agreement to drop the suit.[49] The persevering Light had finally obtained some results. And Rolie Boynton had behaved more like Ronald Finney's personal legal advisor than like the chief prosecutor of the state of Kansas.

GOVERNOR ALFRED LANDON had also been made aware repeatedly that all was not right under his Statehouse dome in the Bond Department. He must have been embarrassed, at the least, that the extensive perfidy that had been taking place daily on the same floor of the same building in which he worked had been revealed by agents of a totally outside authority. How long it would have taken Kansas and Kansans to uncover the monumental duplicity is anybody's guess. Even Governor Woodring had learned of Judge Light's concern in the fall of 1932 but had failed to investigate. The archives' copy of Boynton's November 23 response to Light carries the handwritten note at the bottom, presumably from an aide: "Gov.: I had a conference with Boynton this A.M.—another to follow—will keep you advised."[50]

Since he hadn't received a response over the winter from Boynton,

Judge Light had written to the governor on April 19, outlining the case and stating that the SFC had bought the bonds "from a friend of theirs." Landon responded on April 22 that he had "just talked to the Attorney General about this matter. Apparently there has been fraud in this transaction and I have instructed Mr. Boynton to earnestly and energetically investigate it thoroughly from top to bottom. Will be very happy to have your advice." Encouraged by this, Light had come to Topeka on April 24 with his legal petition drawn up. Landon asked Light to confidentially investigate both the Satanta and the Kismet deals and to report back to him. Light did so on May 4 in a two-page letter which briefed the governor on Kismet primarily. Light assured the governor that "I am willing to get into action at any time I can be of service to you."[51]

Governor Landon had received warnings from at least two other sources that spring. After the explosive meeting of February 6, a furious Frank Ryan had gone to the governor and "talked it over" with him.[52] Ryan apparently also told Landon about Leon Roulier's visit from Thomas County in April. A little later a Wichita banker—through Leslie Edmonds, a prominent Wichita Republican—complained to Landon that his bank had sold some bonds pretty cheap which had later been purchased by the SFC at par. It was too much spread for the banker to take without a squawk. Concerned, Landon again discussed the matter with Boynton.[53] As a result, Boynton had Stanley prepare a list of all the bonds that had been bought "over the counter"—that is, from brokers rather than directly from municipalities—for the period from June 1932 through February 1933. The final score: Finney, 24; all other brokers, 3. "I [just] didn't realize," the enlightened attorney general later cried.[54]

In mid April the *Capital* ran a story that all was not well with the School Fund: "It is understood that Governor Landon has called for some information . . . and it is barely possible that an investigation of bond purchases is in the offing."[55] Ryan, who probably was the Statehouse source for the article, publicly promised to investigate the continuing complaint that "one particular firm seemed to have a monopoly on selling bonds to the commission." "I don't like this favoritism talk," Ryan continued. "Everything perhaps may be all right, probably is, but it is time to stop this talk. . . . And there are going to be no more bonds bought until everything is done in a business-like way."[56] Stanley was fired on April 15, and Ronald Finney made no more deals through the commission.[57] Poor Boynton had to break the bad news to Finney that the commission wouldn't be buying from him anymore. Ronald cheerfully replied that it was O.K., because "I won't be selling any more bonds to the . . . Commission."[58] Of course, by that time, the ingenious entrepreneur had found a much better way to succeed in this world.

While Landon evidently didn't feel that he had sufficient reason to start a formal investigation in his own Statehouse, he did boil over with indignation in late May at "racketeers like Insull, Morgan and Van Swearingen," who, he righteously declared, "will be driven out of finance and industry by the scorn of honest people and the strong arm of government." The gubernatorial hackles had been raised by the recent disclosures at U.S. Senate hearings of the selling of stock to certain privileged people at less than the public market prices. That, the perceptive governor sermonized, "is outright bribery."[59] At that very moment the governor's floor at the Statehouse overflowed with enough "outright bribery" to fill a book.

THE PARALLELISM between the circumstance of Alfred Landon and that of Roland Boynton is striking. Yet the outcomes of their similar circumstances could hardly have been more disparate. For one it meant a major boost to reelection and a presidential candidacy just two short years later; for the other it meant shame, humiliation, and the abrupt termination of a promising career that probably would have culminated in a seat on the Kansas Supreme Court.

Each man served on a state board that had a major responsibility for the state's financial well-being. For Landon, it was the Treasury Board. But the board's inspection duties had become so onerous over the years that they had been pretty much ignored—in the 1870s, for example, the task of auditing the state books had been delegated to a groceryman. Nevertheless, had the board only superficially carried out its duties as prescribed by the Kansas statutes, the Finney operations would have been nipped in the bud, and the bond scandal would have existed only as a figment of a novelist's fertile imagination.

Both the governor and the attorney general had been warned by the Satanta, Kismet, and Thomas County affairs, and both had command of the same unsettling facts during the spring of 1933. Ronald Finney had been a major contributor to Boynton's campaign in 1932; Warren Finney, to Landon's campaign in the same year. Boynton had invested some of his money directly with Ronald Finney; Alf's wife had invested with Ronald Finney through the National Bank of Topeka. Under Boynton's nose, Ronald Finney had looted the public treasury of over $20,000 through his SFC operations over a two-year period; Alf had heard plenty about Warren's banks for years but had never investigated them and had even allowed them to reopen following the bank holiday after certifying them to be in the best of condition. Boynton did not double-check on Tom Boyd, assuming that he was honest; Landon did not check on Boyd or on Koeneke, his bank commissioner, assuming that he was competent. Boynton was a good friend of Ronald Finney's, it was true, but that relationship was no closer, if as close, as that between Alf Landon and Warren Finney.[60]

William Allen White was not slow to note the parallelism in the cases of the two men, both of whom he was close to politically and personally. In a long editorial in mid November, defending Boynton when his case was before the House, White declared that "the state bond board [treasury board] had neglected to examine the bonds in [Boyd's] vaults as provided for by the constitution. That mistake . . . let hundreds of thousands of forged bonds . . . lie undetected in the treasurer's vaults. . . . To impeach him [Boynton] and take away his citizenship is just as wicked, just as revolting as it would be to impeach the bond [treasury] board."[61]

In letters to his close newspaper friends, White spoke more frankly. To Charley Scott in Iola he wrote: "I am unhappy about Roland Boynton. Obviously he has been made the goat. . . . As a matter of fact, any one transaction of his in connection with the sale of the bonds and the Finney family is exactly duplicated by Alf." To Rolla Clymer at El Dorado: "Curiously enough the parallel between Roland and Alf is exact. . . . But circumstantial evidence has surrounded them and the mob is after them. If it gets a taste of blood with Roland you may be sure it will not be satisfied until it gets Alf. Yet Alf talks about political expediency in Rolie's case!"[62]

Fate often intercedes in strange ways in the affairs of men. An infinite series of "What if" questions can be asked. Only one such is raised here: What if Mrs. Landon's check had become public knowledge during the near-hysterical week of August 7 and Boynton's financial dealings with Finney had remained unknown to investigators for a couple of months? What if—?

EVEN MORE DIRECT EVIDENCE of Finney perfidy came to the attention of the attorney general in the spring in the form of four counterfeit bond coupons from Thomas County. Of all the impeachment charges, this incident proved the most difficult for Boynton. It also affords our most complete insight into the *modus operandi* of Ronald Tucker Finney, confidence man *par excellence*.

School District Number 80 at Brewster in Thomas County had an issue of bonds outstanding that bore 4.5 percent interest. They had been purchased by the Farmers State Bank, Wichita, in 1931 in a transaction that had been handled by John Knightley. The small rural district had been charged in the normal fashion for the number 3 interest coupon due on January 15, 1933. But two months later, four more number 3 coupons came in for the same issue. These coupons had also been paid, on March 25, by the state treasury. They bore 4.75 percent interest. No such bonds had ever been issued by School District Number 80.[63]

The Thomas County treasurer called the problem to the attention of the Brewster School Board. The board quickly convened and asked their young, recently elected county attorney, Leon N. Roulier, to go to Topeka to investigate the matter. The twenty-nine-year-old Roulier, who had been born just over the state line in Nebraska, had graduated from the University of Nebraska Law School in 1931. A year later, he had opened a law

Leon N. Roulier, Thomas County attorney (in 1961 as a member of the Kansas Board of Regents)

practice in Colby, the seat of Thomas County. The bachelor lawyer had served as county attorney for less than three months.[64] Inexperienced, but not unaware of the power of publicity, Roulier felt that perhaps this adventure might turn up something that would give a welcome boost to his embryonic career. And he was right—almost.

Leon saddled his favorite white horse and rode full gallop to the state capital on Thursday, April 6. Arriving in midafternoon, he went directly to the Attorney General's Office. He showed Boynton the four duplicate canceled coupons, which he had neatly stapled to a postcard-size piece of paper. Each coupon was for $23.75, a total of $95. Roulier stated flatly that no such valid Thomas County issue existed. The preoccupied attorney general immediately turned the anxious county attorney over to his assistant, Judge Ralston, then promptly dismissed the matter from his mind.[65] "Never thought about it again," he later said ruefully. "I have thought about it since."[66]

Ralston escorted Roulier to the fiscal agency of the treasury, where a clerk confirmed that the coupons had been paid, but he couldn't find to whom. Later it was determined that the payee had been the Fidelity Bank at Emporia. About 5 P.M., Roulier left the Statehouse and walked over to the firm that had printed the original issue, Crane and Company. There a clerk informed him that Crane had printed only one Thomas County issue (at 4.5 percent) and that none had been ordered or printed for John Knightley. If he would return tomorrow, a Mr. Mackey might be able to tell him more.[67]

Roulier then checked in at the Jayhawk Hotel. A couple of hours later he received a phone call from a man who said he was Lester Goodell, the Shawnee County attorney. The man came up, and they chatted; he explained that it was his policy to have the local hotels notify him whenever visiting county attorneys were in town, so that they could get acquainted. Just before the man left, he asked Roulier if he was down on private or public business. "Official county business," Roulier curtly replied. Roulier felt that this had been a most peculiar and somewhat unsettling visit, even though the county attorney had seemed friendly enough.[68]

The next morning, Roulier returned to Crane's, where Tom Mackey promptly handed him twenty $1,000 bonds bearing 4.75 percent interest. Four of the coupon sheets had had coupons clipped off up through those due in July, 1933. The unsigned bonds had been perforated with holes as if canceled. Mackey offered no satisfactory explanation for either the missing coupons or the genesis of the issue that he handed to Roulier. Puzzled, the

HONEST, BUT . . .

intrepid investigator returned to the Jayhawk, still intent on running this thing down.

Roulier, who had been told in Colby that a bond man with whom Knightley worked lived at the Jayhawk, was referred to Ronald Finney at the hotel desk. He went up to the fifth-floor suite, where he found Finney and Caldwell. The 140-pound Roulier came on strong to the 220-pound Finney. He feistily informed the broker that he had been investigating some coupons and that both Finney and Knightley were in big trouble of a criminal nature. The corpulent broker listened patiently as Roulier shot his silver bullets. Then the unscathed quarry started firing back. "He told me not to get tough with him, . . . that I had nothing on him," and that "I had better quiet down," Roulier recalled. "He started in telling me then about his powers and how he knew everything that was going on and how he knew that I was in town the night before and where I had telephoned and just what I had done." When Finney had finished reciting in faithful detail every movement that Roulier had made since he had arrived in Topeka, Leon began to feel that he might be in considerably deeper waters than he had heretofore imagined. He reflected back to the strange visit of the county attorney the night before. Perhaps he had been sent "to ascertain just what my business was and how much I knew," Roulier mused.[69]

After parrying the thrust of his would-be accuser, Finney turned the conversational tone to mellow. For a couple of hours or more they talked —and drank—"in a friendly manner." Ronald gave Leon a mini course in economics—all about how he was getting rich on the rising tide of inflation. He had made a quarter of a million "in big league style" since January 1, Finney bragged to the impressionable young man. Roulier was especially interested in Finney's position on the wheat market, since Roulier's father was a big wheat grower out in Thomas County. He would love to go back and give old dad an inside tip direct from the Topeka highflier. Finney obliged and then indicated that he sure could use regular reports on wheat conditions in western Kansas as the crop matured. In return, perhaps he could help Leon out with some good publicity for the home folks. Ronald then confided that he could fix Leon up with some public utilities (Cities Service) legal work that was soon going to be needed out in Roulier's neck of the woods. Leon thought that that would be a good deal, a very good deal. This Finney sure knew his stuff, and he was real friendly too. All in all, it was a very heady conversation for the young man, almost enough to make him forget what he had come to town for in the first place.[70]

Roulier did not return to the Attorney General's Office that afternoon, though he did go to the Treasurer's Office. Tom Boyd remarked that he had heard of Roulier's visit (we can be sure of that), and he assured Roulier that he would be most happy to reimburse Thomas County the $95 that they had been overcharged (we can also be sure of that). Why hadn't Roulier gone back to the Attorney General's Office? He testified that he thought that probably someone at Crane and Company had taken the coupons; and well, he was still disturbed by his "mysterious caller" of the night before. Perhaps the situation was "too large for me to handle," he said. If that were so, wasn't that all the more reason to have gone back to the attorney general to enlist his aid? Well, probably the school board would want a further investigation, and "I would have a hand in it and not just the attorney-general would get all of the credit."[71] After all, there's no use sharing recognition for your good deeds unless you have to. Boynton's attorneys had another idea as to why Roulier hadn't returned, which they revealed at the trial.

Ronald had invited Leon back to the suite for a friendly dinner that evening. Roulier had accepted, he said, in order to try to find out more about the bond matter. But the Kingfish didn't seem to want to talk any more about such a minor matter, so "the rest of my visit was more or less social."[72] Finney called in his publicity man—Lee Meadows, a former western Kansas newspaperman whom he had recently hired full time—to talk with Roulier, so that Meadows would have the basis for writing a good story on the crusading county attorney. Finney also had a photographer take pictures of Leon—including one of him sitting in the "throne chair."[73] That photograph, which has unfortunately been lost for posterity, gave cause for "considerable merriment" when it circulated through the Senate at the impeachment trial.[74]

After sleeping late the next morning (Saturday), Roulier rose and "debated with myself" whether to go back to the Attorney General's Office to tell what he had learned or to accept an invitation, proffered by Finney, to go to Kansas City with Caldwell and his wife for a weekend of rest and relaxation. Who won the debate? Kansas City.[75] As Roulier entrained on the Union Pacific at the cavernous Kansas City Union Station on Sunday evening for the long "uphill" ride to Colby, he had to be an immensely pleased young man. He had obtained the troublesome bonds that he had come for, and he had solved the mystery of the duplicate coupons—well, more or less. As an unexpected bonus he had become fast friends with one of the most powerful men in Kansas, a man who, along with his connections, could open many a door for an ambitious young lawyer. Yes sir, it had really turned out to be quite a trip.

When Roulier got back to Colby on Monday, he immediately called the members of the Brewster School Board into the county seat and told all (or, at least, most—well, some) of what had happened. Everyone agreed that the bond issue that Leon had so daringly snatched from the clutches of the dark forces in the capital city should be destroyed forthwith. So, there in the Thomas County Courthouse on that cool April morning, in front of God and the school board, the county treasurer, the county clerk, and—of course—the newspaper reporters, the twenty bonds of the 4.75 percent issue duly, solemnly, and officially went up in smoke.[76] Unfortunately for our young hero, those bonds would rise again from their carbonized grave.

An April 19 story about the trip in the *Colby Free Press-Tribune* contained a wild mixture of fact and fantasy, which Roulier later admitted did not speak the truth.[77] Another story in that issue came from the overactive imagination of Lee Meadows, Finney's hired typewriter. The totally fabricated column depicted the valiant county attorney traveling to Topeka to unravel the mysteries of the recently passed cash-basis law for the Thomas County folk:

> Roulier . . . took time by the forelock and journeyed to Topeka last weekend for a conference with . . . Boynton, . . . French and others in an effort [to] ascertain just what the proper procedure will be in carrying out provisions of the new refunding measure. . . .
>
> While in the city he . . . left no stone unturned to secure every bit of possible information for his people. . . .
>
> If Roulier is a fair example of the stock of the county . . . it is no wonder that Colby is one of the outstanding cities of the Western half of the state. . . .
>
> More power to this hustling young chap who believes that anything worth doing is worth doing well—may his tribe increase—upon such young fellows depends the future success of our state and nation.[78]

Although not a single allegedly factual word in that article was true, Roulier kept his own counsel, not admitting the gross inaccuracies until much later, when he had to. Roulier himself even became an author: an article on the infamous trip appeared in October in a new Kansas political magazine, *New Democracy*. At that late date Leon had decided to stick close to the facts.[79]

Roulier wrote to Boynton on April 11, stating that the matter had been "satisfactorily adjusted" and adding that "the state treasurer is the loser in the transaction, and you and he can determine what further action you may wish to take."[80] On May 5 Roulier wrote to Finney, reporting that the requested wire regarding wheat conditions had been sent to Harold Trusler in Chicago and wishing him well in his speculation. ("Here's hoping . . . you hit in big league fashion.")[81] He then apologized for some of the remarks in the Colby paper regarding their meeting:

> I want you to know, Mr. Finney, that I had no intentions then, and have none now, to injure your reputation in any manner. I realize that the only reason you had in checking up on my activities while in Topeka was for the reason that you thought I was down there to sell some Thomas county bonds and that you were interested in making the sale.
>
> If I can be of any service to you in the future, do not hesitate to call upon me, and, likewise, if you can do me any good with Cities Service or with any other connection, I want you to know that I will be deeply and sincerely grateful.[82]

Ronald Finney had made a fast friend, firm admirer, and business associate of the county attorney who, just a month before, had come so close to upsetting the whole Finney applecart.

Later in the spring the Thomas County treasurer complained to a Crane salesman that Finney had not sent his promised reimbursement for Roulier's expenses for his Topeka trip. The treasurer later denied having said that, but he did admit that a money order for $43 for that purpose had been received by his office. When Lester Goodell raided the Jayhawk in August, he found a check written on April 7 by Finney for $100 to cash—in the lower left-hand corner of which was the notation "for Roulier."[83] It came in handy in Kansas City, no doubt.

AS SOON AS HE RETURNED from Europe, William Allen White began to make his presence felt in the Boynton case. Letters to his friends came from White's typewriter at a furious pace. A major theme—in addition to the similarity of Boynton's case to that of Landon—emphasized Boynton's inability to defend himself in a political dogfight. "When I got home, I was just as fussed at Roland as I could be," White told Charley Scott shortly after returning. "He has handled himself horribly. He is subject to criticsm but he should not be impeached nor should he have to resign under fire. His political career is ended and properly so. . . . I am going to advise him never again even to go to an election booth without a guardian and to keep out of politics the rest of his life."[84]

White's most poignant epistle went to his cousin in California, Boynton's mother:

> I am doing everything I can for him, pulling whatever wires I know, but you can't do much good pulling wires in front of a mob. I have

tried ... to get Roland to transfer to the crowd his sense of the cruelty, the injustices and the humiliation which the mob is putting upon him, but he is just deficient in that one quality. He can't fight for *himself*. ...

I also want you to know how helpless I am. That is part of the mechanics of the tragedy. In any other fight I have ever been in I have been equipped for the fray. Here, and now, my very presence instead of his in front of the mob [in] some way seems to prove the case of the mob. Think this over! This is real tragedy.[85]

A few days before the case came before the Senate court of impeachment on January 8, White caused a stir with an editorial, just as he had in November during the House proceedings. He had decided that it would be best for his cousin's case if no further editorial pressure were applied during the course of the trial. In a January 6 essay pleading Boynton's cause, he wrote: "Despite the fact that the wolves who are after Boynton have been yelping since the house impeachment charges were made and despite the fact that their misrepresentations were deliberately cruel, The Gazette and Boynton's friends have not replied. Now on the eve of the trial as a next friend of ... Boynton, The Gazette desires to ask all his friends to refrain from editorial comment of any kind until the verdict is reached."[86]

Bill Clugston and Dutch Shultz didn't receive White's declaration as an unalloyed blessing. "There was such a 'kickback' to the White newspaper activities in the house impeachment proceedings [in November]," Clugston reported, "[that] ... he therefore wants to make it appear 'unethical' ... for other newspapers to keep the public informed."[87] The *State Journal* fumed that "the Emporia *Gazette* ... is up to its old tricks again. With a show of piety, it joins in the exhortation, using it, however, to coat an additional dose of propaganda in favor of [Boynton]. ... [Thus] the last ounce of pressure [is applied] for a favorable decision."[88] Claiming that "the two implacable enemies of Boynton" were after his job "for political purposes," White's response represented a classic example of his noted verbal extravagance:

> Gentlemen, go take your freedom. Pervert the news. Clamor and yammer to your heart's content. It will be all on your side. For Boynton's friends will not form an opposition mob. As the beaters of tom toms, as players of hewgags, as blowers of clarion notes, as sounders of editorial tocsins, the field is yours. ...
>
> So hop to it, Dutch and Clug! And may you burn your pants off in your own witch fires.[89]

RESPONSIBILITY FOR PROSECUTION of the impeachment case, the sixth to be heard in Kansas history,[90] rested with the board of managers, which was drawn from the House of Representatives. It comprised five members, headed by sixty-two-year-old Judge S. C. Bloss of Winfield. One of the top legal minds in the legislature, the tough but fair-minded Bloss had graduated from the University of Kansas and from Harvard Law School. After an eight-year teaching stint at Winfield High School, he began to practice law in Winfield, and he served as its city attorney. The crusty veteran legislator had served three terms in the Kansas House. Other members of the board, who were selected for their legal background and skill, included Edward E. Pedroja, Eureka; J. R. White, Mankato; Matt Guilfoyle, Abilene; and George K. Melvin, Lawrence. As Governor Landon's representatives, Fred Harris and Donald Little provided legal counsel for the board. Boynton retained very able counsel, headed by Will L. Cunningham and Arthur Walker of a respected Arkansas City law firm; A. M. Ebright, Wichita; and Arthur J. Mellot, Kansas City. The four served without remuneration, they publicly proclaimed, so strongly did they believe that their client was innocent of the "outrageous" charges that had been filed against him.[91]

Composed of forty men, sixteen of whom were lawyers, the Senate sat as the impeachment court, judge, and jury. Their decision could not be appealed to any other person or body. No woman sat in either house of the legislature in 1934 (though three had run in 1932), the first time that the legislature had been devoid of females since 1919. Twenty-four Republicans and sixteen Democrats made up the Senate; they ranged in age from thirty-two to seventy-five, with most being in their forties and fifties. Though thirty-five of the forty were freshman senators, several had gained legislative experience from prior service in the House. All were Caucasians and almost all were of Anglo-Saxon descent and Protestant in religion (predominately Methodist and Presbyterian). One member, Simon Fishman, was Jewish. The first dozen names on the alphabetical roll clearly confirm the predominately WASP nature of the assemblage—Baird, Bateman, Beckett, Bender, Benson, Bradney, Cannon, Carter, Coffman, Conkey, Cox, Dale.[92]

Had the senators followed the example of Elmer Hilton at the House impeachment debate, it would have greatly shortened the trial. A representative from Sumner County, the conscientious Hilton had listened carefully to proponents of one side, becoming nearly persuaded of the rectitude of their cause, and then had been pulled in the opposite direction as other House members cogently pleaded their case. What was a simple and direct

Kansas man—one who wanted very much to do the right thing—supposed to do? Hilton had an idea, at once simple yet brilliant. He made an appointment with the attorney general and asked him point-blank if he were guilty as charged. Boynton, point-blank, said no, definitely not. That was good enough for Elmer. On all the subsequent roll calls, the guileless representative steadfastly voted with the small minority against the impeachment of the attorney general, who had declared so firmly that he was innocent.[93]

The charges of misdemeanors against the attorney general were organized into four articles. The first dealt with SFC matters, enumerated in eight specifications, each concerning a different "Finneyized" deal before the commission. The second, the strongest, charged that Boynton had been duly warned by Judge Light and Leon Roulier but had failed to take the proper and necessary steps to investigate the criminal transactions of Finney. Article three, the weakest, claimed that Boynton had entered into a conspiracy with Finney, Boyd, Booth, Knightley, and Caldwell to defraud the state of Kansas. No one—not even the prosecution—took that one very seriously. The last article detailed in five specifications the "intimate social and personal relations" of Boynton and Finney, including the Colorado and Illinois business trips, the Finney contributions to Boynton's campaign, and the market investments, charging that his effectiveness in prosecuting both the criminal and civil cases that grew out of the bond scandal "is destroyed."[94]

A STEADY PARADE of witnesses, many of them colorful, kept the state enthralled for the three-week span of the trial.[95] Flint Hills Peggy said that she had expected the bond salesmen that came to testify to be dashing, Ivy League–type fellows. But, she complained, they turned out to be "hard-boiled, unromantic-looking individuals . . . , [whose] only contact with higher learning and culture seemed to have been at the Wichita Business College."[96] Legal or constitutional hassles frequently arose between counsels, interrupting the flow of the proceedings: "Are these criminal or civil proceedings?" "What constitutes a misdemeanor?" "Just what is an impeachable offense?" The hotly contested issue remained in doubt down to the last day.[97]

As one of the star witnesses for the prosecution, W. H. Stanley startled even the worldly wise senators with the sordid admissions that were extracted from him of persistent and unsavory duplicity in Finney's behalf for a few pieces of silver. The unctuous former preacher typically responded in as evasive, contradictory, and incomplete a fashion as possible. "Yes, I don't"; "Primarily, no"; and "Ordinarily not, yes" represented some of his more lucid responses. Flint Hills Peggy remarked that "if he had said a little more, it would have been slightly less than nothing."[98] E. A. Cornell and W. T. Markham testified about their participation on the SFC. Neither of them could recall much of anything about the key events, thus manifesting very serious cases of amnesia. Former students of Markham, the state's top man in education, must have smiled wistfully to hear so many answers of "I don't know" and "I can't remember" emanating from the forgetful teacher.[99]

Frank Ryan proved to be an aggressive and expansive witness for the prosecution. After the February 6 SFC meeting, which resulted in the Finney "killing," Ryan had gone in and had a long talk with Landon, because there had been Statehouse talk "about my being mandamused"—a reference to Finney's scheme to frame him. After a heated exchange with defense attorney Art Walker, Ryan abruptly turned to the presiding officer and asked who this man was that had been harassing him so. "You remembered my name quite well when I was getting you some votes in Cowley county," Walker shot back.[100]

A subdued Leon Roulier testified with "frankness and candor." Since he represented the key figure in the prosecution's strongest article, the defense gave him a thorough going-over. He admitted that he had become very friendly with Finney and had completely abandoned his primary purpose in coming to Topeka by the afternoon of the second day. Pressing him hard on the fact that he had not returned to see the attorney general on Friday afternoon, the defense insinuated broadly that Finney-induced intoxication had been the real reason. Roulier, ill at ease, admitted only to having had "a few drinks."[101]

The sensation of the trial came when Tom Mackey of Crane and Company took the stand. Since neither side had called him, the Senate itself had subpoenaed the printer, along with his boss, Charles Mitchell. Mackey had already given three different written statements to investigators—declarations that included a number of contradictory assertions and questionable protestations of truth. While the Senate impatiently awaited his imminent arrival in the chamber, the prosecution offered to read his latest statement. To which proposal one senator unkindly responded: "I don't care to listen to a statement . . . that is twenty pages long, and [made by a man] everybody concedes . . . is a damned liar."[102]

Mackey began by admitting that in his earlier statements he had told just "as little as possible." He now testified that on the evening of April 6, the day that Roulier had come to Topeka, Ronald Finney had phoned him at home and urgently asked him for "a favor." Finney told his printer-friend that someone had come in from western Kansas and was raising hell about some Thomas County coupons. Turning his infamous personality up to full voltage, Finney told Mackey that someone in his office had clipped the coupons, that he was embarrassed by that, and that he very much needed Mackey's help to get out of the jam. Finney said that he would like to fool the county attorney—"pull the wool over his eyes"—by giving him what he had come for. The disquieted broker wanted Mackey to go down right that evening and print an entire new issue of the bonds. But Mackey protested that he would have to wait and check with Mr. Mitchell. When he did check with Mitchell the following morning, the boss gave his approval, since Finney was a big businessman and such a good customer of Crane's. After the bonds had been run off, Mackey sent them over to the Jayhawk for Finney's inspection. When the bonds were returned an hour later, coupons had been clipped from four of them, and the gaps corresponded exactly with the coupons that Roulier had been carrying around Topeka in his sweaty palm. Mackey had handed the freshly printed bonds to the unsuspecting county attorney when the latter appeared at the printing office later in the morning.[103] Leon's proud pyrographic exercise in the Thomas County courthouse that April morning had all been in vain.

Following Mackey on the witness stand came Charles L. Mitchell, the manager of Crane and Company. A past president of the National Association of Stationers and of the Topeka Chamber of Commerce, Mitchell held "memberships in more business, civic and fraternal organizations . . . than probably anyone else in [Topeka]." He had proudly served as an honorary aide-de-camp to four governors, including the incumbent. The list of bonds that Crane printed for Finney, which Mitchell had voluntarily offered to investigators in August, did not include the third (April 7) Thomas County printing. Mitchell had boasted at that time that it would be virtually impossible to get a bond forgery through Crane and Company. On the stand he gave vague and devious answers, denying that he had known about a plot to fool Roulier. Much of his testimony directly contradicted Mackey's. Immediately after being embarrassed before the Senate, Mitchell went home and took to his sickbed. Four weeks later he resigned (voluntarily?) as a colonel on the staff of Governor Landon, citing "health" as the reason.[104]

The defendant spent many hours on the stand, elaborating on oral and written statements that he had given earlier, without making any significant additions or subtractions. He continued to maintain steadfastly that he had not had the slightest inkling of what friend Ronald had been up to and to protest that he was completely innocent of any wrongdoing. Of the 110 character witnesses that had been subpoenaed, 14 were placed on the stand or had their statements read into the record. The impressive array of citizens who stepped forward to vouch for Boynton's sterling character included former Governor Ben Paulen; former Lieutenant Governor Dr. J. W. Graybill; K.U.'s chancellor Ernest H. Lindley; two distinguished newspapermen, Roy Bailey of Salina and Rolla Clymer of El Dorado; and the ardent prohibitionist Lillian M. Mitchner.[105]

As the trial moved into its final days, Senator Charles E. Miller, a Tonganoxie Democrat and a man with his eye firmly fixed on the governor's chair, rose to a point of personal privilege:

> We have been led to believe that Governor Landon was going to be called on the witness stand. The papers carried that message to the people of Kansas. Governor Landon knows more about this bond scandal than any other man in this statehouse. He knows it from top to bottom, from the time he went into office until now.[106]

Speaking in support of Miller's subsequent motion to subpoena Landon, Senator Taggart argued: "There are a lot of people who think that the governor has a lot of knowledge that we haven't heard. If he has it, let's hear it. It has been whispered around here . . . that Governor Landon knows a lot of things that none of the rest of us know."[107]

On a standing vote the motion was defeated. The chairman ruled that a roll-call vote was not in order, but his decision was appealed to the entire body. A roll-call vote then followed on the technical ground of sustaining the chair, though the vote basically addressed the question of whether Landon should be called before the Senate. A highly partisan vote of twenty to sixteen sustained the chair. Of the twenty yeas, all were Republicans; of the sixteen nays, thirteen were Democrats.[108]

An occasional spike of levity punctuated the otherwise somber proceedings. At one point Senator Miller asked the attorney general if he had been in "W. W. Finney's house in Emporia with Governor Landon in April, 1932, when Mr. Finney insisted that Governor Landon run for governor." To much laughter, a smiling Boynton replied, "No, sir; I wasn't there that day."[109] When queried about certain bond transactions, W. H. Stanley testified that it was "house business," that is, between different departments of the state. "In what department of the state of Kansas was [Ronald] Finney operating?" "In most of them, apparently," came the wry reply.[110] In his closing remarks, one of Boynton's attorneys asserted that Ronald Finney was on his way to Lansing. "He will probably get there," he added with a straight face, "and organize a corporation and sell Senator Harris and Mr. Bloss some preferred stock."[111]

MATT GUILFOYLE, a Democratic candidate for U.S. district attorney, utilized his summation for the prosecution as a vehicle for displaying his considerable polemical talents. After making a detailed comparison between Ronald Finney and Al Capone, Guilfoyle lashed into the attorney general:

> If the county attorney from Thomas County would have come down to Topeka and told the attorney-general that there was a nickel slot machine running out there, he would have been out there right away with every force at his command, but because it was nothing but forgeries of some of the most sacred instruments that this state has, he didn't act....
>
> Just what do you think we have got an attorney general for? There you come right down to the meat of this case....
>
> Is it a wonder ... the people of this state ... have lost confidence?[112]

In his summary, Senator Harris sounded a more dispassionate note:

> This case should not be decided from a mob standpoint.... We know now ... that Ronald Finney ran wild in this building, that he used various people in his manipulations, and that he was in various departments of this state and used them all for bad ends.... Oh, I don't want to crucify anyone. I am asking you to follow the sequence of these transactions along and then, if you believe that the duty was not done, to so express it in your votes.[113]

The defense claimed that Boynton had been punished enough already by having "his picture published with Finney and Boyd and others standing trial as though he were one of their kind."[114] They quoted liberally and passionately from the Bible, Shakespeare, Omar Khayyam, and "A Man without a Country."[115] Ronald Finney became Boynton's Judas Iscariot, "the man who would impress upon his brow the betrayal kiss."[116] A wicked combine had been lined up against the poor attorney general, composed of "a dishonest printer, Crane, and a dishonest county attorney, Roulier, and a dishonest treasurer, Boyd, and a dishonest broker, Finney."[117]

Will Cunningham—he of ruddy complexion and long white hair—concluded grandiosely for the defense. He argued that Boynton was a victim of circumstances—perhaps too loyal to his friends—and had simply believed that those around him on the second floor of the Statehouse were honest.[118] Cunningham asked the senators to carefully weigh the evidence, weigh it not with the idea of what some man out here in the country might say about you, not what some newspaper might say about you, because all of those things soon pass away, but there is one thing that you can't escape from, and that is your own conscience....

The man . . . who would vote in this case, giving any consideration whatever to the effect that his vote would have upon his personal or political fortunes, or upon the political fortunes of his party, is unworthy of a seat in this body. Those things must be and will be swept from your minds, and all you will consider, I am satisfied, is the evidence in this case.[119]

On January 25 the Senate resolved itself into an executive session. After considerable discussion the articles of impeachment were voted upon. On Article 1 the vote to sustain the charges was sixteen to twenty-four; on Article 2, twenty-two to eighteen; on Article 3, five to thirty-five; and on Article 4, nineteen to twenty-one. Since none of the articles had received a two-thirds vote (twenty-seven), Boynton was acquitted on all charges. The vote did not follow party lines closely. On the critical second article, thirteen (of twenty-four) Republicans joined nine (of sixteen) Democrats in voting to convict Boynton. Though a majority voted against him on this article, he failed by five votes to be convicted. Twenty-five of the forty senators voted to convict on at least one of the counts. Nine Republicans —six of whom had been the special objects of William Allen White's persuasiveness—voted to acquit on all articles.[120]

The reaction to the Senate vote varied predictably depending on one's political predilections. Governor Landon declined to comment, though presumably he was disappointed.[121] The *Parsons Sun* intoned that Boynton was cleared by a senate that "seemed anxious to get at the facts and play as little politics as possible." That was a particularly ironic comment, coming as it did from the *Sun*'s editor, Clyde Reed. On the day before the vote, the former governor had conspicuously entered the Senate chamber—in company with Federal Judge Richard Hopkins—and had grandly positioned himself in a prominent place near the rostrum. "As a grim warning to recalcitrant senators," Marion Ellet asserted.[122] So many letters poured into the *State Journal* protesting the decision that the paper had to stop publishing them and "call it a day."[123] But at that moment the senators hardly had time to reflect on the implications of what they had done. After pronouncing their verdict, they reassembled immediately to hear the case of Will J. French, auditor of state.

13

A Most Helpful Office

THE OFFICE of state auditor was a critical one for Ronald Finney to control. Though it eventually became an integral part of the Finney bond machine, that circumstance did not derive from a warm friendship between Finney and Auditor French.

William James French was born in Sparks, Doniphan County, Kansas, on August 28, 1889, of English-German ancestry. His grandfather had come to northeastern Kansas as a territorial pioneer. The family moved to Stafford County in 1904, where his father became one of the area's leading wheat growers. After graduating from St. John High School, the quiet, reserved French taught school for nine years in Stafford County. While teaching school he took correspondence work with the University of Kansas and the International Correspondence School of Scranton.[1]

After serving two terms as Stafford County clerk (1921–25), French lost a bid for the Republican nomination for state auditor in 1924. After that race, Governor Ben Paulen named him an assistant state oil inspector, in charge of collecting the gasoline tax. In 1926 French came back to win the Republican nomination for state auditor over four contenders and went on to easily trounce his Democratic opponent in the general election. Having been reelected in 1928, 1930, and 1932, the gray-haired, forty-four-year-old auditor was serving his fourth term in 1933. Things had gone well enough during this extended public service except in his second term, when there had been some difficulty growing out of his handling of a state land royalty account. He was accused of having misused the funds but was later acquitted.

Conservative in both politics and personal habits, French was a cautious, fussy man and a teetotaler. His organizational memberships included the

Will J. French, state auditor (Jim French)

Masons, the Odd Fellows, and the First Baptist Church of Topeka. He ran a "tight ship" so far as the personal habits of his staff were concerned, though he was not above employing deserving relatives and St. John friends in his office.[2]

A member of the standpat faction of the party, French had often publicly disagreed with the sitting governor, especially Clyde Reed and Harry Woodring, about the amount of money in the state exchequer and the general state of the public financial health. His political opponents accused him of attempting to discredit the work of progressive administrations with half-truths based on distorted figures. The auditor admittedly was not unaware of the political possibilities inherent in his office. "I . . . found I had done much to defeat Harry Woodring and make possible your election," French proudly wrote to governor-elect Landon, "by releasing certain stories in regard to his expenditures."[3] In the heat of the hard-fought Republican gubernatorial primary campaign of 1930, Governor Reed accused French, along with other prominent conservatives, of being all too anxious to turn control of state government over to the big utility companies. After the bond scandal broke, the progressive Reed, still bitter at his former colleague, remarked sarcastically: "French has one defense that none of the other state officials can make. He is incompetent to begin with, perhaps the least competent official ever to hold that place."[4]

THE FIRST French-Finney interaction, which had been negative, set the pattern for their future relationship. During the 1931 legislative session, French had overheard Finney loudly bragging to an associate in the rear of the Senate Chamber that he would make over $50,000 on the bond-exchange bill that had just passed the Senate.[5] Disturbed at this, French went to George Allen, and together, French claimed, they managed to get the bill altered so as to disallow all brokers' commissions. Realizing that the list of municipalities with bond issues that were eligible for exchange under the act could only have been obtained from his office, French sent a letter to all the bond houses in the state, reminding them that the auditor's records were public and open for inspection by all. He had hoped thereby, he said, to minimize Finney's apparent advantage.[6] So, French didn't like or trust Finney and thought that he was a "sharp dealer." And French and the progressive Tom Boyd in the treasury just across the hall "never had friendly relations at all."[7]

In the summer of 1931, French reported, he had been contacted by Finney, who said that "he would like awfully well to see me."[8] At this juncture the two had never formally met, though French had heard a great deal about the senior Finney—about both his money and his good works—down at Emporia. The next day, French visited Ronald Finney's quarters at the Jayhawk, which at that time consisted of only a single room. Trying to establish a rapport with this key office for his future activities, Finney asked French about some Stafford County bonds in which he had an interest. French was polite enough but wary, answering the broker's questions but never returning after this initial meeting.[9] Since the old charm hadn't worked its usual magic, Finney undoubtedly decided after this encounter to work around the auditor, not with him.

ONE OF THE PRINCIPAL CHARGES against Will French grew out of the role that his office had played in the cancellation of school-district warrants that had been refunded by bonds. In 1931 the legislature had passed some seventeen different statutes enabling a municipality to refund its outstanding indebtedness into bonds. Warrants that were marked "unpaid due to insufficient funds" and were held by the district's creditors—often building contractors, hardware stores, carpenters, and so forth—represented much of the indebtedness. Refunding into bonds generated the funds to pay off the warrants and to spread out the debt over a ten- or twenty-year period. The bond transcript listed the warrants that were to be refunded, though nothing had to be stamped on the warrant itself to indicate that it had in fact been paid. When the bonds were issued, the warrants were to be paid and canceled and then retained or destroyed by the school district. Unfortunately, the law—Chapter 105 of the Session Laws of 1931—was vague about the exact manner in which and by whom the warrants were to be canceled. It merely stated that "such bonds shall also in every case be registered by the county clerk and by the auditor of state, and all evidences of indebtedness funded hereby shall be canceled."[10] That was all; there was nothing more specific. The fate of French, in large part, depended on the interpretation of that statute.

The vagueness in the refunding law represented just the opening that our villain needed in order to engineer still another grand and nefarious scheme. During the summer of 1931 Finney became the official agent for a number of school districts in central and western Kansas to aid and abet the refunding of their outstanding indebtedness into bonds. Instead of turning the canceled warrants over to the district, Finney collected and illegally retained them, later putting them to work for an entirely different purpose. Finney told the local officials that "it was necessary that these warrants be canceled or destroyed in the office of the state auditor." This scheme was foisted off on eight school districts in seven counties for a total of $133,597.[11]

Out in the field, Leland Caldwell and John Knightley purported to represent the Fidelity Bank or the National Bank of Topeka. District Number 49 in Logan County heard from a "Mr. J. F. Charlesworth," who signed himself as receiver in bankruptcy of a Kansas City investment company.[12] On occasion the local officials relinquished the warrants only after a struggle. In one instance, Caldwell and Finney had gone to the house of a member of a rural Logan County school board, to obtain the single warrant that they lacked. "They wanted that warrant, and I told them that unless they paid for it, they couldn't have it," the stubborn farmer related. Finney replied that they had to have the warrant immediately in order to turn it over to the state auditor so that the bonds could be issued. "I tried my level best to get them [the warrants] away from Caldwell before ever I went as far as to sign for the stuff," the perplexed man said, "[but] Mr. Caldwell and

Mr. Finney put up the legislature had passed a new ruling; they had to have them, and that was all there was to it."[13] Another school-board member recalled having been given the characteristic Finney rush by Knightley. "He said that he just had a day or so to get them down in," the board member said, "and that they was damn particular down there [Topeka] and he wanted to get going."[14]

In a few instances, dates on the warrants had to be altered to make them legal and acceptable. Chapter 105 provided that no indebtedness could be refunded which had not existed on March 16, 1931. Five of the warrants that District Number 49 in Logan County wanted refunded bore dates after the cutoff. When members of the school board learned of the problem, they thought that they would have to drop the whole matter since there weren't enough other warrants to justify issuing bonds. But, the ever-helpful Knightley said that they shouldn't worry, "we will take care of that." And true to his word, he did, changing each of the offending dates from 1931 to 1930.[15]

THOUGH THE SCHEME seemed almost foolproof, the natives began to get restless, and they started to complain. School-board members felt uneasy about turning over both the warrants and the bonds to Finney. They began to grumble to Finney or his subordinates about getting back the warrants and about refunds that they felt were due to them. More alarmingly for Finney, they began to write directly to the auditor.[16] Finney decided that another element needed to be added to perfect the plan and to still the complaints coming in from the hinterland.

To accomplish that end, Finney invented something that he called a certificate of destruction. On January 23, 1932, he marched into French's office carrying a large batch of Russell County warrants and a certificate, made out in triplicate, which certified that the listed warrants, totaling $14,543.57, had in fact been "canceled and destroyed in my presence." It was dated and was to be signed by the state auditor. Finney insisted that it was the auditor's solemn duty, as required by law, to sign the certificate after he had witnessed the destruction of the warrants. The cautious French was nonplused and hesitant. No such request had ever been made before, and he certainly did not want to do any special favors for Finney. But the persuasive powers of the young speculator carried the day. French reluctantly signed, though not before he had called in an assistant and asked him to carefully check off the warrants listed on the affidavit as French himself meticulously tore them into very small bits and threw them into the wastebasket. Finney then gave French instructions on how to dispose of the three copies of the certificate: one copy should go into the auditor's vault with the bond transcript; one copy, in a state auditor's official envelope, should go to the school district; and one copy should be retained by Finney for his files. What two of the three men in the office that day didn't know was that at that very moment, warrants of identical description rested peacefully (though working all the while) in the National Bank of Topeka, and had so rested since the previous November.[17]

Five days later—only three days after French's new number-one assistant, Joe Voorhees, had joined the auditor's staff—Finney showed up again with an armful of paper. This time he carried $27,545.22 in Gove County warrants and a similar certificate of destruction. Finney introduced himself to Voorhees, explained to the tyro the office procedures à la Finney, and asked him to sign French's name to the certificate. New on the job and not yet responding fully to the raw power of the Finney charisma, Joe Voorhees played it cautiously. He was sorry, but they would have to go to the boss to get his approval. In the Auditor's Office, Finney and French "argued around back and forth." French began to redden with anger. After a period of such contention, Finney suddenly reached up to a shelf in the office, which was lined with legal documents, and pulled off "some law book." He indignantly flipped it open to an (any) appropriate spot and solemnly began to read a section regarding the auditor's duties, which included the firm necessity of destroying (actually burning, Finney read) old warrants. With supreme self-assurance, he then snapped the book shut and quickly replaced it on the shelf. Impressed by this convincing recitation of his official duties, French instructed Voorhees to check the one hundred warrants off the list, destroy them, sign his (French's) name to the certificate, and imprint the certificate with the auditor's seal. When French later had occasion to consult that statute, he looked high and low but could never lay his hands on it. He even put a young lawyer in his office to work thoroughly checking the most likely places, but to no avail. French, of course, couldn't find what did not exist except in Ronald Finney's fertile imagination. Another cold fact was unknown to French on that critical day of January 28: the Note Department of the National Bank of Topeka held warrants of identical description to those that had been destroyed. Placed in the bank on October 8, 1931, the original warrants had been accepted from Finney as collateral for a $25,000 loan in the name of the Fidelity Bank.[18]

Finney continued to direct the execution of certificates of destruction by the Auditor's Office through the spring and summer—the last ones were issued on August 19, 1932. Except for the first, they were signed by Voorhees with French's name. At the impeachment trial, French and Voorhees gave directly contradictory testimony regarding French's instructions on the matter. French insisted that he had made it clear to his assistant, at least by February, that no more certificates were to be issued. Voorhees denied this, stating flatly that he had never been instructed not to sign the certificates. Office employees testified that Voorhees had done it openly, that Finney had read the warrants while Voorhees checked the list, and that Finney had then cut the warrants into small pieces and deposited them in the nearest wastebasket. In any event, the local districts received signed certificates, listing a total of nearly $135,000, which were designed to assuage any lingering doubts of the "official" warrant-cancellation policy of the Auditor's Office.[19]

WHILE THEY HELPED a good deal, the certificates didn't completely eliminate the static from the system for Finney. Some of the school districts, such as one in Pratt County, continued to give him problems. A district at Coats had issued $25,000 in bonds to cover some much-needed school construction in June, 1931. The district paid for the warrants with drafts on their Fidelity account and then sent the paid warrants to Finney in care of the bank. On January 29, 1932, Voorhees signed a certificate of destruction after having destroyed twenty-six warrants of $500 each. The genuine warrants were unusual—they were the size of a bond and had interest coupons attached. The ones that Voorhees had destroyed were small, the size of a check, and had no interest coupons attached.[20]

One school-board member, J. H. Shriver, became progressively irritated at the failure of the district to receive either a certificate covering the remaining warrants or the warrants themselves. In August, 1932, after a draft to pay a remaining warrant had been turned down at Fidelity, he decided that it was time for action. So, he drove to Topeka, where he found Finney's offices characteristically busy—he recognized Charley Cooke among the "boys." Finney, who was told that his visitor wanted all the warrants located and a certificate of destruction prepared that afternoon, managed to find all but one of them after an hour or so. Pleading that he was about to leave for a vacation in Colorado, he promised that when he returned, he would locate the missing warrant and prepare the certificate. The stubborn Shriver was having none of that. He insisted that he wanted the deal finished that day—right now. After another lengthy "search," the hard-pressed Finney, perspiring a bit due to the sudden appearance of the insistent school-board member with his embarrassing demand, finally "found" the missing warrant.

It was nearly 6:00 P.M. when Finney and Shriver, with the warrants, set out for the Statehouse to obtain the certificate of destruction. And who should they bump into in the corridor just outside the Auditor's Office but the state treasurer. The voluble Tom Boyd explained that he was working late, since he had just returned from a glorious vacation at Finney's ranch in Colorado. While Boyd was expounding on the glorious times they had had out there, Finney politely excused himself and slipped into the auditor's suite. Observing the social amenities, Shriver had to remain in the hall with the talkative Boyd. During the next five minutes he learned more than he cared to know about the joys of southwestern Colorado. Then Finney rejoined them with a smug look of satisfaction, we can be sure, written all over his ample face. As they walked down the Statehouse steps a few moments later, he handed the certificates covering the remaining $12,000 in warrants to Shriver.[21]

Finney had stalled with the "searching" for the missing warrants while he made arrangements to get the genuine articles out of the National Bank of Topeka and over to the Jayhawk Hotel. Warrants of Pratt County totaling $12,000 had gone into the National Bank of Topeka on December 9, 1931 (Fidelity also held $13,000 of the genuine warrants). Perhaps Charles Cooke was the delivery boy; certainly he had done even more questionable favors for Finney. After he had shown those warrants to Shriver, Finney hoped to put him off with the ruse of a missing warrant and the upcoming vacation. This would buy time to prepare duplicate issues for destruction by Voorhees. When Shriver persisted, Finney undoubtedly called Boyd, asking him to stay late and to intercept them in the corridor. Since the certificate bore Joe Voorhees's genuine signature, Finney must have phoned and asked him to stay late as well.[22] Ronald's trained seals had performed magnificently that day.

As a spin-off of the operation of illegally retaining canceled warrants, those of at least four counties (Riley, Gove, Logan No. 5, and Pratt), totaling $88,709, were forged as well. With one exception, none of the forged warrants purported to be a duplicate of any of the warrants that were listed on the transcript of the refunding bonds. "[They] are not carried upon any record anywhere," said Senator Harris. "They are not duplicates of any other thing."[23] The total of the illegally retained and forged warrants came to approximately $222,000.

The Pratt County issue became one of Finney's favorite securities. The warrants that were refunded by the $25,000 bond issue were falsely listed as having been destroyed on the certificates of destruction of January 29 and August 19. Assets of the Finney banks and those in Ronald Finney's safety-deposit box included $60,000 in forged warrants of this issue. In addition the bond issue itself was forged, not once, but twice. All of which added up to $135,000 in illegal securities of that Pratt County country school district which were abroad in 1932/33.[24] The schoolhouses had turned out to be pretty expensive.

RONALD FINNEY sold the illegally retained and forged school-district warrants—sometimes in his own name and sometimes in the name of the Fidelity Bank—to the National Bank of Topeka. The familiar Finney device, the repurchase agreement, had been utilized. Finney received nearly the full face value of the warrants in cash. The first transaction of this nature, which had been approved personally by the president, Carl McKeen, had occurred on September 24, 1931. The other warrants went into the bank later that fall and winter, through February, 1932. The Bond Department, under Charles Cooke, carried these securities until they were transferred to the Note Department on March 25, 1932. All the warrants under these agreements had been withdrawn by Finney by the fall of 1932. But they came back into the bank in the latter part of 1932 as security for county deposits in the three Finney banks. In several instances, forged warrants also entered the bank as security during this period.[25]

On October 7, 1932, the National Bank of Topeka exchanged some bad Finney pears for some worse Finney apples: they accepted from Ronald Finney the forged bonds of a Clay County school district in exchange for the illegally held canceled warrants of the same district. A few months later, in January, the vice-president in charge of the Loan Department, M. A. Ross, happened to be looking at some of the recently acquired bonds and noticed that they had been issued in August, 1931. He recalled that Finney had told him that the bonds had been printed just a short time before the exchange had been effected and that they had been issued to refund the warrants. The Clay County warrants had been owned by the bank from September 24, 1931, until the October, 1932, exchange.[26]

His curiosity and suspicions aroused, Ross made inquiry at the bank at Green in Clay County that handled the issue. The bank officials confirmed that the bonds had indeed been issued in August, 1931, but they could not find out "whether the warrants that were taken up by the bonds had been returned to the school board or not."[27] Ross turned next to the Topeka bank's errand boy, the bond broker Byron Gourley. In the state auditor's vault, Gourley found that the bonds had been issued in 1931 to pay the warrants, which thereby became invalid legal instruments. He also found a certificate of destruction testifying that said warrants had been officially destroyed in the presence of the state auditor on February 18, 1932, nearly eight months before Ross had exchanged them for the bonds.[28]

Ross reported his discoveries to other bank officers, including President McKeen. A few days later he talked with Finney, who had gotten word of the inquiry from his bank grapevine even before he saw Ross.[29] Finney faked indignation, protesting, Ross said, that he wished "I wouldn't have Byron Gourley interfere in his business."[30] Ross asked his principal customer for an explanation of the discrepancy in the dates. "He said that was the regular ... way of handling the thing," the bank officer lamely recalled. "My recollection is that he said there was a mix-up in the dates."[31] That was true enough. Ross didn't even ask about the damning certificate of destruction that Gourley had found. Could not the bank's officers have ascertained unequivocally that either Finney had put forged warrants up with the bank or that he had had forged warrants destroyed in February, 1932, and that, in either event, he had no business with those warrants in his possession after August, 1931? "I didn't come to any conclusion about that," Ross responded at French's trial.[32] Despite this unambiguous evidence that came to the attention of its top management in January, the bank continued to do business, in fact an increased business, with the errant Finney until an outside agency, the national bank examiners, came to town in late June.

THE AUDITOR'S OFFICE had, curiously, turned a deaf ear on recurrent indications of Finney's deceptions. Will French received a steady stream of complaints from the offended school districts from the winter of 1931/32 into the spring of 1933 regarding the operations of Finney and his henchmen.[33] The Logan County attorney, on March 1, 1932, after declaring that he had determined that the dates on five of that district's warrants had been altered, wrote to French: "It seems strange to me that any instrument of this kind should be destroyed, and as a matter of fact they should be returned to the [county] treasurer for cancellation. There has either been a forgery committed, or some crookedness in the procuring of these bonds from the school district."[34] A month later the county attorney told French that "it appears that a criminal action is going to be called for and I would appreciate it very much if you would give me all the information you can."[35]

Not all the letters that came to the auditor were as articulate or grammatically correct as those written by the Logan County attorney, but the message, even in the form of the unrefined Kansas vernacular, was the same:

> Grinnell [Gove County] rural high school trustees, of which I am clerk, had some school bonds drawn against the high school district through Mr. E. R. Nightley, of National Finance Co. These bonds, through you and your reccemendation, were put in escro in the Fidelity State Savings Bank at Emporia, Kans. Said bonds were to be held by said savings bank until all outstanding warnts against desrict of which tye had the numbers were to be called in by said savings bank. . . . Mr. French, will you as state auditor and as you reecemended this savings bank as a very reliable place to hold said bonds. Take the matter up with them ameaditly as the bonds were placed their last summer and the warnts were to be called in by them ameaditly, and the buisness should of been settled by first of Oct. 31.[36]

Auditor French's most persistent pen pal was Mrs. Lucy M. Pottorf, clerk of the school board at the village of Riley in Riley County. Mrs. Pottorf started off in July, 1932, in a polite-enough vein, complaining that Finney had not filed the canceled warrants, as promised, in the Auditor's Office and asking for French's help "in seeing that this matter is attended to promptly." French responded that "I took the matter up with Mr. Finney personally and he states that one of the warrants has not turned up is the reason, and he will take that up following the primary." On this occasion, Ronald Finney had told the truth: an additional warrant did remain outstanding. Mrs. Pottorf found it and mailed it to French on August 25. But to confound the problem and to add to the auditor's embarrassment, he had filed it away, he wrote her in late September, "so securely I cannot find it."[37]

A little later, Lee Caldwell appeared on the Pottorfs' front porch, claiming that French had given him the "lost" warrant and that the school board owed him $800 for it.[38] The plain-spoken Pottorf testified that she and Caldwell had had "quite a bit of conversation" about it. "I told him that he was to keep his contract with us and our contract . . . called for no $800 payment to him." "You don't believe for a minute," she was asked at the trial, "that that man who was trying to bleed you out there . . . had that warrant [in his pocket], do you?" "I thought he did; yes," she responded; "I didn't ask him; I was glad to get away with my pocketbook and everything I had in the house that day."[39]

Mrs. Pottorf persisted regarding the lost warrant. The following May she again wrote to French, stubbornly declaring that she wanted to get the matter settled before her term of office expired. Her tone had changed from that of the original correspondence nine months earlier. "Will it be necessary," she acidly asked French, "to have the attorney-general help us get this record straight?" The frustrated French responded that "the warrant you refer to has been canceled in this office, as per previous statement of having been paid, so that part is absolutely clear."[40] The board of managers made much of that response, which indicated all too clearly that French had acknowledged the fact that warrants were being canceled in his office as late as the spring of 1933.[41]

Given the extensive series of complaints from the school districts and given Will French's acknowledged dislike for Ronald Finney, it was a curious fact that the auditor didn't directly confront the broker about his refunding practices. French never once talked to Finney about his misrepresentations, though Finney was in and about the Auditor's Office on nearly a daily basis. In a subsequent attempt at a defense, the auditor said that "if you sat at my desk and get complaints, coming in on this fellow and that fellow, you get fed up on complaints. It is nothing uncommon for people to write to my office and complain."[42] He did acknowledge that he suspected that Finney "was doing something he didn't have business to."[43] Didn't he know that Finney and his agents had given the "official" word in every school district in Kansas that refunded warrants had to be canceled in the Auditor's Office? "No, I wouldn't say that that was ever in my mind that way."[44] But hadn't the recurrent letters given him direct notice that Finney was claiming that that was necessary? "They do now, they bring them right square to my eye."[45]

The auditor's failure to nip the bud of the warrant enterprise in 1931/32 can be attributed more to the enormous Finney confidence—his intimidating bravado—than to the Finney charm. When Ronald Finney explained something, "there just wasn't any other thing you could possibly want to know about it," an observer had once admiringly exclaimed.[46] Although French had had a good deal of experience—had, in fact, been in office longer than any of the major state officeholders—he still seemed to be unsure of himself in Finney's presence and was readily "bulldozed." This diffidence had prevented him from following through in a decisive manner on the evidence that was "square before his eyes." His failure to do so resulted in a great deal of distress and embarrassment for the school districts, the state of Kansas, and, not least of all, William James French.

WILL FRENCH may not have cottoned to Ronald Finney, but he had an absolute genius for picking top assistants who did. When Finney first began coming around the Statehouse, the assistant auditor had been George Winters. Winters and Finney struck up a warm friendship.[47] Regarding the latter, Winters testified that "outside of the fact that he would always come in there on the rush, want us to do something in five minutes that we should take an hour or so to do, I hadn't seen anything wrong with him at all."[48]

Joseph E. Voorhees had come into the office as assistant auditor, replacing Winters. Voorhees, a middle-aged former county clerk of Leavenworth County (for sixteen years), had also completed a stint as a school teacher. The friendship between the naïve Voorhees and the worldly wise Finney ripened quickly. In addition to cajoling Voorhees into signing the certificates of destruction, Finney asked him to do a variety of favors around the office, including frequent trips over to the bond clerk, W. H. Stanley, to check on how well a given bond deal was progressing. During Voorhees's tenure, Finney became a very common sight in the auditor's suite. Frequently seen at Voorhees's desk with their heads together, they engaged in lengthy, "sort of whispering" conversations. Finney or Caldwell frequently checked bond transcripts out of the auditor's vault. At the time of the disclosures, eight transcripts were checked out, one of which (a big Kansas City condemnation issue) never was recovered. Investigators discovered that numerous pages had been torn from five different ledgers, which held receipts for removal of transcripts—evidently an effort to destroy evidence about Finney's frequent withdrawal of the transcripts.[49]

One of Joe Voorhees's most valuable services consisted of his willingness to let Finney into the auditor's suite on weekends. On the first such occasion, Finney called Voorhees at Leavenworth on a Sunday. Voorhees's wife told Finney that her husband was in St. Joseph (Missouri) visiting his aged mother.[50] Finney called Voorhees and urged him to return. "I hadn't seen my mother for about six months, and I begged not to come," he said, "[but] I finally did."[51] Finney met him at the train station and drove him up to the Capitol. After checking a transcript for just a few moments, Finney cheerfully announced: "That is all I wanted to know." He then drove Voorhees to the bus depot, so that he could return to Leavenworth.[52] Could Finney obtain anything of significance in a minute's time? "He sure could," Voorhees testified, "he was pretty fast."[53] Why couldn't this business have been handled during regular office hours? "I didn't know what transcript [he wanted]; he didn't tell me, and that wasn't my business to find out. I was told to give the service, and I gladly gave it."[54]

What did Voorhees receive as compensation for these sundry services? Part of the recompense rested merely in being an associate, a confidant, of the dashing and powerful Finney. Voorhees's boss, when checking up on Voorhees's activities regarding the ladies, learned from Joe's landlady that he "spent a good deal of time" at the Jayhawk.[55] Once Finney asked Voorhees a lot of "Amos and Andy" questions about the gold standard and other high-level financial doings. "I told him that I was a poor man," Voorhees testified, "I didn't know about these big deals. . . . I couldn't understand why he would ask me . . . about millions."[56] In a more concrete expression of his gratitude, Finney made direct cash payments to Voorhees. When called back on weekends, Voorhees said, he received "a couple of dollars more than my actual expenses."[57] How much money, total, did the assistant auditor receive from Finney? "I don't remember; I think $10 one time, and . . . $15 the next time. . . . He gave me about the usual tip, I imagine, if you want to call it that."[58]

The coziness of Finney and French's assistant auditor for well over a year hadn't seemed to bother French at all. But in the spring of 1933 the auditor heard some news that did disturb him a great deal and led to the dismissal of Voorhees:

> His [Voorhees] wife came over to Topeka and called for Mrs. French and asked her to come down to the hotel, she had something awful she wanted to tell her . . . she told quite a tale there that Joe was not coming home over Sundays and that he was running around with some girl or girls in Topeka. . . .
>
> I took a little time to investigate to find out whether this was a fight between a man and his wife or whether there was something to it, and about three weeks later I told him that I expected he had better find another place.[59]

A few weeks later, Jim Kelsey, Leavenworth County Republican chairman, visited French. Kelsey, who was a law partner of Voorhees's brother, came to make inquiry on behalf of Voorhees as to the auditor's specific reasons for letting him go.[60] French told Kelsey that though Joe's work had been satisfactory, there was "a man in [the] office ahead of him" in seniority and he "had to take care of him." Why had he said that? "I wasn't going to come right out and tell about the girl thing," French testified. "I wasn't going to go into all of the details of why I fired him to a man who might be wanting to start a damage suit. I wouldn't want to be doing that."[61]

THE "MAN IN THE OFFICE ahead of Voorhees" was Ray N. Hardin, who assumed the assistant auditor's position on May 22, 1933. Since 1927, Hardin had been in charge of the sand-and-oil account of the state and had had responsibilities for river surveys. Prior to that he had served for eight years as a deputy clerk and as county clerk of Crawford County. Though the sand-and-oil account was nominally under the Executive Council (which consisted of the state constitutional officers, headed by the governor), Hardin had his desk in the auditor's suite, took his direction from French, and had always been considered to be one of French's employees.[62]

Ray Hardin had joined the Finney circus of trained animals long before he assumed the number-two post in the Auditor's Office. Hardin had first met Finney in Boyd's office in the summer of 1931, when he had dropped by to say hello to the treasurer. They quickly became warm friends. Hardin agreed to go out to Hinsdale County, Colorado, that August to audit the county treasurer's records subsequent to Finney's purchase of the large block of the county's bonds. After a three-week initial visit, Hardin returned in September and once again in December. Finney paid Hardin's expenses and a fee for his services. After the first trip, Hardin, when asking French for the time off, told his boss about his plans and Finney's connection with them.[63]

In March of 1932 Finney approached his buddy Hardin and asked if he would mind doing him another favor. Finney said that he owed $120 to a certain lady down in Crawford County. If he gave Hardin a check for that amount, would Hardin, in turn, send his check to the Frontenac lady? Finney, who had engaged in numerous nefarious transactions since the middle twenties in partnership with his cooperative father, didn't want the offending check to clear through the Fidelity Bank and his father's (worse yet, his blue-nosed mother's) prying eyes. The lady in Frontenac, you see, was one of the leading bootleggers in southeastern Kansas, the heart of bootleg country. When the teetotaler French eventually learned of the liquor transaction, he "criticized" Hardin and shortly thereafter asked him to turn in his keys at the Auditor's Office.[64]

In addition to the more direct payments for his services, Hardin enjoyed the pleasure of Finney's company at the Jayhawk. "I don't suppose I was over there to exceed a dozen times [in 1933]," he testified. What had he gone there for? "Not anything in particular"; he had just dropped in to visit.[65] He and his family took low-cost carefree vacations at the Finney ranch near Lake City. Hardin had been at Lake City in early August, 1933, when he had received a call from his harried boss to return post haste. Hardin had told French with a straight face that his wife's "condition" required the bracing Colorado climate.[66]

The strongest bond between Finney and Hardin came as a result of the broker's real-estate venture. The assets of Finney's company included about sixty rental properties, most of which were in Topeka. Among those properties was a modest four-apartment frame dwelling close by the Statehouse. As early as the fall of 1932 Finney had mentioned the possibility to Hardin of moving into one of these apartments.[67] Finney told him, Hardin said, "that it would possibly be cheaper for me than where I was living at that time."[68] A man of his word, Finney permitted Hardin and his wife to move in rent-free in mid March, 1933. At about the same time, Lee Meadows—the former newspaperman who had done such a fine job of publicizing Leon Roulier's visit to Topeka—moved into the same building at the same rent. Meadows and Hardin became fast friends. When they left Topeka in early January, 1934, they went into partnership in the printing business at Parsons.[69]

One of the major counts against French charged that he had hired Hardin; that Hardin had received "money, free rent and other valuable favors from Ronald Finney"; that "as a result of such payments and favors . . . , special favors were extended to the said Ronald Finney by the said Ray Hardin"; that French "knew, or by the exercise of reasonable diligence should have known, that said Hardin was receiving regular pay from Ronald Finney while performing duties in the auditor's office"; and that French, "by continuing the said Ray Hardin in office under the conditions aforesaid, is guilty of such neglect and mismanagement . . . as to constitute a misdemeanor in office."[70]

Considering the great pressure on his office that autumn, French did manifest an inexplicable difficulty in severing himself from his top assistant. Though the connection between Hardin and Finney had been fully disclosed by the end of August, French kept Hardin as the assistant auditor until the end of October. In fact he kept him on the payroll until mid December, permitting him to do some Sand Department work at the same rate of pay even after asking him to resign as assistant auditor.[71] If Hardin hadn't played middleman between Finney and Mrs. Bootlegger, he might be there yet.

AN IMPRESSION on the back of each of the more than one thousand forged bonds bore the most damning challenge to the integrity of the Auditor's Office. Boynton's signature, giving the attorney general's approval, had been forged; French's signature on the registration form had been forged; and the signatures of local officials and the county clerks' seals had been forged. But the impression of the seal of the State of Kansas was genuine. So swore no less an authority than J. C. Shearman of Wichita.

The meticulous Shearman could give running testimony for three days without taking a deep breath as evidence for his conclusion, if you cared to go into it that deeply. To save themselves that ordeal, both sides at the French trial agreed that the auditor's seal was genuine.[72]

How the genuine seal became affixed to those bogus securities over a period of thirteen months beginning in July, 1932, became a matter of intense interest from the initial stages of the investigation. Hugo Wedell had given the matter his personal attention. He speculated that Finney or one of his minions had gained entry to the auditor's suite by creeping along a ledge that ran around the north side of the Statehouse and slipping through an unlatched window. Fuel was added to that particular fire when, in mid August, a window in the auditor's suite was found unlocked. The aggressive Wedell gave the trembling Statehouse janitors and night watchmen the third degree, but with no concrete results.[73] Another theory had it that a watchman had been intercepted by one person while going his rounds, thus allowing an accomplice to slip in through an open transom. Then there was the lost-key theory. French, who held various combinations of these explanations, recalled that Voorhees had once misplaced his keys for a couple days, claiming later that they had turned up in his room.[74]

Given the Finney personality and *modus operandi*, it is most unlikely that entry to the office had been gained through a transom or by stealthily creeping along a narrow ledge at midnight. Ronald Finney unlocked people—not windows. The great seal, which weighs nearly ten pounds and is several inches wide, was secured to a board that was two feet long and the exact width of the seal. The board resided on a table in the central room of the auditor's suite of four offices, about fifteen feet from the desk of Joe Voorhees. Ray Hardin's desk sat in the adjoining room, near the auditor's vault.[75]

The most direct testimony on this critical question came from two independent sources in the office, each reporting on a different occurrence. French's brother-in-law reported to the auditor, sometime after the crash, that once when he returned a bit early from his noon break, he "had seen Mr. Voorhees and Mr. Finney there using the seal; one of them using the seal and the other feeding the bonds."[76] H. A. Perkins—a civil engineer with the Sand Fund who had known Joe Voorhees for thirty years—testified that in the early spring of 1933, sometime between 1:00 and 1:30 P.M. (the dinner hour ran from noon to 1:30 P.M.), he had observed Voorhees and Finney using the auditor's seal. Finney was using the seal while his accomplice was "poking the bonds into the seal."[77] Since Finney continued to use the seal until August, he had had to make other arrangements after

Voorhees's sudden departure in May. With whom those arrangements were made isn't too difficult to guess. Both Voorhees and Hardin denied having known anything about the illegal use of the seal.[78] In fact, Hardin wasn't totally convinced, he publicly asserted, that the genuine seal had actually been used. "The original seal was placed on the forged bonds, was it not?" he was asked at the trial. "I don't know that it was," he unblinkingly replied.[79] J. C. Shearman would have smiled at that.

ANOTHER MAJOR CHARGE filed against French concerned his role in the Treasury Board meeting of June 23, 1932. With Treasurer Boyd at the controls, the Finney banks had become a most-favored state depository, sometimes holding as much as 10 percent of the total state funds on deposit. However, during the early summer the Fidelity particularly had been hurting for funds, due to the unyielding demand by the Banking Department that they correct various irregularities. The Finneys felt that something had to be done, and quickly. They also were concerned about the shaky Farmers State Bank of Wichita, a friendly institution with which Ronald Finney had done a good deal of bond business.[80]

On that particular morning the state treasurer, at the insistence of Ronald Finney, made a withdrawal of $1,444,875 from the soldier bonus accounts, which were held in all 105 counties of the state. Finney anxiously approached a cashier in the Treasury Department, Garnet Stiers, and asked her how long the withdrawal would take. Stiers, who didn't have much use for Finney, replied that it would be afternoon before she could get to it. A few moments later, Tom Boyd appeared and told her he "had to have it in twenty minutes" and that he would send someone in to help her.[81] That someone turned out to be Leland Caldwell. The former treasury employee helped to prepare the drafts on the counties, and upon the instructions of the treasurer, Caldwell took the checks, totaling almost a million and a half, for deposit in the National Bank of Topeka. That wasn't the first time that Caldwell or Finney had performed such a task, Stiers testified. They had handled checks varying in amounts from $10,000 to $50,000, transferring state funds from one depository to another, beginning as early as August, 1930. Stiers' testimony came from a written statement that she had given in August, 1933. She died on January 30, the night before she was to testify at the French trial.[82]

The Treasury Board held an emergency meeting that June afternoon on the call of Boyd and Finney. The minutes of the meeting told the short, sour story:

Moved by Mr. French that the Fidelity State and Savings Bank and the Farmers State Bank of Wichita be considered banks to take care of the excess deposits, and the state treasurer . . . may deposit in one or both of these banks, without additional security, up to $50,000.[83]

Why would French make such a motion, since no similar resolution naming specific banks for deposits without security had ever been made before? At the trial, his counsel suggested that French had been preoccupied at that time because his wife lay seriously ill in a Topeka hospital.[84] French said simply, and convincingly, "I don't know."[85]

AT THE OUTSET of the trial the *State Journal,* which manifested considerably more sympathy for the cause of French than for any of the other accused, evaluated his situation and took a swipe at the progressive forces:

Suppose . . . that the senate decides it must go home with blood on its hands, the blood the populace demands. Mr. French is the most likely victim. . . .

. . . in Mr. French's case there won't be a former governor on the floor of the senate courtroom; there won't be a federal judge working in his behalf; there won't be the Kansas City Star watching from behind tilted cigars; there won't be William Allen White in emotional eruption.[86]

Judge S. C. Bloss once again chaired the Board of Managers. Other members of the board included R. A. Cox, Augusta; O. P. May, Atchison; W. D. Reilly, Leavenworth; and George Templar, Arkansas City. Jaspar Napoleon ("Poly") Tincher of Medicine Lodge and Hutchinson, who was a long-time friend of the accused, headed counsel for the defense. Tincher had served four successive terms in the U.S. House of Representatives (1919-27) from the "big seventh," the western Kansas district that had sent such notables as "Sockless" Jerry Simpson, Chester Long, Victor Murdock, Jouett Shouse, and Clifford Hope to Washington.[87] The colorful but conservative Tincher had once been hailed as the "prince of Kansas windbags" by Clyde Reed.[88] The defense also included Randal Harvey of Topeka (brother of the assistant Shawnee County attorney, Paul) and Robert Garvin of St. John, both of whom were old friends of the defendant.[89]

The four articles of impeachment included charges that the forged bonds bore a certificate of registration purporting to have been executed in the Auditor's Office with the impress of the genuine seal and the charges that related to Ray Hardin (Article 1); the several charges relating to the canceled warrants and the certificates of destruction (Article 2); the charge growing from the motion made by French at the June 23, 1932, meeting of the Treasury Board (Article 3); the "conspiracy" charge (similar to Article 3 in the Boynton charges), which, as before, no one took very seriously (Article 4).[90]

The trial moved slowly for the first few days, coming as it did in the immediate wake of the Boynton verdict. Tired, restless, and irritable, the senators seemed to show more interest in Dutch Shultz's political column in the *State Journal* than in the proceedings.[91] Senator E. H. Benson announced on the morning of the second day, a Friday, that he wanted to call it quits and go home right then. He had been disturbed by the ugly rumors floating around the hotel lobbies "that the political and the social hook-up of the attorney-general was such that he was to be acquitted, and the respondent here is to be convicted."[92] But by the following Tuesday —the trial was postponed for Kansas Day, January 29—after having been rejuvenated by a weekend of politicking back home, the senators began to feel their oats once again, and the trial proceeded apace.

The Board of Managers introduced in evidence a lengthy statement that had been made by French in September. French had been questioned closely by the state investigators, especially Wedell, and had offered a much more revealing—and damning—explanation of matters than he would give, after reflection, in direct testimony at the trial.[93] Wedell enumerated the major factors that had placed French's office "under a cloud," and he pressed the auditor on why he had not thoroughly interrogated members of his office staff about what they knew. French explained that one day he had called everybody in and said, "Folks, I want you to tell the truth."[94] Not too surprisingly, nothing had come of that. But French had another scheme. "My plans were, if there was anything they knew, I could find it out more by watching them than by questioning them. . . . The person who is guilty will be doing a lot of talking to me." "They haven't done it, at any rate up to now?" the exasperated Wedell asked. "Only when I asked them, and I figured in that way I would be able to find out something," French replied enigmatically.[95]

The first article had detailed the Hardin-Finney tie-up, and held French accountable. Though Joe Voorhees's name did not appear in the articles, he did appear as the star witness for the prosecution. A tense struggle continued throughout the trial as the opposing counsels attempted to prove that the "state's man" (Voorhees) was better or worse than the "defendant's man" (Hardin). The problem stemmed from the fact that the evidence of Voorhees's helpfulness to Finney was the stronger but the linkage of Hardin to Finney in the payoff department was the greater.[96]

Referring to a prosecutor's repeated condemnation of Hardin and his defense of Voorhees, Poly Tincher disgustedly declared toward the end of the trial: "God bless him. He can have them both."[97]

Neither side had called Hardin, who was considered by both to be an unreliable maverick who couldn't be trusted. But on January 31, on a motion by Senator William Schoen, the Senate issued subpoenas for both Hardin and his Parsons printing business partner, Lee Meadows. The summons was telegraphed to the sheriff of Labette County and was promptly delivered to the witnesses.[98] When they hadn't appeared by the next afternoon, the angry Senator Schoen took the floor: "They have had ample time to get here, and this Senate and this Court will be the laughing stock of the state of Kansas if we let this go by a default. I am going to move that we instruct the governor to instruct the militia to go and find these men and bring them in here."[99]

The reluctant witnesses finally showed up on February 2, protesting that they had been held up by a freight train outside of Parsons. Testifying in a low, barely audible voice, Hardin admitted that he had worked for Finney in various capacities since 1931; that he had been a habitué at the Jayhawk; and that he had lived rent-free in an apartment provided by Finney.[100] He then categorically denied that he had known Finney owned the apartment until after the scandal broke. A minute later, he tripped himself by blurting out that Finney had said "that he owned an apartment over there on Tyler."[101] Hardin said that he had spent around $140 on the apartment in order "to be comfortable." This, he claimed, was understood to be in lieu of the $45 per month rent. The $140 outlay included a $75 stove, which the Hardins had taken with them when they moved. Window shades, linoleum, and a light bulb had cost around $40. A sarcastic Senator Harris asked if he had taken the light bulb, too.[102] Near the conclusion, Hardin was asked if Finney was "just a casual acquaintance of yours." "You might term it that, yes," was his incredible response.[103]

Defense motions to quash (on the first day) and to dismiss (five days later) had been badly beaten. But at the conclusion of the state's case on February 2, French's problems diminished considerably. Although a general demurrer to the evidence lost (11 to 28 to 1), specific defense demurrers on articles 1 (22 to 18), 3 (16 to 24), and 4 (33 to 7) were sustained. On the second, and only remaining article, the vote stood at 8 to 31 to 1. On these several defense motions, support for the defendant was generally bipartisan, with somewhat more strength from the Republican side.[104]

The remaining article dealt with school-district warrants and the certificates of destruction. The defense quickly adjusted to the new circumstances, calling only eighteen of the eighty-two witnesses who had been subpoenaed. J. H. Shriver of Pratt County recounted his tale of having extracted a certificate of destruction from Finney in August, 1932. A number of witnesses from the Auditor's Office testified; most of them said that they thought Finney had done a lot more business with Voorhees than with Hardin.[105]

The respondent himself testified for half a day on the morning of February 5, covering much the same ground as in his September statement. His answers now glistened with polish, producing far fewer opportunities for the prosecution to pounce on a slip or expand on a blunder. On a direct question from a senator, French admitted that if the Treasury Board had carried out its prescribed duties and had checked the bonds put up for security, the duplications would have been readily discovered.[106]

Realizing that the trial represented the last formal state action to arise from the scandal and that they had not yet had a chance to interrogate (or even see) Ronald Finney and Tom Boyd, the Senate considered subpoenaing the two major culprits. Senator Miller made the motion on the penultimate day of the trial. The Democrats seemed to show rather more enthusiasm for the proposition than the Republicans, especially the more conservative Republicans.[107] Senator Hansen, a Cloud County Democrat, explained his thinking:

> I think it is only right and proper that a man, who seemingly had the ability to throw the machinery of the state of Kansas into such a turmoil, should at least be questioned a little . . . as to how he did it. I was home over the week-end, and I talked to a lot of people, men who [are] considered smart men. They asked me, "Say, we can understand that one official might go wrong, but how did it happen that the whole caboodle went wrong?" and then they asked me, "Did you ever see that man that was able to do all that?" "No, we haven't." "Well, what have you been doing?"[108]

After some spirited debate, the motion passed, and Ronald Finney was scheduled to appear in the Senate chamber that very afternoon, February 5. The word spread like a prairie fire through the Statehouse and downtown Topeka that Kansas' archfiend would be on the stand at 2 P.M. The galleries, which had been only partially full, quickly filled and spilled over into the aisles and around the perimeter of the chamber. The jam-packed assemblage, Dutch Shultz remarked, "stood goggle-eyed waiting for the grand event."[109]

"Your name is Ronald Finney?" asked Fred Harris. "Yes, sir," answered Finney, wearing his best cynical smile. Whereupon the nimble

John Schenck jumped to his feet and declared (without taking a breath) that whereas his client was now a defendant in a case pending in Shawnee County District Court and in a case on trial (the Caldwell case) and was a defendant in other pending state and federal cases, and whereas the evidence in these cases "might include almost anything," and whereas it would be impossible at this juncture to determine whether any particular question might tend to incriminate him—for all these reasons, "I object to any testimony from this witness." After a short conference the chair asked Finney if it was his desire not to testify at this time. "Yes sir; on advice of counsel," the archfiend quietly responded. The question of whether Finney should be excused from testifying was then put to a roll-call vote and carried 22 to 16 to 2, with rather more Republican support for the proposition. The witness was excused and was returned to jail. A few days later, to buttress his devoutly desired image of poverty, he put in a claim for the $1.50 witness fee. The claim was disallowed on the grounds that since he was a ward of the state, he had no citizenship standing and therefore was ineligible.[110] Poor Ronald—he was frustrated by society even when he tried to earn an honest dollar.

Tom Boyd and his attorney, Tinkham Veale, followed Finney and Schenck with identical reasons, which yielded an identical result. The roll-call vote was 22 to 17 to 1.[111]

IN ITS SUMMATION, the prosecution appealed to the senators' sense of outrage at the bond-scandal events. W. D. Reilly led off for the Board of Managers:

> If you want to say to the people of Kansas that when you enter the statehouse you must bring a bodyguard with you or you will be robbed, if you want to say to the people of Kansas that we will hang a sign over the state capitol, "Honor has no place here," turn this man loose, but if you fairly, unbiasedly, consider the actual evidence in this case, you cannot help but vote to convict him on the second article.[112]

Thirty-year-old George Templar, for the prosecution, made the most poignant statement at either impeachment trial:

> It may be that, because of my youth, I have too high a conception of honor and trust, such as I am sure dwells in the breast of every youth in Kansas, and it may be that sometime these precepts that I hold of high public office . . . which were instilled in my heart in the public schools of Kansas, will become mellowed with the passing of time . . . so that I will overlook the frailties of those who . . . claim the right to lead

my people, but I doubt it . . . , and I can tell you why. You know as well as I that Kansas has long been made the butt of . . . jokes and criticisms from outsiders for what they call our "righteous sternness" and the strict accountability of those rules of conduct which we have set for our people, and that is true. We have been stern. . . . we have expected much from our people, not only from our people, but from those whom we elect to public office. We have not lived in an atmosphere where faithlessness in a public office has been tolerated for a moment . . . , and I want to tell you that I am proud to be a native son of so illustrious a state, and I sincerely hope that whatever action you gentlemen take here, the vision of the youth of Kansas for strict accountability of its public officers will not be shattered by [that] action.[113]

The defense stuck to more mundane matters. They argued that French was not prohibited by law from signing the certificates of destruction; that he had told Finney not to bring any more in after he had signed the first ones; and that he later told Voorhees not to sign any more certificates. They also made reference to the public pressure on the senators. "In the Boynton case we started out with the idea that you were going to have to explain your vote to the groceryman and the drayman and a few other special industries," defense attorney Robert Garvin said in his summation; "but when they started to try Mr. French, for some reason they gave us credit that we will have to explain our votes to the whole people of Kansas. So we are in some respects rather flattered."[114] Toward the conclusion of Garvin's remarks he made reference to Voorhees's penchant for the ladies. Mrs. Voorhees, who was seated beside her husband, suddenly shouted, "That's a lie! It isn't true." The startled Garvin continued, remarking that the cited testimony had not been denied. Whereupon Mrs. Voorhees interjected again with a very firm "I do deny it!" A sergeant-at-arms cautioned her to be quiet, and no further outbursts emanated from the unhappy woman.[115]

Poly Tincher appealed to the senators' conscience in his concluding remarks for the defense:

> Gentlemen of the Senate, I want to ask you to do this: When you come to vote on "guilty" or "not guilty" in this case, vote with your conscience. I do not want some of you to go home and say, "I voted 'guilty' against a man who is not guilty." The only difference in the world to Bill French is that he will be permitted to serve out his term of office . . . , that he may be permitted to go back to Stafford County where we love him and his, and live his life without having on his name and his family's name the stigma of a verdict of "guilty" of a crime that sounds more horrible than death.[116]

The Senate resolved itself into executive session at midday on February 6. Simon Fishman, who was always the first one out of an executive session (it is "against the principles of a man from the wide open spaces of western Kansas"), had been the first with the news. After considerable discussion the vote on the question to sustain the charges in Article 2 had been 18 to 22. Only seven Republicans had joined eleven Democrats to sustain the charges. Will French had been acquitted on all counts. That evening, over two hundred well-wishers came by the Frenches' home to offer their congratulations.[117]

THE RESPONSE to the acquittals in the impeachment trials depended on one's position on the political spectrum. The outcomes pleased William Allen White:

> The Senate is to be praised because it refused to yield to political partisanship and factional bias. [French and Boynton] are to be congratulated because in a time of hysteria their innocence has been established. . . . the State of Kansas is to be congratulated because in future days it may not be said of Kansas that its people officially and in a rage of justifiable shame and proper humiliation, judicially lynched two public servants, who were innocent. . . . But, so long as impeachment was . . . charged . . . , it is well that the trials have gone clear through to this happy ending.[118]

The *Kansas City Star* also was happy with the results, importuning the state to return to normalcy:

> The political prosecutions rising from the Finney affair in Kansas are thus wound up and out of the way. . . . The state is almost ready to turn its back on an unfortunate and humiliating chapter in its history, to apply the lessons painfully learned from it, and embark on a new era with a more vigilant and more healthy mental attitude toward the obligations of state office.[119]

The *Topeka Capital* reflected the sentiments of many Kansans in the wake of the impeachments:

> It cannot be said . . . these trials were a clear loss to the state. It is worth much that the whole story was told and the public has a far better understanding of what happened in the State House. . . . There were questions involved that could not have been entirely cleared up without the impeachment trials. Moreover, without [them], the officials accused if not of actual criminality at least of great lack of diligence and under-

standing of how their offices were being used [,] would have escaped scot free even of censure.[120]

The *State Journal* took a more jaundiced view of the matter and gave some unsolicited advice to the two principals:

> The verdict of acquittal in the French case comes as no surprise. . . . The case . . . admittedly was weaker than the one . . . [against] Boynton. . . . It would be foolish to pretend that the . . . verdict restores either of them to the confidence of the people. . . .
>
> However the close friends of the two . . . may feel, the . . . voters have a very decided opinion as to [their] usefulness in office. Neither specious arguments, official fluster nor the clattering of swords in the cause of future righteousness will change that opinion. If only on the ground of party patriotism, Mr. Boynton and Mr. French should resign.[121]

It remained for the "ring-tailed hellcat" Marion Ellet in her *Journal Post* "Mugwump" column to wreak the most devastation on the forces of goodness and light in a hilarious parody entitled "Prayer Meeting." Marion's rapierlike wit and sarcastic brilliance never shone to better advantage. The piece became a major siege gun in the arsenal of the Democrats as they prepared to slay the Republican dragon in the campaign of 1934.[122]

> Now that Brother Boynton and Brother French have been gathered back into the fold, I suppose we can go right on with the prayer meeting. . . .
>
> Let's see where were we when the prayer meeting was interrupted? Oh, yes, Brother Boynton had just given thanks that he was not as other men—not as little sheriffs who are negligent . . . ; not as gamblers and wastrels who squander their patrimony in nickel slot machines; not as lawbreakers who peddle 3.2 beer. Brother Bill Smith had delivered a sermon on total abstinence and Brother Richard J. Hopkins had rendered, "Home, Sweet Home." Brother Finney was passing the collection plate and the whole celestial choir which is led by the Kansas City Star and the Emporia Gazette and which includes . . . Brother Clyde Reed, Brother Henry Allen, . . . and Sister Lillian Mitchner, was about to sing "Purer Yet and Purer" as a closing hymn.
>
> That was just before the interruption which occurred when it was discovered that Brother Finney and the collection plate were missing. A still hunt revealed that the collection plate wasn't the only thing that was missing. The taxpayers were out a million dollars more or less. . . . And here were the federal authorities clamoring at the very door of the prayer meeting. This was terrible! At least it seemed terrible for a little while.

A MOST HELPFUL OFFICE

But at length it was discovered that the whole wretched business of swindling, filching, conspiracy and willful negligence was carried on by Christian gentlemen. As long as the state had to be looted everyone did hope that it had been looted by the right people. And it had. So that made everything all right. You see, the whole business might have been in the hands of infidels, and that would have been a scandal indeed. But now that there's no scandal, I presume we can go right on with the prayer meeting.[123]

14

Politics

ooooooooooooooooooooooooooooooooooooooooooooooooo

POLITICS reared its ugly head almost immediately after the bond scandal broke. Affecting virtually all the major state offices, the scandal had numerous political ramifications. Frequently a front-page story, the infamy continued to be a major factor down through the general election of 1934.

When Sard Brewster told Alf Landon what he knew on that fateful Monday morning in 1933, the chief executive had to act first and think later. Disregarding the possible repercussions of his actions, he responded instinctively to the crisis in a decisive, uncompromising fashion, and he continued to do so throughout the autumn. As it turned out, his precipitate acts, which the alarming circumstances dictated to be both proper and necessary, marked his most astute political course. Had he delayed his response for days while he pensively ruminated on the matter, he could not have chosen a more circumspect policy to enhance his own political future. The thinking public could hardly have expected the governor to do more; on the other hand, they scarcely would have permitted less. Landon perhaps led them in the cleanup in the same fashion that Napoleon "led" the French troops to Moscow in 1812 or that one jumps in front of a rolling boulder and "leads" it down the mountainside.[1]

In the 1932 campaign Landon had said: "If you do elect me and I find corruption I'll stamp it out if it's the last thing I do."[2] Few politicians ever received as quick an opportunity—or as severe a test— to live up to campaign rhetoric. "When I get through," the intransigent governor declared at the end of the first week of the scandal, "there will be no excuse for anyone to point a finger at any person . . . and say, 'They applied the white wash. . . .' Several persons I personally like are going to get hurt, but I can't help it.

I was elected governor of Kansas and, to me, that means the enforcement of law without fear or favor."[3] The people of Kansas from Hiawatha to Garden City, from Goodland to Baxter Springs—man, woman, and child—stood up and applauded.

The *Topeka Capital* expressed complete confidence in Landon's ability to stand up under pressure from outside sources: "In the bond scandal the people of Kansas place their-reliance upon Gov. Landon. They are right in feeling confident, we believe, that there is no influence powerful enough to intervene anywhere along the line to turn the investigation by the width of a hair from its purpose, or to give any individual, high or low, what is known as a 'break.' "[4] "I tell you," Senator Capper remarked over the radio on August 15, "it means a lot to know that we have a governor who is not afraid to do his duty, no matter who may be affected."[5]

Landon had been under unrelenting pressure since he took office in January. The horde of pathetic job seekers who had frequently disturbed his private life had been followed by the potentially troublesome legislature. The stressful and enormously time-consuming bond scandal came hard on the heels of attempts to solve the vexing relief and beer problems. Then came the kidnapping plot on his family. Finally, the special session of the legislature and the two impeachments. "But a visitor to his office," commented the *Leavenworth Times*, "still finds a pleasant, calm, interested and capable man behind the desk."[6] The *Capital* suggested that his popularity lay in his "humanness, unaffected friendliness and business judgments."[7]

After the first few weeks the governor began to appear less and less frequently in the public eye as regards the scandal. This did not mean, however, that he had turned the cleanup over to Fred Harris and his assistants. Quietly, behind the scenes, he continued to play a dominant role in all the major activities. He directed the state's role in all the criminal and civil cases in which it had an interest; he pushed the investigation of the questionable practices in the Eureka bank; he became directly involved in the complicated financial settlement of Warren Finney's affairs; and he even immersed himself in such detail as asking a district judge for a change in his court calendar so that the ardent Matt Guilfoyle (a Democrat) could serve on the Board of Managers in Boynton's trial.[8] During the impeachment trials, Landon sat alone in his office, refusing to take an overt hand in the prosecution. "And by his door in a steady stream," noted the *State Journal*, "marched the powers that sought to discredit his board of managers. If the impeachment trials defeat Governor Landon this year, it [will be] because he refused to play politics."[9]

The *Atchison Globe* warned that Landon's vigorous prosecution of the principals in the scandal had "aroused powerful enemies against him." "A great effort will be made to embarrass and defeat him for re-election," it continued. "A certain crowd in Topeka will organize against him, for the reason that the bond scandal involves several of their rosy-cheeked pets. That crowd feels the Governor was not diplomatic, that he should have given the guilty a chance to quietly adjust matters."[10] In November the *State Journal,* which had become a warm admirer of Landon due to his firm handling of the affair, admonished that "the real goat [of the scandal] is ... Governor Landon.... Every political finger will point at him in an attempt to discredit him with the voters."[11] Just before the Senate reached a decision in the Boynton case, the *Journal Post* declared emphatically that "a whitewash is coming and ... it will ruin Landon."[12]

IT WAS KANSAS DAY as usual—almost—on January 29, as fifteen hundred of the Republican-party faithful gathered in Topeka to hear the former secretary of the treasury, Ogden L. Mills, as the principal "foreign" speaker. Don C. Little, who had leaped to prominence as one of Fred Harris's assistant investigators, gave a rousing "toast to Kansas" oration. Thirty-seven years earlier that honored duty had been performed by the youthful and innocent Warren Finney.[13]

Held just four days after the Boynton decision, the meeting heard John D. M. Hamilton laud Landon for furnishing honest leadership "without fear or favor." Finney's erstwhile lawyer declared that Kansas Republicans needed to have no fear in the fall election with Landon leading the ticket. The large crowd roared its approval.[14] Bill Clugston reported that "the 'whitewashing' of Boynton brought gloom to the countenances of most leaders as they gathered." They openly expressed fear that the outcome of Boynton's trial would be used as a spearhead to oust them from office.[15] The *Star* observed that the meeting took place "under the most discouraging circumstances of many years." But at the conclusion of the conclave, the leaders of the G.O.P. bravely announced that they intended to go forth into the campaign "with freshly cleaned weapons and a chastened but indomitable spirit."[16]

WHILE LANDON had achieved great popularity with the public, the "without fear or favor" prosecutions of the politically potent had produced some significant realignments within the power structure of the party. Many egos had been bruised; private frustration and hostility ran high. The anti-Landon forces included the remnants of the political machines of Tom Boyd,

Alf Landon enjoying Kansas Day festivities (Kansas State Historical Society)

of Rolie Boynton, of Will French, of the Finneys, and possibly even of William Allen White.[17]

In the early spring the antigovernor coalition attempted to identify a candidate who would run in the primaries against Landon. The improbable name of Will French came tumbling out of the rumor mill. The impeached but exonerated auditor had had second thoughts about his political future and had begun to think seriously about running against Landon, whom, by now, he openly despised. In early March, state Senator William Schoen, who had been among the most active senators at the trials, made a formal announcement of his candidacy but later withdrew. No one seemed to relish the prospect of going into the primary "with the flag of the bond scandal defendants flying above his tent."[18]

"Last summer," Marion Ellet observed, "the 'Progressive Republicans' ... could have accepted the unpleasant fact that [Boynton] had been morally doped ... by one of the biggest crooks who ever set foot in Kansas, and they could have asked their attorney general to resign, [or] they could sacrifice the party and Landon in order to vindicate [Boynton]. . . . [They did the latter] because they couldn't face the music of disgrace . . . [and] they didn't want to break their line of succession from attorney general to supreme bench."[19] Knowledgeable observers of the political scene, recalling the cooperative spirit that had existed in the past between the progressive Republicans and the Woodring-Helvering Democrats, expected to see "that alliance renewed this year and the Boynton strength thrown behind a Democrat candidate acceptable to William Allen White who emerges from the impeachment trial a tower of strength instead of a discredited political leader, as some persons saw him a few months ago."[20]

AFTER HIS CLOSE CALL in the Senate, Roland Boynton took time to reflect on his current condition and future prospects. He found the presence of the Landon-appointed Fred Harris a daily affront. After all, Harris had been doing—and continued to do—what the attorney general should have done and should now be doing. And who had abruptly appointed Harris in the first place, arbitrarily usurping Boynton's legitimate authority in those dark days of early August, a usurpation that had led directly to all his problems? Contemplation of his present plight and past tormentors led Boynton to seriously consider aiding and abetting the anti-Landon forces, now a cause busily looking for a leader.

This potential development had caused a deep frown to furrow the brow of the famous cousin. On February 13 Mr. White gave "Rol" some friendly, paternal advice:

> About Harris: Do try to work out your relations with Harris. I know it is terrible. But unless you are prepared to be the center of a big state row and defend yourself almost against the united opinion which the Governor can swing, it would be disastrous for you to make a public break.
>
> Political fighting is not your fort or hold. I don't see how you can do it. But on the other hand, I realize the stress you are under. If you come out best with yourself and with Harris in the spiritual tussle that you will have to make, for which you are equipped, it will be better than to make the public break.[21]

White had not shared the full extent of his alarm with his protégé. He had been concerned enough—though not nearly so much as his outraged son—at the governor's alleged interference with the sentencing of his friend Ronald Finney in December and with the vigorous prosecution of Boynton, which had been inspired if not literally led by the hard-nosed governor. But White had cannily surveyed the wreckage on the postscandal political scene—he had sniffed the factional wind and counted the partisan house—and had determined unequivocally that he wanted to stay firmly hitched to the governor and to the dominant Republican power structure. Boynton's posttrial threats to break publicly with the governor, therefore, had been a good deal more unsettling to the surrogate "father" than the "son" could have imagined. So the distressed editor called on a member of the family to carry an urgent, confidential message to Boynton—a move that would ultimately prove to be successful. The man chosen for this delicate mission had carried more confidential messages and held more sensitive political information in his forebrain than any other unelected man in Kansas history —White's brother-in-law and Landon's confidant, Lacy Haynes.[22] White, the old political war-horse, asked Lacy to explain a thing or two to the recalcitrant and unappreciative attorney general.

> [Tell him] that I strained myself as hard as I could, and pledged myself as far as I dared with [Guy] Helvering, to get those Democrats not to make a political issue of this impeachment, but to listen to the evidence....
>
> [Tell him] that I used every ounce of influence I had with the Kansas newspapermen. And . . . that I cannot budge a step further in this matter without crippling myself for further usefulness, and that the nearer he comes to a public break with Harris and with Landon . . . the nearer he comes to putting an impossible task on me and ruining my usefulness for many years....
>
> But whether I help him in the break or not I would be crippled by his break and that he must see.[23]

White had indeed pulled out all the stops in his frenzied attempt to save Boynton's hide. After the favorable outcome of the trial, he had written to his old political foe, the standpatter John Hamilton, currently the Republican National Committeeman, thanking him for favors rendered and acknowledging a major political debt:

> I want to thank you specifically . . . for your kindness in helping Boynton get a fair hearing. I realize that but for you, if factionalism had entered the vote, Boynton would have been impeached [that is, convicted] and I feel that you persuaded seven or eight of your conservative Senatorial friends to listen to the evidence and not be counselled by factional prejudice. When men like Maloney [Delaney], Knapp, Bradney, Russell and Dale line up for a man who has had progressive support in the past, it is a sign that these men are not considering anything but the evidence and I know that your good offices have helped....
>
> Again let me express my gratitude to you for all that you have done and let me tell you that you have deposited in my bank and I will acknowledge your check.[24]

THOUGH BOYNTON privately brimmed with frustration, the public saw a newly energized attorney general after his acquittal. He turned his watchful puritanical eye, once again, on possible infringements of the state's liquor and gambling laws. "Boynton is on the job," the *Gazette* proudly proclaimed in mid February, "with full steam ahead and will continue on the job until next January. He has a right to show the state that he can make good; and he will show it."[25] The road for the attorney general in that final year wasn't always smooth, however. In May he criticized the Pittsburg Police Department for its alleged failure to protect unemployed workers in a riot in which several had been injured. Boynton wrote the mayor, asking that "every effort be taken to prevent future disorders." "Roland Boynton," the mayor loudly and publicly proclaimed, "can go to hell."[26]

The attorney general did not heed this advice, however, and served out the remainder of his term in relative harmony. At the conclusion of it, he went into a law partnership in Topeka with an assistant attorney general. The *Gazette* acknowledged that Boynton wouldn't be returning to Emporia: "Lyon County loses one auto license tag that has been bought here for 15 years, and one good citizen, and the 'sojer boys' a good fellow. . . . 'There will be one vacant chair'. . . . This town needs his kind. But business is business and he has to go where the business is. So goodbye Rolie; take care of yourself!"[27]

Frustrated by the controlling realities in his desire to see his favorite cousin on the Supreme Court bench, the undaunted Mr. White turned his attention to the upcoming vacancy in the Attorney General's Office. Encouraged by the reaction to the early soundings, the *Gazette* in February gave a "home town boost" to the impending candidacy of the Lyon County attorney and Finney prosecutor C. V. Beck. "When he played first base on the Americus [Lyon County] ball team, he was 'Prunes' Beck," the *Gazette* chortled, "now he is C. V. Beck, and if he gets to be attorney general he will be Mr. Clarence Victor Beck."[28]

With assurance of the *Gazette*'s backing, Beck announced officially on June 1. "He has never belonged to The Gazette's faction," the paper noted, "but he is a straight, brave, able young man. This is no time for factionalism and if the Republicans win in this campaign, they must get together."[29] Although Beck had been an obscure county attorney before the Finney scandal, he had handled the prosecution of Finney so well that he had attracted widespread attention across the state. And during the primary and the fall campaign he didn't let the voters forget his sterling accomplishment. In late October the populace was again reminded of the association when Beck announced that he had been forced to halt his campaign in order to prepare a response to W. W. Finney's appeal to the Kansas Supreme Court.[30]

FROM THE VERY OUTSET the Democrats sought to take full advantage of the scandal that had been dropped in their undernourished laps like manna from political heaven. Speaking at a Eudora picnic a week after the initial revelations, Thurman Hill, a Democratic gubernatorial aspirant, charged that if the state officials had done their duty, Kansas wouldn't have been "mulcted of over a million dollars. . . . The attorney general failed in his duty because he approved apparently forged bonds; the auditor was negligent in permitting duplicates to be registered and the governor was negligent in failing to make a thorough monthly inspection of the records of the . . . treasurer."[31] Hill, in a speech at Coffeyville on August 30, charged that it was Landon's duty to ask for the resignation of five state officials. The Republicans, he said, would doubtless like to shift the blame to the Woodring administration, but "unfortunately for them none of the forged bonds was deposited in the [treasury] until March 3."[32] That refrain would be picked up later in the fall by another prominent Democrat, much to his regret.

The Democratic invective gained both in color and in force as the autumn leaves fell and the winter set in. Occasionally an unkind soul or unfriendly newspaper referred to the governor as "Alfred Finney Landon." One partisan cried, "Is the Emporia *Gazette* going to continue its policy of holding a soft spot in its heart for the desperadoes of Kansas?" A resolution of a Young Democrat group in Manhattan assailed the Landon administration as "venal, corrupt and wasteful." At a mid-December rally, both Thurman Hill and Senator Charles Miller excoriated the administration for its handling of the bond scandal, charging that "the governor should have been impeached before Boynton and French." The final formal effort to associate the Republicans and the scandal even more firmly in the public eye came in late winter at a short special legislative session, called primarily to extend the moratorium on farm mortgages. The Democrats offered a resolution that would have forced Governor Landon to initiate an investigation of the connection between Republican Jesse Greenleaf and the Finneys, but it never got out of committee.[33]

The little Democratic weeklies regularly added their small but febrile voices to the partisan outcry. The *Western Spirit* at Paola gleefully pointed out that "all connected with the steal, directly or indirectly, are Republican politicians now in control of Kansas."[34] The Democratic weekly in Emporia, the *Emporia Times,* editorialized: "This paper joins with many others in commending the vigor of the Landon clean-up; but we can't help feeling that some of this pent up condemnation might have been loosed a little sooner. . . . An office-holding clique for years has run the state house, about as it pleased, with the first attention to the selfish interests of the office-holders."[35] Lynn Broderick, the Democratic National Committeeman, growled in his *Marysville Advocate-Democrat:* "The state house bond scandal has shocked the state, but it is not at all surprising. The stage has been set for just such a sordid scene for years. . . . Republican office holders can get away with murder in Topeka. Each is allowed to rule his own roost. The Press is docile, harmless, and of the same faith."[36] "Out in this part of the state," declared the *Leoti Standard,* "when a pigpen gets so rank that anybody can notice it, the pig owner moves the pen over onto some clean grass. Why not move the state capitol out of Topeka, dip it, delouse it, and plant it on some clean spot."[37]

The optimistic Democrats gathered, two thousand strong, for their traditional Washington Day rally on February 22 in the Jayhawk Hotel. At every mention of the revered Franklin Delano Roosevelt, they cheered lustily and jeered the names of his critics just as heartily. Senator Charles Miller asserted that it had taken years to build up the Republican machine which permitted the Finney operations, and that disgrace wouldn't be lived down by the state for one hundred years. Matt Guilfoyle suggested that "Clean out the state house" should be the Democrats' slogan for the campaign. "It does look like for the first time in Kansas," he cheerfully observed, "the Democratic party will be able to elect an entire state ticket."[38] Dudley Doolittle, Kansas' National Committeeman, said that people everywhere were asking whether there had really been a cleanup in the Statehouse. The bond scandals, he predicted, would occupy a prominent place in the campaign. They might overshadow everything else.[39]

A good deal of talk at the Washington Day rally centered on the position of U.S. district attorney. Early in the fall, stories had circulated that certain "friends of Finney" were working to secure an early appointment of a Democrat to replace Sard Brewster, a holdover Republican. The implication was clear that anyone who was likely to be indicted would earnestly seek to have him retired to private life.[40] The Democrats strained to get Brewster replaced in order to garner some of the laurels in prosecuting the "bad guy" Republicans. On the other hand, a premature change could seriously jeopardize the prosecution of the criminal cases. Word came from Washington in the fall that no Republican officeholder would be immediately replaced. In the early spring, Senator George McGill submitted a list of "eligibles" to Washington, which reportedly included Representative Matt Guilfoyle and Summerfield S. Alexander of Kingman. On March 16 the announcement came that the new U.S. district attorney would be Alexander, a long-time friend of McGill's. Alexander's appointment became official on May 4; and the veteran Brewster returned to his old law practice in Topeka.[41]

In early April, to no one's surprise, Senator Charles E. Miller, the inveterate questioner at the Senate trials, tossed his hat into the gubernatorial ring along with those of Thurman Hill and the mayor of Topeka, Omar Ketchum. The people didn't trust their state government, Miller said, because of "trickery, dishonesty, hypocrisy and deceit." If elected, he promised to pursue "the Topeka State House Gang" relentlessly until the capital was completely purged of corruption.[42] Later, the senator would grandly claim that when Landon ("[who] knows more about the Finneys and the bond scandal than any man in Kansas") refused to testify before the Senate court of impeachment, "he took the full responsibility for all of it on his shoulders."[43]

THE DEADLINE for filing for state offices, June 20, was rapidly approaching, and still no primary opponent to the incumbent governor had come forward. Weak and in disarray as a result of the scandal cleanup, the anti-Landon forces had been unable to persuade anyone of substance to make what almost certainly would be a futile effort. William Allen White and Lacy Haynes had successfully cooled Roland Boynton's fevered brow, and Will French had made other plans. Just when it appeared that a gubernatorial contest would have to await the general election, who should appear in the bright-blue southern Kansas sky—in a celestial chariot drawn by eight magnificent white goats (nannies we may assume, since billies could be put to better use)—none other than the goateed, red-haired old wizard himself: Doctor John Romulus Brinkley. In the person of Burt Comer, a Wichita lawyer and candidate for the Republican nomination for attorney general, Brinkley filed for governor in the Republican primary on the day of the deadline. "If I had not filed," the old doc modestly but accurately noted, "the campaign would have been a droll affair."[44]

Running for governor as a belated write-in candidate in 1930 and as an independent in 1932, the unlicensed medicine man had attracted nearly 430,000 votes of desperate Kansans in those two contests. He had repeatedly preached, over the radio and in person, that the Statehouse was rotten, a den of iniquity chock-full of dishonest and conniving politicians. Certainly not much had happened in the past year to disabuse the people of that. His slogan—"Clean Out, Clean Up and Keep Kansas Clean"—seemed especially appropriate at this hour.[45] Nevertheless, the move caught most everyone by surprise. Mr. White—an implacable foe of Brinkley's—had said goodbye to the would-be governor in a February editorial ("The Last of Brinkley") after Brinkley had dropped his multimillion dollar lawsuits against the *Kansas City Star* and the American Medical Association and had moved his radio station south of the border into Mexico. "Ever so often the sort of people who are fooled by Brinkley . . . , scare the rest of us to death," the *Gazette* reflected. "[But] it is vastly better to have folks go wrong on the various types of Brinkleys . . . , than to have the channels . . . clogged by . . . prohibitions that deny democracy the blessed and educative privilege of making its own mistakes." The sadder and wiser White concluded that "we all get fooled now and then one way or another. No one is infallible."[46] Amen. Given his recent experience with his Emporia friends and relatives, he knew whereof he spoke.

A few days after Brinkley had filed, a Salina man lodged a formal protest with the secretary of state, charging that Brinkley was not a bona fide resident of Kansas. Giving his home as Milford on the filing form, Brinkley stated that he had been "temporarily living in Del Rio, Texas." Though there were solid grounds for challenging Brinkley's Kansas residency, the Republican leadership decided that they wouldn't aid and abet the good doctor in his bid for martyrdom by denying his candidacy on what many folks might feel was a mere technicality. On July 6 the state's Contest Board (the secretary of state, the attorney general, and the auditor) denied the protest, and Kansas had a Republican primary gubernatorial contest.[47]

Another surprise occurred when Will French—conveniently forgetting the assurances he had given at his Senate trial—announced that he would once again seek the nomination for state auditor. Asking to be elected to his fifth consecutive term "on his record," he declared that he had been "the victim of persecution by a clique in state politics ever since he first took the office in 1927."[48] Later in the campaign he asserted that "circumstances over which I had no control made it necessary I should again ask the people of Kansas for their opinion as to my conduct." The relationship between the auditor and the governor had continued to degenerate; they were now scarcely on speaking terms. French admitted that "there may have been some misunderstanding between the governor and myself as to whether or not I should run for state auditor." Above all else, he piously exclaimed, "we must do right."[49]

WHAT HAD BEEN a lethargic campaign began belatedly to pick up steam toward the first of August. A Democratic gubernatorial candidate, George E. Rogers of Wichita, assailed William Allen White, calling him a "soured, prejudiced Republican, fermenting under Democratic rule in which he is allowed no part." Rogers had been upset with the journalist's spring commencement address at the University of Kansas, which, he said, attempted to turn the graduates against Roosevelt and the Democrats. "White is sore at me because I told the truth about his University of Kansas speech . . . ," Rogers complained; "he wants K.U. to graduate Republicans."[50] No denial of that charge ever came from Emporia.

Things really began to heat up when Dr. Brinkley opened a seven-day drive for votes on July 31 with a radio address over a three-station network. Advance notice indicated that the talks would emphasize reforestation and the attraction of new industries to Kansas.[51] But the millionaire doctor had more important things on his mind. He intoned in his best "Pecksniffian" voice that the people of Kansas had been warned two years ago that conditions in the Statehouse were rotten. "An awful lot of whitewash [has been] used in the state house in the past year and a half," he said. Asserting that both Finneys were "personal chums of the governor," he claimed that it was "his honest belief" that if Landon were to be reelected, he would soon pardon Ronald Finney.[52] Then he turned to an item that had continued to plague Landon and his supporters:

> Just a few days before the public learned of the extent to which Finney had corrupted state officials, . . . [he] had paid over to Governor Landon the sum in excess of $10,000 with high interest. Mr. Landon promptly hid behind his wife's skirts; he tried to explain that Mrs. Landon had loaned Finney $10,000 through some bank or other. The alibi is too thin, too naive and too lacking in sincerity or even probability to be swallowed by the voters of Kansas.[53]

A number of prominent Republicans immediately rushed to Landon's defense against the "dirty and base insinuations" of the goat-gland specialist. Clif Stratton published an article giving, once again, the facts about the transaction, which had been fully disclosed the prior fall. Sard Brewster branded as false the Brinkley claim. "I know of my own personal knowledge that the charge is without foundation," Brewster emphatically stated.[54] In an editorial entitled "Landon Luck," Mr. White predicted that it would all work out to Landon's advantage:

> Every night on the radio Brinkley rushes out barking at the cars
> And the car that enrages him most bears the Landon tag. . . .
>
> In these six days, while Brinkley is blowing poison through the microphone, Kansas will realize how inexplicably mean and disreputable this insinuation is. But Brinkley will perform a real service for Governor Landon. Brinkley will immunize the Governor to that particular phase of the bond scandal during the campaign. . . .
>
> Right now Landon is suffering from this miserable Brinkley itch. Next Tuesday it will be gone—and gone forever. Landon luck![55]

Brinkley had one more incendiary volley to fire. On August 4 he charged that he had been forced to eliminate part of his radio address on the previous night because threats of libel had been made against the originating station in Kansas City. The station manager confirmed that he had ordered Brinkley to cut out the part of his remarks that dealt with the scandal after the station's attorney reported "hearing that libel suits might follow."[56] In his 1936 booklet "The Tale of a Fox"—a vitriolic diatribe against Landon and his presidential bid—Burt Comer claimed that the pressure on the station came from Landon sources. Comer related that the station manager wailed that "today a couple of tough looking guys came down here from Topeka and said, if I let one word be said about Landon and the Finney $10,000.00 check, they would sue me for libel and have my broadcasting license revoked."[57]

Brinkley, who managed to put in a good word for Will French most every night in his radio broadcast,[58] warned that he intended to be around for a while, win or lose:

> I did not intend to make an active campaign this year and only permitted my name to be placed in nomination with a view to the future. But when the Topeka clique started to question my citizenship, I'm going to deal them a lot of misery from now until the November election and perhaps longer.
>
> If I'm defeated this time I intend to stay in Kansas. I have several political debts to settle, involving certain of my enemies who have yet to learn what may happen when I'm fully aroused, as I am at this time.[59]

Aroused or no, the Kansas voters preferred Landon, 234,000 to 59,000.[60] Contrary to his recently stated word, Brinkley did not stay in Kansas, and he played no further role in state politics. Before he disappeared in his sixteen-cylinder car in late October, he issued a formal statement urging Kansans to vote for repeal of prohibition and defeat of the Republicans. "If the Republican party would clean house of such personages as Mrs. Mitchner [the WCTU leader] and William Allen White," the old doc advised before he left the Kansas scene forever, "there are a lot of self respecting people who formerly voted the Republican ticket that would vote it again."[61]

BY LATE AUGUST, both party platforms had been drawn up. The Republican platform included a bond-scandal plank: "We commend the thoro vigorous and effective investigation of the bond forgeries by the state administration and the speedy prosecution of those involved. By this prompt action for honest government, the fair name of our state and its credit have been protected."[62] The Democrats, falling short of directly pinning the scandal on Republicans, demanded "a high standard of honesty and efficiency" on the part of public officials and employees, "to the end that public faith and confidence in state government, which is at a low ebb, be restored."[63]

Just before he opened the fall campaign, "Lucky" Landon remarked that he had been anything but lucky during his first term. In the years to come he would just sit back in his easy chair, he mused, and "console myself by saying that I was governor when Kansas had the biggest bond scandal, the worst drouth, the hottest weather, the most terrific relief problems and the most days of a legislature it ever had."[64] And the Good Lord has given him a number of years to do just that.

Landon opened the campaign with a speech in Abilene on September 5. He spoke in his terse, straightforward manner, which was devoid of bombast and hyperbole, fully utilizing the Kansas idiom, of which he was a master. Landon reminded his audience that most of the bogus bonds were in the treasury when he came into office, and he went on to laud the investigators whom he had appointed. "I call your attention to the fact that the prompt and vigorous investigation has resulted in the conviction and sentencing of the four principals involved to the Kansas state prison for long terms. The state investigators and prosecuting officers are entitled to much credit for their service."[65]

Landon repeated his Abilene speech, more or less, to an overflow crowd in Emporia on October 3. This time the introduction was not handled by W. W. Finney. Hugo Wedell stood by to speak in the governor's stead, in case Landon's bad cold would prevent him from going on. "As shameful and as sorrowful and disgraceful to every prideful Kansas citizen as the bond forgeries are," the governor rasped, "they were no respectors of political parties."[66] In spite of his cold, Landon gave a rip-roaring talk—"the best political speech we ever heard," admiringly wrote the Farm Woman Down on the Neosho in her *Gazette* column.[67]

Out on the hustings the candid governor found that a grateful people frequently alluded to the scandal with a "Thank you" or a "God bless you, governor." At one courthouse stop a big burly man in bibbed overalls elbowed his way up to Landon, stuck out his calloused hand, and exclaimed, "Let me shake your honest paw."[68] In reply to Democratic claims that it was the federal, not the state, investigators, who had uncovered the scandal, Landon frequently reminded his audiences along the hot, dusty trail that it was he who had declared martial law in the state treasury and had ordered the arrest of Tom Boyd and Ronald Finney. He also attempted to give the lie to the whispering campaign that he had ordered that Ronald Finney be accorded special privileges in the State Penitentiary.[69] Since the celebrated prisoner currently worked "like a mule" in the prison coal mine, that charge didn't seem to carry much substance.

On October 24 Senator Harris took to the WIBW (Topeka) airwaves to give details of the scandal investigations, since, he said, some Democratic campaigners evidently had been "misinformed or are deliberately trying to deceive the public." Harris said that between July, 1932, and January 9, 1933 (the end of the Woodring regime), there had come into the treasury vault a net total of $379,000 in forged bonds. By August 8 this had grown to $426,000, a net increase during the Landon administration of only $47,000. The prosecutions and convictions, Harris proudly added, "as an example of speedy action and perfect results, is unequalled in the history of this or any other state."[70]

Harris went on to discuss publicly for the first time the pressure that bondholders had put on his office during the previous fall:

> A great part of the time of the office which we were conducting was taken up with matters relating to these bond owners over the country. They came, they wrote, they wired. Conferences were had with bankers over the state. . . . Finally, . . . payments resumed and . . . the value of Kansas bonds on markets of the world resumed the high place which they had held . . . and the fears of most of our people of the direful results did not materialize. Today, the bonds of good communities in this state . . . command as high a price as the bonds of the United States.[71]

In late September at Pawnee Rock, Omar B. Ketchum, the young Democratic gubernatorial candidate, asserted: "If I am elected . . . , there shall be no man on a state payroll who ever took a dime of Ronald Finney's money. I'll further promise that no Democratic campaign fund shall ever be enriched by anybody who has had anything to do with the Finney fortune." The former mayor of Topeka criticized Landon for retaining Jesse Greenleaf as a member of the Kansas Corporation Commission "when it is an established fact that Greenleaf, while employed on the same post, was in the employee of Ronald Finney. . . . Do you people of Kansas want such public officials when they know of that official's connections with the man who was the central figure in one of the most disgraceful and nefarious scandals ever perpetrated upon the state of Kansas?" The answer, Ketchum suggested, was no, they didn't.[72]

Miss Ann Laughlin, who was a Democratic National Committeewoman, the vice-chairman of the state committee, and a cousin of Congresswoman

Kathryn O'Loughlin McCarthy, charged that state highway personnel had been forced to stop work in order to lay out huge Landon signs on the hillsides with stone and whitewash. The whitewash, the fiery Irishwoman made bold to suggest, had been left over from the bond-scandal investigations. She declared that the full explanation of the $10,000 check, which the Republican press had promised, had not been forthcoming. "That check went into the Landon home the same day the governor signed the cash basis law. Following this law, communities hastened to issue bonds. Could this situation have been worth $10,000 to Mr. Finney?"[73] Some said that the lady delivered the most brilliant and most vilifying speeches on the stump that fall. Mr. White noted that she was "not meticulously observing the Queensbury rules of fighting. She bites, scratches, gouges and fudges in her rhetorical flights."[74] The lady was certainly no lady on the stump.

In late October the Democratic State Committee released a nine-page pamphlet entitled "Landon's Remarkable Record in the Bond Scandal." Reportedly authored by Senator Miller, it took Landon to task for a variety of sins related to the late unpleasantness. "We are informed by a Republican who was present," the circular exclaimed, "that Governor Landon was put into the Republican race for Governor at a meeting in Warren Finney's house . . . in the spring of 1932. There was also considerable talk at that time about Finney running for Governor after Landon had completed his four years." Reference was made to Mrs. Landon's loan to Ronald Finney and the fact that the governor had failed to carry out his formal responsibilities as a member of the Treasury Board. Liberal sections of the record of Boynton's trial were reproduced in the brochure, highlighting the attempt of the senators (mostly Democrats) to call Landon to testify: "He refused to walk up one flight of stairs and tell the people of this sovereign state, what he knew about the bond scandal. He therefore took full responsibility for this disgraceful page in Kansas history upon his own shoulders."[75]

A WORRIED OMAR KETCHUM canceled his campaign engagements for a few days in late October and hurried East in response to a real or imagined "call from Washington." The Republicans appeared to have the lead; his campaign badly needed a boost. He went to Washington to seek help and to link his name with that of the magical FDR in a press release. Introduced by Guy Helvering, commissioner of the Internal Revenue Service, he met with the President on October 29 to discuss "the progress of the Recovery program in his state."[76]

At about this time the dapper Harry Woodring appeared on the Kansas scene with a rip-snortin' New Deal speech in his hip pocket.[77] Before

Woodring left Washington, Guy Helvering had encouraged him to stick to New Deal economic policies and to leave the bond scandal alone. "You can't beat Landon on that," Helvering warned.[78] Had Woodring followed his friend's advice and stayed with his original plan, the outcome might have been different, since the Republicans hardly held a commanding lead. But immediately upon his arrival, Woodring huddled with members of the Democratic State Committee, which included the omnipresent Senator Miller. They asked if he had heard the terrible things that the Republicans had been saying that linked his administration with the bond scandal. No, Harry hadn't heard. When he took to the platform the next day, the now-aroused assistant secretary of war kept FDR and economic recovery in his hip pocket.[79]

The peaceful Kaw countryside was disrupted by Woodring's initial blast at Lawrence on October 29:

> It has been called to my attention that the present Governor of Kansas has in public statements, tried to cast away some of the stigma and responsibility of the State House bond scandal and smear the preceding Democratic administration and myself as governor. . . .
>
> Upon further statements or controversy I shall be forced to ask the U. S. attorney's office in Washington to immediately send a representative to join the U. S. attorney's office in Kansas for an immediate and thorough reopening of this investigation. . . .
>
> I shall not tolerate further statements by the governor of Kansas which intend to smear my administration with the stigma of the Finney bond scandal.[80]

The following day at Emporia, Woodring stepped up his attack and made a serious blunder that a little homework would have prevented:

> I cannot let go unchallenged the statement of the Governor of Kansas that $379,000 of fraudulent forged bonds were in the treasury when he went into office. There is not a word of truth in that. There wasn't a fraudulent bond printed in Topeka until January 10, 1933, after I went out of office. I cannot believe that the present governor of Kansas, who is a friend of mine and a neighbor, could knowingly have made that statement. I think he has been misinformed.[81]

In remarks that evening at Topeka, Woodring reiterated his charges against Landon: "It is my information, and I intend to have the matter checked, that none of the forged bonds in the treasurer's office was printed until after January 10, 1933."[82] It did seem to be a little late for checking.

Woodring had played into the Republican hands perfectly. Landon had been pointing out since mid August of 1933 that most of the forgeries had been in the vault when he took office. On August 19 he had written to Drew McLaughlin of the *Miami Republican* (Paola): "As a matter of fact, the greater part of the forgery occurred in 1932. There has been little comment on that. You might use this in your second run."[83] A year later he wrote to a Lawrence man: "It might be interesting for you to tell some of these folks that the first forged bonds . . . went in under Governor Woodring's administration in the amount of more than $350,000."[84]

The publicly indignant but privately joyful Republicans immediately picked up the gauntlet that the Democrats had thrown down. Clif Stratton referred Woodring to the Senate journal on the Boynton trial and then proceeded to list in the *Capital* every one of the fraudulent bond issues and their date of deposit. Sard Brewster challenged Woodring to bring forth any new evidence in the scandal, if he had such.[85] The following day the U.S. district attorney, S. S. Alexander, countered that Brewster had drawn a defective indictment against Carl McKeen, which had enabled McKeen and the other indictees to slip through. And, he asked paradoxically "If Landon knew these forged bonds were in the [treasury], when Woodring left office, as he now claims, why did he not make it public before . . . August, 1933?"[86]

The erstwhile state prosecutors quickly came to Landon's defense in an orchestrated response. In a broadcast from Coffeyville, Hugo Wedell asserted that "any effort by Woodring to besmirch Landon could only result in his own besmirchment, two for one."[87] Fred Harris issued a low-key, measured statement, which included the exact dates that the forged bonds had gone into the treasury.[88] From Winfield, Judge Bloss declared that if Woodring "will read the records, he will find the facts."[89] And from down at Emporia, Woodring received some Sage advice. Editorializing about his favorite Democrat, White commented that "somebody did him a bad turn when he came to Kansas. . . . And he pranced out in front of the people of Kansas with great unction and denied that the forged bonds were in the State House when he was there. . . . C'mon Harry, be a good fellow; fess up. It will be to your credit and people will think more of you." Woodring finally did drop his ill-founded charges, though not until after the damage had been done.[90] All in all, it would be accurate to state that Harry Woodring didn't do much, at least on the positive side, for Omar Ketchum's lagging campaign.

THE CAMPAIGN moved at a furious pace during the last week as the bond scandal shoved federal relief measures and the prohibition amendment from center stage.[91] "We have no Finney stains on our ticket," Omar Ketchum announced proudly at Concordia, "[and] no Finney contributions to our campaign funds."[92] Two days later at the Holton Courthouse, to the largest political meeting ever held in Jackson County, young Ketchum stubbornly defended Woodring, even though doing so meant flying directly in the face of the record. "The bond scandal belongs to the present Republican administration," Ketchum shouted; "there is no proof that any of the forged bonds in the state treasury were placed there before Landon became governor."[93] In a speech over WIBW, Sard Brewster lashed back at his detractors. After lamenting the fact that the Democrats were still talking about the $10,000 check, he observed: "One of the Finney attorneys [E. R. Sloan] yesterday . . . stated that it was the new deal conscience that brought to light the bond scandal. I am surprised that he did not claim that the investigation was made personally by [Jim] Farley under direct orders from the president at the request of Finney."[94]

In a drizzling rain at Topeka on the Saturday before the November 6 election, a crowd of twenty-five hundred heard Landon systematically review his record. When he came to his handling of the bond scandal, he showed "just a trace of indignation." "I would just call your attention to one other thing," he said. "In the Democratic state platform there is not one word of criticism of the manner in which my office handled the bond forgery investigations. . . . Because in that party council there were many honest, self-respecting Democrats who knew the facts in the case, and who would not have stood for one instant for the kind of a campaign on that subject that has been waged by certain persons since the Democratic party council adjourned."[95]

Chaired by John D. M. Hamilton, the damp but enthusiastic crowd heard some stirring remarks from Tom McNeal, the well-known journalist:

> Dr. Brinkley threw all the mud that he could find to throw in the primary campaign and the people repudiated him by a vote of four to one. . . . And then the Democratic campaign managers began picking up the dried and deodorized filth that Brinkley had scattered about and imagined that they could use it again. They began the old refrain, "He was a friend of the Finneys." What if he was. It showed more courage by far to insist that his former friends should be exposed and prosecuted than if they had been his political enemies. . . .
>
> . . . To defeat Governor Landon after this record would give courage to every racketeer and gangster to come here and prey on Kansas. If a governor, no matter who he might happen to be, should attempt to drive them out they would say, "Look what happened to Landon."[96]

On the day before the election, Ketchum wound up his campaign at the Topeka City Auditorium before a large and noisy crowd. He reviewed the reasons that Kansans should vote Democratic in 1934. He then attacked the *Topeka Capital* as "the most rabid, bitterly partisan newspaper in the whole United States." The *Kansas City Star,* he added, had become "linked to The Daily Capital." Ann Laughlin, who lived up to her brilliant reputation as a political-stump speaker, followed the mayor. She devoted most of her time to the bond scandal, making the same impassioned speech that she had made in over ninety counties to more than 150,000 people since June.[97]

Even at this hour of the national Democratic high tide, the people of Kansas clung with determination to their traditional Republican values. Landon defeated Ketchum comfortably (422,000 to 361,000), and Clarence Beck won the attorney generalship by a margin of 35,000. Unprecedentedly, the Democrats took two state offices when W. T. Markham won as superintendent of public instruction and Ed Powers of Salina defeated Will French for state auditor.[98]

GOVERNOR LANDON had appointed J. J. ("Jake") Rhodes, a Council Grove lumberman, as Treasurer Jardine's successor on April 1. Rhodes defeated his Democratic opponent for the regular term in the general election but did not declare for the short term which ran from November to January. That honor went to George McDonald, a Kansas City accountant, who ran unopposed. After the election, McDonald announced that he could not make his $500,000 bond until his bonding company had been reassured, through an audit, about the current status of matters in the treasury. Rhodes, who continued in the office pending developments, refused to allow the audit until McDonald had qualified for the bond. Trapped in a "catch-22" situation, McDonald filed a mandamus action with the Kansas Supreme Court in early December to compel Rhodes to allow him to make the audit. The Supreme Court denied the writ, declaring that McDonald was not entitled to the run of the treasury until he had qualified according to law. Thus McDonald went into history as the only person ever elected to a state office in Kansas who was unable to perform the duties of the office for even a day.[99]

Earlier in the year, Rhodes, responding to the public clamor for tightened security in the Statehouse, had installed a "burglar-proof" cage around the entrance to the treasury vault. He put up additional bars for the windows, moved the fiscal agency into the same room as the vault, and permitted access to the area through only one electronically controlled door.[100] Did Treasurer Rhodes really believe that the remodeling would be enough to keep a Ronald Finney out? A more sensible policy would have been to require all Statehouse employees to take a short course in the ways and wiles of confidence men.

The new Democratic auditor, Ed Powers, announced a revised policy regarding warrants. Henceforth, they would be canceled and checked daily, rather than weekly, thus giving immediate notice if a forgery were to occur. Powers, it developed, had some problems of a more personal nature. A $3,500 shortage had been discovered in his books when he had been treasurer of Saline County. Admitting the shortage, Powers declared that a portion had already been repaid and that the problem never would have arisen if an illness had not kept him out of the office for an extended period of time. In mid December the Saline County attorney, upon the recommendation of Roland Boynton, announced that he would file criminal charges against Powers. The auditor was acquitted the following September of a charge of misuse of public funds. Powers died on November 2, 1935, following several weeks of hospitalization for an undisclosed illness. Landon appointed George Robb of Salina—one of only two Kansans who then held the Congressional Medal of Honor—to the office ten days later. Thus the Republicans quickly recaptured one of the two state offices they had lost in the election.[101]

AT THE INAUGURATION in January, Mr. Clarence Victor Beck solemnly pledged that his office would be run as a legal department, not as a political office. "Political fixers, crooked lawyers and dishonest officers have no place in Kansas," the prosecutor righteously declared.[102] Two days after making this august pronouncement, Beck's mail included a congratulatory letter from Mr. White ("I did not go . . . to witness your inauguration . . . but nevertheless when the hour came . . . , I was thrilled with pride"). After giving the new attorney general some unsolicited advice about who should be retained in his office, White spoke optimistically of the future: "If any matters come up in which you think I can help you over, please come to me. I have your good fortune at heart. You have a flare for politics. . . . If you have political ambitions, there is no good reason why they should not be further enjoyed."[103]

Beck soon faced a problem that he couldn't quite manage; nor, presumably, could Mr. White. In early February, "in the interests of public health," Beck officially canceled a jack-rabbit hunt scheduled in Lane County for a Sunday. With a rather definite feeling that it was their own damn business whether they hunted the menacing rabbits or not, the locals adamantly went ahead with the affair, which involved ten thousand farmers (live) and forty thousand jack rabbits (dead). They announced another "hunt" (actually a roundup, since the chief weapons were clubs, not guns) for the following week, and in a stroke of boldness and mirth, they invited the attorney general to participate. Recognizing that he was soundly whipped on the issue, Beck accepted. Credited with five killed (or maimed) rabbits in the roundup, he received an engraved hickory club in a Chamber of Commerce ceremony at the conclusion of the day's work, the better to kill more rabbits with.[104] Meanwhile, the biggest quarry of all continued to hop around down in Emporia in an attempt to stay ahead of his creditors and out of the Kansas State Penitentiary.

15

Victory

∘∘

THE LEGAL BLIZZARD of civil lawsuits that descended on the Warren Finneys during the fall of 1933 continued well into 1934 and beyond. The suits ranged in magnitude from a few hundred dollars, for collection on the Emporia hotel bill for Finney's trial attorneys, through a $25,000 Lyon County Commissioners' judgment up to amounts as great as the $131,000 Fidelity suit. The crowded docket of the Lyon County District Court included eighty-eight civil cases through the spring of 1936 that either involved the Finneys or stemmed directly from their problems.[1] When the criminal actions and the suits outside Lyon County are included, the total comes to over one hundred. Probably more legal action stemmed from the scandal than from any other single source in the state's history. The lawyers did indeed have a field day.

In May, 1934, Warren Finney unsuccessfully sought a change of venue on a dozen of the civil cases. His attorneys argued that their client couldn't receive a fair and impartial hearing in Lyon County because of the publicity about his troubles that had been given in the pages of the *Gazette;* because he was linked in the public mind with the bond scandal; because he was president of the local bank that had closed; and because the judge was biased, since he had presided over the embezzlement trial.[2] But the good Judge McCarty had the final word. He allowed as how he had lived in Lyon County all his life and devoutly believed that the jurors in said county were "better than the average." "If I were in the defendant's position," he ingenuously asserted, "I would want to have this taken care of here." Surprisingly, the judge even threw in a good word about Mr. Finney. The jurors knew that the defendant was "a man of a high type," he said, and they all recognized "his desire to do the right thing."[3]

SETTLEMENT with the state's Banking Department, on the double liability of the two banks ($51,700); with the federal government, on its income-tax claims ($60,000); and with Bell Telephone Company, on its Fidelity-accounts claims ($30,500) remained the key elements in effecting an overall solution to the complicated financial entanglements. Governor Landon played a major role in the prolonged attempts to reach a bank settlement. One of the Finney attorneys, Owen Samuel, proposed a full-payment settlement to the governor in December, 1933, whereby the state would immediately receive $40,000 from the sale of Finney-owned telephone stock to Bell, with the remainder to come in monthly installments of $1,000. Samuel warned that Bell would probably not have to pay at all unless the state acted quickly. Landon responded that he would "be glad to give this matter serious consideration, except that I am frank to say if there is any way we can get the whole $50,000 for the benefit of the depositors of the bank[,] I think it is the thing to do." In early March, Fred Harris wrote the governor that "on Saturday evening Mr. William Allen White called me again concerning the affairs of the receiver of the Emporia bank. He says there was a conference held in Emporia a week or more ago concerning a proposed adjustment.... He is convinced that the proposition offered was most advantageous to the bank and a great mistake was made in not making the adjustment.... He was quite insistent that I transmit his suggestion to you."[4]

In mid April the Fidelity's receiver wrote the governor regarding recent developments. "I am very sure that the definite stand which you took on the matter that was discussed in your office last Saturday relative to a compromise settlement with W. W. Finney, which had been suggested by Mr. Finney and considered by the Banking Department, was well taken. I sincerely believe that every resource of W. W. Finney should be exhausted for the benefit of the depositors of the bank. If this policy is followed vigorously I am quite certain that the depositors will be better satisfied than they would in case of a compromise settlement on any basis."[5]

Landon's "definite stand" had apparently forestalled a settlement. An exasperated Mabel Finney issued a public statement on April 18, explaining the Finney side of the negotiations and repeating the Finney offer of December last:

> We have been in almost continuous conference for the last two

months with the bank commissioner . . . trying to work out a settlement of Mr. Finney's double liability and all other claims involved. Unless one has had experience along these lines they cannot realize how hard it is to reach any agreement about anything where every action is weighed in the scales of political expediency. . . .

If some settlement is not made, and that at once, the lawyer's fees and court costs will eat up practically every cent and the depositors will get very little or nothing.[6]

By early summer, Landon had begun to look at the Finney offer in a more favorable light. At the governor's request, Senator Harris studied the problem in depth and reported on June 4 that "if this settlement can be made without further expense or litigation on the part of the receiver, that it should be promptly done." Landon accepted Harris's advice and promptly wrote back to his investigator: "The bank commissioner and Senator Rees, in a conference yesterday on the Emporia–Neosho Falls bank situation, both agreed with me as to the advisability of accepting the Finney offer. The Bank Commissioner doubts that they will be able to go through with it but thinks that we should at least give them the opportunity, especially as the national government is getting ready to file liens on its income tax claims."[7]

The federal government had in fact filed an income-tax lien on March 3 for $19,385.66 in unpaid 1930 taxes against all of Warren Finney's property. Subsequent federal tax claims on unpaid 1932 taxes brought the total to about $60,000. In August, 1934, the U.S. district attorney filed a civil suit to collect on the 1930 taxes. The suit tied up the titles to all Finney real estate, since the government claimed a prior charge against all their property. The suit listed 108 defendants, every person and corporation that had any claim whatever against Finney property. Since the federal government had a first lien, plaintiffs against the Finneys in the state district court hesitated to push their cases to trial while the federal case was pending.[8]

In February, 1935, the U.S. district attorney called a conference in Topeka among all interested parties to work toward a settlement, but no satisfactory agreement was reached. Then, on the date set for hearing the federal income-tax suit, May 20, word came that a complete settlement might be at hand. The comprehensive settlement was announced on May 24. After the dramatic events that occurred two weeks later, the agreement threatened to come unglued. After much additional bargaining and legal maneuvering, the final settlement was consummated on April 21, 1936.[9]

The key element in the settlement was the sale of the 133 shares of stock in the Emporia Telephone Company. In February, 1932, Warren

Finney had entered into an agreement to sell the stock to Southwestern Bell on January 2, 1934, for $50,000. In anticipation of the big legal problems that he perceived on the horizon, he made an assignment of $45,000 of the proceeds to Mrs. Finney and to his lawyer, Owen Samuel, a few days after the Fidelity Bank had closed. Of this amount, $25,000 was to be used by Samuel for his own fees and fees of attorneys that he might hire. On the agreed-upon date, Bell refused to pay on the contract, claiming that the Finneys could not give clear title. In April, 1934, Mabel Finney had filed against Bell, alleging breach of contract.[10]

In the final settlement, Bell agreed to buy the stock for $38,000, the discount in satisfaction of their $30,500 claim on the funds of the three phone companies that had been frozen in Fidelity. All Bell suits against Finney were dropped. The federal government received $16,000 from the Bell sale, plus $3,500 in cash from Mrs. Finney. In return they agreed to grant a full release from the government liens on Finney property. Finney's attorneys received a $24,000 judgment and credit on the judgment of $7,000 from the Bell payment. Mrs. Finney agreed to make up the difference between the amount paid and the final judgment.[11]

The remaining $15,000 from Bell went to the bank receiver, to be applied on the $34,000 judgment against Finney's double liability. The additional $19,000 due to the receiver came from the sale of a farm to which the Finneys had clear title, from the sale of cattle, and from the sale of town properties. All Banking Department suits against the Finneys were dropped. Had the Banking Department agreed to the 1933/34 Finney offer that was proposed to the governor, depositors in the failed bank would have received from the Finneys a settlement 50 percent greater than what they in fact did receive.[12] The governor's "definite stand" had backfired.

In addition to accepting the $34,000 judgment, the Finneys relinquished all their claims against the two banks. They agreed to assign to the receiver all the dividends that might be due from their deposits in the future. These deposits, on which they took assignment in the hectic days following the bank's closure, amounted to about $35,000 (at different times, Finney had claimed varying amounts up to twice that). Bad paper taken out of the banks over the years by the Finneys and replaced by personal funds on orders from either the bank directors or the state Banking Department, it was acknowledged, had come to about $96,000 for Fidelity and $58,000 for the Neosho Falls Bank.[13]

The Finneys received settlement thereby on the $131,000 suit by Fidelity, the $51,700 double-liability judgment, and a judgment on two notes due to Fidelity for $13,500. The only real estate of any substantial value that the Finneys retained free and clear was the 80-acre farm just east of Emporia on which was situated their modest summer cabin with its screened-in porch. In addition, under the decrees, ten small pieces of property in which Finney owned an equity were not subject to judgment. All the remainder of the Finney property had been sold under mortgage foreclosures.[14]

BY AUGUST, 1935, Fidelity had accumulated over $100,000 in cash assets, which were to be made available for paying a dividend to its long-suffering depositors. In late November the bank receiver announced that $132,000 would be paid in mid December to depositors of the three Finney banks that had closed. Those thrifty depositors who had joined the Fidelity's Christmas Savings Club in good faith in 1933 would now get back fifteen cents on their savings dollar just before Christmas of 1935.[15] "It's not much but I'll give it to the county treasurer on my taxes," one grateful depositor sighed. An old woman who had deposited $155 in gold in March, 1933, said that the money had been saved to help pay for her funeral expenses. Another related that her money had gone in as part of Roosevelt's gold-devaluation order. But she added charitably, "I doubt if Roosevelt had anything to do with this." Still apprehensive about possible mischief from the bank's president, she wondered if Mr. Finney's name would be on the check.[16]

THOUGH BROKEN AND HUMBLED in the public eye, the still-proud Warren Finney gamely held his head high as he moved briskly along Commercial Street during 1934. His status in the town could hardly have changed more drastically. He had been a pillar of his church and community, a shining example of rectitude for youth and his fellow-man. The magic name, which had formerly been shouted with vigor in the halls of power, was now only whispered with embarrassment behind closed doors. The fallen idol even had to read in the *Gazette,* with a mixture of anger and ignominy, that members of his Lyon County jury and their spouses had held a square-dancing party at the home of one of the jurors—evidently in order to recall the good old times at the courthouse.[17]

Important as the civil suits were, since they involved all his worldly possessions, the appeal on the criminal conviction remained basic to all else. His "galaxy of lawyers" now bent every effort to secure a reversal of the district court's sentence from the state's highest tribunal. Notice of the appeal was taken immediately after the sentencing on December 1; the appeal itself was filed on January 3, 1934. Immediately after the trial the court reporter, Miss May Larson, began to transcribe the massive testimony in her spare time. The transcript would include virtually every word spoken by the judge, lawyers, witnesses, and jurors. From the transcript an abstract would be prepared by the defendant; a counter abstract, by the state. Initially Larson had expected the transcript to be ready for the April hearing. But in late March came the announcement that the work was still unfinished; so the hearing was continued until October. In late July, Larson finally completed the 2,802-page document, the largest ever prepared in Lyon County. The full record comprised 3,600 pages plus 300 exhibits. The exhibits—which included bank records, checks, affidavits, and contracts—weighed more than twenty pounds.[18]

When the defense failed to file the abstract in early September, thirty days before the scheduled hearing, Attorney General Beck moved to dismiss the appeal. Since the transcript had not been picked up by defense attorney Roscoe Graves until two weeks after it had been completed, the state suspected that the defense was dragging its feet. The defense argued that it needed additional time to complete the lengthy abstract. At the September 21 hearing on dismissal of the appeal, the court granted a continuance until November 2, though the defense asked for a longer delay. The 474-page abstract was filed on October 11, and the 165-page counter abstract was filed ten days later. Candidate Beck had to cancel all his campaign engagements during October in order to come to Topeka to supervise the preparation of the counter abstract and the brief.[19] The Kansas Supreme Court heard the case on November 2. E. R. Sloan, a former justice of the Supreme Court, presented essentially the same arguments before his former colleagues that had been made before Judge McCarty in arguing for a new trial. The state attorneys, Beck and Wedell, contended that the basic rights of Warren Finney had not been compromised and that "concerning his guilt there can be no doubt." The High Court's decision, originally scheduled for December 8, was postponed until January 26.[20]

A COUPLE OF WEEKS before the decision came down, Finney diverted his attention from the case in order to vent his ire on one of his chief tormentors, the *Kansas City Journal Post*. On January 10 the paper had published an extensive front-page story under the heading "Finney Bank Depositors out of Luck." The story told about the recent sale of $65,000 in Hinsdale County bonds for $600 at a Lyon County sheriff's auction. Since the bonds had been placed in Fidelity as security for deposits, the depositors were realizing only one cent on the dollar, the story claimed. "So thoroughly did . . . W. W. Finney loot the Fidelity bank," the paper lamented, "the depositors probably will not receive more than 15 per cent of their funds." Actually the sale had been held to dispose of the property as part of an $89,000 judgment by the bank against Ronald Finney. The bonds, which had been taken from his personal lockbox, had never been part of the bank's assets.[21]

Falsely accused in this instance, Warren Finney dashed off a heated letter to the paper, getting a related matter off his chest in the process. The *Journal Post* obligingly published the letter in the same prominent front-page position as the earlier story:

> The entire article is false, misleading and slanderous and must have been known to be false by your Emporia correspondent when it was written . . . the article was written and published maliciously and with utter disregard of truth. . . .
>
> There may have been a dissipation of the bank assets—I don't know yet exactly what happened to the bank's bonds. But this I do know—if the bank's good bonds were substituted—it was done in Topeka and not in Emporia. I further know that I had no knowledge of it or part in it nor did I profit by it. . . .
>
> I have had trouble enough the last year and half and am not desirous of further litigation but I cannot and will not let this article pass unchallenged.[22]

THE SUPREME COURT'S DECISION—written by Justice William A. Smith—was handed down on January 26, 1935. It upheld the prosecution on all counts. The Court decreed that the trial judge had not been prejudiced and that the behavior of counsel had been only what "might be expected from a vigorous prosecutor." Where an overdraft of the bank president's account is covered by a fictitious deposit, "the court will consider the overdraft and the making of the fictitious deposit together, and where the result is that money is taken out of the bank with nothing given in return it will be held to be embezzlement." With reference to the defense's contention that the defendant had restored, or intended to restore, the funds that he had removed from the bank, the Court held that "evidence of acts done by defendant after he has taken the money from the bank and placed it beyond its control is not admissible to prove lack of intent to defraud the bank. . . . People to whom money is intrusted cannot be heard to say they used the money but intended to put it back. If this should be the rule every embezzler would say that."[23]

Immediately after the decision was rendered, Warren Finney—bravely declaring that "we have just begun to fight"—announced that a motion would be filed for a rehearing. He also issued a bitter public statement:

> The Supreme Court has spoken and every one must bow to its mandate. The fact that a citizen with a long lifetime of decent and neighborly living has been given a life sentence for a crime nearly everyone knows he did not commit is not by itself perhaps an unknown thing. . . .
>
> What I was prosecuted for, and a conviction railroaded, was for some unknown and unseen connection with the bond scandal on account of family connection. As to the bond scandal, I knew nothing, profited nothing. . . .
>
> Fighting for a year and a half to clear my name on account of my wife and daughter . . . , I have, at every turn, run up against a stone wall of politics. Ambitions of men to be president, congressman, governor, state or county officer have prevented them . . . from doing their official duties, and influential friends have refused to help for fear of being drawn into the political vortex of fury and hate. All sat with the servants and warmed themselves at the fire.[24]

THEN FOLLOWED long and drawn-out legal maneuvering by Finney's attorneys in a valiant attempt to forestall the inevitable. Negotiations regarding the financial settlement waxed and waned during the late winter and early spring, but the wheels of criminal justice ground inexorably on. On February 12 the Kansas Supreme Court granted a 30-day extension for filing the application for a rehearing. On March 14 the Court extended the continuance until April 2. The rehearing motion, filed on April 2, was denied on April 12. The next day the mandate of execution was stayed "until further order of the court." On April 17 the Court stayed the mandate until April 19. The next day the Court ordered the mandate continued until April 29 to give Finney additional time to decide whether to take an appeal to the United States Supreme Court.[25]

Harry Colmery, of the respected Topeka firm of Doran, Kline, Colmery and Cosgrove, had gained an enviable reputation around Kansas as a successful attorney in taking cases on appeal to the United States Supreme Court.[26] (Colmery had been approached in early February by Tom Boyd's attorneys about the possibility of taking his case to the higher court. He had told them that "there are no grounds for the petition and that he had better let his family have the money which would be spent in printing costs and other expenses.")[27] After the motion for Finney's rehearing had been denied in mid April, John Schenck and E. R. Sloan had contacted Colmery in Finney's behalf, asking him to review the record to determine whether or not there existed "proper grounds for filing petition for certiorari in the Supreme Court of the United States."[28] A few days later, Colmery was visited by Warren Finney himself, with whom he had become acquainted through state YMCA work. Accompanied by his wife, Finney reaffirmed the request that his lawyers had made to Colmery. Fixing the attorney in an unblinking gaze with his deep brown eyes, and with a nod toward Mrs. Finney, he stated matter-of-factly that if the appeal should fail, "Mrs. Finney and I agree that life would not be worth continuing." A grim Mabel Finney said nothing. The Finneys politely thanked Colmery for his consideration and then glumly filed out, leaving the stunned attorney to his own thoughts.[29]

Shortly thereafter, Colmery informed Justice Bill Smith that he had the record under review. On April 26 he wrote to Smith that "it would only be fair to stay the execution [of the sentence] for . . . a period of 60 days"—adding in an underlined phrase recalling the recent disconcerting Finney interview: "This man is going over for life."[30] Three days later, on the day that the order was to be executed, the Court once again stayed the mandate, for thirty days, to May 29.[31] This extension postponed the order for commitment until after the federal income-tax hearing on May 20.

After reviewing the record during free periods at the Mayflower Hotel in Washington, where he had gone on other legal business, Colmery wrote to the Finney lawyers in late May that, in his considered view, an appeal would be futile. On May 29, the deadline, the Court ordered the mandate to be stayed until further notice, pending a second application by Finney for a rehearing. Roscoe Graves, Finney's Emporia lawyer, optimistically explained that at this rehearing, "evidence not presented at the first hearing will be introduced."[32]

Then suddenly—though not totally unexpectedly—the Kansas Supreme Court announced on June 5 that the mandate had been mailed to the Lyon County court for immediate execution upon receipt. On the next morning, Finney's dejected Emporia attorneys reported that all avenues had been exhausted: the mandate could not be further delayed. Downtown on an errand later that morning, the preoccupied and distraught Finney stepped off the curb directly into the path of an oncoming car, narrowly avoiding a serious accident. (The shaken driver went home and told his family that he had almost run over old man Finney. "Too bad you didn't," they said.) Around noon there came renewed hope. Judge McCarty told the attorneys that he would need two or three days to examine the mandate carefully for errors and that he would not act on it before the following Monday, June 10. Rumors circulated around the courthouse in early afternoon that a rehearing had been scheduled for June 12.³³

At about 4 P.M. the clerk of the district court received an urgent call from Topeka. It was the attorney general of the state of Kansas, Mr. Clarence Victor Beck. The Finney prosecutor declared that the case was now beyond the jurisdiction of Judge McCarty: he ordered the sheriff to serve the commitment papers on Mr. Finney immediately and to accompany him forthwith to the State Penitentiary. At about 4:30 P.M., Sheriff Roy Davis and his deputy dutifully drove over to the large Finney home on the corner of Tenth and State.³⁴

Since the Finneys had been heartened by the earlier news that the papers would not be served for a few more days, the sheriff's appearance caught them almost totally unprepared. Mabel Finney met the officer at the door and asked him if he was the sheriff (she knew that he was) and if he had the commitment papers (she knew that he did). They conversed "at length." The sheriff did not see Mr. Finney, though he was told by Mrs. Finney that he was "upstairs playing cards with his daughter." The sheriff did see the Congregational minister in the living room, who had arrived just a few moments before in response to an urgent telephone summons from Mrs. Finney. The minister later reported that he had heard Mr. Finney's voice upstairs but had not seen him. The very frightened, but very composed, Mabel Finney beseeched the sheriff to please allow the family an hour to be alone together. "I hesitated," the sheriff recounted later, "and told her that I would not want anything to happen to Mr. Finney. She understood what I meant, and insisted that nothing would happen." The soft-hearted sheriff finally acceded to her insistent pleadings. "In giving them an hour together," he said, "I was trying to extend to the Finney family the same courtesy that I would extend to any other family in the same circumstances." The sheriff left, noting that Finney's car was parked in the driveway behind the house. The disquieted minister left "immediately" after.³⁵

When they were only "a block away," the sheriff and his deputy, thinking better of their actions in having left the house, returned to it with the intention of "guarding Mr. Finney" for the requested hour. This time they were met at the door by the twenty-one-year-old daughter, Mary Jane. She informed them that her father was not at home and that her mother was indisposed and could not see them. The now-alarmed sheriff insisted on coming in. Miss Finney went upstairs and brought her mother down. The faithful spouse, displaying nerves of iron, remembered that Mr. Finney "had gone down town after some medicine." The sheriffs noted that the car which had been so reassuringly parked in the driveway on their initial visit was now gone. The law-enforcement officers then began a thorough search of the house "from basement to garret," opening the doors to all the rooms and closets. After a futile 30-minute search, on which they were accompanied by a very cooperative Mary Jane, the frustrated officers appealed directly to Mrs. Finney. Where on earth could Mr. Finney be? Perhaps he had gone out to one of his farms, she responded. Which farm? It might just be the one east of Emporia, where the summer cabin was, she volunteered. At that moment the phone rang. Warren Finney had been found shot and was near death in the cabin.[36]

Young Bill White traced the last miles of Mr. Finney in the *Gazette* the next evening:

> At a few minutes after 5 o'clock . . . a car driven by a lonely man bumped over the Katy crossing on Sixth avenue, going east. From these tracks to the Finney farm the distance is a little less than five miles. The familiar buildings and landmarks, clear in the sloping sun, swam by, one by one with the miles—filling stations, happy farms, luxuriant elm trees. . . .
>
> Then came the last mile of that solitary ride, the flickering girders of the Neosho river bridge, the grade, the gentle curve and at last on his right the sprawling rail fence along the hillside. . . .
>
> Again he turned the wheel to the right. The car wheels crushed the thick green prairie sod of the little hill, on whose summit that last mile ended.
>
> That little hill commands a spacious view at any time, but in waning daylight of that afternoon its lonely occupant commanded a far wider horizon. Sixty busy, active years stretched away from that little hilltop; most of them happy and useful, a few of the ones closest to that last mile bitter with humiliation, betrayal and black despair.
>
> But before he closed the car door and left the engine ticking away its heat on the hilltop, the lonely man must have paused for a minute to look at that view; must have glimpsed beyond that last sad mile, back to the sun-bathed hills and valleys of many happier decades.[37]

On arriving at the hilltop, Mr. Finney had pulled out the front seat of the car—retrieving two heavy manila envelopes—and had entered the cabin. He took a Savage .38 revolver from one envelope, removing it from its holster. Tearing off a corner of the other envelope, he poured the contained cartridges onto the table and loaded the gun. He then stepped out onto the screened-in porch and, with the aid of a small mirror, positioned himself precisely on the canvas-covered divan. Clutching the mirror in his right hand and pressing the gun's muzzle tightly against the iron-gray hair of his left temple, he quickly pulled the trigger. A pool of blood, which barely touched his body or clothing, formed neatly on the divan beside the slumped figure. Though suffering from the extensive loss of blood, he was still alive when found a few moments later by a friend who had happened by to discuss a business matter. He died that night at 7:40 in an Emporia hospital.[38]

THE *GAZETTE* VIVIDLY DESCRIBED Mr. Finney's state of mind and his strategy during those last bitter months:

> Warren Finney from the day the bank was closed contemplated and later planned suicide. To his lawyers, to his friends, and to acquaintances, he reiterated his statement that he would never go to the penitentiary. . . . No one near to him doubted his determination to avoid the humiliation of bars and locks. He was a proud man. Never in one unguarded moment did he let slip from his lips a phrase, even a syllable, which would acknowledge the slightest guilt in connection with the closing of the bank. . . . Naturally with this capacity to uphold and defend himself in his own heart, he could not have gone to Lansing unless he had been carried by force nor could he have been kept there except under constant surveillance.[39]

The June 7 edition of the *Gazette,* crammed with news of the tragedy, estimated that Mr. Finney had left his wife "something like $200,000 of life insurance." The next morning an incensed Mabel Finney released a statement of her own: "With reference to the article in last night's Gazette, I wish to state and have published in an equally conspicuous place, the statement that the maximum amount of insurance ever carried by Mr. Finney, for me, was less than half the amount stated in last night's Gazette. . . . On this insurance we have had to borrow large sums, and have been unable to keep up the premiums. Last night's article was very unfair to me and I am making this statement for the purpose of correcting it."[40]

Family plans for the suicide had been so premeditated and precisely arranged that Mr. Finney had left specific instructions that details of the funeral should be kept out of the papers. The private services, which were held in the Finney home on June 8, were conducted by the Congregational minister. Attendance was by invitation only. Former governor Clyde Reed and other old friends attended; son Ronald and the Whites did not. Burial was in the family plot at Neosho Falls. Ten automobiles bearing the grieving friends and relatives of the self-condemned man accompanied the long black hearse on its lonely journey to the Falls.[41]

So strong was the legend of Finney power and influence that for years after his death many otherwise sober and intelligent Kansas citizens refused to believe the "official" account of the suicide. They believed, instead, that Warren Finney had bought off the sheriff and other local officials with his ill-gotten gains and had hightailed it to Mexico or some other "foreign port." The weight of the coffin, so the story ran, came from a medical-school cadaver made up to look like Mr. Finney or (in a closed-casket version) from rocks of a Neosho River gravel bar.[42]

AS WITH HIS CELEBRATED "MARY WHITE" ESSAY, written fourteen years earlier, Mr. White, with material help from his wife, Sallie, drafted the editorial-obituary for his friend.[43] "It was a hard editorial to write," the grieving editor later wrote, "he was my friend . . . that I knew and loved." White prided himself on having some insight into human nature—as indeed he had. During the Harding administration, for example, he had had an opportunity to meet Secretary of the Interior Albert B. Fall, of Teapot Dome ill-fame. "A cheap, obvious faker," White had quickly and astutely noted, "I could hardly believe the evidence of my eyes."[44] Yet he had been badly and persistently fooled by the civic leader and businessman with whom he had lived cheek by jowl for nearly three decades.

Both Will and Sallie White had been profoundly fond of the Finneys and had remained loyal despite the horrendous difficulties. "He could not know the heartbreak that I felt at the thought of his sad fate," White wrote after the tragedy.[45] But trying to be an intimate of the Finneys during those last stressful months could tax the strongest bonds. In the twenty months following the Whites' return from Europe, their contacts with the Finneys had become limited and strained. The Finneys continued to press their "God damned crazy, unreasonable and embarrassing" demands on the Whites—urgent requests that legitimate news be suppressed and futile pleas that the editor use his considerable influence to effect a reversal of the criminal sentence. While White played a minor supportive role in the financial negotiations, repeatedly urging that the Finneys' offer be accepted, he resolutely refused to intervene in the judicial process with his friend Justice Bill Smith or with anyone else. Though White actually did little enough, rumors persisted through 1934/35 that he had, in fact, trespassed to thwart the ends of justice at the criminal trial and subsequently with Clarence Beck, Justice Smith, and others.[46]

Mr. White's lengthy and poignant obituary appeared in the *Gazette* on June 10:

THE GREAT KANSAS BOND SCANDAL

What follows is frankly a tribute to a friend. As I recollect it now the last time I saw him was the day before his death. He had on a light suit and a white hat, set at the usual jaunty angle that pleased him, and he was walking swiftly and with the familiar click of confidence in his heels, with some ghost in his carriage of the gay, challenging swagger which marked his gait when I first saw him as a young member of the legislature in his twenties nearly 40 years ago. As he clicked along the street Wednesday, a cocky, defiant figure with his full six feet drawn up in unconquered pride, I knew what he knew, that he walked deeply in the shadow of death. . . .

The tragic waste, so unnecessary, yet so inevitable! Warren Finney was, as all of us are, a curious compound—no more and certainly no less than every man, is of strength and weakness. It is hard to draw a balance, to place even blame honestly, to bestow praise justly, for one knows so little of another's heart. Each heart knoweth its own bitterness. During the years when I knew him best, possibly for 20 years, I think I knew his strength. I believed that in the end it would triumph over his weaknesses. His strength lay in his daring. He had a vast spiritual audacity. He loved conflict. He delighted in taking a chance. He was happiest breasting a storm. . . . I never saw him at his best or happiest that he was not in combat, sometimes fighting men, sometimes causes, sometimes the devil's own luck of the game he was playing, business or politics, or what not. Of course that mounting consuming fever in the end burned him up. That story is a tale that is told. Let it be buried with his bones. . . .

There is another story, and if I know this first one, now let me bear testimony to the second: With all this mania for danger, personally he was a gentle spirit. He liked to do little kindnesses, often mischievously unknown to the recipients. And he was generous. . . . He was public-spirited in the best sense. I know his enemies say it was easy to splurge with other people's money, but the money he gave to this town was unimportant. It was the time he gave, the vision for public welfare that he followed not with his money but with his energy. . . . His affection for his fellowmen and particularly for the underdog was not hypocritical. It is unfair to say that. For in the last stages of the game the poor whom he honestly cherished, suffered for his weakness. Well, so did he—if that means anything. He never thought that he or they would pay the price. His enormous self-confidence shielded him from a sense of the realities of danger into which it took them and him. . . . That kind of fear was a blank spot in his makeup. It was too bad. It was a terrible element of weakness. . . .

His life ended in the inevitable cataclysm of his qualities, good and bad. He ran a true course to the very last incident of his stormy life, but he never lowered his flag. He meant his death to be the sign of his victory. He would rather be dead than to be downed. He had his way. His last prayer was answered.

He took his name into the bankrupt court of death. He settled everything there. It is the universal court through which all men must pass and having passed their names are clear. . . . And so God saves and frees us all for the uses of this sad old earth—in the end.[47]

A few days later Mr. White wrote to an old journalistic colleague, Walt Mason,[48] about the suicide ("I still think he was worth all he cost to this town. But oh, my dear Walt, the cost has been deep and bitter. And poor devil, he paid it all").[49] Mason gave a fitting benediction to the tragedy:

> I haven't been able to think of anything else since I read the brief dispatch this morning. No doubt a lot of cold-blooded people have exulted in his misfortunes, but I have been sorry for him since his troubles began. I have found it hard to believe that he was a deliberate scoundrel. He was always prominent in good works when I knew him, and seemed a generous, clean man, and now that he is dead, I have only compassion for him.
>
> "Nobody knows the trouble we seen. Nobody knows but Jesus."[50]

To which we can only add—"Amen."

16

Redemption

ooooooooooooooooooooooooooooooooooooo ooooooooooooooooooooooo

ON MAY 31, 1934, when Ronald Finney stood once again before Judge Paul Heinz in the Shawnee County Courthouse, the scene differed markedly from that of the final hectic days of his trial and sentencing. The noisy crowds that had jammed the building six months earlier were now gone. With only his wife and attorneys in attendance, the resigned defendant stood emotionlessly in the deserted courtroom as the judge solemnly repronounced the original sentence. Afterwards, in Lester Goodell's office, Finney said that he "was sorry the judge was not able to keep his agreement on the sentence. I can't understand, after the supreme court clarified for him . . . the 137th Kansas, why he went back on his agreement to sentence me to 15 years." A few hours later, Finney took the longest ride of his young life—sixty miles—to begin serving the second-longest sentence in state history, 31 to 635 years.[1]

The boys in the jailhouse would miss their generous fellow prisoner. "Santa Claus" had been a benefactor to many of the down-and-out inmates to whom he repeatedly gave food, clothing, and money. Just the day before he left, a farewell party had been staged for the "elephant man" in cell block number 2. And guess who bought the ice cream and cake? Bets were being taken on Topeka's Kansas Avenue by the smart-money boys that young Finney wouldn't serve five years in the "big house." Some observers predicted that a pardon would emerge as a major issue in the 1936 gubernatorial campaign. Many believed that the young financial wizard still retained much of the wealth that he had amassed in his operations and that after a short, perfunctory stay at Lansing, he would be freed through

313

political pull to cruise the highways once again in his Pierce-Arrow and conspicuously consume his ill-gotten gains.[2]

With a brave air of sanguineness the new inmate passed through the gate of the gray-walled prison, carrying a box of books for his mental health (including *The Marks of an Educated Man* and Roget's *Thesaurus*) and a box of baking soda for his physical well-being.[3] In the record office he spied a familiar face. "Pay me a social call at your first opportunity," Finney told his former employee and fellow prisoner. "I sure will just as soon as they will let me," answered Leland Caldwell.[4] Finney joshed good-naturedly with the guards and vowed to newspaper reporters that he intended to be a good prisoner and to do as he was told. He allowed as how he was mighty pleased to leave the Shawnee County Jail and to have a chance to work off some of his recently acquired poundage (he weighed in at nearly 250).[5]

THE PRISON OFFICIALS proved to be very accommodating. They immediately granted the wish of prisoner number 4224 to work off his excess adipose tissue. His work assignment was to the coal mine. Unique among the forty-eight states, the Kansas State Penitentiary had a coal mine whose shaft opened within the prison walls. The men who were assigned to the mine worked in teams of three: one dug the coal from the 2-foot seam, one loaded it onto a car, and the third pushed the car to a point where the ceiling was high enough for a mule to pull it the remainder of the distance to the vertical shaft. The last job was assigned to Finney. Each day from 6:30 A.M. to 4:00 P.M. he performed the "mule's job" effectively and without complaint.[6] It was quite a fall for Kansas' most favored son—from the fifth floor of the Jayhawk Hotel to the bottom of the 720-foot mine shaft.

Seven months after he entered Lansing, Finney found himself playing a new role in his multifaceted career. The five hundred convicts in the mine had become increasingly restive. Because they performed such physically exhausting work, they demanded more protein in the form of red meat. The situation became acute. Warden Lacey M. Simpson, a Landon political appointee whose term was marked by frequent charges of incompetence, went down into the mine to confer with their leader—a former bond broker who was just now down a bit on his luck. After some talking back and forth, the conflict was peacefully resolved. The authorities credited Finney with bringing it off.[7] Santa Claus had become a labor negotiator.

Six months later, on June 18, 1935, the prison miners struck for better-cooked food and a new prison physician. A law passed by the 1935 Legisla-

Ronald Finney as a prisoner (Kansas State Penitentiary)

ture, which sharply curtailed so-called good-time allowances, had also upset them. Under the new regulations a convict could not be paroled until he had served at least two-thirds of his minimum sentence. Two-thirds of thirty-one was twenty and two-thirds. Anticipating the strike and concerned about the possibility of violence, Finney decided that June 18 would be a perfect day to get some much-needed dental work done. He spent the day in the infirmary.[8]

Young Bill White took this occasion to reflect editorially on penological matters, in both their anthropological and zoological aspects:

... the strike in the Kansas penitentiary ... yielded two tiny pearls of enduring wisdom, which are these:
    Pearl 1.—that Ronald Finney, Emporia's representative in Lansing, ... reported to the prison sick call to have some dental work done the night before the trouble started. Nice work, old boy, nice work.
    Pearl 2.—. . . the state has chiseled out mule-rolls in those mines,

several hundred feet below the ground. . . . Mules must roll daily . . . [for] their physical well-being and their spiritual hygiene. So the proud state of Kansas bowed before the dictates of mule-biology. Rather than waste decades breeding a race of mine mules that didn't need to roll, it proved cheaper to chisel mule-rolling-places. . . .

These two pearls of wisdom coalesce into a third: if human nature received the same intelligent treatment in American prisons which is accorded mule-nature, there wouldn't have been any riot.[9]

VISIBLY SHAKEN by the news of his father's suicide in the summer of 1935, Ronald elected to go down in the coal mine as usual rather than to accept the standard privilege of a day off that was accorded to bereaved prisoners. "It will help me pass the time more quickly," he told the warden. "If Mrs. W. W. Finney requests that Ronald be permitted to go to his father's funeral, he will be allowed to go," the warden announced. Whatever the reason, Ronald did not attend.[10]

Two days after Warren Finney's death, his will was filed in probate court. Son Ronald was not included in his bequests. Dated January 23, 1935 (about the time of the Supreme Court's decision), the document left all his real and personal property "unto my beloved wife, Mabel T. Finney." In the event that she should predecease him, all the property would go to Mary Jane. "In making this disposition, I am not unmindful of my other heirs, but I have discussed my affairs thoroughly with my wife and daughter and they are familiar with my wishes as to the management of my affairs after my decease, and I therefore leave it to the discretion of the one of them that shall take under this will, to carry out my wishes."[11] So spoke the voice from the grave.

The Finney family suffered a series of medical emergencies during Ronald's first few years of confinement. Winifred continued to have trouble with her chronic ear problem, which required several operations. In May, 1935, Ronald was allowed to visit his nine-year-old daughter in a Kansas City hospital, where she lay gravely ill following a mastoid operation. On February 29, 1936, his six-year-old son, while bicycling near his home, was struck by a drunken driver. His jaw was shattered; a jagged fragment of bone containing two teeth lay in the street. Winifred, Mabel, and two friends rushed the boy to a Kansas City hospital. Accompanied by Deputy Warden Stubblefield, Finney was again allowed to visit a stricken offspring in the hospital. The boy eventually recovered, though he had to undergo a long series of corrective surgical operations. At the hospital,

Winifred told reporters that she intended to stay in Emporia for the foreseeable future. "I have the finest friends in the world there," she exclaimed.[12]

A NEW ASSIGNMENT for Lansing's best-known citizen in September, 1936, created a public uproar. After toiling in the mines for nearly sixteen months, the slimmed-down Finney had been reassigned to the library in September, 1935. A year later, Deputy Warden Stubblefield, who had grown to respect Finney for his uncomplaining toughness, assigned him to a hospital job. Dressed in hospital garb, he was to administer intelligence tests to incoming prisoners, with the promise, so the incensed state Board of Administration claimed, of "an easy time."[13] As soon as the board heard of the new assignment, they promptly rescinded it and issued a terse public statement:

> The Board has a policy of no favoritism in prisoner treatment. The advancement of Ronald Finney, who is under a heavy sentence for embezzlement [sic], to an important post in the hospital was made without the Board's knowledge or authority. Immediately on learning of this assignment . . . the Board instructed the warden to rescind the action and remove Finney from the assigned place. The Board is investigating the matter.[14]

Will T. Beck, who was the Republican state chairman and a member of the board, explained to the public that "Finney's crime, his long sentence and the notoreity of his case does not entitle him to such a position. Ordinarily, Stubblefield assigns the prisoners but in the case of such a prominent prisoner as Finney, we feel he should consult us before acting."[15] And of course, it might have proven an embarrassment to the governor, who at that hour was vigorously seeking no less an office than that of the presidency of the United States of America.

Although Beck intimated that Finney might be sent back to his old job in the mines, he was detailed as a "dormitory night runner" instead and never again pulled the "mule's duty." His later responsibilities, which were sometimes clerical in nature, became progressively less demanding. By 1941 he had charge of the wood lot, where he energetically split boxes into kindling wood and wrote in the adjacent shack during his spare time. Nearby, the former highflier—who had rented garden space for Emporia's down-and-outers in 1932—cultivated a victory garden of huckleberries, tomatoes, and peppers.[16]

After a few years of confinement, number 4224 began to see and admit the error of his ways, but in some fundamental respects his behavior

A mid-1930s Christmas card from Ronald Finney

remained pure, unmitigated Ronald Finney. After a visit to Lansing, some of his friends reported that "his head was filled with a number of schemes, all of them plunges."[17] He continued to work innocent little deals and angles, though primarily for the profit of his friends. Some of his admirers imagined that he would soon have the prison organized and paying out dividends. "If Ronald Finney is running Lansing," one of them quipped, "I'm going to buy stock in it."[18]

IN THE SPRING of 1938 the prison's most famous denizen had to take to his bed, though not because he was the victim of the flu or had another toothache. He had read a book, and its initial impact was more than he could handle. Young Bill White, with the close cooperation of his wife, Kathrine, had written a novel, *What People Said*. Though the names of the people and places had all been changed and though some circumstances had deliberately been altered, the book presented an impressionistic, but quite detailed, accounting of selected facets of the bond scandal.[19] Bill wrote to his mother-in-law about the principal's reaction: "Today I heard from Ronald. Just a note, for he couldn't write yet about the book. He said when he first read it it put him to bed, but when he had thought it over and re-read it he decided it was grand, and that Winifred had had the same reaction. And of course I'm very glad about that, too."[20]

The novel, which was widely read and well received by critics both in Kansas and in New York, was a Book-of-the-Month Club selection and gained the national best-seller list.[21] (William Allen White, who was one of the original judges for the club, abstained from voting on the book.) The leftist New York literary crowd thought that it was fine social commentary—a telling indictment of decadent capitalism and the mores of small-town plains-state culture. Despite the author's statement that he had not intended to portray any actual persons, Kansans quickly perceived that it followed the events of the bond scandal very closely indeed. Paul Jones, editor of the *Lyons News,* thought that White had written a mighty fine book. But—referring to White's claim that it was strictly a work of fiction—the veteran newspaperman declared that "it starts off with a ——— lie." All the major characters in the bond scandal and many minor ones could be readily identified. In the following months it became a popular Kansas parlor game, especially around Topeka and Emporia, to try to identify a neighbor, or hopefully oneself, in the novel.[22]

WITH THE ENCOURAGEMENT of Kathrine and Bill White, Finney began to develop some latent writing talents of his own. He enrolled in a University of Kansas extension course, "The Short Story," in the fall of 1938, and he took several additional writing courses over the next three years. The *Thesaurus* was finally being put to good use. A story that he wrote for one of these courses was readily accepted by the *Kansas Magazine,* a respected Kansas literary journal published at Kansas State College. With the announcement that the 1940 issue would include a work of fiction by the notorious prisoner, a heap of criticism came down around the head of its editor, a Kansas State professor of journalism.[23] In a prefatory paragraph to the stories, the editor defended his choice:

> This short story is printed by the Kansas Magazine solely on its literary merits. For more than a year its author, a prisoner in the state penitentiary as every Kansan knows, has been learning to write. The following story received high praise from . . . W. L. White, who first called it to the attention of the editors. . . . In accepting it for publication the editors were guided by purely literary standards and they hope that the readers in judging it will do the same.[24]

The editor asserted that "many other publications have encouraged the literary work of persons trying, even in prison, to save something from their lives." He went on to cite John Milton and O. Henry as outstanding examples.[25] Ronald suddenly found himself traveling in pretty fast company. The *Capital* concurred with the editor's literary judgment but objected to his promotional techniques. "His advance publicity concerning this new contributor," said Arthur Capper's paper, "smacked too much of yellow journalism. And Kansans do not particularly care for the ballyhoo method of advertising its outstanding literary magazine."[26]

The story in question carried the unimaginative title "Two Short Stories"; it in turn was divided into "The First Story" and "The Second Story." The simple plot concerned the devotion of a married woman to a deceased child who had been conceived, presumably out of wedlock, from an earlier liaison. The underlying theme was forgiveness. The magazine published additional short stories by Finney in 1941 and in 1943. The 1941 story, entitled "The Inspectors," involved a nervous bank president who received what he erroneously believed was a surprise visit from the bank examiners. The chief inspector was a beady-eyed man named Harris. Entitled "Twin Beds," the 1943 piece portrayed a middle-aged couple's attempt to revitalize a ten-year-old marriage.[27] Finney manifestly hadn't had to reach far for his plots.

While these pieces demonstrated an unmistakable flair for writing, the erstwhile bond broker had no desire to join the legions of poor, aspiring creative writers. But he found in this vehicle a psychologically satisfying and monetarily rewarding activity in the form of expository writing for commercial trade journals. While less glamorous than writing fiction, this more mundane outlet opened up the possibility of a steady income to a diligent writer of some talent. Best of all, it promised an immediate creative outlet for the enormous nervous energy of the high-strung, ambitious inmate, who had been shut away from humanity for an indefinite period for his prior antisocial acts.

Finney would study the trade magazines and then he would write to them with ideas for a story. When they expressed an interest, he would contact business firms for data and facts, enclosing a self-addressed stamped envelope to encourage replies. The subjects of the articles ranged from the intricacies of building a birdhouse or running a laundry, through the problems and joys of stratospheric flying, to analyses of factors that make for a bank's solvency—or insolvency. Appropriate illustrations and other assistance came from friends on the outside. In this and other matters, his greatest friend and ally was his mother. Mabel Finney served as his outside "agent," making almost daily contributions to her son's new-found interest.

Everything was done by mail. He often received more mail than did the warden. By 1941 as many as forty letters a day came pouring out of the Finney word factory. To reduce the chance of embarrassment or declinations from the solicited firms, he elected to use a Lansing post-office-box number and a pseudonym in his correspondence. With malice aforethought he chose Lon Fanald as his nom de plume.[28] Apparently, Ronald had a fondness for anagrams—but no love for a certain former chief executive.

The commercial writing, which developed rapidly, became his life's work after his release. It gave him a trade outside those in which his greatest natural talents lay but which would henceforth be legally barred to him—namely, salesmanship, banking, and finance. "Thanks to Bill, and to reading every editorial you have written in the past four or five years," the grateful and now-subdued prisoner wrote to William Allen White in the early forties, "I've learned to write in a good enough hack way." In January, 1942, he and his new vocation received lengthy coverage as a Sunday feature in the *Kansas City Star*. In the incipient stages of the enterprise he earned only a few hundred dollars a year, but his income grew steadily. In 1941 the ingenious entrepreneur took in $900; in 1942, about $2,000; in 1943, over $3,000; and in 1944 he made over $7,000. The earnings were promptly and proudly turned over to Winifred, who, with the children, had left Kansas and moved to California.[29]

IN AUGUST, 1940, the boys at Lansing received a special treat when war correspondent W. L. White agreed to talk to them on his recent, celebrated experiences in Finland and the other European war zones. Sandwiched in between religious services, the noted journalist gave a witty, informative talk to a large and appreciative audience in the chapel. After the formal presentation, he had a chance to talk to an old friend,[30] who tried to help him understand how it was on the inside:

> Nothing ever happens [here] to laugh at. Now you, on the outside, you probably laugh three or four times a day. But I'll bet most of those fellows hadn't laughed for a week. Because there's nothing ever funny about these places. If you're in for a short time, you think how awful it's going to be when you have to get out and face all the fellows you knew. And if you're in for a long time, you keep wondering how long the folks on the outside that still write to you are going to live, or how soon they will quit getting a kick out of writing to a fellow that's in the penitentiary and forget all about you. . . .
>
> It's not what they do to you in these places that makes them so tough. It's not that they ever beat you with clubs, or starve you. That

would be something new—you could get mad about that. It's just being in them, and the same thing happening, day after day, nothing ever funny, and knowing it will go on just the same, year after year.[31]

Bill used the occasion not only to enlighten the inmates on conditions in Europe but also to enlighten the citizens of Kansas about something called justice. In an article telling about the events of that Sunday, he began his public campaign to free his friend, a campaign that would not bear fruit for several years.

> My old friend ... [has] an unusual sentence, but his was an unusual offense, for he embezzled several hundred thousand dollars from the State Treasury, unlike Richard Whitney, who embezzled more money from private individuals and got only three years, or Boss Tom Pendergast, of Kansas City, who embezzled his from the Federal Government and got only one year, or unlike Al Capone, who in the process of cleaning up several million dollars had to have a number of people machine-gunned and has already finished his ten-year sentence....
>
> But now of course I exaggerate a little. For while my friend has a maximum sentence of 635 years, in point of fact with good behavior he may get out when he has served his minimum of thirty-one years, ready to start life anew at the age of seventy-six [sic], after having paid the penalty for having done, seven years ago, a very silly, stupid, crazy thing, and for not having been smart like Richard Whitney was, or Tom Pendergast was, or Al Capone was.[32]

TOM BOYD became the first of the three incarcerated principals of the bond scandal to leave prison. The former treasurer had entered Lansing in an acrimonious and truculent mood. "I haven't anything to say to anybody," he snapped as he began his four-to-ten-year sentence in March, 1935. He was first assigned to ditchdigging; later he was transferred to the dairy department. Though he mellowed a bit as his years in prison passed—on occasion flashing some of his old-time wit—Boyd continued to be resentful, repeatedly insisting that he had been the fall guy.[33]

As he moved into his sixties, Boyd made repeated but unsuccessful attempts to gain executive clemency (December, 1936) and parole (December, 1937, and February, 1939). In his applications for parole he tersely declared that he "was a victim of circumstances, and have nothing more to state at this time." Though he suffered some from chronic lumbago, prison doctors pronounced his state of health to be "generally good."[34]

With time off for good behavior the once-popular Statehouse politician completed his maximum sentence in September, 1941. After gaining his freedom, Boyd returned to Topeka, where he spent the remainder of his life. He sold his Shawnee County farm and lived primarily on his Santa Fe pension. He did little or nothing in his declining years—becoming something of a recluse as he carefully nursed his passionate hatred for his erstwhile "brother," Ronald Finney. An old and embittered man, he died at the age of eighty-four, on December 17, 1961, in a Topeka hospital.[35]

RONALD FINNEY made his first formal plea for executive clemency in the fall of 1941. Advertising in the newspaper as the law required, he petitioned Governor Payne Ratner for a commutation of his minimum sentence from thirty-one to fifteen years. With allowances for good behavior, that would make him eligible for parole after serving about ten years.[36]

In support of the request, William Allen White raked over the still-smoldering coals of the controversial sentencing on the editorial page of the *Gazette:*

> Finney is asking that the sentence be reduced to the period for which he pleaded guilty under a definite agreement with the court. The agreement was violated after Finney pleaded. . . . His attorney and the prosecuting attorney definitely agreed to this 15-year sentence in the presence of the judge of the court—a procedure usual in such cases. . . .
>
> If he had committed an offense against an insurance company or a bank or a railroad, taking from them the money he tried to take from the state, he would have got a 10-year sentence and would be out today. But Finney committed a crime against the state. He is a political prisoner.[37]

White followed the editorial with a letter to the governor a few days before the hearing. He repeated his arguments from the editorial and called Ratner's attention to the fact that no unfavorable reaction to the editorial had been registered around Emporia ("I asked the reporters to report any comment upon it, favorable or unfavorable").[38]

Mabel Finney appeared at the January hearing in her son's behalf. She said that they had no funds for a lawyer, but "money won't help in this case and we have no money." She charged that the state had "double-crossed Ronald." "The state promised a 15-year sentence and went back on its word," the bitter mother declared. She said that her son had earned a thousand dollars from selling magazine articles and that he had an offer of a job in Kansas City. But she declared, "You can't go on and on in a place like Lansing without deteriorating. I hope and pray to get him out and to rehabilitate him." Though she left the hearing room in tears, Mabel

Finney had made a clear-eyed and forceful statement to the officers representing the governor.[39]

A surprise witness accompanied the mother—the Finney prosecutor, Lester Goodell. "I have always felt that good faith was not kept with Finney," the former Shawnee County attorney testified;[40] "it was a very serious offense but, on the other hand, there was a lot of public hysteria."[41] Five days later, Governor Ratner declined to commute the sentence.[42] The first round had been fought and lost.

During this period, Finney and W. A. White established a regular and lively correspondence. The Emporian helped to keep the prisoner abreast of family events ("your mother . . . is looking well") and tried to keep Ronald thinking positively about the future ("keep your dauber up"). The publisher sent carefully selected books by the boxful to the grateful inmate ("I honestly believe that the men who read books regularly in here enjoy them more than they possibly could on the outside"). With White's help, Finney lined up some jobs at manpower-hungry defense plants, though not without some misgivings ("It seems cheap to me to . . . mention the war in trying to get out"). After the initial attempt at commutation had failed, White wrote: "I am satisfied that your friends, among whom I am which . . . can go up and see the Governor some time and talk turkey and tell him it just ought to be done in all decency."[43]

In a March, 1942, epistle to White, Finney reflected on his general circumstance:

> I am doing fine. I don't think there is a man in jail in the world who is doing better. I'm not worried a great deal and . . . I'm doing as well as 75 per cent of the people on the outside. I am making money and I am using that money to support my wife and kids. BUT, regardless of all this, I want out. I can think all day of reasons why. . . . But they sum up to the same reasons why every man in wants out. There's no difference. I have less reasons, really, than most. But that does not in any way soften the desire.[44]

Finney advertised a second time for executive clemency in the fall of 1942; the hearing was set for December. White published another editorial in the *Gazette*, repeating his charge that Finney was a political prisoner. He quoted Jack Harris of the *Hutchinson News*, who had recently commented: "Finney continues to serve time less for his misdeeds than for his fame. Probably the average Kansan today either favors Finney's release or at least would have no objection to it. There are enough Kansans who might not, however, to keep anyone with the pardon and parole authority for some years to come from taking the chance of offending them."[45]

At about this juncture, Mr. White decided to enlist some help from an influential and knowledgeable quarter in his continuing quest to free the son of his dear friend. He contacted his long-time political associate and close personal friend William A. Smith, justice of the Kansas Supreme Court. White had helped to launch Smith politically as attorney general and had continued to be one of his strong supporters over the years. ("You know, of course, that he made me attorney general," Smith later acknowledged.)[46] A man of wide interests, Attorney General Smith had successfully prosecuted the state's case against Doc Brinkley when the quack was stripped of his medical license in 1930.[47] The jurist was one of that small inner circle of political friends whom White contacted between general elections, before the formal party caucus, to line up an unofficial, but usually successful, slate. ("Dear Judge Bill: . . . We must be thinking about a

William A. Smith, justice of the Kansas Supreme Court (Kansas State Historical Society)

candidate for Supreme Court next year. What would you think of ———?")[48]

Smith, who himself had been close to the Finneys in their halcyon days, having attended Rotary luncheons as Warren Finney's guest when he was visiting in Emporia, responded immediately and favorably to White's request: "Command me when I can be of any help."[49] He then reflected on past events and urged White to contact the reluctant governor:

> I told Governor Ratner about what was said . . . with reference to our friend who is at Lansing. He said he appreciated the way you felt and thought, himself, in fairness something should be done, but he said that he hated to do anything just in the latter part of his term. . . .
> I think if you request it he will do it. . . .
> This thing should be done in common decency and I don't know of anything better you could do just now than to see that Payne does the thing . . . he should do. . . .
> Les Goodell has always insisted to me that there was an out and out agreement that if [Finney] would plead guilty the minimum sentence would be 15 years. A good many people have criticized Goodell but I have never heard anybody say he would lie or fail to keep his word. He is a fanatic in that respect. I have myself been convinced that the agreement was made.[50]

Confidence that the governor would do "the thing which in common decency he should do" was not well placed. On the day after the hearing at which Mabel Finney appeared alone on behalf of her son, Governor Ratner wrote to White that he had denied Finney's application:

> I have given this case a great deal of thought the past few weeks. I have even given it some prayer. . . .
> I can't help but have a very real indignation in regard to Finney's behavior. I believe that he was and is completely immoral. That is, there was a complete absence of the scruples and conscience which deter the average citizen from committing a crime. I do not believe Finney has overcome that attribute of character. . . .
> Tom Boyd, another Finney tool, served his maximum before being released. I was forced to resist the strongest kind of political pressure in his case. . . .
> I regret more than I can tell you the necessity of refusing any request that you might make, but knowing you as I do, I know you would not want me to do anything I cannot do conscientiously.[51]

And so the second round, though fought more vigorously than the first, had also been lost.

In late December the eternally optimistic Mr. White wrote to his incarcerated pen pal in an attempt to bolster his sagging spirits:

> I am not laying down on this job. I believe that in the next ten or twelve months we can find reason for substantial hope. There is just one thing I want you to do: Keep yourself in hand. Don't let down. Don't get discouraged. As long as Bill and I and Mrs. White are on earth, you have got someone to depend on. And we will be here.[52]

Finney quickly responded, suggesting that abstract justice wasn't the only criteria used in deciding whether a prisoner would be released or not:

> I feel that the reason I was turned down was not one but ten thousand. I was told here, as you know, that it would take twenty. That of course was out of the question. Then both Mother and I were told that ten would do the job. . . . I felt then and I feel now that even had we been able to pay the money, doing it would have been a great mistake. . . . Business of that sort is what landed me in here in the first place. Surely, after nearly ten years, I should learn something, even if the learning it requires that I spend many more years in prison.[53]

Prior to the 1943 "season" for requesting executive clemency, Mr. White underwent a major operation at the Mayo Clinic.[54] "Just before he went on the operating table (he didn't expect to come off alive)," Young Bill wrote to Lacy Haynes, "he told mother and me that there were only two things in his life left undone. First, he had hoped to be able to finish his autobiography. . . . Secondly, he said that, even more than the book, he had wanted to see Ronald Finney free, now that he has served ten years."[55] The medical prognosis following the operation indicated that the aging editor could only be expected to live a short time. So, in his father's stead, Young Bill began to work closely with Justice Bill Smith on the clemency project.

During the fall, Bill shuttled back and forth between his New York activities and Emporia, where he ran the *Gazette* and also directed the Finney enterprise. Encouraged by the election of a new governor, he had decided to reopen the matter, he wrote Smith, by approaching the recently appointed parole attorney, a veteran of the bond scandal.

> When I get out there, I going to talk to Judge Bloss, whom I know and have always respected. He is, thank God, an honest man and a courageous one and I thought, in general an excellent appointment. By that I don't mean I have any reason to think he would be unduly lenient to Ronald. It isn't a matter of leniency because after all the poor boy has been in there ten years. . . .
> I suppose you know that he has already been in prison longer than any man in the United States convicted of a civil crime, i.e., not murder, rape or other crimes of violence.[56]

Smith decided to sound out the parole attorney in a casual manner.

Bloss told Smith that he thought "perhaps Ronald should serve about fifteen years." "I do not think this is a fixed idea of Judge Bloss," the somewhat disconcerted Smith immediately wrote to Young Bill. "He looks on these things as legal questions and under his apparent crust he is a very humane person. . . . The best way to handle the thing is for your father to have a personal talk with Andy [Schoeppel, the governor] when he gets strong enough to do so and I am turning over in my mind whether any of us should talk to Andy before that. . . . As it is, I do not have the remotest idea how Andy feels."[57]

When Finney had advertised the first time in 1941, no written objections had come to the governor or to the Board of Administration from any quarter. The subsequent *Gazette* editorial and Mabel Finney's statement at the hearing emphasized that Finney had been "double-crossed." The judge had gone back on his solemn word, they loudly and publicly proclaimed. When Finney advertised in 1942, a strong written protest had been registered. It came from a still-disturbed Judge Paul Heinz.[58] He wrote again in the same vein in 1943:

> I tried this case and I must say that in all of the years that I have been connected with criminal prosecutions I never came into contact with a more flagrant violation of the law than this man has been guilty of. I think his crime probably reached more people causing serious sorrow and in at least three instances the death of parties who were directly affected by his operations. I am firmly convinced that he should pay in accordance with the magnitude of his operations while he was going good.[59]

Finney wrote to Young Bill White in early November, recalling some ancient legal history:

> This is the judge . . . who agreed to a ten-year minimum, then after Landon's attorney kicked, said in the presence of seven men that he would give me a *fifteen* year sentence. Over the weekend, between the time of my plea of guilty and receiving sentence, this judge was with Landon three times (we had him followed), and when I was brought into court I was given the 31 to 600 year sentence. . . .
>
> At the time I was sentenced, before I appealed to the supreme court, this judge sent . . . an attorney friend of Heinz and also a friend of mine, over to the jail, and [he] said that he had come from the judge, and that he, the judge, hated to do what he did, but it couldn't be helped, and if I would NOT appeal, after two years, he, the judge, would do everything he could to get a reduction of the sentence to the ten years he had originally suggested and which he felt was ample.[60]

In a letter to Lacy Haynes, Young Bill remarked that he objected to approaching the governor, or anybody else, in this matter "as something which should be done only because it gratifies a wish of my father. It would be fairer to present it as something which, as a matter of abstract justice, should have been done long ago."[61] Bill sent a copy of the letter to Smith. In return he received from the distinguished jurist a pragmatic lecture on the relative values of abstract justice and political expediency. William Allen White would have heartily approved.

> I imagine the ends of both of us will best be served by talking frankly.
>
> I note you say it would be fairer to deal with our friend's release as a matter of abstract justice.
>
> This might sound very well to your publisher and would no doubt make a fine line in an essay, but I understood what we wanted was to get Ronald out of the penitentiary. . . .
>
> The painful fact is that men are not released from the penitentiary as a matter of abstract justice; nor do I remember when any public official has acted in any particular way in any particular situation as a matter of abstract justice in this state or in any other. . . . The truth of the matter is that all decisions are swayed by personal interests or bias or viewpoint of him who has to make the decision. . . .
>
> . . . It is perfectly safe not to act, that is, there won't be any criticism at all if he doesn't do anything. Ronald is in the penitentiary and that is all there is to it. Outside of a few people like you and some of us who are interested in him on account of you and your family nobody cares about his fate anymore. So Andy could just as well do nothing and he would be certain not to incur any criticism. On the other hand, there is always a little danger of criticism if he does act.
>
> On account of your father's reputation for rightness and his interest in good government generally, I say a request from your father that some action be taken would carry great weight. . . . Andy will understand pretty well that the other newspapers would not criticize the governor too much for doing something that your father wanted done. . . .
>
> Remember this, your father is the greatest idealist this state ever produced, but when the situation demands it he can spit on his hands and knock heads with the best of them and be just as realistic as an auctioneer in Georgia in 1850 selling slaves in the market place.[62]

On December 3 William Allen White, who was gravely ill, sent identical letters to about two dozen of his closest newspaper friends, asking for their support in the Finney matter:

> I am sick and unable to go to Topeka, so I am writing Governor Schoeppel in behalf of Ronald Finney. . . .

> The bitterness which surrounded him at the time of his sentencing has now largely passed, and while I don't think it would be either fitting or proper that I should ask the Governor to do this as a favor to me, I am telling him that it would personally gratify me more than anything he can ever do for me....
>
> I don't ask that you tell the Governor that you are in favor of this pardon. I only ask you to give me assurances for him that if he thinks it should be made you . . . will not offer any criticism or protest.[63]

A gratifying response came as a result of the call, eloquent testimony to the great esteem and affection in which the *Gazette*'s editor was held by his journalistic colleagues. Senator Arthur Capper responded in a personal vein:

> I am glad to respond to your call for help in the Finney matter and I enclose a letter that you are at liberty to show the Governor. . . . I have talked this over with Clif [Stratton]. . . .
>
> Will, I do not believe there will ever be a time when I would not respond to your call. I feel I owe you more than any other man in Kansas and will always welcome a chance to help on anything in which you are interested. I have a good many fine friends in Kansas, but you have gone further for me than anyone else. I never can forget that kind of friendship.[64]

The editorial response was modest but positive. The *Leavenworth Times* reflected the thoughts of many:

> At the time Finney was sentenced, feelings ran high against him and the public cried out for his blood. The unheard of severity of the sentence he received met with popular acclaim. . . . But now the public has had time to cool off and to consider the term of the sentence more calmly, Finney's record in the prison, and the full score of the punishment he has suffered for his wrong doing. . . .
>
> Ronald Finney has given every evidence of deeply repenting the wrong he did. There is no reason, whatsoever, to believe that he ever will break the law again. So what is gained by keeping him in prison?[65]

SOMETIME during the fall, Judge Bloss suggested to Young Bill that a statement from Finney regarding his role in the bond scandal and his disposition of the money might strengthen his chances for getting the sentence commuted. Finney willingly responded, receiving the help of Young Bill in the early stages of drafting a statement. The fifteen-page document, dated December 9, presents a straightforward "confession" of the duplicity and deceit that had led to his downfall. Finney implicated no one else except, indirectly, his father. The seminal problem, he said, rested in the bad loans that the Emporia and Neosho Falls banks had floated during the twenties. Losses from imprudent notes to farmers and cattlemen totaled upwards of a million dollars, he claimed. Profits from his bond operations, legitimate and spurious, went to take up the bad paper in the banks and, he admitted, to support his cost of high living.[66] Essentially, he exchanged the bad paper in the banks for worse paper in the state treasury.

The penitent Finney appeared to be making an honest attempt to explain the crazy events, insofar as he could explain them:

> To me now, it all seems much like carrying a heavy load and running to get away from a wind cloud which raced along over you. You grabbed up one end (Cattle) and ran with it, then another (land) and ran with it, all the while trying to get away, or do something about the cloud. And all the time you are living in a sort of crazy world which is like nothing I can explain, or want to. . . . I know that it was all wrong, rotten, crooked, and senseless.
>
> . . . I do not think there has been a day since I came to prison when I have not thought about the suffering and loss and grief caused—thought about it many times each day. I doubt if there will ever be a day so long as I live when I will not think about it in detail. I say this in no attempt to gain sympathy.
>
> However, I do not think that this self criticism either helps me atone for what I have done, or makes me better fitted to go out of prison and make a living for my family and conduct myself as a decent citizen.[67]

Then the remorseful prisoner addressed the question, still debated by the public, of how many millions the Finneys had salted away. "I have heard it said or hinted, that there was a large amount of money that I had saved or hidden before the crash. Or had left from the crash. I can see how this is a natural sort of thinking process but it is not the truth."[68]

A detailed breakdown of his current financial situation followed. The Finneys were hard-pressed, he said, due to extensive insurance loans that had been arranged by his father in order to pay off bank depositors; the heavy losses resulting from the banks' closing (which Mabel Finney was still struggling to meet); and the mammoth medical expenses stemming from the children's and Win's major operations. "My mother and my wife and family, and my sister and her family," he said, "have lived in very moderate circumstances since 1933. I have heard it said that this was, of course, the thing to do. I do not believe that people can do things consistently for over ten years, 'Because it is the thing to do.' Particularly people who have been used to another way of living."[69] He had, he said, net assets of only $3,510, of which $2,000 came from an equity in a Topeka apartment house.[70]

After Judge Bloss had read the original statement, he asked for a further financial accounting—especially of $240,000 that the broker had received from Jackson Brothers, Boesel and Company in late July, only a couple of weeks before the crash. In response to the request, Finney added a two-page supplement to the original document. He swore that $70,000 had gone to meet a debt at a Kansas City grain company; that $150,000 had gone to Fidelity (he evidently meant Eureka) to meet the treasurer's check withdrawing state funds; that $15,000 was kept as credit at the brokerage firm; and that he couldn't account for the other $5,000. The record, however, indicated that only $50,000 ever went back to the Eureka bank in the "$150,000 caper."[71]

AT THE CLEMENCY HEARING before Judge Bloss on December 16, 1943, Mrs. Finney, W. L. White, and Douglas Hudson, a Fort Scott attorney, appeared for the petitioner. Mabel Finney and Bill White had met with Governor Schoeppel just a couple of days before.[72] Hudson, who had done the legal work for Bell Telephone in the W. W. Finney case, protested that "the punishment suggested for Hitler and Mussolini, that they be locked in cages and exhibited to the public, is no more horrible than being locked in a prison cell for ten years."[73] White testified that Finney had demonstrated a marked bent for commercial writing. "Finney's development in this work is simply amazing," he said.[74]

Leland Caldwell's latest bid for parole was taken up at the same hearing. Caldwell's sentence had been commuted to fifteen to fifty years in November, 1941, but his repeated attempts to gain parole had been stymied since that time. His attorney made bold to suggest that perhaps there had been political reasons for Caldwell's not having been paroled heretofore. Provoked by the remark, Judge Bloss huffed that the prisoner wasn't being kept in Lansing because of politics but due to the "sentence of the courts."[75] Deciding that discretion was the better part of valor, the attorney quickly beat a strategic retreat. "If there was politics involved," he hedged, "it was long before my connection with the case." After the hearings, Governor Schoeppel announced that he would receive Bloss's recommendations within the next few weeks and that he personally intended to give the cases intensive study.[76]

Though the hearings had seemed to go well enough, on his way back to New York on the following day an apprehensive Young Bill, in an effort to make the case as strong as possible, wrote to Alf Landon, who was now a respected senior statesman in the national Republican party. It was a letter that White hated to write. He still angered at the thought of the governor's influence on the sentence in December, 1933. On the other hand, a quiet word at this hour from the still-influential former governor to the somewhat nervous incumbent could make all the difference. Previously, Bill had discharged some of his hostility in remarks to important eastern politicians during the 1936 presidential race and in his unsympathetic portrayal of the governor in *What People Said*.[77] But the letter—with its repeated references to events buried in the painful past—revealed clearly the full depth of his feeling:

> I do not ask you for favors for the same reason that I do not [write] checks on a bank where I don't keep an account; we have a

Alf Landon enjoying one of William Allen White's stories (Kansas State Historical Society)

mutual friend who got into trouble by doing that. . . .

My father is dying of cancer and he . . . is most anxious to secure the release of Ronald Finney, who now, with good behavior allowances, has already served more than the fifteen years he was told the judge had agreed to give him when he pled guilty. You know more about the circumstances of that sentence than I do. . . .

I can see no reason why Governor Schoeppel should be asked to lose votes in this matter; after all he didn't know any Finneys—he grew up in western Kansas in blissful ignorance of the pleasures and/or profits to be derived from their society—it certainly isn't *his* baby.

. . . if you came out, the day following Ronald's release, with a one sentence statement saying that the ends of justice had been served and you approved the Governor's action, Governor Schoeppel would lose no votes whatsoever.

. . . you might do this if father asked you to, but I have not suggested it to him, because on the other hand you might not, and in his present condition I do not care to have him rebuffed.[78]

Two weeks later, Bill, who had received no response to his acrimonious letter, sent a copy to Bill Smith, with an appended note: "I haven't heard from Alf and at this late date, don't expect to. But I'm glad that letter is on the record because I don't want him ever to tell me how much he would have liked to do this had he only known the circumstances."[79] Later, White wrote to Smith: "I am sure . . . that if Alf had gotten into this with real vigor . . . Bloss would have caved in."[80] Eventually, in late January, a two-paragraph response from Landon did arrive. "The first paragraph said some very nice things about his old friendship with father," Bill White wrote to Smith. "The other paragraph was as follows: 'I am sorry, but the tone of your letter makes it impossible for me to discuss the Ronald Finney matter with you.' "[81]

ON JANUARY 21 Governor Schoeppel announced his decision. Finney's sentence would be commuted to eighteen to thirty-six years, making him eligible for parole, with allowances for good behavior, in February, 1945. In his lengthy statement the governor explained the reasons for his decision. He had dug through the voluminous records of the case in detail and had "read a lot of law." He acknowledged that a number of persons had talked to him about the matter, but he insisted that he had tried to decide it "strictly on the basis of the record."[82]

> Finney freely admits all the wrong doing charged. He is unable to account for the money obtained by his frauds. In the ten years, neither

the federal government, for income collection purposes, nor the state, nor individual losers have been able to locate any of the money or the property he obtained. . . .

His sentence was in effect . . . a life sentence. . . . When Finney entered Lansing he was 34 years old [actually he was thirty-five]. If he should live out a traditional life of three score and ten years, he would stay a prisoner for 36 years. . . . I think it just to Finney and the public that with statutory allowance for good time, he should serve at Lansing one-half of the above allotted years.[83]

On the same day, Schoeppel announced a parole for Leland Caldwell, so that he could join the merchant marine at Port Arthur, Texas. Caldwell's release had generally been assumed to be a precondition for the release of Finney. At the time when he commuted Caldwell's sentence in 1941, Governor Ratner had commented that "Caldwell, an accomplice, should not have a greater term than Finney, the principal." Caldwell continued to be a working merchant seaman for a number of years thereafter.[84]

Finney's relatives and friends were greatly pleased by the news, though it did mean an additional term of thirteen months in prison, at the least. Advised of the governor's action in Topeka where she now lived, the grateful Mabel Finney, "in a voice choked with emotion," said that she preferred not to make any public statement.[85] Justice Smith wrote the senior Whites that the chief executive had received a number of letters on the Finney matter, none of them critical. Many had been written with a lead pencil on tablet paper, he reported, indicating that they came from people of modest means, or at least from people without a secretary.[86]

After the good news had been savored and digested, Young Bill extended his gratitude to his coworker in good deeds. "It couldn't have been done without you," he wrote to Smith. "You went the whole distance, and didn't wiggle, squirm, alibi, or ever once point out that after all it was no skin off of your large pink bottom. . . . The nicest thing of all was that I was able to tell father, truthfully, that they all absolutely intend to go through with this and let Ronald out in February of 1945."[87] On Kansas Day, eight days after the governor had made his announcement, William Allen White died, peacefully secure in the knowledge that the errant son of his old and errant friend should soon be a free man.

Concordia's Gomer T. Davies openly praised the governor's action in the *Kansan:* "There may be those who will criticize, but we venture to say that the great majority of Kansas citizens will commend Governor Schoeppel's disposition of the cases. This scribe will go farther, by expressing our admiration for the frank, fearless, courageous manner in which he disposed of a delicate—or at least that would appear to a politically minded executive—situation."[88] In an editorial headed "Justice above Mercy," Young Bill reflected on the decision, assuring everyone that "no politics entered into it." "There are few people in the state who would [not] say that not only the ends of justice, but also the more savage ones of vengeance, have now been fulfilled," he wrote. "When Judge Bloss after many weeks of study, concurs in the decision to release Leland Caldwell and to cut Ronald Finney's time . . . , Kansas can be sure that . . . this case has been settled strictly on its merits, as these are impartially viewed by one of the best legal minds in Kansas."[89]

THE BOARD OF ADMINISTRATION granted Finney his promised parole in mid February, 1945. Bill White and his mother attended the hearing. "Judge Bloss intimated that it might be wise for me to be there as there had been protests," he wrote to Smith, "and Mother insisted on going because she said father would have been there if he could."[90] The written protest had been lodged by the persistent Judge Heinz. "I had no objection to the commutation of his sentence," he stated, "but now that he has had that favor shown him I do want to enter my protest to a parole being granted to him."[91]

A few days after the hearing, White told Smith of his relief that it had finally ended:

> Well, it's over. It was the last thing father asked of anybody and the Governor fulfilled the promise he gave you a year ago to the letter. . . .
>
> I have also written the Governor telling him I'll be personally responsible for any advice or help which Ronald may need, although my judgment is that he will need none at all. But anyway from here on out it will be my worry and not his or yours.[92]

A few days later, Justice Smith rang down the curtain from his end with a reminder to White of their earlier discussion about abstract justice:

> You remember you and I exchanged letters once about substantial justice and I scoffed a little at the likelihood of that elusive happening. I want to tell you now that I feel in this case that substantial justice was done but in the interest of philosophy, Bill, won't you admit that substantial justice had to have at least a gentle nudge from a few rough necks? If you will admit that, then our philosophical views will be in accord.[93]

REDEMPTION

AFTER NEARLY TWELVE YEARS of confinement, including several at hard labor, the overbearing, swaggering "Kingfish" of the high-rolling Jayhawk days had disappeared. The metamorphosis in character had been complete. "To say that I am ashamed and sorry for all the trouble and worry I have caused," the subdued Finney had written to Mr. White, "doesn't explain how deeply I feel it. Maybe you know how I feel without my saying anything. I hope you do."[94] On another occasion he wrote to his long-term older friend: "I sincerely have a feeling that I do not deserve what has been done for me. I mean that. I don't believe you could possibly ever understand how a man feels who has been called an s-o-b at every turn of the road for . . . years (don't think either that I'm not mindful that it was all coming) and then all at once he is not called that anymore, or anyway not by so many or so much."[95]

On the crisp morning of February 18, with nary a backward glance, the thinner (at 184 lbs.), wiser, and wearier central figure of the infamy walked through the main gate at Lansing to freedom. With $22 in accumulated pay in his pocket, the forty-six-year-old erstwhile bond broker immediately went to visit his ailing mother, who was resting in a Topeka hospital, recovering from a major operation.[96]

After a short visit with the thankful mother, he headed for southern California, where his wife and two children were living. "I'd like nothing more than going ten thousand miles away and crawling in a hole," he had said before his release, "[but] a job would be better." Still unemployed a couple of months later, he visited Bill and Kathrine White for several weeks at their New Jersey farm and in their New York house. Full of his old nervous energy, the jumpy parolee expressed grave concern for the Whites' safety in New York City, insisting that new locks and bolts be placed on all the doors. Often within moments of being introduced to a new acquaintance, he would candidly blurt out that he had just "got out of the penitentiary." For a time he sent his clothes back to Lansing to be laundered, evidently finding it more difficult to break that umbilical cord than he ever could have imagined.[97]

Finney eventually returned to the West Coast, where he got a job with a trade journal. A major condition of his parole had been that he not become engaged in any financial operations that involved the public; another required that he attend church regularly. A year or so after his release, the nearly twenty-five-year-old marriage of Winifred and Ronald was dissolved. Winifred later married the old high-school beau whose father had been a horse trader.[98]

Finney had employed a schoolteacher-photographer as one of his journalistic researchers when he was in residence at Lansing. Since he worked from a Lansing box number, Selma had had no idea that he was in prison. Later they met in Detroit and subsequently were married. For a time he and his young wife ("very much like his mother") lived in a rustic cabin on a lake in the Oregon woods. He wrote, while she photographed the local scenery and the picturesque salmon-fishing. The union, described by a friend as "an extremely happy one," lasted until "death did them part." Ronald waggishly observed that she was "just the girl for me, because she had been a teacher in a home for delinquent boys."[99]

MABEL TUCKER FINNEY died in December, 1947, at the age of seventy-five in the West Coast home of her daughter.[100] Kansas has had its share of heroines over the decades—Sara Robinson, Mary Elizabeth Lease, Carry Nation, and Lilla Day Monroe, to name but a few. Surely Mabel Tucker Finney deserves a small footnote in the historical heavens. To the manner born, the redoubtable lady had been reared and educated as the eldest daughter of the leading citizen of Greenwood County. As a serious and dignified young woman, she met and married an intelligent and ambitious young man, who quickly took them both to the very apex of the Kansas financial, social, and cultural pyramid. "A perfect lady at all times," recounted one admirer, "one who could have been on the front cover of Amy Vanderbilt's book."[101]

Mabel Finney had borne a son who soon exhibited many of his father's strengths and who at a precocious age seemed to be outdistancing even his accomplished sire. Then followed the unspeakable shame and humiliation, as the whole magnificent edifice came tumbling down about her proud head. Most mortals placed in her situation in the fall of 1933 would have collapsed or, at the very least, let out long, impassioned whines of despair. But Mabel Finney did neither of these. Beneath that aristocratic, ladylike exterior she possessed a toughness—the steely toughness of the survivor. In earlier and happier days she had spent a fair amount of her time and talents worrying about who was smoking or drinking or doing you-know-what around Emporia. But after the crash, the doughty matron quickly reordered her priorities. She determined to become fully knowledgeable about the family business and legal affairs, which were as complicated and hopelessly tangled as one could ever expect to find. As the months passed and her beleaguered husband's spirit waned, she assumed an increasingly important role in attaining a just and fair financial settlement. Then she was forced to participate directly in the most agonizing piece of business any woman could ever be called upon to perform—the planned suicide of the man she loved.

After that tragedy she helped her daughter-in-law weather the several medical emergencies that beset the family, and she generally tried to keep their collective heads above water—financially, spiritually, and otherwise. Working almost daily on Ronald's magazine-article projects, the devoted mother mailed to Lansing an endless stream of clippings, photographs, and other essential items that he needed as his new calling developed. Behind the scenes she labored quietly, but unceasingly, to effect for him as early a release from prison as possible. With a resolute chin, our heroine bravely went before the Pardon Board in 1941 and 1942 as the principal witness in behalf of her incarcerated son. By the mid forties she had become terminally ill with cancer. In the end, God in His infinite mercy did send one ray of sunshine in her direction—she lived to see her beloved son released from the Kansas State Penitentiary.

IN NOVEMBER, 1949, Finney applied for a full pardon. That same month, Governor Frank Carlson commuted his sentence to twenty-four years, and in December he granted him a citizenship pardon.[102] A penitentiary official wrote to Finney: "[this] is in effect your final discharge from this Institution. In closing, we desire to assure you that it has been a pleasure to extend to you our friendly interest in your behalf."[103] Citizenship pardons were routinely granted to all Kansas prisoners after their full responsibilities to the institution had been fulfilled. It carried no ethical connotation. The practical consequence was that he no longer needed to report to a parole officer.

In the mid 1950s Finney and his second wife bought a house on the west coast of Florida, where they continued their work with trade journals. For several years they spent summers in Oregon and winters in Florida. They led a quiet, unobtrusive life; Ronald never again had to face a hostile prosecuting attorney. The Pacific Northwest and New Port Richey, Florida, were about as far as one could remove oneself from the Kansas heartland and still remain in the forty-eight states. Nevertheless, they did occasionally visit old and loyal Kansas friends, of which he still had quite a few. On October 1, 1961, at the age of sixty-three, Ronald Finney died of acute bronchitis, complicated by pulmonary emphysema, in a St. Petersburg, Florida, hospital.[104] His lifelong habit of heavy smoking had finally caught up with him.

THE GREAT KANSAS BOND SCANDAL

Ronald Finney, about 1955 (Kathrine White)

After the death was reported in Kansas, Bill White wrote a heartfelt tribute to his boyhood friend:

> Ronald Finney, one of this writer's oldest and warmest friends, is dead at the age of 63. He left one dying request which we were glad to honor, and this was that for the sake of his children whom he deeply loved, that we carry no obituary notice of him; that even in death he should remain as gone and forgotten in the town in which he grew up, as though he had never existed. . . .
>
> But what should now be set forth is not this ancient and atoned-for scandal, but of the Ronald Finney who emerged from it. . . .
>
> There has been, in this later second life, which was entirely of his own making, no hint of scandal. Shortly after he began it, his first marriage went on the rocks—understandably, considering the strains of separation under these tragic circumstances. But he then made a most successful and happy second marriage with a hard-working, intelligent and sensitive young woman. . . .

So those few left in Emporia who remember Ronald Finney should now be deeply proud of him. In the past 15 years he was able, on the shaky foundations of a wrecked career, to rebuild a happy, useful life —as it always could have been, and would have been except for circumstances beyond his control.

Few of us get this chance—he made the most of his.[105]

17

Epilogue

○○○

SHORTLY AFTER the initial revelations had been made, Governor Landon assigned to the Attorney General's Office the task of ameliorating the massive state losses by bringing action against the surety companies, on Treasurer Boyd's bond, and against the National Bank of Topeka. The eastern-based bonding companies and the state's attorneys attempted to negotiate a settlement from the winter of 1933/34 into the following summer. The companies raised their initial $150,000 offer to a final, unacceptable $350,000. In July, negotiations broke down completely. The Attorney General's Office then filed suit to recover approximately $700,000 on the $1 million treasurer's bond ($500,000 on each of Boyd's last two terms). Out-of-court negotiations were resumed and continued intermittently for over a year. On November 25, 1935, a settlement of $450,000 was announced.[1]

Ironically, after all the returns had been counted, the state actually realized a small profit. It received $201,000 in dividends and realized assets from the three Finney banks in addition to the surety companies' settlement to apply against their total frozen deposits of $701,000. This left a $50,000 deficit. But some of the deposits in Fidelity had been in a protested inheritance-tax account. For years, Kansas had been collecting inheritance taxes from "foreign"—that is, out-of-state—owners of common stock in Kansas corporations. In 1933 the U.S. Supreme Court declared these levies unconstitutional and ordered that the impounded funds, which often involved stock in the Santa Fe Railroad, be returned. Sixty-six thousand dollars of these funds had never been reclaimed by the original taxpayers, thus producing a "profit" of $16,000 for the state government. The state's books were at long last closed on the scandal when that amount was transferred to the General Fund in 1941.[2]

Controversy continued to surround scandal activities even in the mop-up stage. When Governor Landon accepted Attorney General Beck's recommendation to settle with the surety companies for $450,000, Democratic Senator Joe McDonald objected that the settlement was "an outrage" and demanded that there be a thorough legislative investigation. Since that opinion wasn't widely shared around the state, the partisan issue quickly died. Another ruckus was kicked up in 1937, when attorney Arthur Walker presented his bill of $25,000 to the legislature for services rendered in connection with the state's recovery suits. Just a few days after his acquittal, Roland Boynton—ever appreciative of his friends and apparently learning little from his harrowing experience—had hired Walker, his personal attorney and one of the defense lawyers in his impeachment trial, as a special assistant attorney general to help recover on Boyd's bond. After heated discussion and further cries of outrage, the legislature eventually did approve payment of only $11,000 on Walker's claim.[3]

The state filed a civil action against the National Bank of Topeka in February, 1934, claiming that the bank "did knowingly and fraudulently take and apply to a personal indebtedness . . . of one Ronald Finney . . . the sum of $150,000 of the moneys and credits of the state of Kansas [on] deposit in said bank and did thereby misappropriate and misapply . . . said sum . . . belonging to the state of Kansas."[4] As a stipulation in the 1935 settlement with the state, one of the eastern surety companies gained the right to maintain the action against the bank under the state's name. An out-of-court settlement, which was announced in March, 1938, indicated that both parties were "satisfied," though the basis of the settlement was not disclosed.[5] The bankrupt Chicago brokerage firm of Jackson Brothers, Boesel and Company brought a $237,000 civil action against the National Bank of Topeka in U.S. District Court in January, 1934. The plaintiffs transferred the petition to the Shawnee County District Court two months later, hoping to obtain speedier action. The defunct financial house alleged that the bank knew of the bogus nature of the many Finney bonds in their possession in the spring and summer of 1933. The bank became liable for subsequent losses incurred by others, they claimed, when the securities were allowed to reenter the stream of commerce. The suit was dismissed in May, 1938, on motion of the plaintiff. The nature of the settlement, if any, was never divulged.[6]

THE COST of the investigations and subsequent trials had been uppermost in the minds of the budget-conscious public and legislature from the beginning. The two impeachment trials cost $23,000, while the state investigations headed by Fred Harris came to only about $20,000—a real investigative bargain. The state also reimbursed Emporia Teachers College for 50 percent of its funds that had been impounded in Fidelity, a total of about $10,000. The cost of the federal investigations and indictments was substantial, though the exact amount is not known. The four criminal trials cost the two counties a total of about $10,000. The commissioners of both counties made futile attempts to obtain refunds from the state, arguing that the trials basically represented state cases.[7] Actually, the trials represented a great judicial bargain. If one divides the total cost of the criminal trials by the sum of the maximum sentences received, each year of sentence cost the public less than $5. That had to be an attractive cost-benefit ratio, even for the Depression years.

The unfortunate individual depositors in the three Finney banks bore the brunt of the losses connected with the scandal. The initial 1935 dividends were followed by somewhat smaller distributions in 1936 and 1937. The books closed on the three star-crossed institutions after the final payments were made in September, 1938. Fidelity paid a total of 26.6 percent on its deposits of $863,994; Eureka paid 34.6 percent on deposits of $571,893; and Neosho Falls paid 37.9 percent on deposits of $89,984. The total loss for depositors came to over $1 million (Fidelity, $634,258; Eureka, $374,018; Neosho Falls, $55,879).[8] Adjusting for the surety companies' settlement to the state, total losses suffered by the general public (including the banks' stockholders) and the county governments came to $752,000. To that total should be added the large losses suffered by Jackson Brothers, Boesel ($285,000) and Mitchell-Hutchins ($36,000) and the amounts paid by the National Bank of Topeka in their out-of-court settlements. It was, indeed, a million-dollar phenomenon.

AT HIS "BEST" (e.g., in the Roulier affair), Ronald Finney's duplicity matches that of other leading confidence men on the national and international scene. Along with Doc Brinkley, he bears the Kansas colors in the national rascals' hall of fame—joining there such luminaries as the immortal Ponzi ("America's best-known con man"), "Yellow Kid" Weil ("I never cheated an honest man"), "Wily" Wilby ("he had a sincere way of talking"), and the ingenious Oscar M. Hartzell of Madison County, Iowa. Hartzell successfully solicited thousands of dollars from numerous duped Americans named Drake, claiming that he had located a descendant of an illegimate son of Sir Francis Drake, who had a fortune of $25 billion coming, which he was most anxious to share with his kinfolk.[9]

At the time of the events in Kansas, a remarkably similar phenomenon, though with its own inimitable character, was occurring in France. The central figure was Serge "Handsome Alex" Stavisky, a "mysteriously powerful" personage and confidence artist *par excellence*. Through his highly placed connections on the political left, which included the chief prosecutor in Paris, who was the brother-in-law of the premier, Stavisky would get himself named agent of a bond issue by an unsuspecting municipality, then would secure the bonds with "creative" bookkeeping. Later, the securities would be sold for cash at a friendly Paris bank. All of which would sound familiar to anyone acquainted with the Kansas scene. After several years of such deception, the public belatedly began to clamor for action. Then events took a decidedly non-Kansas course. Incensed at the revelations of the swindles and the disclosures of official cover-ups in the highest offices in the land, angry mobs took to the streets and forced the resignation of the premier. Thousands of irate Frenchmen filled the Paris streets in late January, at the very hour when the Kansas Senate was calmly rendering its verdict in the case of the attorney general and was placidly taking up the charges against the auditor. "If Topeka was the capital of a French province," Mr. White puckishly suggested, "there would have been rioting up and down Jackson street, when Boynton was acquitted, . . . probably . . . led by . . . Colonel Bloss."[10]

A CURIOUS SIDELIGHT to the Kansas scandal, which should be of interest to researchers in psychosomatic medicine, was the abnormally high frequency of illness and death among the principals during the investigations and trials . Though no influenza epidemic or anything like it appeared among the general population, several jurors, females in every instance, became ill during each of the four criminal trials. In addition, a dozen attorneys and witnesses "enjoyed poor health" for varying periods of time. Five deaths of key witnesses occurred between August, 1933, and the following January. The former bank commissioner Roy Bone, who had suffered through so many difficulties with Finney's banks, died shortly after the initial disclosures. Then followed Arthur Jackson, of the bankrupt brokerage firm, and three clerical employees of Tom Boyd's Treasury Office. When the third, youngish, employee of that twenty-person office died in January, 1934, not a few public eyebrows were raised, and an autopsy was ordered. But as in the other cases, only natural causes could be identified, though severe stress from the disclosures of the fraudulent practices of Boyd and Finney was deemed to be a contributing factor in this and one other death among the employees in the Treasury Office.[11]

In sifting through the cold ashes of the scandal, we find no major laws stemming therefrom, but only a few minor changes in bureaucratic procedure. In comparison with the Brinkley phenomenon, the financial loss to the people of the state did not approach the estimated $12 million that went into the coffers of that master medical charlatan. However, the loss in confidence in state government and the political and personal devastation that was wreaked on a few were infinitely greater.[12] The affair revealed something of the nature of the many as well as the perfidy of the few. The angry demands of the shocked people and the consequent harsh sentences bear witness to the reaction of the collective puritanical mind to a crisis during a period of extreme economic duress. The people perceived grave problems in their state government—many of which were real, and a few of which were imagined—and they reacted accordingly. In that hysterical climate, the politicians and judges found it almost impossible to impose a penalty on the wrong-doers that the public would consider severe enough.

Not all the disclosures exposed the dark side of human nature. Several of those who were drawn into the eye of the fast-paced events conducted themselves in exemplary, even heroic, fashion. The roster of the staunch and courageous includes Lester Goodell, Fred Harris, Judge Bloss, Frank Ryan, Judge Light, Clif Stratton, and Mabel Finney, as well as Alf Landon, Clarence Beck, and Hugo Wedell. The last three received their rewards in political form almost immediately from the appreciative populace. The Whites and Justice Smith deserve honorable mention for their persistent, thankless, and initially unpopular efforts to obtain the release of Ronald Finney after he had served a lengthy sentence for a white-collar crime. The roll call of the intrepid would not be complete without mention of the "little people"—those unpaid public servants such as Lucy Pottorf and J. H. Shriver who doggedly resolved that their impoverished constituencies would not be hoodwinked out of their hard-earned dollars.

The state received a pointed and well-publicized lesson that crime and connivance in crime do not pay. Sunday School teachers had a field day with the plethora of well-documented examples of unethical conduct and un-Christian behavior. That nothing remotely approaching its magnitude has recurred over the intervening years can, arguably, be ascribed to a lesson well learned. Could it happen again? The answer remains a self-evident proposition so long as greed and gullibility continue as salient traits of *Homo sapiens,* even in its *kansensis* variety.

The scandal developed very much as a Kansas affair, bounded almost exclusively by the political borders of the state and having an impact on numerous communities within the state. Though disturbing enough in its revelations, it did furnish a kind of vicarious pleasure for the reading public during the joyless Depression years—something akin to following the escapades of John Dillinger or "Pretty Boy" Floyd, though it had more local immediacy and generated a great deal more hostility and righteous indignation. As a "family affair," it served further to integrate the commonwealth as a cultural unit—providing still another unique and distressful experience shared by its long-suffering people.

It is axiomatic that a historian chronicles life—that is, life of the human species—in its several aspects. This narrative portrays a selected facet of human life as it was manifested at a particular time by a special people on a certain imperfect rectangle on the globe. All the principals in the bond scandal have either died or long since retired from the active scene. Their deeds and misdeeds have become part of the cultural heritage and have faded into the dim halls of time—like the Norman Conquest, the War of 1812, or Lincoln's imperfect relationship with his father. The Moving Finger writes; and having writ moves on.

Appendix

LIST OF FORGED OR ILLEGALLY RETAINED MUNICIPAL BONDS AND WARRANTS:

Issue	Bonds			
	Original Amount	Date of Original Issue	Date of Duplication(s)	Total Amount Forged
Cheyenne County S.D.* No. 1 (St. Francis)	$ 9,000	June 1, 1931	July 23, 1932	$ 9,000
Clay County R.H.S.D.† No. 4 (Green)	16,000	Aug. 1, 1931	July 29, 1932 Sept. 24, 1932	32,000
Eureka (City) Refunding	45,000	Jan. 1, 1933	Dec. 28, 1932	45,000
Gove County R.H.S.D. No. 2 (Grinnell)	30,000	June 1, 1931	July 27, 1932	30,000
Hutchinson (City) Park Improvement	30,000	Feb. 1, 1932	Oct. 22, 1932 July 31, 1933	60,000
Johnson County S.D. No. 92	51,000	July 1, 1932	July 13, 1932 unknown date	102,000
Kansas City (City) Condemnation, Seventh St.	177,070	Dec. 1, 1931	Nov. 4, 1932 July 22, 1933	337,070
Kansas City (City) General Improvement, Seventh Street	52,858	Oct. 1, 1932	March 2, 1933 May 4, 1933	105,716

APPENDIX

Issue				
Logan County S.D. No. 5 (Monument)	20,000	Aug. 1, 1931	July 28, 1932	20,000
Logan County S.D. No. 49 (Page City)	11,700	Aug. 1, 1931	July 28, 1932	11,700
Norton (City) Internal Improvement	55,853	Aug. 1, 1931	Feb. 1, 1933	55,853
Pratt County R.H.S.D. No .5 (Coats)	25,000	June 1, 1931	Oct. 19, 1932 July 27, 1933	50,000
Riley County R.H.S.D. No. 4 (Riley)	15,250	Aug. 1, 1931	July 29, 1932 Sept. 24, 1932	30,500
Russell County S.D. No. 50 (Waldo)	16,000	Aug. 1, 1931	July 28, 1932 Oct. 12, 1932	32,000
Salina (City) Board of Education	20,000	July 1, 1932	Oct. 22, 1932 July 31, 1933	40,000
Stevens County Center Township (Hugoton)	18,000	Sept. 15, 1932	June 20, 1932	18,000
Thomas County S.D. No. 80 (Brewster)	20,000	July 15, 1931	July 27, 1932 April 7, 1933	40,000
TOTALS	$612,731			$1,018,839

	Warrants		
Issue	Amount Illegally Retained	Date of Certificate of Destruction	Forged Amount
Cheyenne County S.D. No. 1	$ 8,250	Feb. 3, 1932	—
Clay County R.H.S.D. No. 4	15,284	Feb. 18, 1932	—
Gove County R.H.S.D. No. 2	27,545	Jan. 28, 1932	20,000
Logan County S.D. No. 5	18,603	Feb. 3, 1932	5,000
Logan County S.D. No. 49	10,700	Feb. 3, 1932	—
Pratt County R.H.S.D. No. 5	25,000	Jan. 29, 1932 Aug. 19, 1932 (2)	60,000
Riley County R.H.S.D. No. 4	13,671	Aug. 17, 1932	3,709

APPENDIX

Russell County S.D. No. 50	14,544	Jan. 23, 1932	—
TOTALS	$133,597		$88,709

SOURCES: Kansas, Senate, *Trial of Roland Boynton, Attorney-general of the State of Kansas* (Topeka: State Printer, 1934), pp. 467–71, 472–75; Kansas, Senate, *Trial of Will J. French, Auditor of the State of Kansas* (Topeka: State Printer, 1934), pp. xiv, 50, 100–108, 400–401.
* S.D.—School District
† R.H.S.D.—Rural High-School District

Notes

ooooooooooooooooooooooooooooooooooooooooooooooooo

ABOUT THE SOURCES:

Since nothing approaching a full historical treatment of the bond scandal has ever appeared, secondary sources were of limited value. Sketchy accounts appear in the White biographies and in several books and articles treating Kansas in the 1930s. The most complete and accurate account previously available can be found in Donald McCoy's coverage in his biography of Alf Landon.

Contemporary newspapers constitute the best single source of information on the scandal and its ramifications. The *Emporia Gazette,* the *Topeka Capital,* the *Topeka State Journal,* the *Kansas City Star,* and the *Kansas City Journal Post* were the principal, though scarcely the only, papers consulted. The *Gazette* was searched systematically, page by page and column by column, from November, 1931, through April, 1936, for news about the scandal and for items of interest on the local scene. I also made numerous forays into the Emporia paper for other periods, especially 1911/12. The *Capital* was similarly searched systematically for the period June, 1933, through November, 1934, and for other limited periods. The Kansas State Historical Society has two volumes of newspaper clippings on the scandal, arranged chronologically up into the 1950s. In addition, and of inestimable value, were the eight notebooks of clippings, averaging 200 pages each, that were prepared by Mrs. Randal Harvey, the wife of one of Will French's defense attorneys. Assigned by her husband's law firm the task of clipping all items about the scandal that she could find, she continued the extensive project well into 1934 and later presented the carefully prepared material to the Kansas State Historical Society.

Legal records and private correspondence provided invaluable information. The official transcripts of the two impeachment trials, which total nearly 1,500 pages of fine type, proved a rich source of reliable information not only about the respondents Roland Boynton and Will French but also, more broadly, about many facets of the Finneys' bond and warrant operations. The indictments, trials, and appeals of W. W. Finney, Ronald Finney, and Tom Boyd generated extensive and valuable legal records. The Governor Landon Papers in the Kansas State Archives include several hundred letters and official documents pertaining to the scandal. Approximately thirty of the over one hundred statements taken by the state and federal investigators are extant. The useful information from most of the remaining statements are available in other modes. The William Allen White letters from the Library of Congress, which are available on microfilm in the Kansas Collection at the University of Kansas, were extensively consulted. Several collections in the Manuscript Division of the Kansas State Historical Society included correspondence of value. In two of these (the Cecil Howes and the Lacy Haynes papers) was found the text of Fred Harris's lengthy summaries of the evidence that was presented to the House of Representatives committees in October and November, 1933. A number of checks that had been written by Ronald Finney, as well as other relevant financial records from the Jayhawk suite, were brought forward by Gerald Goodell, son of Lester Goodell.

Upwards of 150 Kansans were contacted regarding their direct knowledge of the events. In only one instance did the person who was approached refuse to cooperate, presumably fearing adverse publicity even at this late date. Some useful information came from about forty individuals. Much of it confirmed or extended data and insights that I had obtained from other sources. Kathrine White provided a great deal of useful background information and many keen insights into the events.

W. L. White's novel *What People Said* follows closely selected events of the bond scandal. It was written in 1936/37 in New York City without recourse to records, notes, or newspapers, just with the collective memory and impressions of its author and his wife. The names of all the people and places were altered in the *roman à clef*. As a nonfiction novel, it presents a problem for the historian, as do other more recent works of this genre. Since it often relates in minute and accurate detail the actual events and since the author occupied a seat that was very close to the center of the real-life story—at times having become a part of the story himself—the book cannot be ignored with impunity. On the other hand, some of the events that are depicted reflect reality imperfectly or incorrectly. In certain instances the facts were deliberately altered in order to jar the fit with reality so as to avoid possible lawsuits. For example, in the novel, the fictional substitute for Warren Finney has a sister, that for Ronald Finney has three children, and those for the senior Whites travel around the world on their 1933 trip. None of these were true, as W. L. White well knew. With the aid of Kathrine White and the well-established facts, the true and the untrue have been sorted out, at least as regards the significant events. *What People Said* has been cited—cautiously and prudently, I hope—at various points in the text, but almost never as a sole source and only where it can reliably add a background note.

ACRONYMS USED IN THE NOTES:

EG   *Emporia Gazette*
KCJP   *Kansas City Journal Post*
KCS   *Kansas City Star*
KCT   *Kansas City Times*
KSA   Kansas State Archives, Topeka
KSHS   Kansas State Historical Society, Manuscript Division, Topeka
TC   *Topeka Capital*
TSJ   *Topeka State Journal*

Preface

1. Bureau of Labor Statistics, *Handbook of Labor Statistics* (Washington, D.C.: Department of Labor, 1975), p. 313; Department of Labor, Bureau of Labor Statistics, *Consumer Price Index.*
2. Francis W. Schruben, *Kansas in Turmoil, 1930–1936* (Columbia: University of Missouri Press, 1969), pp. 69, 71; *EG*, July 1, 1933, November 30, 1934, and January 17, 1935.
3. *EG*, December 24, 1935; Donald R. McCoy, *Landon of Kansas* (Lincoln: University of Nebraska Press, 1966), p. 151.
4. McCoy, *Landon*, p. 192; *EG*, March 2, 1935; *TC*, April 15, 1934; Keith D. McFarland, *Harry H. Woodring* (Lawrence: University Press of Kansas, 1975), p. 270.

Chapter 1

1. *EG*, September 30, 1932; William E. Leuchtenburg, *Franklin D. Roosevelt and the New Deal, 1932–1940* (New York: Harper & Row, 1963), pp. 26, 118–42; Ruth Friedrich, "The Threadbare Thirties," in *Kansas: The First Century,* ed. John D. Bright (New York: Lewis Publishing Co., 1956), 2:89–110.
2. *EG*, June 17 and August 3, 1933, and March 14, 1934; *TC*, May 31, 1933.
3. Donald R. McCoy, *Landon of Kansas* (Lincoln: University of Nebraska Press, 1966), pp. 144, 176; Francis W. Schruben, *Kansas in Turmoil, 1930–1936* (Columbia: University of Missouri Press, 1969), pp. 47–49.
4. McCoy, *Landon*, pp. 66, 106–13; Schruben, *Kansas*, pp. 79–103; Friedrich, "Threadbare Thirties," pp. 94–95; W. A. White, "Landon: I Knew Him When," *Saturday Evening Post*, July 18, 1936, pp. 5 ff.
5. McCoy, *Landon*, pp. 120–29, 123–24, 192; *EG*, August 15, 1933, and July 2, 1935; Alf Landon, interview with D. McCoy and G. Griffin, March 29, 1976.
6. *EG*, July 2, 1935.
7. McCoy, *Landon*, pp. 125–27; *EG*, March 7, 1933; Friedrich, "Threadbare Thirties," pp. 95–96.
8. Alf Landon to Charles H. Trapp, December 10, 1932, KSHS.
9. McCoy, *Landon*, p. 121.
10. Robert W. Richmond, *Kansas: A Land of Contrasts* (St. Charles, Mo.: Forum Press, 1974), pp. 63–66, 169.
11. *EG*, July 13, 1933.
12. *EG*, July 5, 12, and 27, 1933.
13. *EG*, December 22, 1931.
14. *EG*, July 15, 1932, April 27 and August 3, 4, and 5, 1933; Kansas, Senate, *Trial of Roland Boynton, Attorney-general of the State of Kansas* (Topeka: State Printer, 1934), pp. 109–10; Keith D. McFarland, *Harry H. Woodring* (Lawrence: University Press of Kansas, 1975), p. 55.
15. Kansas, Senate, *Trial of Will J. French, Auditor of the State of Kansas* (Topeka:

State Printer, 1934), p. 464; Charles Rooney, Sr., interview, May 17, 1979; Friedrich, "Threadbare Thirties," p. 93.
16. Lulu Wood statement, October 13, 1933, KSA.
17. Pamphlet, Republican State Committee of 1932, KSHS; W. G. Clugston, *Rascals in Democracy* (New York: Richard R. Smith, 1940), p. 259; Will J. French to Alf Landon, November 10, 1932, KSHS; *EG,* January 20, 1932.
18. Kansas, Senate, *Trial of Will J. French,* pp. 179–80, 329–31.
19. *EG,* August 3, 1933.
20. *EG,* August 4, 1932, and August 2, 3, and 7, 1933; Frank C. Clough, *William Allen White of Emporia* (New York: Whittlesey House, 1941), p. 165; Charles E. Webb, "A Caravan of Culture: Visitors to Emporia, Kansas," *Heritage of Kansas,* vol. 12, no. 3 (summer 1979), pp. 3–7.
21. *EG,* January 29, 1912, December 17, 1931, March 9 and 25, April 25, and November 13, 1933.
22. *Hutchinson News,* February 24, 1934.
23. *EG,* June 6, 1931, March 1, June 3, July 4, and August 17, 1933.
24. *EG,* September 26, 1932.
25. *EG,* July 4, 1933.
26. Walter Johnson, *William Allen White's America* (New York: Henry Holt & Co., 1947), pp. 475–500; *TC,* April 13, 1934; *EG,* November 7, 1930, December 17, 1931, and February 5, March 14, April 27, and November 10 and 22, 1932.
27. Johnson, *William Allen White's America; EG,* November 7, 1930, February 1 and 9, May 23, and September 17, 1932, and March 21, 1933; Kenneth S. Davis, "The Sage of Emporia," *American Heritage,* vol. 30, no. 6 (October/November, 1979), pp. 80–96; W. A. White, "Landon: I Knew Him When," *Saturday Evening Post,* July 18, 1936, pp. 5 ff.
28. Johnson, *William Allen White's America,* pp. 350–56.
29. *EG,* May 27, 1933; *TSJ,* August 31, 1933; W. L. White, *What People Said* (New York: Viking Press, 1938), p. 10.
30. Johnson, *William Allen White's America,* p. 354; *EG,* March 11, 1932; W. A. White to Robert Hazlett, February 19, 1916, W. A. White Collection, Library of Congress.
31. *EG,* June 19, 1933.
32. *EG,* February 16 and July 25, 1932, and April 13, 1933; Kathrine White, interview, February 17, 1979; White, *What People Said,* pp. 10–11, 66.
33. Clough, *William Allen White,* pp. 223–27; *EG,* September 12, 1933.
34. Clough, *William Allen White,* pp. 225–26; Elizabeth P. Leonard to author, March 30, 1980; Everett Rich, *William Allen White: The Man from Emporia* (New York: Farrar & Rinehart, 1941), pp. 236–37; White, *What People Said,* pp. 156–58, 173–86.
35. William Allen White, *The Autobiography of William Allen White* (New York: Macmillan, 1946), p. 555; Rich, *William Allen White,* p. 236; White, *What People Said,* pp. 11–14, 237–38.
36. Clough, *William Allen White,* p. 227; Kathrine White, interview, February 17, 1979.
37. *EG,* June 10, 1935; White, *What People Said,* p. 10.
38. *Parsons Sun,* August 9, 1933.
39. *EG,* January 26, 1932, June 14 and July 6 and 17, 1933.
40. Kansas, Senate, *Trial of Roland Boynton,* p. 762.
41. *TC,* August 9 and 10, 1933; *TSJ,* August 10 and 11, 1933.
42. Russell George, interview, August 12, 1978; Clugston, *Rascals,* p. 255; Charles Rooney, Sr., interview, May 17, 1979.
43. *EG,* July 31 and August 4 and 7, 1933; Gayle Mott, interview, January 9, 1979; *Time,* August 21, 1933.
44. *TC,* August 1, 2, 3, and 4, 1933; *EG,* August 3 and 4, 1933; White, *What People Said,* pp. 350–56.
45. Clugston, *Rascals,* pp. 261–65; *EG,* August 7, 1933; *TC,* August 5 and 6, 1933.

Chapter 2

1. *KCT,* August 8 and 12, 1933; *TC,* August 8, 1933; *KCS,* August 8, 1933; *TSJ,* August 12, 1933; W. H. Stanley statement, August 23, 1933, KSA.
2. Alfred M. Landon interview, January 23, 1979; *TC,* August 8, 1933.
3. *TC,* August 8, 1933.

4. Alf Landon to Lester Goodell, August 7, 1933, KSA; *TC*, August 8, 1933.
5. *TC*, August 8, 1933.
6. *TSJ*, August 8, 1933; *Chicago Tribune*, August 9, 1933.
7. *TSJ*, August 8, 1933; *KCS*, August 8, 1933.
8. *EG*, August 8, 1933. Hamilton became chairman of the Republican National Committee during Landon's 1936 presidential campaign.
9. *TC*, August 9, 1933; Charles Rooney, Sr., interview, May 17, 1979.
10. Democratic State Committee, "Landon's Remarkable Record in the Bond Scandal," Democratic campaign pamphlet, 1934, KSHS.
11. Richard B. Fowler, *Deeds Not Deficits: The Story of Alfred M. Landon* (Kansas City: R. B. Fowler, 1936), pp. 76–79; W. A. White, "Landon: I Knew Him When," *Saturday Evening Post*, July 18, 1936, pp. 5 ff.
12. *TSJ*, August 8 and 9, 1933; *TC*, August 9 and 10, 1933; *EG*, August 8, 1933; *KCT*, August 9, 1933; *Time*, August 21, 1933.
13. *TC*, August 10, 1933.
14. *TC*, August 9, 1933.
15. Kansas, Senate, *Trial of Will J. French, Auditor of the State of Kansas* (Topeka: State Printer, 1934), pp. 250–51, 407.
16. Ibid., p. 251.
17. Supreme Court of the State of Kansas, case no. 31,876, *State of Kansas* v. *T. B. Boyd*, Counter Abstract of the Record, p. 4; *TC*, August 9, 1933.
18. *TC*, August 9, 1933.
19. Ibid.
20. Alfred M. Landon interview with Donald McCoy and George Griffin, Kansas Collection, University of Kansas, March 9, 1976, pp. 15–16; *TSJ*, August 9, 1933.
21. Landon interview with McCoy and Griffin, March 9, 1976, p. 16.
22. *TSJ*, August 9, 1933; *TC*, August 10, 1933.
23. *TSJ*, August 9, 1933.
24. Governor's Executive Order, August 9, 1933, KSA.
25. Landon statement, August 9, 1933, KSA; *TSJ*, August 9, 1933.
26. *TC*, August 12, 1933; *TSJ*, October 4, 1933.
27. *TC*, August 10, 11, and 12, 1933; *TSJ*, August 10, 1933.
28. *TC*, November 28, 1933.
29. *TSJ*, August 10, 1933; *TC*, August 11, 1933; *Chicago Tribune*, August 11, 1933.
30. *TC*, August 10 and 11, 1933; *TSJ*, August 10 and 11, 1933; *KCS*, August 10, 1933.
31. *TSJ*, August 11, 1933.
32. *TSJ*, August 10 and 11, 1933; *TC*, August 10 and 11, 1933.
33. *TSJ*, August 11, 1933.
34. *TSJ*, August 10 and 11, 1933.
35. *TC*, August 12, 1933.
36. Kansas, Senate, *Trial of Roland Boynton, Attorney-general of the State of Kansas* (Topeka: State Printer, 1934), p. 769; William L. White, *What People Said* (New York: Viking Press, 1938), pp. 377, 390–91.
37. *KCS*, August 10, 1933; *TC*, August 11, 1933; *KCT*, August 18, 1933.
38. *TC*, August 11, 1933.
39. Kansas, House, *House Journal, Special Session, 1933* (Topeka: State Printer, 1933), p. 199; *TC*, August 13, 1933.
40. *Time*, August 21, 1933; *TC*, August 11, 1933.
41. Landon to Boynton, August 11, 1933, KSA; Landon to French, August 11, 1933, KSA; Landon to Markham, August 11, 1933, KSA; *KCT*, August 12, 1933; *TC*, August 12, 1933.
42. *KCT*, August 12, 1933.
43. *TSJ*, August 9, 1933; *KCT*, August 10, 1933.
44. The term "municipal" will herein refer to all public securities, including those of the state, a county, a city, a school district, a sewer district, a fire district, etc.
45. *House Journal*, pp. 237–38; *EG*, August 17, 1935; Charles H. Landrum, "A History of the Kansas School Fund," *Kansas Historical Collections, 1911–1912*, vol. 12, pp. 195–217; *House Journal*, pp. 133, 238; *TC*, August 9, 1933.
46. *TC*, August 12, 1933.
47. *TSJ*, August 11, 1933.
48. *KCS*, August 16, 1933; *TC*, August 13 and 14, 1933; a list headed "Forged

Bonds" definitely located on August 14, 1933, KSA.
49. Landon to Goodell, August 14, 1933, KSA; *TSJ*, August 14, 1933; *KCT*, August 15, 1933; *TC*, August 15, 1933.
50. Landon to Boyd, August 14, 1933, KSA.
51. *TC*, August 15, 1933.
52. Landon to Claude C. Bradney, August 11, 1933, KSA.
53. Boyd to Landon, August 15, 1933, KSA; *TC*, August 16, 1933.
54. *TC*, August 16, 1933.
55. *TC*, August 15 and 16, 1933.
56. *House Journal*, pp. 275-76; Kansas, Senate, *Trial of Roland Boynton*, p. 640; *Kansas Statutes*, Revised 1923, Section 75-612.
57. *TC*, August 15, 1933.
58. Donald R. McCoy, *Landon of Kansas* (Lincoln: University of Nebraska Press, 1966), pp. 123, 129; Clyde W. Coffman to Landon, August 11, 1933, KSA; *TC*, August 15, 1933; *KCT*, August 16, 1933; Ruth Friedrich, "The Threadbare Thirties," in *Kansas: The First Century*, ed. John D. Bright (New York: Lewis Publishing Co., 1956), 2:100.
59. *TSJ*, August 16, 1933; *KCT*, August 16, 1933; *TC*, August 16, 1933.
60. *TC*, August 16, 1933.
61. *KCS*, August 18, 1933; *TC*, August 18, 20, 26, 1933; *KCT*, August 19, 1933; *Chicago Tribune*, August 13 and 20, 1933; *EG*, September 2, 1933.
62. Landon to U.S. Comptroller of the Currency, August 22, 1933, KSA.
63. *TC*, August 23, 1933.
64. *TC*, August 24, 1933.
65. *TC*, August 23, 1933.
66. *TC*, August 23, 24, and 25, 1933; *TSJ*, August 21 and 24, 1933; *KCS*, August 24, 1933; *Chicago Tribune*, August 25, 1933.
67. *TC*, August 25, 1933.
68. *TSJ*, August 24, 1933; *TC*, August 25, 1933.
69. *TC*, August 27, 1933.
70. *KCT*, August 25, 1933; *KCS*, August 27, 1933; *TC*, August 28, 1933.
71. *TC*, August 31, 1933.
72. *TC*, August 27, 1933.
73. *TC*, August 27 and 30, 1933.
74. *EG*, August 28, 1933.
75. *KCS*, August 28, 1933; *TC*, August 29, 1933.
76. *EG*, August 14, 1933.

Chapter 3

1. *TC*, August 20, 24, and 27, September 5, 1933; *KCS*, September 3, 1933.
2. *KCT*, August 8, 1933; *TC*, August 9 and 26, 1933; *Chicago Tribune*, August 10, 1933; *KCJP*, August 9, 1933; *TSJ*, October 10, 1933; *Wichita Eagle*, August 10, 1933.
3. *TSJ*, September 6, 1933.
4. *KCS*, October 1, 1933; *TC*, September 15 and October 2, 1933. Shawnee County District Court, *Jackson Brothers, Boesel* v. *National Bank of Topeka*, case no. 49,884, Plaintiff Petition, pp. 7, 12, 18.
5. R. Finney to W. L. White, November 8, 1943, KSHS; Democratic State Committee, "Landon's Remarkable Record in the Bond Scandal," Democratic campaign pamphlet, 1934, KSHS; *TSJ*, August 15 and 22, 1933; *EG*, August 11, 1933; *KCS*, November 22, 1933; W. H. Stanley statement, August 23, 1933, KSA.
6. *TC*, August 11, 1933; *TSJ*, August 10 and 11, 1933; *Chicago Tribune*, August 24, 1933. Hinshaw was one of Mr. White's "boys." He had carried the *Gazette* as a boy and later was closely associated with White in the Progressive campaign of 1912. A Quaker, he had become a confidant of President Hoover in the late twenties. His wife, Augusta Wiggam, the older sister of Winifred, had written an article on White in 1930; he would be the author of a full-length biography of White in 1945.
7. *EG*, May 6, 1933.
8. *EG*, March 24, 1932.
9. *TC*, August 29, 1933.
10. *EG*, August 29, 1933.
11. *EG*, August 8, 1933; Donald R. McCoy, *Landon of Kansas* (Lincoln: University of Nebraska Press, 1966), pp. 39-43, 106, 112; Keith D. McFarland, *Harry H. Woodring* (Lawrence; University Press of Kansas, 1975), pp. 30, 89-92.
12. Alf Landon interview, January 23, 1979; Wayne Estes statement, August 11, 1933; *TC*, August 16 and 31, 1933,

January 18 and February 15, 1934; *KCT*, January 18, 1934; James M. Rhodes to Alf Landon, August 18, 1933, KSA; Walt Markley, *Builders of Topeka* (Topeka: Capper Printing Co., 1934), p. 201.
13. *TSJ*, September 2, 1933.
14. *EG*, October 1 and November 28, 1932; *TC*, January 18, 1934; *KCS*, October 29, 1933; W. L. White, *What People Said* (New York: Viking Press, 1938), pp. 125–26.
15. *TSJ*, August 31, 1933.
16. *TC*, September 1, 1933.
17. *TC*, September 4, 1933; *KCT*, September 7, 1933.
18. *TC*, September 9 and 10, 1933; *TSJ*, September 9, 1933.
19. *TC*, September 13 and October 8, 1933; *EG*, October 29, 1932. A repurchase agreement is a device whereby a bank can make a loan to a favorite customer without labeling it as such. The customer deposits (technically sells) securities with the bank and receives cash (a loan) in return. An agreement is made by which the seller (borrower) may repurchase the security when the loan is repaid. If the bank wants to sell the security before the customer has repaid the loan, he is given first refusal before the security is put on the open market. All of Finney's repurchase agreements were made orally.
20. J. F. T. O'Connor to Landon, August 28, 1933, KSA; Landon to O'Connor, September 2, 1933, KSA; O'Connor to Landon, September 6, 1933, KSA; telegram, Landon to O'Connor, September 16, 1933, KSA; telegram, O'Connor to Landon, September 16, 1933, KSA; *TC*, September 17 and 19, 1933; *TSJ*, September 18, 1933.
21. *TC*, September 19, 1933.
22. *TC*, September 6, 1933.
23. *TC*, September 13, 1933.
24. *TSJ*, September 7, 1933; *TC*, September 16, 1933.
25. *TC*, September 20, 1933.
26. *KCT*, September 21, 1933; *TC*, September 21, 1933; *TSJ*, September 20 and 22, 1933; *KCS*, September 24, 1933; W. A. White, "Landon: I Knew Him When," *Saturday Evening Post*, July 18, 1936, pp. 5 ff.
27. McCoy, *Landon*, pp. 38–39, 114; *EG*, March 18, 1933.
28. *Hamilton Grit*, August 3, 1933.
29. *TSJ*, August 12 and September 25, 1933; *TC*, September 26, 1933; McCoy, *Landon*, p. 123; Fidelity State and Savings Bank records, in my possession; J. W. Greenleaf statement, September 27, 1933, KSA.
30. *EG*, September 2, 1933; *KCS*, September 2, 1933; *TC*, September 3 and 23, 1933.
31. *TC*, September 22, 1933.
32. See Appendix; *TC*, August 18, 20, and 26 and September 2 and 9, 1933, and January 19, 1934; *EG*, September 2, 1933; *KCT*, August 19 and September 2, 1933; *Chicago Tribune*, August 13 and 20, 1933.
33. *EG*, September 20, 1933.
34. *EG*, September 1 and 14, 1933.
35. *EG*, September 21 and 25, 1933.
36. *EG*, September 21, 22, and 26, 1933; *TC*, September 26, 1933.
37. *TC*, September 22 and October 23, 1933; *KCT*, October 10, 1933.
38. *EG*, November 11, 1933.
39. *TC*, September 16, 20, and 24, 1933; J. J. Kindscher to Landon, September 6, 1933, KSA; Landon to Kindscher, September 9, 1933, KSA; George A. Widder to Landon, September 12, 1933, KSA; Landon to Widder, September 14, 1933, KSA.
40. *TC*, September 22, 24, and 27, 1933; *KCS*, September 24, 1933; *TSJ*, September 25, 1933.
41. *TC*, September 27, 1933.
42. *Plain Talk*, September 29, 1933.
43. *TC*, September 28, 1933.
44. *TC*, September 29 and 30, 1933.
45. Arthur M. Schlesinger, Jr., *The Crisis of the Old Order, 1919–1933* (Boston: Houghton Mifflin Co., 1957), p. 108; Alf Landon interview, January 23, 1979; *TC*, October 1 and 2, 1933; *St. Louis Globe-Democrat*, October 11, 1980.
46. *TC*, October 2, 1933.
47. *TC*, October 3, 1933.
48. *TSJ*, October 4, 1933.
49. *TC*, October 6, 1933.
50. E. O. Hahn to W. H. Jardine, October 11, 1933, KSA; *TSJ*, October 2, 1933; *TC*, October 3, 27, and 31, 1933; Jar-

dine to Landon, December 19, 1933, KSA.
51. *TC*, October 28, 1933, and January 28, March 8, and April 22, 1934.
52. *TSJ*, September 28, 1933; *TC*, September 29 and October 18, 1933.
53. *TC*, September 22, 1933.
54. Theo Cobb Landon statement to Fred Harris, September 20, 1933, KSHS; *KCS*, September 28, 1933; *TC*, September 29, 1933.
55. *KCT*, September 30, 1933; *TC*, September 30, 1933.
56. *TC*, October 1, 1933.
57. Kansas, Legislature, *Laws of the Special Session, 1933* (Topeka: State Printer, 1933), p. 10.

Chapter 4

1. *EG*, August 15, 1933.
2. *TC*, September 5, 1933.
3. *TC*, September 9, 1933.
4. *TC*, September 29, 1933.
5. *TC*, August 9, 1933.
6. *TC*, August 16, 1933.
7. *TSJ*, August 9, 1933.
8. Donald R. McCoy, *Landon of Kansas* (Lincoln: University of Nebraska Press, 1966), pp. 161-62; *TC*, September 8 and 17, 1933.
9. *TC*, September 22, 26, and 28 and October 25, 1933; *KCJP*, September 24, 1933; *KCT*, September 28 and October 24, 1933; *KCS*, October 25, 1933.
10. *TC*, September 30, 1933; W. T. Markham statement, August 14, 1933, KSA.
11. *EG*, December 10, 12, and 23, 1932; *TSJ*, October 12, 1933.
12. *TC*, October 3, 1933; Jesse Underwood statement, September 12, 1933, KSA.
13. *TC*, September 10, 1933.
14. Fred M. Harris statement to Legislative Council Investigating Committee (Bloss Committee), October 2, 1933, KSHS, p. 2.
15. *TC*, October 4, 1933.
16. Harris statement, October 2, 1933; *TC*, October 3 and 4, 1933.
17. *TC*, October 5, 1933; W. H. Stanley statement, August 23, 1933, KSA.
18. *TSJ*, October 5, 1933; *TC*, October 5, 1933; Harris statement, October 2, 1933, p. 11. Ryan, a Leavenworth Republican, held the office for three successive terms (1923 to 1929). After two terms by E. A. Cornell, Ryan had regained the office in January, 1933. Ryan had been a special target of the Ku Klux Klan in the 1924 election, but had been staunchly defended by W. A. White, among others.
19. *TSJ*, September 13, 1933.
20. *TC*, October 6, 1933.
21. *TC*, October 3, 1933.
22. *TC*, October 6 and 7, 1933.
23. *TC*, October 3, 7, and 8, 1933.
24. *TC*, October 7 and 8, 1933.
25. Legislative Investigative Committee Resolution, October 4, 1933, KSA; *KCT*, October 16, 1933.
26. *KCT*, October 24, 1933; *TC*, October 25, 1933.
27. Harris Statement, November 7 and 8, 1933, *KSHS*, pp. 1–12; *TSJ*, October 25, 1933; *KCS*, October 25, 1933; *TC*, August 19 and October 26, 1933; *KCT*, October 27, 1933; *EG*, October 26, 1933; Kansas, House, *House Journal, Special Session, 1933* (Topeka: State Printer, 1933), pp. 173–76.
28. *TC*, October 27, 1933; *KCT*, October 27 and 28, 1933.
29. *TC*, October 27, 1933.
30. *KCJP*, October 29, 1933.
31. *TC*, October 31 and November 1, 1933.
32. *KCT*, October 24, 1933; *TC*, November 2, 1933.
33. *House Journal*, pp. 173–76, 426; *EG*, August 30, 1933; *TC*, October 29 and November 2, 1933; *TSJ*, August 30 and 31 and November 1, 1933; *KCJP*, September 23, 1933.
34. *KCS*, November 13, 1933.
35. *House Journal*, p. 427; *TSJ*, November 14, 1933.
36. *House Journal*, p. 169; *TC*, November 18, 1933.
37. *TSJ*, November 17, 1933.
38. *TC*, November 18, 1933.
39. *TSJ*, November 16 and 17, 1933; *TC*, November 18, 1933.
40. *House Journal*, pp. 176–77.
41. *TC*, November 3, 1933.
42. Harris Statement, November 7 and 8, 1933, KSA; *TC*, November 8 and 9, 1933.
43. *TC*, November 14, 1933.
44. *TC*, November 15, 1933.
45. *TC*, November 17, 21, and 22, 1933.

46. *House Journal*, p. 221.
47. *TC*, November 23, 1933.
48. *House Journal*, pp. 227, 236–45; *TC*, November 24 and 26, 1933.
49. *House Journal*, pp. 250–51.
50. *House Journal*, pp. 264, 270–79; *TC*, November 29, 1933.
51. *EG*, October 30 and November 14, 17, 20, and 24, 1933.
52. *EG*, October 30, 1933.
53. *TSJ*, November 1 and 16, 1933; *KCJP*, November 26, 1933.
54. *House Journal*, pp. 281–82; also in *TC*, November 29, 1933.
55. *KCJP*, October 29, 1933.
56. *TSJ*, September 13 and October 9, 1933.
57. *TC*, October 28 and November 3, 1933.
58. *KCS*, October 5, 1933; *KCT*, November 3, 1933.
59. *TC*, September 18, 1933.
60. John D. Bright, *Kansas: The First Century* (New York: Lewis Historical Publishing Co., 1956), 2:439; Rolla A. Clymer, "Thomas Benton Murdock and William Allen White," *Kansas Historical Quarterly* 23 (1957): 255.
61. *TSJ*, October 13, 1933.
62. Kansas, Legislature, *Laws of the Special Session, 1933* (Topeka: State Printer, 1933), p. 170; *KCS*, November 29, 1933.
63. *Laws*, p. 167; *House Journal*, pp. 218–19.
64. *Laws*, pp. 42, 70, 138; *TC*, November 8 and 15 and December 10, 1933.
65. *House Journal*, pp. 420, 422; *TC*, November 3, 9, 23, and 28, 1933; *KCT*, November 3, 1933.
66. McCoy, *Landon*, p. 121; *TC*, August 11, September 4 and 14, and November 14 and 30, 1933; *EG*, August 16, 1933; *TSJ*, November 4, 1933.
67. *Laws*, pp. 10, 11, 13–14; *TC*, November 23 and 28, 1933; *KCT*, November 7 and 27, 1933.
68. *KCS*, October 15, 1933; *Parsons Sun*, August 16, 1933.
69. *TC*, October 1 and 16, 1933; Secretary of State, *Kansas Directory, 1977* (Topeka: Secretary of State, 1977), pp. 70, 73; McCoy, *Landon*, pp. 31, 56–57; W. G. Clugston, *Rascals in Democracy* (New York: R. B. Smith, 1940), pp. 207–20; Walter Johnson, *William Allen White's America* (New York: Henry Holt, 1947), p. 441; Sara M. and Robert M. Baldwin, eds., *Illustriana Kansas* (Hebron, Nebr.: Illustriana, Inc., 1933), p. 551.
70. *TC*, October 20 and 25, November 1 and 2, and December 1, 1933; *TSJ*, October 21 and 24 and November 2, 1933; *KCS*, October 29, 1933.
71. *KCS*, November 22, 1933; *TC*, December 1 and 3, 1933.

Chapter 5

1. Kenneth S. Davis, *Kansas: A Bicentennial History* (New York: W. W. Norton, 1976), pp. 1–6; Carl L. Becker, *Everyman His Own Historian* (New York: F. S. Crofts & Co., 1935), pp. 1–28; Dudley T. Cornish, "Carl Becker's Kansas: The Power of Endurance," *Kansas Historical Quarterly* 41 (1975): 1–13.
2. Davis, *Kansas*, pp. 164–67; *EG*, August 15, 1896. The editorial "What's the Matter with Kansas?" caught the eye of Mark Hanna, McKinley's campaign manager, who had thousands of copies distributed throughout the country. The piece helped to propel McKinley into the White House, where he stayed for five years, and White into national prominence, where he stayed for forty-eight.
3. *EG*, November 22, 1930.
4. Davis, *Kansas*, pp. 37–38; R. W. Richmond, *Kansas: A Land of Contrasts* (St. Charles, Mo.: Forum Press, 1974), pp. 63–66; W. F. Zornow, *Kansas: A History of the Jayhawk State* (Norman: University of Oklahoma Press, 1957), pp. 67–69; W. H. Carruth, "New England in Kansas," *New England Magazine* 16 (March, 1897): 3–21; Nyle H. Miller, "Kansas Newspapers to 1900," in John D. Bright, ed., *Kansas: The First Century* (New York: Lewis Historical Publishing Co., 1956), 1:531.
5. Richmond, *Kansas*, pp. 129–34, 169; Zornow, *Kansas*, pp. 159–73; W. A. White, "Fifty Years of Kansas," *World's Work* 8 (June, 1904): 4870–72, "Kansas: A Puritan Survival," *Nation* 114 (April 19, 1922); 460–62, and "The Glory of the States: Kansas," *American*

Magazine 81 (January, 1916): 41 ff.; Clarence Woodbury, "What Happened: Kansas Rocked the Nation When They Revolted against Their 70-year-old Dry Law," *American Magazine* 147 (January, 1949): 20–21, 115–19; *Chicago Tribune*, October 21, 1923; H. L. Mencken, "The Last of the Victorians," *Smart Set* 29 (October, 1909): 153–55; Cornish, "Carl Becker's Kansas," p. 2.

6. Charles B. Driscoll, "Major Prophets of Holy Kansas," *American Mercury* 8 (May, 1926): 18–26; Davis, *Kansas*, pp. 53–65; Richmond, *Kansas*, pp. 169–70, 175, 180–81, 202–3; W. G. Clugston, *Rascals in Democracy* (New York: Richard B. Smith, 1940), pp. 141–60, 221–45; Homer E. Socolofsky, *Arthur Capper* (Lawrence: University of Kansas Press, 1962); Gerald Carson, *The Roguish World of Doctor Brinkley* (New York: Holt, Rinehart & Winston, 1960); Walter Johnson, *William Allen White's America* (New York: Henry Holt & Co., 1947); Donald R. McCoy, *Landon of Kansas* (Lincoln: University of Nebraska Press, 1966).

7. Jonathan W. Bell, ed., *The Kansas Art Reader* (Lawrence: University of Kansas, 1976), pp. 3–10; Lora D. Reiter, *From the North Slope of the Solomon* (Lawrence, Kans.: Coronado Press, 1967); Joanna L. Stratton, *Pioneer Women* (New York: Simon & Schuster, 1981).

8. *EG*, October 14, 1933.

9. Secretary of State, *Kansas Directory, 1977* (Topeka: Secretary of State, 1977), pp. 65–72; *TC*, September 13, 1933.

10. *KCT*, August 16, 1933; *TC*, August 16 and 17, 1933; *TSJ*, August 16, 1933.

11. *TC*, August 17, 1933; *TSJ*, August 16, 1933.

12. J. H. Jenson to Landon, August 12, 1933, KSA; M. U. Ramsburg to Landon, September 22, 1933, KSA; *TC*, August 17, 1933; S. C. Holmes to Landon, November 10, 1933, KSA; V. J. Rowe to S. C. Bloss, October 4, 1933, KSA.

13. J. C. Stephenson to Landon, August 20, 1933, KSA; *TC*, August 17, 1933.

14. *TC*, August 16, 1933.

15. G. H. Harvey to Landon, August 31, 1933, KSA.

16. M. C. Todd to Willard Mayberry, August 26, 1933, KSA; L. Seacot to Landon, August 11, 1933, KSA; C. Caldwell to Landon, August 14, 1933, KSA; A. Connelly to Landon, August 11, 1933, KSA; J. F. Trazzare to Landon, August 12, 1933, KSA.

17. T. H. Brown to Landon, August 15, 1933, KSA.

18. W. M. McMullen to Landon, August 14, 1933, KSA; see Landon gubernatorial papers, KSA.

19. Landon to Fred M. Harris, October 25, 1933, KSA.

20. J. Stafford to Landon, September 12, 1933, KSA.

21. J. B. Sanders to Landon, August 11, 1933, KSA; E. Fickertt to Landon, August 14, 1933, KSA.

22. O. C. Colvin to Landon, August 22, 1933, KSA; S. O. Oyler to Landon, August 19, 1933, KSA; E. Walker to Landon, August 16, 1933, KSA; T. W. Rule to Landon, August 17, 1933, KSA; S. K. Williams to Landon, September 30, 1933, KSA.

23. A. H. Gillis to Landon, August 9, 1933, KSA; D. Van Ness to Landon, August 11, 1933, KSA; W. D. Ferguson to Landon, August 19, 1933, KSA.

24. J. C. Stephenson to Landon, August 20, 1933, KSA.

25. *KCT*, August 16, 1933.

26. Landon to Walter McGugin, September 25, 1933, KSA.

27. R. G. Walters to Landon, August 19, 1933, KSA.

28. S. M. Brewster to R. G. Walters, August 24, 1933, KSA; Brewster to Landon, August 24, 1933, KSA.

29. George Bordenkircher to Landon, November 21, 1933, KSA.

30. *TC*, August 12 and September 7, 1933.

31. *TC*, September 27, 1933.

32. Kansas, Senate, *Trial of Roland Boynton, Attorney-general of the State of Kansas* (Topeka: State Printer, 1934), p. 875.

33. *Marysville Advocate-Democrat*, August 24 and October 12, 1933.

34. *TSJ*, December 2, 1933.

35. *Pink Rag*, August 11 and November 3, 1933.

36. *TC*, October 15, 1933.
37. *TSJ*, August 29, 1933.
38. *EG*, November 2, 1933.
39. *TC*, October 4, 1933.
40. Bootleg whiskey was often flavored with ginger ("jake") root. In April, 1930, five hundred people in Wichita were affected with a motor paralysis known as Jake leg, which was caused by drinking the illegal brew. Francis W. Schruben, *Kansas in Turmoil, 1930–1936* (Columbia: University of Missouri Press, 1969), pp. 76–77.
41. Kathrine White interview, February 17, 1979.
42. *TC*, October 2, 1933.
43. *EG*, October 7, 1933.
44. *KCJP*, September 21, 1933.
45. *EG*, February 26, 1934.
46. *Newsweek*, August 19, 1933; *Time*, August 21, 1933; *TC*, September 5, 1933.
47. *KCJP*, February 1, 1934; *TSJ*, October 21, 1933.
48. *TSJ*, October 21, 1933.
49. *Chicago Tribune*, August 20, 1933.
50. McCoy, *Landon*, p. 183. Ned and Martha's brother Will, who was co-editor of the *Recorder*, was named Republican state chairman in 1934.
51. *TC*, September 16, 1933.
52. *TSJ*, August 14, 1933.
53. *Wichita Eagle*, August 13, 1933.
54. *Leoti Standard*, October 26, 1933.
55. The people around Neosho Falls couldn't complain that they weren't warned. In the spring an ad for the Farmers State Bank asked: "Are you preparing for the fall?" *Neosho Falls Post*, March 9, 1933.
56. *Neosho Falls Post*, August–November, 1933, issues.
57. *Eureka Herald*, August–November 1933, issues; *Eureka Democratic Messenger*, August–November, 1933, issues.
58. *EG*, August 9, 11, 12, and 15, September 8, 9, 23, 25, 26, 27, 29, and 30, and October 28, 1933; W. L. White, *What People Said* (New York: Viking Press, 1938), pp. 431–38, 473–77.
59. Kathrine White interview, February 17, 1979; White, *What People Said*, pp. 448–69, 471–72.
60. Kathrine White interview, February 17, 1979.
61. White, *What People Said*, p. 471.
62. *EG*, August 25, 1933.
63. *EG*, September 6, 1933.
64. Schruben, *Kansas*, p. 94; *EG*, September 26, 1934; *Wichita Beacon*, August 9 and 13, 1933.
65. *Wichita Eagle*, August 10, 1933.
66. Schruben, *Kansas*, pp. 91–95; *KCJP*, September 4, 17, 18, and 24, 1933; *EG*, December 5, 1932, July 31 and September 26, 1934; Sara M. and Robert M. Baldwin, eds., *Illustriana Kansas* (Hebron, Nebr.: Illustriana, Inc., 1933), p. 235.
67. *KCJP*, September 4 and 17, 1933.
68. *KCJP*, September 17, 18, 19, 20, 21, 22, 23, and 24, 1933.
69. *KCJP*, September 9 and 18, 1933.
70. Clugston later (1940) published many of his political views in expanded form in a book that deserves more attention than it has received, *Rascals in Democracy*. He goes hard after almost all of the Kansas saints: Charles Robinson, W. A. White, Henry Allen, Carry Nation, Alf Landon, and others—even Arthur Capper. It is clear whom Clugston is against, but whom is he for? Brinkley, for one.
71. *KCJP*, September 18, 1933.
72. Marian Ellet interview, March 9, 1979; *EG*, June 11, 1935.
73. Schruben, *Kansas*, p. 94; *EG*, July 31, 1934, and April 10, 1933; Carson, *Roguish World*, p. 146.
74. Kathrine White interview, February 17, 1979.
75. *KCS*, October 5, 1933.
76. *TC*, August 9, 10, 12, 20, and 31 and October 3, 1933; *TSJ*, January 18, 1934; Supreme Court of Kansas, *State of Kansas v. T. B. Boyd*, case no. 31,837, Counter Abstract of the Record, p. 4; Landon to S. M. Brewster, January 8, 1934, KSA.
77. *TC*, August 13, 1933.
78. McCoy, *Landon*, pp. 41, 44, 97.
79. McCoy, *Landon*, p. 396; *EG*, February 6, 1934.
80. *TSJ*, August 9 and 17, 1933.
81. *TSJ*, August 31, 1933.
82. *Pittsburg Sun*, August 11, 1933.

Chapter 6

1. Howard Finney, Sr., *Finney—Phinney Families in America* (Richmond, Va.: William Byrd Press, 1957).
2. Finney, *Finney*, pp. 85, 231, 232, 249–50, 254–55; Affidavit of Jacob Heath, April 18, 1917, David W. Finney's pension records, National Archives.
3. Hill P. Wilson, *A Biographical History of Eminent Men of the State of Kansas* (Topeka: Hall Lithographing Co., 1901), pp. 381–83.
4. David W. Finney's military service record, War Department, National Archives; Rev. J. E. Brant, *History of the Eighty-Fifth Indiana Volunteer Infantry* (Bloomington, Ind.: Cravens Bros., 1902); Wilson, *Biographical History*, pp. 382–83; David W. Finney, autobiographical statement, John Hopkins's file, St. Simons, Georgia.
5. Woodson County (population 4,720 in 1980) holds the distinction of having a higher proportion of subscribers to *Penthouse* magazine than any 'other of the 3,078 counties in these United States. Clark S. Judge, *The Book of American Rankings* (New York: Facts on File, 1979), item no. 228; Woodson County clerk, records, Yates Center, Kansas. Finney's military record; Republican Party Clippings, vol. 1 (1870–82), p. 1169, KSHS; Heath affidavit; Finney's autobiography.
6. Lela Barnes, ed., "An Editor Looks at Early-Day Kansas," *Kansas Historical Quarterly* 26 (1960): 141–42; Edwin C. McReynolds, *The Seminoles* (Norman: University of Oklahoma Press, 1957), pp. 305–6.
7. Wilson, *Biographical History*, pp. 381–83; Andreas, *History*, p. 1195; Finney's autobiography.
8. Wilson, *Biographical History*, pp. 381–83; David W. Finney's pension records, National Archives; Daniel W. Wilder, *The Annals of Kansas, 1541–1886* (Topeka: T. D. Thatcher, 1886), pp. 466, 472, 657, 670, 742, 754; *Kansas Historical Collections* 3 (1881–84): 415–16, and 10 (1907–8): 256, 270.
9. Republican Party Clippings, vol. 1 (1870–82), p. 1169, KSHS; *EG*, July 1, 1935; *Atchison Champion*, September 3, 1880.
10. *Kansas History* 3 (Spring, 1980): 3–6.
11. *Atchison Champion*, September 3, 1880.
12. *Commonwealth*, September 2, 1880; Stephen Z. Starr, *Jennison's Jayhawkers: A Civil War Cavalry Regiment and Its Commander* (Baton Rouge: Louisiana State University Press, 1973), pp. 27–42.
13. *Atchison Champion*, September 3, 1880; Sara M. and Robert M. Baldwin, eds., *Illustriana Kansas* (Hebron, Nebr.: Illustriana, Inc., 1933), p. 605.
14. Wilson, *Biographical History*, pp. 381–83; Wilder, *Annals*, pp. 908, 938.
15. Wilder, *Annals*, pp. 998, 1015; Robert W. Richmond, *Kansas: A Land of Contrasts* (St. Charles, Mo.: Forum Press, 1974), pp. 164, 170–71; Kirke Mechem, *The Annals of Kansas, 1886–1925* (Topeka: Kansas State Historical Society, 1954), 2:276.
16. *Kansas Historical Collections* 7 (1902): 472, and 10 (1908): 170.
17. Wilson, *Biographical History*, p. 383; *Kansas Historical Collections* 8 (190): 529, 541; Finney's autobiography.
18. *Atchison Champion*, September 3, 1880; Republican Party Clippings, vol. 1 (1870–82), p. 116g, KSHS; Wilson, *Biographical History*, p. 381.
19. Maurine Rowe Lauderback to Anne Butler, June 30, 1979, Anne Butler files, University of Missouri–St. Louis; W. G. Clugston, *Rascals in Democracy* (New York: Richard B. Smith, 1940), pp. 248–50.
20. Hellen H. McConnell, affidavit, May 14, 1917, David Finney's pension records, National Archives; Wilson, *Biographical History*, p. 383; Andreas, *History*, p. 1191; Finney's autobiography.
21. *EG*, December 3, 1931.
22. Warren Wesley Finney, death certificate, State of Kansas Board of Health, Division of Vital Statistics, Topeka; Registrar, Washburn University, official records; *Washburn Mid-Continent*, October, 1893, p. 9, December, 1893, p. 12, June, 1894, p. 13, and August, 1894, p. 1; *Argo-Reporter*, April 21, 1893.
23. *Washburn Mid-Continent*, June, 1895, p. 10; Kansas Supreme Court, *State of Kansas v. W. W. Finney*, case no. 31,780, Abstract of Appellant, p. 178; *EG*, Oc-

tober 8 and November 12, 1912, and October 4, 1932.
24. Richmond, *Kansas,* pp. 178-79; William F. Zornow, *Kansas: A History of the Jayhawk State* (Norman: University of Oklahoma Press, 1957), pp. 201-2; Handbook of the 1897 Kansas Legislature, biographical sketch of W. W. Finney, p. 84, KSHS.
25. Richmond, *Kansas,* pp. 181-82; Mechem, *Annals of Kansas, 1886-1925,* 1:262; *EG,* June 10, 1935.
26. *EG,* January 29, 1932; *The Kansas Day Club, Addresses, 1892-1901,* p. 226, KSHS.
27. *Kansas Day Club,* p. 229, KSHS. Among the 133 in attendance on that cold January night were four future governors—H. J. Allen, W. J. Bailey, A. Capper, C. M. Reed; four future U.S. senators—H. J. Allen, J. L. Bristow, A. Capper, C. M. Reed; two future congressmen—W. J. Bailey, C. F. Scott; several prominent newspapermen—C. M. Harger, W. Y. Morgan, T. B. Murdock, C. M. Reed, C. F. Scott; and other notables or soon-to-be notables, including C. C. Baker, W. L. Huggins, Dr. C. F. Menninger, E. S. Leland, D. W. Mulvane. Also in attendance was the speaker's brother Glen, his future brother-in-law George Tucker, and the future father-in-law of his yet unborn son, J. H. Wiggam.
28. *Kansas Day Club,* pp. 226-29, KSHS.
29. Frank W. Blackmar, *Kansas: A Cyclopedia of State History,* vol. 3, pt. 1 (Chicago: Standard Publishing Co., 1912), pp. 282-83; Registrar, Washburn University, official records.
30. *Eureka Herald,* July 6, 1876, and August 21, 1948; John S. Dawson, "The Legislature of 1868," *Kansas Historical Collections* 10 (1908): 278; William E. Connelley, *A Standard History of Kansas and Kansans,* vol. 5 (New York: Lewis Publishing Co., 1918), p. 2298; Registrar, Washburn University, official records.
31. Mildred Thrall interview, May 30, 1976; Blackmar, *Kansas,* pp. 282-83; Laura M. French, *History of Emporia and Lyon County* (Emporia, Kans.: Laura M. French, 1929), p. 82.
32. *EG,* January 25, 26, and 28, February 8 and 10, and March 5, 1909; W. A.

White to W. W. Finney, March 16, 1909, W. A. White Collection, Library of Congress.
33. *EG,* March 13, 1909; W. A. White to W. W. Finney, March 16, 1909, W. A. White Collection, Library of Congress.
34. *EG,* January 3 and 27, 1911.
35. *EG,* January 4 and 19, 1911.
36. *EG,* January 16, 19, and 20, 1911.
37. *EG,* January 20, 1911.
38. *EG,* January 20, 1911.
39. *EG,* January 23, 1911.
40. *EG,* January 24, 1911.
41. *EG,* January 28, 1911. One of Finney's attorneys—H. E. Ganse, who had recently arrived from Coffey County—had "convicted more jointists and saloon druggists than the jail would hold; they were actually waiting their turn to serve their terms." As a state senator he had attracted some attention to himself by slapping fellow senator George Hodges in a committee room after Hodges, earlier in the day on the Senate floor, had called him a liar. Hodges was elected governor in 1912. *EG,* February 12, 1909, and January 30, 1911.
42. *EG,* February 11, 13, and 27, 1911; Kansas Supreme Court, *City of Emporia v. Emporia Telephone Company,* case nos. 17,859 and 18,604.
43. *EG,* November 8, 1911.
44. Mrs. J. C. McKinney to author, May 29, 1979; Mrs. J. C. McKinney interview, May 29, 1979.
45. Kansas, Supreme Court, *State of Kansas v. W. W. Finney,* case no. 31,780, Abstract of Appellant, pp. 178-80; *EG,* April 5, 1930, and June 7, 1935; Blackmar, *Kansas,* pp. 282-83.
46. French, *History of Emporia,* pp. 82, 120; Finney case, Abstract, pp. 179-80, 262-64; *EG,* October 8, 1933; James F. Noble to W. A. White, June 29, 1927, and J. L. Hunt to W. A. Smith, June 27, 1927, Kathrine White's files.
47. W. A. White to W. A. Smith, in *EG,* October 28, 1933, based on a draft that was later introduced in Lyon County District Court at the W. W. Finney trial, the original being unavailable; George T. McDermott to W. L. White, October 9, 1933, Kathrine White's files.
48. *Finney* case, Counter Abstract, pp. 61-

66; *EG*, October 28, 1933; George T. McDermott to W. L. White, October 11, 1933, Kathrine White's files.

49. French, *History of Emporia*, p. 121; Ronald Finney's statement, December 9, 1943, pp. 4–6, KSHS; Biennial Reports, State Bank Commissioner (1914–34), Fidelity State and Savings Bank, Emporia, Farmer's State Bank, Neosho Falls, and Eureka Bank, Eureka; W. L. White, *What People Said* (New York: Viking Press, 1938), pp. 71–73, 260–62.

50. *EG*, November 19 and December 8, 1912, April 16, 1914, September 5, 1930, November 26, 1931, May 12, June 21, and December 9, 1932, January 2, April 14, and June 20, 1933; *KCT*, June 7, 1935; White, *What People Said*, pp. 264–66.

51. *EG*, December 1, 1930, December 15 and 29, 1931, January 26, March 14 and 31, April 13, July 25, October 12, and November 17, 1932, January 4 and September 7, 1933, and June 6, 1935.

52. *EG*, October 24 and November 18, 1930, November 26, 1931, July 23, 1932, and March 14, 1933; White, *What People Said*, p. 67; Kathrine White interview, February 17, 1979.

53. *TSJ*, August 31, 1933; *KCJP*, August 17 and September 1, 1933; W. A. White to Richard J. Hopkins, December 19, 1930, KSHS; White, *What People Said*, p. 73.

54. Warren W. Finney, *The Farmer's Unjust Tax Burden* (Emporia, Kans.: W. W. Finney, 1930), a thirty-two-page pamphlet.

55. Finney, *Farmer's Unjust Tax Burden*, p. 2.

56. *EG*, November 1, 4, and 27, 1930; *TC*, November 4, 1930; Richard J. Hopkins to W. W. Finney, November 19, 1930, KSHS.

57. *EG*, July 13, October 29, and November 1 and 8, 1932.

58. *EG*, November 1, 1932.

59. Alfred M. Landon interview, January 23, 1979; *KCJP*, August 17, 1933.

60. Alf Landon to W. W. Finney, July 26, 1929, KSHS; W. A. White, "Landon: I Knew Him When," *Saturday Evening Post*, July 18, 1936, pp. 5 ff.

61. *EG*, January 4, 1914, and July 26 and August 30, 1932; Alf Landon to Henry F. Draper, August 17, 1934, KSA; John Hopkins to author, January 25, 1979.

62. J. M. Landon to W. W. Finney, September 22, 1932, KSHS.

63. Telegram, W. Finney to Alf Landon, November 12, 1932, KSHS.

64. W. W. Finney to Alf Landon, December 3, 1932, KSHS.

65. Alf Landon to W. W. Finney, December 8, 1932, KSHS.

66. *EG*, March 14, 1933.

67. Herbert Hoover, *Memoirs . . . the Cabinet and the Presidency, 1920–1933* (New York, 1952), pp. 119–20; *TC*, February 6, 1932.

68. *TC*, February 9, 1932.

69. Telegram, W. A. White to Frank Knox, undated (early February, 1932), Library of Congress, W. A. White Collection.

70. *EG*, February 13, 17, and 26 and March 1, 3, 5, 8, 9, 16, 19, and 24, 1932.

71. W. A. White to Frank Knox, March 29, 1932, W. A. White Collection, Library of Congress.

72. Included were the venerable chief justice of the Kansas Supreme Court, William A. Johnston; Judge George McDermott of the U.S. Circuit Court of Appeals; Judge Richard J. Hopkins of the U.S. District Court; Governor Harry Woodring; George Allen, Jr., state superintendent of public instruction; Emerson Carey, Hutchinson salt tycoon; Dr. Charles M. Sheldon, famed Topeka Congregational minister and author; the eminent journalists W. A. White (Emporia), Oscar Stauffer (Arkansas City), Roy Bailey (Salina), Charles Sessions and Harold T. Chase *(Topeka Capital)*, Arthur Carruth, Jr. *(Topeka State Journal);* Dan Casement, prominent Manhattan cattleman; J. H. Mercer of the Livestock Sanitary Commission; the heads of the Prairie Oil and Gas Co. (a Standard Oil subsidiary), the Kansas Chamber of Commerce, the American Legion, the Kansas Bar Association, the Kansas Farm Bureau, the Kansas Farmers Union, the Kansas Grange, the Santa Fe Railroad, the Kansas Bankers' Association, the Associated Industries, the Young Men's Hebrew Association, and the Building and Loan League; the presidents of the University of Kansas, Washburn Col-

lege, the State Federation of Women's Clubs, the Business and Professional Women's Clubs, Kiwanis Clubs, Lions Clubs, and Cooperative Clubs; and labor representatives from the Brotherhood of Locomotive Engineers and the Brotherhood of Railway Trainmen. *TC*, March 1, 1932; *EG*, March 1, 1932.

73. *TC*, March 1, 1932; *EG*, March 1, 1932.

Chapter 7

1. Ronald Tucker Finney, birth certificate, county clerk, Woodson County, Kans.; Mildred Thrall interview, May 30, 1976; Mrs. Walter J. Keeler, January 18, 1979; *EG*, December 22, 1913; Mrs. Richard B. Stevens interview, August 3, 1980.
2. Howard Holtz interview, December 7, 1978; Mildred Thrall interview, May 30, 1976; Walter Cole interview, March 10, 1980; Mrs. Walter J. Keeler, January 18, 1979; *EG*, August 11 and 23 and September 23, 1913, January 1 and 4, April 17 and 21, June 30, and July 14, 1914, and November 27, 1915; Emporia High School graduation records; Emporia High School yearbooks, 1916 and 1917; William L. White, *What People Said* (New York: Viking Press, 1938), pp. 9–14, 21–22.
3. Registrar, Washburn University, official records; *KAW* (Washburn College Yearbook), 1918, 1919; *TC*, August 11, 1933.
4. Registrar, Cornell University, official records.
5. "Kiting" commonly refers to a practice whereby an individual or institution effects financial transactions for the sole purpose of maximizing the "float." A float is a form of credit that is created by the lag between the time a check is deposited in a payee's account and the time funds are actually transferred from the payor's account. W. D. Kinnaman to Alf Landon, September 2, 1933, KSA; Metta Boughton interview, February 15, 1979; W. A. White to Erwin Canham, October 27, 1933, KSHS; *KCS*, August 9 and 30, 1933; Ronald Finney statement, December 9, 1943, pp. 1–5, KSHS; White, *What People Said*, pp. 76–84.
6. Ronald Finney statement, December 9, 1943, pp. 4–6, KSHS.
7. Ibid., p. 6.
8. Ibid., p. 4.
9. Marriage license of Ronald Tucker Finney and Winifred Wiggam, Lyon County Probate Court, April 21, 1923; *EG*, March 2, June 3, August 8, and September 28, 1932, January 21 and June 2, 1933, and October 30 and November 2, 1934; Mrs. J. C. McKinney to author, May 29, 1979; Sara M. and Robert M. Baldwin, eds., *Illustriana Kansas* (Hebron, Nebr.: Illustriana, Inc., 1933), p. 1221.
10. *KCS*, March 1, 1936; Registrar, Washburn University, official records; O. R. Stites interview, December 7, 1978; Gayle Mott interview, January 9, 1979; Kathrine White interview, February 17, 1979; Baldwin, *Illustriana*, p. 1221; White, *What People Said*, pp. 14–29.
11. Mildred Thrall interview, May 30, 1976; Frances Kesner interview, October 15, 1979; White, *What People Said*, pp. 84–85; *Phillips County Review*, August 24, 1933.
12. *Four Counties Paper*, June 25, July 25, and September 28, 1927.
13. *TSJ*, September 4, 1933; *KCJP*, September 1, 1933; *Phillips County Review*, August 24, 1933; Kansas Supreme Court, *Farmers State Bank of Aliceville* v. *Fidelity State and Savings Bank*, case no. 28,740, Abstract of Appellant, pp. 34–35.
14. *Aliceville* case, Abstract of Appellant, p. 25; *Phillips County Review*, August 24, 1933.
15. *Aliceville* case, Abstract of Appellant, p. 35.
16. Ibid., pp. 34–36.
17. Ibid., pp. 25–33, 36–41, 43–48; Kansas Supreme Court Reports, vol. 129 (July, 1929), case no. 28,740, pp. 79–81.
18. *Phillips County Review*, August 24, 1933.
19. Mrs. F. W. Boyd to Alf Landon, August 31, 1933.
20. Ronald Finney statement, December 9, 1943, p. 7, KSHS; *TC*, August 31, 1933; White, *What People Said*, pp. 103–9.
21. *Phillips County Review*, August 24, 1933.

22. Russell George interview, August 12, 1978.
23. *Phillips County Review*, August 24, 1933; Ronald Finney statement, p. 7; U.S. District Court, Civil Docket, vol. P, case no. 3,592, *Ronald Finney v. Pyramid Life Insurance Company*, Federal Archives, Kansas City, Mo.; Kansas, Senate, *Trial of Roland Boynton, Attorney-general of the State of Kansas* (Topeka: State Printer, 1934), pp. 843-44; Finney statement, p. 7.
24. Mildred Thrall interview, May 30, 1976; Kathrine White interview, February 17, 1979; Howard Holtz interview, December 7, 1978; White, *What People Said*, pp. 85-90; *Phillips County Review*, August 24, 1933.
25. Howard Holtz interview, December 7, 1978.
26. *EG*, November 21, 1930; *TSJ*, August 11, 1933; White, *What People Said*, pp. 219-25; Finney statement, p. 7; *Pittsburg Sun*, August 15, 1933.
27. Finney statement, p. 1; *TC*, November 24, 1933.
28. Finney statement, pp. 7-8; Kansas Statutes, Session Laws, 1931, chap. 256; Kansas, Senate, *Trial of Will J. French, Auditor of the State of Kansas* (Topeka: State Printer, 1934), p. 241; White, *What People Said*, pp. 173-86.
29. Senate, *Trial of Will J. French*, pp. 17, 20, 48; Finney statement, p. 7; Donald R. McCoy, *Landon of Kansas* (Lincoln: University of Nebraska Press, 1966), pp. 129, 169; *KCJP*, August 12, 1933.
30. Finney statement, p. 7.
31. *KCT*, August 12, 1933; *TC*, August 12, 1933; Jesse Underwood statement, September 12, 1933, KSA; David Neiswanger statement, September 14, 1933, KSA.
32. *TC*, September 10, 1933; Senate, *Trial of Roland Boynton*, p. 102; Charles Rooney, Sr., interview, May 17, 1979.
33. Finney statement, p. 9; *KCJP*, August 12, 1933; *Wichita Eagle*, August 15 and 16, 1933; *TC*, August 11 and 16, 1933; *EG*, August 10 and 16 and September 7, 1933.
34. Senate, *Trial of Will J. French*, pp. 335-36; *Time*, August 21, 1933; *TC*, August 14 and 18, 1933; *TSJ*, August 10, 1933.
35. *EG*, September 7, 1933.
36. Gayle Mott interview, January 9, 1979.
37. Ibid.; *TC*, August 9, 1933, and March 21, 1934; *EG*, May 1, 1933; *TSJ*, August 10, 1933; Robert Maynard interview, February 20, 1979; Elizabeth P. Leonard to author, March 30, 1980; *Time*, August 21, 1933; White, *What People Said*, pp. 237-40, 272-74, 325-29.
38. *Eureka Herald*, July 27, 1933; *EG*, July 18, 1932; Ellsworth Collings, *The 101 Ranch* (Norman: University of Oklahoma Press, 1937), pp. vii-xxi, 161-88.
39. O. R. Stites interview, December 7, 1978; *TSJ*, August 10, 1933; *Wichita Eagle*, August 14, 1933; *KCT*, August 10, 1933.
40. *TSJ*, August 30, 1933; *Wichita Eagle*, August 14, 1933; W. G. Clugston, *Rascals in Democracy* (New York: Richard B. Smith, 1940), p. 260; *TC*, January 18, 1934; Clyde Schenck interview, May 24, 1979.
41. *TC*, August 9, October 12, and November 22, 1933; *EG*, May 31, 1933, and February 17, 1934.
42. Fidelity State and Savings Bank records, 1932-33; *EG*, August 8, 1933; *Wichita Eagle*, August 21, 1933; *KCT*, June 7, 1935; White, *What People Said*, pp. 276-79; *Time*, August 21, 1933.
43. Senate, *Trial of Will J. French*, p. 387.
44. *TSJ*, August 10 and 30, 1933; *TC*, August 9 and November 24, 1933; Emma Bailey statement, August 26, 1933; White, *What People Said*, pp. 279-85.
45. *TSJ*, August 10, 1933; Emma Bailey statement, August 26, 1933; *TC*, August 10, 1933; Leigh E. Garver statement, August 9, 1933, KSA; Charles Rooney, Sr., interview, May 17, 1979; David Neiswanger statement, September 14, 1933, KSA.
46. *TC*, August 10, 1933; *EG*, August 10, 1933; *Wichita Eagle*, August 11, 1933; Vivian Jeanne Tracey statement, August 11, 1933, KSA; N. L. Sifers statement, September 16, 1933, KSA.
47. *TSJ*, August 12, 1933; *Chicago Tribune*, August 12, 1933; Emma Bailey statement, August 26, 1933; Senate, *Trial of Roland Boynton*, pp. 107, 252, 799; Charles Rooney, Sr., interview, May 17, 1979.

48. Senate, *Trial of Roland Boynton*, pp. 107, 799; Senate, *Trial of Will J. French*, p. 178; White, *What People Said*, pp. 227–33; Kathrine White interview, February 17, 1979; *EG*, April 20, 1933; *TC*, December 3, 1933.
49. *TSJ*, August 30, 1933.
50. *Wichita Eagle*, August 21, 1933; *KCS*, August 27, 1933; *TC*, August 10 and September 26, 1933; *EG*, March 18, 1933; *TSJ*, September 25, 1933; Walter Cole interview, March 10, 1980; Ronald Finney checks, Fidelity State and Savings Bank, 1931–33; White, *What People Said*, pp. 289–99; Wayne Estes statement, August 11, 1933, KSA; Jesse Greenleaf statement, September 27, 1933, KSA.
51. *TC*, December 3, 1933.
52. Emma Bailey statement, August 26, 1933; *Chicago Tribune*, September 30, 1933.
53. *KCS*, August 8, 1933.
54. *TC*, August 16 and 31 and October 2, 1933; *KCS*, October 1, 1933.
55. Finney statement, pp. 10–11; Leigh E. Garver statement, August 9, 1933, KSA.
56. *Wichita Eagle*, August 12, 1933; *Democratic Messenger* (Eureka), September 14, 1933.
57. *TC*, August 31, 1933.
58. Kathrine White interview, February 17, 1979; White, *What People Said*, pp. 233–40, 302–3; *EG*, May 31, 1933; Charles Rooney, Sr., interview, May 17, 1979.
59. *EG*, April 1, July 31, and August 5, 1933; Democratic State Committee, "Landon's Remarkable Record in the Bond Scandal" (Topeka: Democratic State Committee, 1934).
60. *EG*, July 25 and 27, 1933; *TSJ*, August 19, 1933; Kansas, Supreme Court, *State of Kansas* v. *W. W. Finney*, case no. 31,780, Counter Abstract of Appellee, p. 26; Abstract of Appellant, pp. 152–54, 202, 206, 356–60.

Chapter 8

1. Kansas, Supreme Court, *State of Kansas* v. *W. W. Finney*, case no. 31,780, Abstract of Appellant, pp. 153, 204, and Counter Abstract of Appellee, p. 26; *KCS*, November 22, 1933; *EG*, October 26, 1933.
2. *EG*, August 8, 1933.
3. *EG*, August 9, 1933, and August 7, 1936; *TSJ*, August 9, 1933; *Time*, August 21, 1933.
4. *EG*, August 9 and 10, 1933; Alf Landon to Fred Harris, August 12, 1933, KSA.
5. *KCS*, August 9, 1933; *TSJ*, August 9, 1933; *Parsons Sun*, August 9, 1933; *Pittsburg Sun*, August 15, 1933.
6. *EG*, August 9, 10, 11, 12, and 17, 1933.
7. W. W. Finney to Fred Heath, August 9, 1933, Deloy Heath files, Emporia.
8. *EG*, August 24, 1933; *TSJ*, August 24, 1933; *TC*, August 25, 1933.
9. *Finney* case, Abstract, pp. 455–56; *EG*, December 6, 1933.
10. *TC*, August 27, 1933.
11. *EG*, August 18 and 28, 1933; *TC*, August 30, 1933.
12. *EG*, September 2, 1933.
13. *EG*, September 11, 12, 13, and 18, November 23, December 2 and 12, 1933.
14. *EG*, September 2, 7, 11, 21, 22, and 26 and December 28, 1933; *TC*, December 16, 1933.
15. *EG*, September 7 and December 31, 1933, February 10, 1934, and September 14, 1935.
16. *EG*, October 3, 5, and 7, 1933; *Finney* case, Abstract, pp. 7–33.
17. *Finney* case, Abstract, pp. 7–33; *EG*, October 9, 1933.
18. *EG*, October 9, 10, and 19, 1933.
19. *EG*, May 11 and 27, 1933.
20. Walter Johnson, *William Allen White's America* (New York: Henry Holt & Co., 1947), pp. 438–40; *TC*, October 20, 1933; *EG*, May 11 and October 23, 1933.
21. W. A. White to Erwin Canham, October 27, 1933, KSHS.
22. William L. White, *What People Said* (New York: Viking Press, 1938), pp. 493–501; Kathrine White interview, January 17, 1979. The "little jangle" had to do with the news reports of the telephone company's tax check. The Finneys did all they could to prevent that from being published in the *Gazette*, but to no avail.
23. W. L. White to Lacey (*sic*) Haynes, August 29, 1933, KSHS.

24. Telegram, W. A. White to W. L. White, October 19, 1933, KSHS.
25. Clyde Schenck interview, May 24, 1979; *TC*, October 20, 1933; Kathrine White interview, January 17, 1979; White, *What People Said*, pp. 517-25; *EG*, October 23, 1933.
26. *KCJP*, September 21 and 23, 1933.
27. *EG*, September 11, 1933.
28. *Leoti Standard*, October 12, 1933.
29. W. A. White to Erwin Canham, October 27, 1933, KSHS.
30. *EG*, June 10, 1935; W. A. White to Harry Bowman, July 26, 1934, Kansas Collection, University of Kansas Libraries.
31. *Finney* case, Abstract, pp. 262-64, 363; *EG*, November 6, 1933; W. A. White to Hugh C. Bryan, October 25, 1933, Kansas Collection.
32. Donald R. McCoy, *Landon of Kansas* (Lincoln: University of Nebraska Press, 1966), pp. 50-51. Sloan, a Democrat, had been defeated in a heated contest for the state senate in 1928 when Republican state chairman Alf Landon flooded Sloan's district on election day with handbills linking him to the wets, the railroads, and out-of-state agitators.
33. *Finney* case, Abstract, title page; Secretary of State, *Kansas Directory, 1977* (Topeka: Jack H. Brier, 1977), p. 73; Clyde Schenck interview, May 24, 1979.
34. Sara M. and Robert M. Baldwin, eds., *Illustriana Kansas* (Hebron, Nebr.: Illustriana, Inc., 1933), pp. 87, 1203; *EG*, March 4, 1932, and August 31, 1933; *Kansas Governmental Journal*, vol. 34, no. 9 (September, 1948), p. 22; *Emporia Times*, August 17, 1933.
35. *EG*, October 4, 1933.
36. *Finney* case, Abstract, pp. 7-33.
37. Ibid., p. 32.
38. *EG*, October 25 and November 2, 7, and 10, 1933; *TC*, November 8, 1933.
39. *TC*, October 26, 1933. One of President Roosevelt's most controversial programs, the National Recovery Act restricted the number of hours of employment for individuals so that more jobs would be created. The NRA symbol, the Blue Eagle, was displayed in the windows of cooperating firms.
40. *Finney* case, Abstract, pp. 303, 457-59, and Supplemental Abstract and Brief of Appellant, pp. 140-43, 159-60; *EG*, November 3 and 4, 1933; *TC*, October 27, 1933.
41. *Finney* case, Abstract, pp. 33-40; *EG*, October 31, 1933.
42. *Finney* case, Abstract, pp. 40-146, 150-51, 152-54, 158-60, and Counter Abstract, pp. 2-8, 9-29, 107-22; *KCS*, October 25, 1933; *EG*, October 25, 1933.
43. *Finney* case, Abstract, pp. 161-62, and Counter Abstract, pp. 137-54.
44. Ibid., Abstract, pp. 154-56, and Counter Abstract, pp. 53-85; *EG*, November 2, 1933.
45. *Finney* case, Abstract, pp. 156-58, and Counter Abstract, pp. 85-106; *EG*, October 25, 27, and 31, 1933.
46. *Finney* case, Abstract, pp. 156-58, 357-58, and Counter Abstract, pp. 53-85, 86-106; *EG*, October 27 and November 2, 1933.
47. *Finney* case, Abstract, p. 146, and Counter Abstract, pp. 29-35; *EG*, October 30, 1933.
48. *Finney* case, Abstract, pp. 146-48, 149-64; *EG*, October 27 and November 8, 1933; E. H. Rees to W. A. White, October 16, 1933, Kathrine White's files.
49. *Finney* case, Abstract, p. 331.
50. Ibid., pp. 327, 330-32; *EG*, October 28, 1933.
51. *Finney* case, Abstract, pp. 150, 165-70.
52. *EG*, November 1, 1933.
53. *Finney* case, Abstract, pp. 178-340; *EG*, October 30 and November 1, 2, 3, 4, and 6, 1933.
54. *EG*, November 2, 1933; *KCS*, November 2, 1933; *Finney* case, Abstract, p. 337.
55. *Finney* case, Abstract, pp. 178-297, 298-99, 324-35, 337-40; *EG*, November 1 and 4, 1933; White, *What People Said*, p. 532.
56. *Finney* case, Abstract, pp. 299-324; *EG*, November 3, 1933.
57. *Finney* case, Abstract, pp. 299-324, 336; *EG*, November 3, 1933.
58. *KCS*, November 3, 1933; *EG*, November 3, 1933.
59. *EG*, November 6, 1933.
60. *EG*, November 7, 1933.
61. Ibid.
62. *EG*, November 8, 1933.
63. *Finney* case, Abstract, pp. 450-51; *EG*, November 8, 1933.

64. *Finney* case, Abstract, pp. 388–416; *EG*, November 7 and 8, 1933.
65. *Finney* case, Abstract, p. 429.
66. *EG*, November 8, 1933.
67. *Finney* case, Abstract, pp. 431–32; *EG*, November 9, 1933.
68. Hugo Wedell to Alf Landon, November 9, 1933, KSA.
69. Wedell to Landon, November 4, 1933, KSA.
70. *Finney* case, Abstract, pp. 432, 433; *EG*, October 24, 1933.
71. *Finney* case, Abstract, pp. 434, 435.
72. Ibid., p. 437.
73. Ibid., pp. 438–39; *EG*, November 9, 1933; White, *What People Said*, pp. 525–37; *EG*, June 10, 1935 (first draft of editorial).
74. *EG*, November 9 and 10, 1933.
75. Fred M. Harris to Alf Landon, December 5, 1933, KSA.
76. *EG*, November 6 and 10, 1933.
77. *EG*, November 15, 18, and 29, and December 1, 1933.
78. Landon to Beck, December 16, 1933, KSA.
79. *Finney* case, Abstract, pp. 442–43.
80. *EG*, December 2, 1933, and January 3, 1934; *TC*, December 2, 1933.

Chapter 9

1. W. L. White, *What People Said* (New York: Viking Press, 1938), p. 455.
2. *KCT*, October 13, 1961; Ronald Finney statement, December 9, 1943, p. 8, KSHS; Alf Landon to W. D. Kinnaman, September 6, 1933, KSA.
3. Kansas, Senate, *Trial of Will J. French, Auditor of the State of Kansas* (Topeka: State Printer, 1934), pp. 109–10, 310; W. H. Stanley statement, August 23, 1933, KSA.
4. Senate, *Trial of Will J. French*, pp. 329–31, 335–36, 364, 440–41, 455–56; Kansas, Senate, *Trial of Roland Boynton, Attorney-general of the State of Kansas* (Topeka: State Printer, 1934), pp. 101, 107, 111, 228–29, 384–86, 410–11; Fred M. Harris statement to Bloss Committee, October 2, 1933, pp. 3–8, KSHS; *TC*, December 22, 1933; *TSJ*, January 24, 1934; Kansas Supreme Court, *State of Kansas v. T. B. Boyd*, case no. 31,876, Abstract of the Record, pp. 54–55; N. L. Sifers statement, September 16, 1933, KSA; W. H. Stanley statement, August 23, 1933, KSA.
5. *TC*, September 16, 1933, and February 8, 9, 10, 11, and 13, 1934; *KCT*, February 8 and 14, 1934; *TSJ*, February 8 and 10, 1934.
6. Senate, *Trial of Roland Boynton*, pp. 162–63; Kansas, House, *House Journal, Special Session, 1933* (Topeka: State Printer, 1933), pp. 237–38; W. H. Stanley statement, August 23, 1933, KSA.
7. Senate, *Trial of Will J. French*, pp. 121–22, 127–28; *TC*, September 10, 1933.
8. Senate, *Trial of Roland Boynton*, pp. 467–71, 472–75; Senate, *Trial of Will J. French*, pp. 207, 400–401; Appendix.
9. *KCJP*, February 14, 1943. Charles Ponzi, a notorious swindler, had a get-rich-quick scheme in which millions of dollars were lost in 1920. He was released in 1934 to be deported, having spent nearly one-third of his fifty-two years behind bars. Ivan Krueger was the unscrupulous Swedish match king. Wallingford was a popular fictional character of the period who had a get-rich-quick scheme.
10. *TC*, August 9, 1933; *KCJP*, August 12, 1933; *TSJ*, November 9 and December 16, 1933, and January 1 and 26, 1934; *KCT*, December 25, 1933; Senate, *Trial of Roland Boynton*, pp. 505, 528; Gayle Mott interview, January 9, 1979.
11. *TSJ*, September 5, 1933.
12. *TSJ*, September 28, 1933.
13. Ibid.; *KCS*, August 27, 1933; *TC*, August 27 and 31, 1933; N. L. Sifers statement, September 16, 1933, KSA.
14. *KCS*, December 24, 1933.
15. Gayle Mott interview, January 9, 1979.
16. *TC*, November 18, 1933.
17. Jesse Greenleaf statement, September 27, 1933, KSA.
18. *TC*, November 18, 1933.
19. *KCT*, September 26, 1933; *EG*, December 8 and 18, 1933; *TC*, December 14 and 17, 1933.
20. *TC*, December 2, 10, and 12, 1933.
21. *TC*, December 12, 1933; Walt Markley, *Builders of Topeka* (Topeka: Capper Printing Co., 1934), p. 101; Alf Landon memorandum, December 11, 1933, KSA;

KCS, December 18, 1933; Fred Harris to Alf Landon, December 5, 1933, KSA.
22. Markley, *Builders*, p. 114; *TC*, September 8 and December 10, 1933.
23. *TC*, December 10, 1933; *TSJ*, December 16, 1933.
24. *KCS*, December 11, 1933; *TC*, December 12, 1933; *TSJ*, December 13 and 22, 1933.
25. *TC*, November 4, 1974.
26. *TC*, December 13, 1933. Zula Bennington Greene—"Flint Hills Peggy"—had just commenced writing a column for the *Capital*. She moved to Topeka with her family in the fall of 1933 from Cottonwood Falls, where she had written for the *Chase County Leader*. The impeachments and the Ronald Finney trial were her first assignments from *Capital* editor Charles Sessions. Nearly fifty years later she still was writing a widely read column for the same paper.
27. *KCS*, December 12, 1933; *TSJ*, December 13 and 15, 1933; *TC*, December 12, 13, and 15, 1933.
28. *TC*, December 14, 1933.
29. *TC*, December 16, 1933.
30. *TC*, December 16 and 18, 1933.
31. *TC*, December 16, 18, and 19, 1933.
32. *KCS*, December 19, 1933; *EG*, December 19, 1933; *TSJ*, December 19, 1933; *TC*, December 20, 21, and 22, 1933; Shawnee County District Court, *Jackson Brothers, Boesel* v. *National Bank of Topeka*, case no. 49,884, Plaintiff Petition, pp. 17–18; Senate, *Trial of Roland Boynton*, pp. 467–75.
33. *TC*, December 19, 1933.
34. Kansas, Supreme Court, *State of Kansas* v. *Ronald Finney*, case no. 31,785, Abstract of Appellant (March 12, 1934), pp. 26–28; *TSJ*, December 20, 1933, and February 9, 1934; *TC*, December 20 and 21, 1933.
35. *TC*, August 24 and December 21 and 22, 1933; *KCT*, December 21, 1933.
36. *TC*, December 22, 1933.
37. *KCT*, December 21, 1933.
38. Ibid.; *TC*, December 21, 1933.
39. *TC*, December 22, 1933.
40. *TC*, December 22 and 24, 1933.
41. Finney case, Abstract, pp. 29–31; *TC*, December 23 and 24, 1933.
42. Finney case, Abstract, pp. 30–32.
43. Ibid., p. 32; *TC*, December 24, 1933.
44. *EG*, December 25, 1933.
45. *TC*, December 24, 1933; *TSJ*, December 25, 1933.
46. *KCS*, December 24, 1933.
47. *TSJ*, December 25, 1933.
48. Ibid.; *TC*, December 25, 1933; *EG*, December 20 and 25, 1933.
49. *TSJ*, December 26, 1933.
50. *TSJ*, December 28, 1933.
51. B. H. Bennett to Alf Landon, January 4, 1934, KSA.
52. *TSJ*, December 30, 1933; *TC*, December 31, 1933.
53. *TSJ*, January 1, 1934.
54. Finney case, Abstract, pp. 14–24; Kansas, Supreme Court, *Reports*, vol. 139, case no. 31,785, May 5, 1934, pp. 585–86; *TC*, January 3, 1934.
55. Finney case, Abstract, p. 14.
56. Ibid., p. 15.
57. Ibid., pp. 16–19; *TC*, January 3, 1934.
58. Finney case, Abstract, pp. 20, 22.
59. *TC*, January 3, 1933; *KCT*, January 3, 1934.
60. Finney case, Abstract, pp. 22–23.
61. Ibid., pp. 23–24.
62. Ronald Finney to W. L. White, November 8, 1943, KSHS; Clyde Schenck interview, May 24, 1979; Kathrine White interview, February 17, 1979; Walter Johnson, *William Allen White's America* (New York: Henry Holt & Co., 1947), p. 442.
63. Finney case, Abstract, p. 38; *TC*, January 3, 1934; *KCT*, January 3, 1934.
64. Finney case, Abstract, p. 39.
65. Ibid., pp. 39–40; *TC*, January 3, 1934.
66. *TC*, January 3, 1934.
67. *EG*, January 3, 1934.
68. Hugo Wedell to Alf Landon, February 2, 1934, KSA.
69. Fred Harris to Alf Landon, March 5, 1934, KSA.
70. Kansas, Supreme Court, *Reports*, pp. 578–99.
71. Ibid., p. 588.
72. Ibid., pp. 588–89; Ronald Finney prison record, Lansing, no. 4,224; *EG*, May 31, 1934; *TC*, June 1, 1934.
73. *TSJ*, January 3, 1934.
74. *KCS*, January 3, 1934.
75. *TC*, January 4, 1934.

76. Lester M. Goodell to Alf Landon, January 5, 1934, KSA.
77. Secretary of State, *Kansas Directory, 1977* (Topeka: Secretary of State, 1977), p. 73; *EG,* July 1, 1935; *Journal of the Bar Association of Kansas,* vol. 23, no. 3 (February, 1955), pp. 213–14; Alf Landon to Branch Rickey, February 16, 1945, KSHS.
78. Alf Landon to Lester Goodell, January 6, 1934, KSA.
79. *TC,* January 7, 1934; *TSJ,* January 3, 1934.
80. Ralph L. Funk to Alf Landon, January 6, 1934, KSA.
81. *TSJ,* January 3, 1934.
82. *TC,* January 5, 1934.

Chapter 10

1. Republican pamphlet, State Central Committee, 1932, KSHS; T. B. Boyd, Kansas State Penitentiary record, no. 4,673, Lansing; Secretary of State, *Kansas Directory, 1977* (Topeka: Secretary of State, 1977), p. 69; Charles Rooney, Sr., interview, May 17, 1979; *EG,* March 2, 1932.
2. *EG,* July 30, 1932.
3. *TSJ,* August 16 and October 12, 1933, and January 22, 1934; *EG,* July 30, 1932; Mrs. Clif Stratton interview, March 8, 1979.
4. Lulu Wood statement, October 13, 1933, KSA; *TC,* August 9, 1933; Coryell Gove to Alf Landon, November 15, 1932, KSHS; Edward E. Pedroja to Alf Landon, August 8, 1933, KSA; Charles Rooney, Jr., interview, May 17, 1979; *TC,* January 18 and 19, 1934; N. L. Sifers statement, September 16, 1933, KSA.
5. Fred M. Harris statement to Kansas House, November 7 and 8, 1933, p. 18, KSHS; Frank Beach statement, September 17, 1933, p. 4, KSA; Lulu Wood statement, October 13, 1933, KSA.
6. Harris statement, November 7 and 8, 1933, pp. 18 ff.; Lulu Wood statement, October 13, 1933, KSA; *TSJ,* August 14, 18, 19, and 23, 1933; *TC,* August 20 and November 8, 1933; *KCS,* January 19, 1934; F. M. Agard statement, September 17, 1933, KSA; Frank Beach statement, September 17, 1933, KSA; J. W. Finney statement, September 16, 1933, KSA.
7. Fred M. Harris statement to Bloss Committee, October 2, 1933, pp. 3–4, KSHS; Harris statement, November 7 and 8, 1933, pp. 20–23, KSHS; *KCS,* October 2, 1933.
8. *TC,* August 9, 1933.
9. *TSJ,* August 13 and 14, 1933; *KCT,* August 14, 1933.
10. *TSJ,* August 9, 1933.
11. Lulu Wood statement, October 13, 1933, KSA; Harris statement, November 7 and 8, 1933, p. 19, KSHS; Ronald Finney statement (draft), December 9, 1943, p. 4, Kathrine White files; Kansas Supreme Court, *State of Kansas* v. *T. B. Boyd,* case no. 31,876, State of Kansas, Counter Abstract of the Record, pp. 11–12; *TSJ,* March 18, 1932; *KCJP,* August 13, 1933; *TC,* January 18, 1934; Ruth Friedrich, "The Threadbare Thirties," in John D. Bright, ed., *Kansas: The First Century* (New York: Lewis Publishing Co., 1956), p. 93.
12. Walt Markley, *Builders of Topeka* (Topeka: Capper Printing Co., 1934), p. 329; Robert W. Richmond, *Kansas: A Land of Contrasts* (St. Charles, Mo.: Forum Press, 1974), p. 65; *TSJ,* January 6, 1925, and December 4, 1933; William E. Treadway, *Cyrus K. Holliday* (Topeka: Kansas State Historical Society, 1979).
13. Markley, *Builders,* p. 174.
14. William E. Connelley, *History of Kansas, State and People* (New York: American Historical Society, 1928), vol. 5, p. 2278.
15. John E. Kirk to Alf Landon, November 30, 1932, KSHS; William F. Zornow, *Kansas: A History of the Jayhawk State* (Norman: University of Oklahoma Press, 1957), p. 194; Markley, *Builders,* p. 174; Wayne Estes statement, August 11, 1933, KSA; W. H. Stanley statement, August 23, 1933, KSA. Several departments of the state of Kansas, including that of the state treasury, occupied the building as of 1981. Ironically, the then treasurer, Joan Finney, had her office just a few feet from the spot where the "$150,000 caper" took place. Neither

Mrs. Finney nor her husband is related to the Warren Finney family.

16. Kansas Senate, *Trial of Will J. French, Auditor of the State of Kansas* (Topeka: State Printer, 1934), pp. 121–28, 129–37; *EG*, October 29, 1932; Wayne Estes statement, August 11, 1933, KSA.

17. *TC*, September 10 and 11, 1933.

18. *TC*, September 12, 1933.

19. J. F. T. O'Conner to Alf Landon, August 28, 1933, KSA; Senate, *Trial of Will J. French*, pp. 380–81; Fred M. Harris statement to Bloss Committee, October 2, 1933, pp. 4–5, KSHS; Fred M. Harris statement to Kansas House, November 7 and 8, 1933, pp. 23–24, KSHS; *TC*, August 12, 16, and 23, September 10 and 11, and December 3, 1933; U.S. District Court, District of Kansas, First Division, December 2, 1933, case nos. 5,931, 5,935, 5,936, Federal Archives, Kansas City, Mo.

20. *TSJ*, August 23, 1933; *TC*, August 23 and September 9, 1933.

21. *TSJ*, August 23, 1933.

22. Senate, *Trial of Will J. French*, pp. 114–17; Harris statement, October 2, 1933, p. 5; Harris statement, November 7 and 8, 1933, p. 24; *TC*, August 12 and September 10, 1933, and February 3, 1934.

23. *Boyd* case, Counter Abstract, pp. 12–15; *KCT*, August 10, 1933; *KCS*, January 20, 1934; Senate, *Trial of Will J. French*, pp. 380–81; *TC*, August 8, 1933.

24. Harris statement, October 2, 1933, p. 5; Harris statement, November 7 and 8, 1933, pp. 24–25; Kansas Supreme Court, *State of Kansas v. T. B. Boyd*, case no. 31,876, T. B. Boyd, Abstract of the Record, pp. 18–30, and Counter Abstract, pp. 7–8, 9–11; *TC*, September 10, 1933; *KCS*, September 9, 1933.

25. Harris statement, November 7 and 8, 1933, p. 25; *Boyd* case, Abstract of the Record, pp. 18–30, and Counter Abstract, pp. 7–8; *KCT*, September 9, 1933.

26. Harris statement, November 7 and 8, 1933, p. 25; *Boyd* case, Counter Abstract, pp. 7–8.

27. *Boyd* case, Abstract of the Record, p. 23.

28. Ibid., pp. 26–27.

29. Harris statement, November 7 and 8, 1933, pp. 25–26; *Boyd* case, Abstract of the Record, pp. 26–29, and Counter Abstract, pp. 7–8; *TC*, September 19, 1933; Shawnee County District Court, *Jackson Brothers, Boesel v. National Bank of Topeka*, case no. 49,884, Plaintiff Petition, p. 11.

30. Harris statement, November 7 and 8, 1933, p. 26.

31. Harris statement, October 2, 1933, p. 6; Harris statement, November 7 and 8, 1933, pp. 26–27; *Boyd* case, Abstract of the Record, pp. 45–49, and Counter Abstract, pp. 3, 6, 18–19; *TC*, September 9 and October 3, 1933.

32. Harris statement, October 2, 1933, p. 8; Harris statement, November 7 and 8, 1933, pp. 27–28; *Boyd* case, Counter Abstract, p. 6; *KCT*, January 18, 1934; *Chicago Tribune*, September 29 and 30, 1933; *New York Times*, September 29, 1933; Arthur S. Jackson, death certificate, Department of Health of the City of New York; W. G. Clugston, *Rascals in Democracy* (New York: Richard B. Smith, 1940), p. 273; *Jackson Brothers* case, Plaintiff Petition, pp. 7, 12.

33. District Court, Shawnee County, *State of Kansas v. T. B. Boyd*, records case no. 14,848; *TC*, January 7 and 16, 1934.

34. Sara M. and Robert M. Baldwin, eds., *Illustriana Kansas* (Hebron, Nebr.: Illustriana, Inc., 1933), p. 145; Markley, *Builders*, p. 29; William E. Connelley, *A Standard History of Kansas and Kansans* (New York: Lewis Publishing Co., 1918), 3:1290; Kansas, House, *Journal*, Thirty-first Biennial Session (January–April, 1939), concurrent resolution no. 21, relating to death of S. M. Brewster, p. 346; *KCJP*, January 7, 1934; *EG*, March 5, 1936; *Pink Rag*, March 23, 1934; *Journal of the Bar Association of the State of Kansas* 4 (May, 1935); 338.

35. *TSJ*, January 11, 1934.

36. Zornow, *Kansas*, p. 240; Richmond, *Kansas*, p. 226; *TSJ*, January 3, 1934; *Boyd* case, Abstract of the Record, title page; Baldwin, *Illustriana*, p. 570.

37. *TC*, January 6, 9, 10, and 11, 1934.

38. *TC*, January 14, 1934.

39. *TC*, January 10, 11, 16, and 17, 1934.

40. *TC*, January 18 and 19, 1934; *KCT*, September 1, 1933, January 19, 1934; *Boyd* case, Counter Abstract, pp. 3–15.

41. *Boyd* case, Counter Abstract, p. 12;

KCT, January 19, 1934; *TC*, January 20, 1934.
42. *Boyd* case, Counter Abstract, p. 15; *TSJ*, January 20, 1934.
43. *TC*, January 21 and 22, 1934.
44. *TC*, January 21, 22, and 26, 1934; *TSJ*, January 22, 1934.
45. *TSJ*, January 22, 1934; *TC*, January 23 and 26, 1934.
46. *TSJ*, January 24, 1934; *TC*, January 25, 1934; *Boyd* case, Abstract of Record, pp. 54–55; Ruth Pennick statement, August 15, 1933, KSA.
47. *TC*, January 25, 1934.
48. *TC*, January 26, 1934.
49. *TSJ*, January 26, 1934.
50. *TC*, January 27, 1934; *Pink Rag*, January 19, 1934.
51. *TC*, January 27, 1934.
52. Ibid.
53. Ibid.
54. *TC*, January 27 and 28, 1934.
55. *TC*, January 28, 1934.
56. *Wichita Beacon*, January 28, 1934.
57. *TC*, February 17 and 18, 1934.
58. *TSJ*, February 17, 1934.
59. *TC*, February 18, 1934.
60. Kansas, Supreme Court, *Reports*, vol. 140, case no. 31,876, pp. 623–35; *KCS*, December 8, 1934; *TSJ*, February 2, 1935; Supreme Court Docket, no. 68, T. B. Boyd v. *State of Kansas*, p. 76; Harry W. Colmery to William A. Smith, April 26, 1935, KSA; T. B. Boyd, Kansas State Penitentiary record, no. 4,673, Lansing; *EG*, June 2 and 6, September 29, October 12 and 30, and December 8 and 28, 1934, February 2 and 4 and March 8, 9, and 11, 1935.
61. *TC*, December 3, 1933; *TSJ*, December 5, 1933.
62. U.S. District Court, First Division, State of Kansas, Criminal Docket, case no. 5,931, Federal Archives, Kansas City, Mo.
63. U.S. District Court, First Division, State of Kansas, Criminal Docket, case no. 5,931, Judge Hopkins, *Memorandum Decision*, p. 8, Federal Archives, Kansas City, Mo.; *TC*, March 3, 1934.
64. *TC*, November 1, 1934.
65. *Pink Rag*, March 30, 1934; *TC*, March 10, 1934.
66. *TC*, March 25 and June 3, 1934; *EG*, June 2 and 26, 1934.
67. Hopkins, *Memorandum Decision*, pp. 22, 25, 27.
68. U.S. District Court, First Division, State of Kansas, Criminal Docket, case nos. 5,931, 5,932, 5,933, 5,934, 5,935, 5,936, Federal Archives, Kansas City, Mo.; *EG*, April 4 and 9 and December 3 and 4, 1934; Alf Landon to Roland Boynton, March 20, 1934, KSA.

Chapter 11

1. State Penitentiary Records, Leland C. Caldwell, no. 4,105; *TSJ*, August 25, 1933, and November 20, 1940; *TC*, February 14 and 15, 1934; *KCT*, February 14, 1934.
2. Lulu Woods statement, October 13, 1933, KSA; *TC*, October 27, 1933; Charles Rooney, Sr., interview, May 17, 1979.
3. Vivian Jeanne Tracey statement, August 11, 1933, KSA; Emma Bailey statement, August 26, 1933, KSA; Frank Ruby statement, September 17, 1933, KSA; *TSJ*, August 10, 1933; Kansas, Senate, *Trial of Will J. French, Auditor of the State of Kansas* (Topeka: State Printer, 1934), pp. 152, 154, 164–65, 251–54; *TC*, January 20, 1934; *KCS*, February 14, 1934. Kansas, Senate, *Trial of Roland Boynton, Attorney-general of the State of Kansas* (Topeka: State Printer, 1934), p. 426.
4. *TSJ*, August 19, 1933; *KCT*, February 8, 1934; *TC*, December 19 and 20, 1933, and February 8, 1934; Senate, *Trial of Roland Boynton*, p. 692.
5. *TC*, December 23, 1933; *KCT*, December 23, 1933; *TSJ*, February 10, 1934.
6. *TC*, December 12, 1933, and January 11 and February 5, 1934.
7. *TC*, February 10 and 16, 1934.
8. *TC*, February 6, 1934; *KCT*, February 14, 1934; District Court, Shawnee County, records, case no. 14,765.
9. *TC*, February 7, 1934.
10. *TC*, February 8, 9, and 10, 1934.
11. District Court, Shawnee County, case no. 14,765; *KCT*, August 29, 1933; *TC*, February 11 and 13, 1934.
12. *TSJ*, February 13, 1934.
13. *KCT*, February 14, 1934; *TC*, February 14, 1934; *KCS*, February 14, 1934.

14. *KCS*, February 14, 1934.
15. *TC*, February 15, 1934.
16. Ibid.
17. Ibid.
18. Ibid.
19. *TC*, February 16, 1934.
20. *TC*, February 17, 1934.
21. *TSJ*, February 15, 1934; *TC*, February 16, 1934; *Pink Rag*, February 23, 1934.
22. *TC*, February 16, 1934.
23. District Court, Shawnee County, records, case no. 14,765; *TC*, March 4, 1934.
24. *TC*, March 4, 1934.
25. Ibid.
26. *TSJ*, March 5, 1934.
27. *TSJ*, March 7, 1934.
28. State Penitentiary Records, Leland Caldwell, no. 4,105, Lansing; *EG*, March 10, 1934; *KCS*, March 12, 1934; District Court, Shawnee County, case no. 14,765.
29. *TC*, March 9, 1934.
30. G. L. Stahl to Alf Landon, February 19, 1934, KSA.
31. Glen C. Austin to Alf Landon, February 21, 1934, KSA.
32. J. S. Martin to Alf Landon, March 5, 1934, KSA.
33. Landon to Martin, March 9, 1934, KSA.
34. *TC*, March 4 and 6, 1934; *EG*, March 5, 1934; *KCT*, March 6, 1934.

Chapter 12

1. Sara M. and Robert M. Baldwin, eds., *Illustriana Kansas* (Hebron, Nebr.: Illustriana, Inc., 1933), p. 134; W. A. White, *The Autobiography of William Allen White* (New York: Macmillan, 1946), p. 6; University of Kansas, *Graduate Magazine*, vol. 31, no. 5 (February, 1933); *EG*, November 15, 1932; Kansas, Senate, *Trial of Roland Boynton, Attorney-general of the State of Kansas* (Topeka: State Printer, 1934), p. 99.
2. *Illustriana Kansas*, p. 134; Republican Central Committee, *Republican State Candidates for 1932*, pamphlet, 1932, KSHS; Senate, *Trial of Roland Boynton*, pp. 100, 682–83; Secretary of State, *Kansas Directory, 1977* (Topeka: Secretary of State, 1977), p. 70.
3. *Illustriana Kansas*, p. 134; K.U., *Graduate Magazine* (February, 1933); Senate, *Trial of Roland Boynton*, p. 823.
4. W. A. White to Alf Landon, July 29, 1929, KSHS; Charles Rooney, Sr., interview, May 17, 1979.
5. W. A. White to Alf Landon, July 29, 1929, KSHS; White to Walter Neibarger, February 9, 1931, Kansas Collection, microfilm, University of Kansas.
6. Senate, *Trial of Roland Boynton*, pp. 100–101, 776, 684–85; W. L. White, *What People Said* (New York: Viking Press, 1938), p. 453.
7. Senate, *Trial of Roland Boynton*, pp. 111, 776, 813.
8. Ibid., pp. 101, 111–13, 234, 686–87, 734.
9. Ibid., p. 814.
10. Ibid., pp. 104–5, 482–83, 686; *TSJ*, September 11, 1933.
11. Senate, *Trial of Roland Boynton*, pp. 107–8, 761–63.
12. Ibid., p. 762.
13. Ibid., pp. 108–9, 762–63.
14. Kansas, House, *House Journal, Special Session, 1933* (Topeka: State Printer, 1933), p. 237; Senate, *Trial of Roland Boynton*, p. 163; *EG*, February 21, 1934; *KCT*, September 1, 1933.
15. *House Journal*, p. 238.
16. Senate, *Trial of Roland Boynton*, pp. 152, 219; W. H. Stanley statement, August 23, 1933, KSA.
17. Senate, *Trial of Roland Boynton*, pp. 219, 228–29, 239, 253, 656, 666; W. H. Stanley statement, August 23, 1933, KSA.
18. Senate, *Trial of Roland Boynton*, pp. 258, 287, 499–500, 812.
19. Ibid., pp. 67, 230, 778; White, *What People Said*, pp. 173–86.
20. Senate, *Trial of Roland Boynton*, pp. 138–40, 146–47, 148–49.
21. *TC*, June 14, 21, 23, and 25 and July 2 and 3, 1931.
22. *TC*, June 21 and July 2 and 3, 1931; W. H. Stanley statement, August 23, 1933, KSA.
23. Senate, *Trial of Roland Boynton*, pp. 140, 149.
24. *House Journal*, pp. 238–39; Senate, *Trial of Roland Boynton*, pp. 66, 83.
25. Senate, *Trial of Roland Boynton*, pp. 831–32.
26. Ibid., pp. 832–33.
27. Ibid., pp. 834–35.

28. Ibid., p. 835; *House Journal*, p. 239.
29. Senate, *Trial of Roland Boynton*, pp. 218, 288–90, 297–98, 311, 322–26; *House Journal*, p. 239; W. H. Stanley statement, August 23, 1933, KSA.
30. Senate, *Trial of Roland Boynton*, pp. 69, 282, 290, 305, 528–29.
31. *House Journal*, p. 239; Senate, *Trial of Roland Boynton*, pp. 74, 348–50, 352, 489.
32. *House Journal*, p. 239.
33. Senate, *Trial of Roland Boynton*, p. 228.
34. Ibid., pp. 232, 350, 360–61; G. L. Light to Alf Landon, May 4, 1933, KSA.
35. *Kansas Directory*, p. 67.
36. Senate, *Trial of Roland Boynton*, pp. 269–70.
37. *House Journal*, p. 241; Senate, *Trial of Roland Boynton*, pp. 136, 200, 252, 384–86, 815; W. H. Stanley statement, August 23, 1933, KSA.
38. Senate, *Trial of Roland Boynton*, pp. 270, 562; W. H. Stanley statement, August 23, 1933, KSA.
39. Senate, *Trial of Roland Boynton*, pp. 136, 244, 271.
40. Ibid., pp. 190, 246–47, 260, 535–36.
41. Ibid., pp. 271, 275, 278, 757; *House Journal*, p. 241.
42. *House Journal*, pp. 236–42; *KCT*, November 23, 1933.
43. Senate, *Trial of Roland Boynton*, p. 193.
44. Ibid., p. 194; *TSJ*, October 25, 1933.
45. Senate, *Trial of Roland Boynton*, pp. 282, 299, 616–17; W. H. Stanley statement, August 23, 1933, KSA.
46. G. L. Light to Roland Boynton, November 10, 1932 (*Trial of Roland Boynton*, pp. 288–90); Boynton to Light, November 23, 1932 (ibid., p. 291).
47. *Trial of Roland Boynton*, pp. 295, 296, 297–99, 307.
48. Ibid., pp. 129–30.
49. Ibid., pp. 296–97.
50. Roland Boynton to G. L. Light, November 23, 1932, KSA.
51. G. L. Light to Alf Landon, April 19 and May 4, 1933, KSA; Landon to Light, April 22, 1933, KSA.
52. Senate, *Trial of Roland Boynton*, p. 281.
53. Ibid., pp. 134–35, 435, 787.
54. Ibid., p. 134; W. H. Stanley statement, August 23, 1933, KSA.
55. *TC*, April 19, 1933.
56. *EG*, April 19, 1933.
57. Senate, *Trial of Roland Boynton*, pp. 135, 152.
58. Ibid., p. 135.
59. *EG*, May 26, 1933.
60. Senate, *Trial of Roland Boynton*, p. 640; Cortez A. M. Ewing, "Notes on Two Kansas Impeachments," *Kansas Historical Quarterly* 23 (1957): 282.
61. *EG*, November 14, 1933.
62. W. A. White to Charles Scott, October 27, 1933; White to Rolla Clymer, December 6, 1933, both in Kansas Collection, microfilm, University of Kansas.
63. *House Journal*, p. 243; *Colby Free Press-Tribune*, April 12, 1933; Senate, *Trial of Roland Boynton*, p. 414.
64. Senate, *Trial of Roland Boynton*, pp. 404–6; Woman's Kansas Day Club, *Lawyers through the Years*, January 29, 1963, KSHS.
65. Senate, *Trial of Roland Boynton*, pp. 405–6.
66. Ibid., p. 151.
67. Ibid., pp. 405–7.
68. Ibid., pp. 408, 422, 423, 434–35.
69. Ibid., pp. 408–10, 422, 435.
70. Ibid., pp. 410, 424–25, 435.
71. Ibid., pp. 410, 422, 428.
72. Ibid., p. 411.
73. Ibid., p. 418.
74. *TC*, January 17, 1934.
75. Senate, *Trial of Roland Boynton*, p. 425.
76. Ibid., p. 411.
77. Ibid., p. 420; *Colby Free Press-Tribune*, April 12 and 19, 1933.
78. *Colby Free Press-Tribune*, April 19, 1933.
79. Senate, *Trial of Roland Boynton*, pp. 420–22.
80. Leon N. Roulier to Roland Boynton, April 11, 1933 (*Trial of Roland Boynton*, p. 150).
81. Leon N. Roulier to Ronald Finney, May 5, 1933 (*Trial of Roland Boynton*, pp. 424–25).
82. Ibid.
83. Senate, *Trial of Roland Boynton*, pp. 426, 429, 437.
84. W. A. White to Charles Scott, October 27, 1933, Kansas Collection, microfilm, University of Kansas.
85. W. A. White to Gwen Boynton, Novem-

ber 9, 1933, Kansas Collection, microfilm, University of Kansas.
86. *EG*, January 6, 1934.
87. *KCJP*, January 8, 1934.
88. *TSJ*, January 9, 1934.
89. *EG*, January 12, 1934.
90. Cortez A. M. Ewing, "Early Kansas Impeachments," *Kansas Historical Quarterly*, vol. 1, pp. 307-25, and "Notes on Two Kansas Impeachments," *Kansas Historical Quarterly* 23 (1957): 281-97. Governor Charles Robinson, Secretary of State John W. Robinson (no relation), and State Auditor George S. Hillyer had been impeached in 1862, Treasurer Josiah Hayes in 1874, and Judge Theodosius Botkin in 1891. John Robinson and Hillyer were convicted by the Senate; Charles Robinson and Botkin were acquitted; and Hayes resigned before his trial.
91. George Mack, Jr., *The 1933 Kansas Legislative Blue Book* (Lawrence: George Mack, Jr., 1933), p. 49; *KCT*, November 3, 1933; *TC*, November 9, 1933; Senate, *Trial of Roland Boynton*, p. iv; O. R. Stites interview, December 14, 1978.
92. Mack, *1933 Kansas Legislative Blue Book*; *EG*, November 16, 1932.
93. *TC*, January 12, 1934.
94. *House Journal*, pp. 236-45.
95. *TC*, January 9, 1934.
96. *TC*, January 19, 1934.
97. Senate, *Trial of Roland Boynton*, passim.
98. Ibid., pp. 151-269; *TC*, January 13, 1934.
99. Senate, *Trial of Roland Boynton*, pp. 560-88; *TC*, January 26, 1934.
100. Senate, *Trial of Roland Boynton*, pp. 279-81.
101. Ibid., pp. 404-40, 419, 420, 883, 884.
102. Ibid., p. 681.
103. Ibid., pp. 693-97, 701, 703.
104. Ibid., pp. 715-32; *KCS*, February 20, 1934; Walt Markley, *Builders of Topeka* (Topeka: Capper Printing Co., 1934), p. 188.
105. Senate, *Trial of Roland Boynton*, pp. 597-602, 648, 649, 682-88, 733, 734-820; *TSJ*, January 2, 1934.
106. Senate, *Trial of Roland Boynton*, pp. 847-48.
107. Ibid., p. 848.
108. Ibid., pp. 848-51.
109. Ibid., p. 818.
110. Ibid., pp. 180-81.
111. Ibid., p. 891.
112. Ibid., pp. 496-97, 872, 874.
113. Ibid., pp. 885, 888; *TC*, January 22, 1934.
114. Senate, *Trial of Roland Boynton*, p. 881.
115. Ibid., pp. 881-84.
116. Ibid., p. 505.
117. Ibid., p. 493.
118. Ibid., p. 897; *TC*, January 19, 1934.
119. Senate, *Trial of Roland Boynton*, p. 898.
120. Ibid., pp. 908-9.
121. *TC*, January 26, 1934; *EG*, January 27, 1934.
122. *Parsons Sun*, January 26, 1934; *KCJP*, January 26, 1934.
123. *TSJ*, February 3, 1934.

Chapter 13

1. William E. Connelley, *History of Kansas* (New York: American Historical Society, 1928), 3:1394-95.
2. *TC*, November 9, 1933; *Democratic Messenger* (Eureka), November 2, 1933; Charles Rooney, Sr., interview, May 17, 1979; Secretary of State, *Kansas Directory, 1977* (Topeka: Secretary of State, 1977), p. 68; *Parsons Sun*, August 12, 1933; Sara M. and Robert M. Baldwin, eds., *Illustriana Kansas* (Hebron, Nebr.: Illustriana, Inc., 1933), p. 423; Connelley, *History*, 3:1394-95.
3. *EG*, January 9 and 20, 1932, and September 16, 1933; Will J. French to Alf Landon, November 10, 1932, KSHS.
4. Donald R. McCoy, *Landon of Kansas* (Lincoln: University of Nebraska Press, 1966), p. 62; *Parsons Sun*, August 12, 1933.
5. Kansas, Senate, *Trial of Will J. French, Auditor of the State of Kansas* (Topeka: State Printer, 1934), p. 241.
6. Ibid., pp. 241-42, 385-86.
7. Ibid., p. 387, 407.
8. Ibid., pp. 386-87.
9. Ibid.
10. Ibid., pp. 17, 409; Kansas, House, *House Journal, Special Session, 1933* (Topeka: State Printer, 1933), pp. 272-73.
11. Senate, *Trial of Will J. French*, pp. 50-

51, 113; *House Journal*, p. 272; Appendix.
12. Senate, *Trial of Will J. French*, p. 143.
13. Ibid., pp. 165–68.
14. Ibid., p. 454.
15. Ibid., pp. 143, 164.
16. Ibid., pp. 141–50.
17. Ibid., pp. 94, 100–101, 317, 419, 467.
18. Ibid., pp. 50, 125–26, 169, 173, 222, 378.
19. Ibid., pp. 170, 184, 378–79, 389–90; *House Journal*, p. 273.
20. Senate, *Trial of Will J. French*, pp. 70, 106–7, 113, 170, 222, 462, 466; *KCS*, August 16, 1933.
21. Senate, *Trial of Will J. French*, pp. 462–68.
22. Ibid., pp. 122–23, 131–32, 400, 493.
23. Ibid., pp. 400–401; Appendix.
24. Senate, *Trial of Will J. French*, pp. 400, 461, 472.
25. Ibid., pp. 121–25, 127–28, 129–39, 304, 400.
26. Ibid., pp. 314–15; Kansas, Senate, *Trial of Roland Boynton, Attorney-general of the State of Kansas* (Topeka: State Printer, 1934), p. 474.
27. Donald Davies to M. A. Ross, January 19, 1933 (*Trial of Will J. French*, p. 314).
28. Senate, *Trial of Will J. French*, pp. 103–4, 307–8; Shawnee County District Court, *Jackson Brothers, Boesel* v. *National Bank of Topeka*, case no. 49,884, Plaintiff Petition, p. 4.
29. Senate, *Trial of Will J. French*, pp. 317–18.
30. Ibid., p. 317.
31. Ibid., pp. 315–16.
32. Ibid., p. 316; *Jackson Brothers* case, Plaintiff Petition, p. 4.
33. Senate, *Trial of Will J. French*, pp. 141–47.
34. C. A. Spencer to Will J. French, March 1, 1932 (*Trial of Will J. French*, p. 143).
35. C. A. Spencer to Will J. French, March 30, 1932 (*Trial of Will J. French*, p. 144).
36. R. E. Brown to William J. French, January 22, 1932 (*Trial of Will J. French*, p. 141).
37. Lucy M. Pottorf to Will J. French, July 23, 1932 (*Trial of Will J. French*, p. 145); French to Pottorf, August 1 and September 27, 1932 (in ibid., pp. 145, 146); Senate, *Trial of Will J. French*, pp. 105–6, 145–47, 252.
38. Lucy M. Pottorf to Will J. French, October 7, 1932 (*Trial of Will J. French*, p. 147).
39. Senate, *Trial of Will J. French*, pp. 252, 254.
40. Lucy M. Pottorf to Will J. French, May 2, 1933 (*Trial of Will J. French*, p. 147); French to Pottorf, May 10, 1933 (in ibid., p. 147).
41. Senate, *Trial of Will J. French*, pp. 148, 222–23, 390.
42. Ibid., p. 220.
43. Ibid., p. 217.
44. Ibid.
45. Ibid.
46. Charles Rooney, Sr., interview, May 17, 1979.
47. Senate, *Trial of Will J. French*, pp. 241, 439–41; J. W. Finney statement, September 17, 1933, KSA.
48. Senate, *Trial of Will J. French*, p. 441.
49. Ibid., pp. 168, 169, 180, 231, 446; W. H. Stanley statement, August 23, 1933, KSA.
50. Senate, *Trial of Will J. French*, pp. 179–80, 183–84.
51. Ibid., p. 183.
52. Ibid., p. 184.
53. Ibid.
54. Ibid., p. 179.
55. Ibid., p. 241.
56. Ibid., p. 178.
57. Ibid., p. 181.
58. Ibid.
59. Ibid., pp. 393–94.
60. Ibid., pp. 419–20, 423.
61. Ibid., p. 420.
62. Ibid., pp. 322–23, 333, 336, 350.
63. Ibid., pp. 323–26.
64. Ibid., pp. 296, 326–29, 341; Frank C. Clough, *William Allen White of Emporia* (New York: Whittlesey House, 1941), p. 165.
65. Senate, *Trial of Will J. French*, pp. 329–30.
66. Ibid., pp. 335–36, 339, 342.
67. Ibid., pp. 189–91.
68. Ibid., p. 329.
69. Ibid., pp. 190–91, 329; David Neiswanger statement, September 14, 1933, KSA.

70. Kansas, House, *House Journal, Special Session, 1933* (Topeka: State Printer, 1933), p. 272.
71. Senate, *Trial of Will J. French*, pp. 267, 271, 296, 333–34; *KCT*, November 21, 1933.
72. Senate, *Trial of Will J. French*, pp. 257–65; *KCS*, October 8 and 11, 1933; *TC*, September 16, 1933.
73. Senate, *Trial of Will J. French*, pp. 52, 64, 229; J. W. Finney statement, September 16 and 20, 1933, KSA; Frank Beach statement, September 17, 1933, KSA; L. F. Hukill statement, September 17, 1933, KSA; Frank Ruby statement, September 17, 1933, KSA.
74. Senate, *Trial of Will J. French*, pp. 239–40.
75. Ibid., pp. 171, 187, 189, 211.
76. Ibid., p. 228.
77. Ibid., pp. 362–63.
78. Ibid., pp. 188, 343–44; J. W. Finney statement, September 16, 1933, KSA; Frank Ruby statement, September 17, 1933, KSA.
79. Senate, *Trial of Will J. French*, p. 344.
80. Ibid., pp. 196–98; *House Journal*, pp. 275–76; Fred M. Harris statement to Kansas House, November 7 and 8, 1933, pp. 1–12, KSHS; Kansas, Supreme Court, *State of Kansas* v. *T. B. Boyd*, case no. 31,876, T. B. Boyd, Abstract of Record, pp. 33–37.
81. Senate, *Trial of Will J. French*, pp. 196–98.
82. Ibid., pp. 197–98; *EG*, January 31, 1934.
83. *House Journal*, p. 275.
84. *House Journal*, pp. 275–76; Senate, *Trial of Will French*, pp. 68, 202, 243.
85. Senate, *Trial of Will J. French*, p. 242.
86. *TSJ*, January 27, 1934.
87. *House Journal*, p. 300; Senate, *Trial of Will J. French*, p. 3; Secretary of State, *Kansas Directory, 1977* (Topeka: Secretary of State, 1977), p. 62.
88. Francis W. Schruben, *Kansas in Turmoil, 1930–1936* (Columbia: University of Missouri Press, 1969), p. 24.
89. Senate, *Trial of Will J. French*, p. 3.
90. *House Journal*, pp. 271–76.
91. Senate, *Trial of Will J. French*, pp. 36, 43–46.
92. Ibid., pp. 44–45.
93. Ibid., pp. 210–51.
94. Ibid., p. 240.
95. Ibid.
96. Ibid., pp. 168–89, 282, 291, 293, 296.
97. Ibid., p. 296.
98. Ibid., pp. 267, 282, 302.
99. Ibid., pp. 302, 312.
100. Ibid., pp. 321–54.
101. Ibid., p. 329.
102. Ibid., pp. 331–32.
103. Ibid., p. 326.
104. Ibid., pp. 42, 97, 359–61.
105. Ibid., pp. 362–71, 371–79, 426–34, 437–70.
106. Ibid., pp. 385–426, 424.
107. Ibid., pp. 402–5.
108. Ibid., p. 404.
109. Ibid., pp. 405, 434; *TSJ*, February 6, 1934; *TC*, February 6, 1934.
110. Senate, *Trial of Will J. French*, pp. 434–36; *TC*, February 6 and March 6, 1934.
111. Senate, *Trial of Will J. French*, pp. 436–37.
112. Ibid., p. 476.
113. Ibid., p. 284.
114. Ibid., pp. 476–90.
115. Ibid., p. 481; *TSJ*, February 6, 1934; *Wichita Eagle*, February 7, 1934.
116. Senate, *Trial of Will J. French*, pp. 489–90.
117. Ibid., pp. 496–97; *TC*, February 7 and 8, 1934.
118. *EG*, February 7, 1934.
119. *KCS*, February 7, 1934.
120. *TC*, February 7, 1934.
121. *TSJ*, February 7, 1934.
122. *Pink Rag*, March 9 and 23, 1934.
123. *KCJP*, February 10, 1934.

Chapter 14

1. Leo Tolstoy, *War and Peace* (New York: Simon & Schuster, 1942), pp. 1330–33.
2. *KCS*, August 13, 1933.
3. Ibid.
4. *TC*, August 12, 1933.
5. *TC*, August 16, 1933.
6. *TC*, October 17, 1933.
7. *TC*, April 7, 1934.
8. Alf Landon to C. M. Clark, December 15, 1933; see references in chaps. 10 and 15.
9. *TSJ*, January 27, 1934.
10. *TC*, November 14, 1933.
11. *TSJ*, November 18, 1933.

12. *KCJP*, January 24, 1934.
13. *TC*, January 28, 29, and 30, 1934.
14. *TC*, January 30, 1934.
15. *KCJP*, January 28, 1934.
16. *KCS*, January 29, 1934.
17. *TSJ*, October 5, 1933.
18. *TSJ*, March 3 and 8 and August 8, 1934.
19. *KCJP*, January 24, 1934.
20. *TSJ*, January 26, 1934.
21. W. A. White to Roland Boynton, February 13, 1934, KSHS.
22. Jay Sullivan interview, May 14, 1979; Donald R. McCoy, *Landon of Kansas* (Lincoln: University of Nebraska Press, 1966), pp. 94–95, 221, 223, 229. Some have claimed that for a twenty-year period, Haynes "ran Kansas." During the thirties and forties he seemed to get handed down automatically as a confidant from one governor to another. Much like the furniture or the silverware in the Governor's Mansion, Lacy seemed to come with the job. Haynes became a prominent member of the innermost circle of Landon advisors in his 1936 presidential campaign.
23. W. A. White to Lacy Haynes, February 13, 1934, KSHS.
24. W. A. White to John Hamilton, February 12, 1934, KSHS.
25. *EG*, February 9, 1934.
26. *EG*, May 12, 1934.
27. *EG*, October 3, 1934.
28. *EG*, February 9, 1934.
29. *EG*, June 1, 1934.
30. *TC*, July 29, 1934; *EG*, October 20, 1934.
31. *EG*, August 17, 1933.
32. *TC*, August 31, 1933.
33. *TC*, December 17, 1933, and March 2, 1934; Ruth Friedrich, "The Threadbare Thirties," in *Kansas: The First Century*, ed. John D. Bright (New York: Lewis Publishing Co., 1956), 2:102; *KCJP*, September 23, 1933.
34. *Western Spirit* (Paola), August 11, 1933.
35. *Emporia Times*, August 24, 1933.
36. *Marysville Advocate-Democrat*, August 17, 1933; *EG*, March 14, 1936.
37. *Leoti Standard*, August 31, 1933.
38. *TC*, February 23, 1934; *TSJ*, February 22, 1934.
39. *TSJ*, February 22, 1934.
40. *TSJ*, August 24, 1933.
41. Ibid.; *KCS*, September 17, 1933; *TC*, March 16 and 17, 1934; *EG*, March 31, 1934.
42. *TC*, April 5, 1934.
43. *EG*, July 13, 1934.
44. *TC*, June 21, 1934; Gerald Carson, *The Roguish World of Doctor Brinkley* (New York: Holt, Rinehart & Winston, 1960), p. 13.
45. Keith D. McFarland, *Harry H. Woodring* (Lawrence: University Press of Kansas, 1975), pp. 34, 75; Carson, *Roguish World*, p. 157; *Pink Rag*, September 22, 1933; Francis W. Schruben, *Kansas in Turmoil, 1930–1936* (Columbia: University of Missouri Press, 1969), p. 31.
46. *EG*, February 17, 1934.
47. *TC*, June 21 and 26 and July 7, 1934.
48. *TC*, July 15, 1934.
49. *TC*, August 26, 1934; Alf Landon interview, January 23, 1979.
50. *EG*, August 1, 1934.
51. *EG*, July 31, 1934.
52. *EG*, August 1, 1934; *TC*, August 1, 1934; Kenneth S. Davis, *Kansas: A Bicentennial History* (New York: W. W. Norton, 1976), p. 183; Alf Landon to James M. Rhodes, June 19, 1934, KSA.
53. *EG*, August 1, 1934.
54. *TC*, August 2 and 3, 1934; *EG*, August 3, 1934.
55. *EG*, August 3, 1934.
56. *EG*, August 4, 1934; *TC*, August 7, 1934.
57. Burt Comer, *The Tale of a Fox* (Wichita, Kans.: Burt Comer, 1936), pp. 76–77.
58. *TC*, August 7, 1933.
59. *EG*, August 4, 1933.
60. *TC*, August 21, 1934.
61. *TC*, October 27, 1934.
62. *TC*, August 29, 1934.
63. *EG*, August 29, 1934.
64. *EG*, July 23, 1934.
65. *TC*, September 6, 1934.
66. *EG*, October 3, 1934.
67. *EG*, October 17, 1934.
68. *TC*, September 22, 1934.
69. *EG*, October 17, 1934.
70. *TC*, October 25, 1934.
71. Ibid.
72. *EG*, September 28, 1934.

73. *EG*, October 3, 1934.
74. *EG*, October 22, 1934.
75. Democratic State Committee, "Landon's Remarkable Record in the Bond Scandal" (Topeka: Democratic State Committee, 1934), KSHS; *TC*, October 30, 1934.
76. *TC*, October 27 and 30, 1934.
77. *EG*, October 29, 1934; *TC*, October 30 and 31 and November 1 and 4, 1934.
78. Alf Landon interview with D. R. McCoy and G. Griffin, March 22, 1976, Kansas Collection, University of Kansas.
79. *TC*, November 1, 1934; Alf Landon interview with D. R. McCoy and G. Griffin, March 22, 1976.
80. *EG*, October 29, 1934.
81. *EG*, October 30, 1934.
82. *TC*, October 31, 1934.
83. Alf Landon to Drew McLaughlin, August 19, 1933, KSA.
84. Alf Landon to Henry F. Draper, August 17, 1934, KSA.
85. *EG*, October 30, 1934; *TC*, October 31, 1934.
86. *TC*, November 1, 1934.
87. *EG*, October 31, 1934.
88. *TC*, November 1, 1934; *EG*, November 1, 1934.
89. *EG*, October 31, 1934.
90. *EG*, November 2, 1934; McCoy, *Landon*, pp. 185-87.
91. *EG*, November 1 and 8, 1934; *TC*, November 6, 1934.
92. *EG*, November 1, 1934.
93. *TC*, November 3, 1934.
94. *TC*, November 1, 1934.
95. *TC*, November 4, 1934.
96. Ibid.
97. *TC*, November 6, 1934.
98. *EG*, November 27, 1934.
99. *EG*, March 15 and December 7 and 8, 1934, and January 14, 1935; *TC*, April 3, 1934.
100. *EG*, December 22, 1934.
101. *EG*, December 10 and 14, 1934, and January 23, March 6, and November 4 and 12, 1935; Secretary of State, *Kansas Directory, 1977* (Topeka: Secretary of State, 1977), p. 68.
102. *EG*, January 14, 1935.
103. W. A. White to C. V. Beck, January 15, 1935, Kansas Collection, University of Kansas.
104. *EG*, February 15 and 20, 1935.

Chapter 15

1. Lyon County District Court, civil dockets L and M and case nos. 18,448, 18,467, 18,468, 18,513, 18,592, 18,936; *EG*, September 22 and October 27 and 30, 1933, July 11 and October 22 and 24, 1934, and January 1, February 9, and May 22, 1935.
2. *EG*, May 1, 3, 11, and 12, 1934.
3. *EG*, May 12, 1934.
4. Owen S. Samuel to Alf Landon, December 15, 1933, KSA; Landon to Owen Samuel, December 19, 1933, KSA; Fred Harris to Landon, March 5, 1934, KSA; U.S. District Court, Kansas First Division, *U.S.A.* v. *W. W. Finney*, case no. 1903-N, Federal Archives, Kansas City, Mo.; *EG*, May 24, 1935, and April 22, 1936.
5. Scott S. Bateman to Alf Landon, April 17, 1934, KSA.
6. *EG*, April 18, 1934.
7. F. M. Harris to Alf Landon, June 4, 1934, KSA; Landon to Harris, June 7 (?), 1934, KSA.
8. *EG*, March 5, July 9, August 17, and November 2, 1934, March 27, 1935, and April 22, 1936; federal case no. 1903-N.
9. *EG*, March 1, April 17, and May 20, 21, and 24, 1935, and April 22, 1936.
10. *EG*, April 27, 1934, May 24, 1935, and April 22, 1936; federal case no. 1903-N.
11. *EG*, May 24, 1935, and April 22, 1936; federal case no. 1903-N; Lyon County District Court, case nos. 18,444, 18,445, 18,446.
12. Federal case no. 1903-N; *EG*, May 24, 1935, and April 22, 1936; Lyon County District Court, case no. 18,585.
13. Federal case no. 1903-N; *EG*, May 24, 1935; *KCJP*, January 14, 1935.
14. Federal case no. 1903-N; *EG*, May 24, 1935; Lyon County District Court, case nos. 18,467, 18,468, 18,585, 18,557, 18,621.
15. *EG*, August 10, November 28, and December 2, 7, and 19, 1935.
16. *EG*, December 19, 1935.
17. *TC*, November 11, 1933; *EG*, January 18, 1934.
18. Supreme Court docket no. 67, p. 480, case no. 31,780; *EG*, January 25, February 3, March 21, April 7, June 24,

July 26, and September 19, 1934; F. M. Harris to Alf Landon, December 5, 1933, KSA.
19. Supreme Court docket no. 67, p. 480, case no. 31,780; *EG*, September 19 and 20 and October 11 and 23, 1934.
20. *EG*, November 2, 1934.
21. *KCJP*, January 10, 1935; *EG*, January 17, 1935.
22. *KCJP*, January 14, 1935; *EG*, January 17, 1935.
23. Reports of the Supreme Court of the State of Kansas, vol. 141, pp. 12, 15, 36, January 26, 1935; *EG*, January 26, 1935.
24. *EG*, January 26, 1935.
25. Supreme Court docket no. 67, p. 480, case no. 31,780; *EG*, February 12, March 14, and April 2, 12, 13, and 18, 1935.
26. Donald R. McCoy, *Landon of Kansas* (Lincoln: University of Nebraska Press, 1966), pp. 251, 548; Harry Colmery interview, March 1, 1979. In 1936 Colmery became the second Kansan in five years to be named national commander of the American Legion. He was a member of the Kansas delegation to the 1936 Republican Convention and an enthusiastic Landon supporter, though later his ardor cooled. In 1950 Colmery, with Landon's support, ran unsuccessfully in the primary for a U.S. senatorial seat against Frank Carlson.
27. Harry Colmery to W. A. Smith, April 26, 1935, KSA; Supreme Court records, case no. 31,780; *EG*, February 4, 1935.
28. Colmery to Smith, April 26, 1935.
29. Harry Colmery interview, March 1, 1979.
30. Colmery to Smith, April 26, 1935.
31. Supreme Court docket no. 67, p. 480, case no. 31,780; *EG*, April 29, 1935.
32. Harry Colmery interview, March 1, 1979; *EG*, May 29 and 30, 1935.
33. *EG*, June 5, 6, and 7, 1935; *TC*, June 6, 1935; *Wichita Eagle*, June 6, 1935; Gayle Mott interview, January 9, 1979.
34. *EG*, June 6, 1935.
35. *EG*, June 7, 1935.
36. Ibid.
37. *EG*, June 8, 1935.
38. *EG*, June 6 and 7, 1935.
39. *EG*, June 7, 1935.
40. *EG*, June 7 and 8, 1935.
41. *EG*, June 8 and 10, 1935; O. R. Stites interview, December 14, 1978; William Allen White to Walt Mason, June 11, 1935, Kansas Collection, University of Kansas.
42. W. G. Clugston, *Rascals in Democracy* (New York: Richard B. Smith, 1940), p. 273; Hellen M. Cox interview, June 18, 1960.
43. Kathrine White interview, March 13, 1979.
44. W. A. White, *The Autobiography of William Allen White* (New York: Macmillan Co., 1946), p. 620; W. A. White to Clara B. Davis, July 11, 1935, Kansas Collection, University of Kansas.
45. Draft, W. W. Finney obituary, *Emporia Gazette* files.
46. *EG*, June 10, 1935; W. L. White to Lacy Haynes, August 29, 1933, KSHS; F. M. Harris to Alf Landon, March 5, 1934, KSA; Kathrine White interview, March 13, 1979; W. L. White, *What People Said* (New York: Viking Press, 1938), pp. 590–93; W. A. White to Harry Bowman, July 26, 1934, Kansas Collection, University of Kansas.
47. *EG*, June 10, 1935.
48. Walter Johnson, *William Allen White's America* (New York: Henry Holt, 1947), p. 240.
49. W. A. White to Walt Mason, June 11, 1935, Kansas Collection, University of Kansas. Mason—whom White called the "Homer of the Midwest"—had come to the *Gazette* in 1907 as a talented but alcoholic writer, down on his luck. White took "Uncle Walt" under his wing and helped him to sober up and to start a new life. By the time Mason moved on to California in the twenties, he had established a solid reputation throughout the country for his short stories and especially for his syndicated prose poems.
50. *EG*, June 11, 1935.

Chapter 16

1. *EG*, May 31, 1934.
2. *TC*, June 1, 1934.
3. *EG*, June 1, 1934.
4. *TC*, June 1, 1934.
5. Ibid.

6. *EG*, June 4, 1934; *KCS*, October 7, 1934; *TC*, September 27, 1934.
7. *EG*, January 2, 1935; *Wichita Beacon*, January 28, 1934.
8. *EG*, June 18, 1935; *KCS*, June 18, 1935.
9. *EG*, June 20, 1935.
10. *EG*, June 7 and 8, 1935.
11. Lyon County Probate Court, W. W. Finney's will, filed June 10, 1935.
12. Ronald Finney statement, December 9, 1943, p. 13, KSHS; *KCS*, March 1, 1936; *EG*, March 16, 1936.
13. Kansas State Prison Records, inmate no. 4,224, Lansing; *EG*, September 14, 1936; *KCS*, September 15, 1936; O. R. Stites interview, December 14, 1978.
14. *KCS*, September 15, 1936.
15. Ibid.
16. Prison Records, no. 4,224; *KCS*, January 25, 1942; R. Finney to W. A. White, July 20, 1943, W. A. White Collection, Library of Congress; Kathrine White to author, April 13, 1981.
17. Mary McKinney to author, May 29, 1979.
18. Frances Kesner interview, October 15, 1979; O. R. Stites interview, December 14, 1978.
19. W. L. White, *What People Said* (New York: Viking Press, 1938); Kathrine White interview, January 17, 1979.
20. W. L. White to Mrs. Klinkenberg, n.d. (April, 1938), Kathrine White files.
21. Kathrine White to author, April 13, 1981.
22. *New York Times Book Review*, April 10, 1938, p. 2; *Progress in Kansas*, vol. 4, no. 5 (April, 1938), p. 11; Charles A. and Mary R. Beard, *America in Midpassage* (New York: Macmillan Co., 1939), 2:676; Kathrine White interview, January 17, 1979.
23. University of Kansas Extension Records, no. 138; Robert Senecal to author, May 4, 1979; *TSJ*, December 15, 1939; *Kansas Magazine*, 1940, pp. 7-9; Kathrine White interview, January 17, 1979.
24. *Kansas Magazine*, 1940, p. 7.
25. *TSJ*, December 15, 1939.
26. *TC*, January 12, 1940.
27. *Kansas Magazine*, 1940, pp. 7-9; 1941, pp. 139-40; and 1943, pp. 49-50.
28. W. L. White to Arthur Capper, January 10, 1944, KSHS; *KCS*, January 25, 1942; Ronald Finney statement, December 9, 1943, p. 14, KSHS.
29. W. L. White to Arthur Capper, January 10, 1944, KSHS; *KCS*, January 25, 1942; *KCT*, October 13, 1961; *TSJ*, January 14, 1942; R. Finney to W. A. White, November 7, 1942, W. A. White Collection, Library of Congress.
30. *TC*, August 5, 1940.
31. Ibid.
32. Ibid.
33. *EG*, March 11, 12, 13, and 18, 1935; Kansas State Penitentiary Records, no. 4,673, Lansing.
34. Kansas State Penitentiary Records, no. 4,673; *KCS*, December 21, 1937.
35. Kansas State Penitentiary Records, no. 4,673; *TSJ*, July 30, 1941; *TC*, September 9, 1941; Charles Rooney, Sr., interview, May 17, 1979; *Wichita Eagle and Beacon*, December 17, 1961.
36. *KCT*, November 18, 1941.
37. *EG*, November 20, 1941.
38. W. A. White to Payne Ratner, January 12, 1942, Emporia State University Collection.
39. *TSJ*, January 14, 1942.
40. Ibid.
41. *TC*, January 15, 1942.
42. *TSJ*, January 20, 1942.
43. W. A. White to R. Finney, January 22, 1942, and January 5, 1943; R. Finney to W. A. White, March 20, September 26, and December 17, 1942; Webb Wilson to Parole Board, December 19, 1942—all in W. A. White Collection, Library of Congress; much additional correspondence during the 1941-43 period, in W. A. White Collection, Library of Congress.
44. Ronald Finney to W. A. White, March 20, 1942, W. A. White Collection, Library of Congress.
45. *KCT*, December 16, 1942; *EG*, December 31, 1942.
46. W. A. Smith to Sallie White, February 1, 1944, KSHS; W. A. White to W. A. Smith, November 30, 1942, KSHS.
47. Hal D. Sears, *The Sex Radicals: Free Love in High Victorian America* (Lawrence: Regents Press of Kansas, 1977), p. 106; Gerald Carson, *The Roguish World of Doctor Brinkley* (New York:

Holt, Rinehart & Winston, 1960), pp. 148-50.
48. W. A. White to W. A. Smith, December 4, 1934, KSHS.
49. W. A. Smith to W. A. White, November 30, 1942, KSHS; *EG*, February 21, 1933.
50. W. A. Smith to W. A. White, November 30, December 1, 1942, KSHS.
51. Payne Ratner to W. A. White, December 17, 1942, KSHS.
52. W. A. White to Ronald Finney, December 29, 1942, Emporia State University Collection.
53. Ronald Finney to W. A. White, January 2, 1943, W. A. White Collection, Library of Congress.
54. Walter Johnson, *William Allen White's America* (New York: Henry Holt & Co., 1947), p. 572.
55. W. L. White to Lacy Haynes, October 23, 1943, KSHS.
56. W. L. White to W. A. Smith, October 29, 1943, KSHS.
57. W. A. Smith to W. L. White, November 6, 1943, KSHS.
58. R. Finney to W. L. White, November 8, 1943, KSHS.
59. Kansas State Penitentiary Records, no. 4,224, Board of Administration, February, 1945, meeting.
60. R. Finney to W. L. White, November 8, 1943, KSHS.
61. W. L. White to Lacy Haynes, November 9, 1943, KSHS.
62. W. A. Smith to W. L. White, November 15, 1943, KSHS.
63. W. A. White to Fred Brinkerhoff, December 3, 1943; identical letters to other newspapermen in W. A. White Collection, Library of Congress.
64. W. L. White to Gomer T. Davies, February 8, 1944, Kathrine White files; W. L. White to M. M. Levand, February 17, 1944, Kathrine White files; W. L. White to W. A. Smith, n.d. (about January 20, 1944), KSHS; F. W. Brinkerhoff to W. A. White, December 4, 1943, KSHS; Arthur Capper to W. A. White, December 7, 1943, KSHS; Henry Allen to W. A. White, December 6, 1943, and Victor Murdock to W. A. White, December 8, 1943, W. A. White Collection, Library of Congress.
65. *Leavenworth Times*, December 13, 1943.
66. Ronald Finney statement, December 9, 1943, pp. 6-7, KSHS; W. L. White notes on the statement, fall, 1943, Kathrine White files; Kathrine White to author, July 7, 1981.
67. Finney statement, p. 12.
68. Ibid., p. 13.
69. Ibid.
70. Ibid., p. 14.
71. Finney statement, December 15, 1943, pp. 1-2, KSHS; Kansas Supreme Court, *State* v. *T. B. Boyd*, case no. 31,876, Abstract of Record, p. 30, Counter Abstract of Record, p. 8.
72. *KCT*, December 15 and 17, 1943.
73. *KCT*, December 17, 1943.
74. *TSJ*, December 17, 1943.
75. Kansas State Penitentiary Records, no. 4,105, Lansing; *TSJ*, December 17, 1943; *KCT*, December 17, 1943.
76. *KCT*, December 17, 1943.
77. Harold L. Ickes, *The Secret Diary of Harold L. Ickes: The First Thousand Days, 1933-1936* (New York: Simon & Schuster, 1953), pp. 667-68; White, *What People Said*, pp. 329-38.
78. W. L. White to Alf Landon, December 17, 1943, KSHS.
79. W. L. White to W. A. Smith, December 31, 1943, KSHS.
80. W. L. White to W. A. Smith, n.d. (about January 23, 1944), KSHS.
81. Ibid.
82. *EG*, January 22, 1944.
83. Ibid.
84. *KCT*, January 22, 1944; *KCS*, November 19, 1941; Kansas State Penitentiary Records, no. 4,105, Lansing.
85. *EG*, January 22, 1944.
86. W. A. Smith to Sallie White, February 23, 1944, KSHS.
87. W. L. White to W. A. Smith, n.d. (about January 23, 1944), KSHS.
88. *Kansan*, January 27, 1944.
89. *EG*, January 24, 1944.
90. W. L. White to W. A. Smith, February 12, 1945, KSHS.
91. Kansas State Penitentiary Records, no. 4,224, Board of Administration, February, 1945, Lansing.
92. W. L. White to W. A. Smith, February 20, 1945, KSHS.
93. W. A. Smith to W. L. White, March 1, 1945, KSHS.

94. R. Finney to W. A. White, December 20, 1942, W. A. White Collection, Library of Congress.
95. R. Finney to W. A. White (undated), W. A. White Collection, Library of Congress.
96. Kansas State Penitentiary Records, no. 4,224, Lansing; *KCT*, February 19, 1945; *EG*, February 19, 1945.
97. Kathrine White interview, January 17, 1979; Kathrine White to author, April 1, 1981; R. Finney to W. A. White, January 2, 1943, W. A. White Collection, Library of Congress.
98. Kansas State Penitentiary Records, no. 4,224, Lansing; *TSJ*, December 13, 1947; *KCT*, November 23, 1949, and October 13, 1961; Mary McKinney interview, May 29, 1979; Kathrine White to author, September 24, 1980, and July 7, 1981.
99. *KCT*, October 13, 1961; Florine Minturn to author, March 15, 1979; Kathrine White to author, April 1, 1981.
100. *TSJ*, December 13, 1947.
101. DeLoy Heath to author, May 31, 1979.
102. Kansas State Penitentiary Records, no. 4,224, Lansing; *KCT*, November 23, 1949; *Wichita Eagle*, December 2, 1949.
103. C. W. Wilson to Ronald Finney, December 10, 1949, Kansas State Penitentiary Records, Lansing.
104. Mr. and Mrs. Lloyd Herdman interview June 21, 1979; *TSJ*, October 12, 1961; Florine Minturn to author, March 15, 1979; death certificate of Ronald Tucker Finney, Bureau of Vital Statistics, State of Florida, Jacksonville, Fla.; Kathrine White to author, April 13, 1981.
105. *KCT*, October 13, 1961.

Chapter 17

1. Alf Landon to Roland Boynton, September 9 and October 14, 1933, KSA; *TC*, February 2, March 17 and 18, July 17 and 20, 1934, and November 26, 1935; *EG*, March 9, May 11, and July 2, 3, and 17, 1934, February 15 and October 1 and 17, 1935.
2. *TSJ*, June 3, 1941; *KCT*, June 3, 1941; Clarence Beck to Alf Landon, November 25, 1935, KSA.
3. *EG*, November 26, 1935; *TSJ*, March 12 and 13, 1937.
4. *EG*, February 28, 1934.
5. *TSJ*, March 3, 1938.
6. *TSJ*, January 9, 1934; *TC*, March 10 and 27, 1934; *KCS*, September 26, 1937; U.S. District Court, civil docket, vol. R, case no. 3,894, Federal Archives, Kansas City, Mo.; Shawnee County District Court, *Jackson Brothers, Boesel v. National Bank of Topeka*, case no. 49,884, journal entry, May 9, 1938.
7. *KCT*, March 6, 1934; *TC*, November 25, 1933, and March 6, 1934; *EG*, November 10, 1933; *TSJ*, March 10, 1934.
8. Kansas State Banking Department, receivership book, Fidelity State and Savings Bank (Emporia), Eureka Bank, and Farmers State Bank (Neosho Falls).
9. Alexander Klein, *Grand Deception* (New York: J. B. Lippincott, 1955), pp. 299–303; Alexander Klein, *The Double Dealers* (New York: J. B. Lippincott, 1958); St. Clair McKelway, *True Tales from the Annals of Crime and Rascality* (New York: Random House, 1950), pp. 1–48.
10. William L. Shirer, *The Collapse of the Third Republic* (New York: Simon & Schuster, 1971), pp. 184–90; *TC*, January 6, 1934; *EG*, January 29, 1934; *TSJ*, February 15, 1934.
11. *TC*, August 19, September 13, and October 13, 1933, and January 18 and 31, 1934; *TSJ*, October 12, 1933, and January 31, 1934; *KCT*, October 24, 1933; *EG*, October 9 and 24, 1933, and January 31 and February 24, 1934; W. G. Clugston, *Rascals in Democracy* (New York: Richard B. Smith, 1940), p. 273.
12. Gerald Carson, *The Roguish World of Doctor Brinkley* (New York: Holt, Rinehart & Winston, 1960), p. 120 (facing).

Index

Abilene Reflector, 86
Alexander, Summerfield S., 203, 283–84, 292
Aliceville Bank, 127
Allen, E. F. ("Jack"), 38–39, 49, 191
Allen, George A., 63, 65, 220, 222–23, 225
Allen, Henry J., 92, 146
Altoona Telephone Co., 77, 111, 154, 157
Angle, Roy, 207, 209
Arma, Kans., 222–23
Atchison Champion, 101
Atchison Globe, 61, 276–77
Attorney general. *See* Boynton, Roland
Auditor. *See* French, Will J.

Bailey, Roy, 244
Baird, Fred, 141, 155
Bank commissioner. *See* Bone, Roy; Koeneke, H. W.
Banking Department, 66, 143–44; investigation of, 69–70, 85; W. Finney's settlement with, 298–301
Barnes, James, 223
Beck, Clarence V. ("Prunes"), 40, 53–54, 127, 142–43, 347; and W. Finney trial, 150–51, 153, 155, 158, 160; elected attorney general, 281–82, 294, 295–96
Beck, Martha, 89
Beck, Ned, 88–89
Bell Telephone Co. *See* Southwestern Bell Telephone Co.
Beloit Gazette, 57–58
Benson, E. H., 266

Berry, George, 127
Betzer, Harry, 173
Bixler, Harold, 159–61
Bloss, S. C., 36–37, 67, 70, 292, 347; head of Board of Managers, 72, 240, 265; and clemency for R. Finney, 327–28, 330, 332, 336
Bloss Committee, 62, 64–69, 70, 73
Board of Treasury Examiners. *See* Treasury Board
Bodley, F. G., 126–27
Bond-exchange law, 249–50
Bonds, totals of forged, 19, 20, 21–22, 29, 34, 53, 167
Bone, Roy, 66–67, 115, 128, 346
Booth, Robert, 223–24, 228–29
Bordenkircher, George, 85
Boyd, G. McDill ("Huck"), 127
Boyd, Helen, 186, 199
Boyd, Tom: friendship of, with R. Finney, 5, 25–26, 185–89; as state treasurer, 27–28, 55–56, 173–74, 194–95, 264; state charges against, 34–35, 47–48, 58; federal charges against, 39–40, 76, 77, 203; and Landon, 50–51, 118; trial and prison term of, 195–202, 322–23
Boyd, Tom, Jr., 50–51
Boynton, Catharine, 215
Boynton, Roland, 50, 94, 131, 213–14, 279–80; as attorney general, 4, 114, 215–16, 281; friendship of, with R. Finney, 4–5, 30–31, 65, 72–73, 217–19; and School Fund Com-

387

INDEX

mission, 33, 219, 221–22, 228–32, 234, 237; impeachment of, 65, 67–68, 70–72, 240–46
Bradney, Claude, 34–35
Branam, Coyle, 224
Brewster, George, 130–31
Brewster, Sardius M., 22, 30, 84–85, 127, 283–84, 293; and Landon, 17, 19–20; and Boyd trial, 183, 195–96, 200; and Caldwell trial, 207, 210
Brinkerhoff, Fred, 97
Brinkley, Dr. John R., 59, 81, 86, 94; as candidate for governor, 2, 93, 284–87
Broderick, Lynn, 85–86, 283
Burlington Telephone Co., 111

Caldwell, Leland, 45, 250–51, 257; as R. Finney's office manager, 15, 129, 135, 205–7; state charges against, 28, 35, 49–50; federal charges against, 39–40, 76, 203; trial and parole of, 207–12, 332, 335, 336
Capper, Arthur, 24, 82, 83, 276, 330
Carlson, Frank, 118, 339
Certificates of destruction, 64, 65, 71, 72, 251–54, 267–68
Chase, D. A. N., 27
Chicago Tribune, 88–89
Citizens State Bank of North Topeka, 49, 52, 170, 173
Clarke, Sidney, 101
Clugston, William G., 16, 93–94; on R. Boynton, 73, 94, 239, 277
Clymer, Rolla, 74, 244
Cobb, Sam, 59, 189
Colby Free Press-Tribune, 237
Coley, Mary E. (Mrs. R. Boynton), 216
Colmery, Harry, 304–5
Comer, Burt, 284, 287
Cooke, Charles L., 48, 59, 67, 130, 190–92; federal charges against, 76, 203
Cornell, E. A., 63, 220, 222, 242
Cowie, Dan, 203
Cox, R. A., 265
Crane and Co., 29–30, 234, 236, 242–43
Cunningham, Will L., 240, 245

Davidson, George, 72
Davies, Gomer T., 335–36
Doherty, Henry, 92, 93
Doran, Kline, Colmery and Cosgrove, 304

Ebright, A. M., 240
El Dorado Times, 89. *See also* Clymer, Rolla
Election of 1934, 282–94
Ellet, Marion, 94, 246, 272–73, 278–79

Emporia Gazette, 7, 9, 86–87, 134–35, 142, 281; on R. Boynton, 72, 281; on R. Finney, 90, 181; on W. Finney, 115–16, 161–62, 308–11. *See also* White, William Allen; White, William Lindsay
Emporia State Teachers College, 52, 87, 345
Emporia Telephone Co., 14, 77, 107–10, 111–12, 118, 299–300; false entries in the accounts of, 53, 144, 154, 155, 157
Emporia Times, 282–83
Eureka Bank, 21, 52, 107; bonds removed from, 26, 48, 193–95, 332

Farmers State Bank of Neosho Falls, 112, 124; *See also* Neosho Falls State Bank
Farmers State Bank of West Wichita, 138, 233, 235, 264
Fidelity and Casualty Co. of New York, 52
Fidelity State and Savings Bank of Emporia, 112, 124; irregularities in, 34, 40–41, 52–54, 66–67, 77, 142–46, 153–58, 191–95; state funds assigned to, 65, 67, 72; claims against, 298–301, 345
Finney, David W., 54, 99–103, 107
Finney, Mabel (Mrs. Warren), 14–15, 90, 107, 125, 298–300, 308, 338–39, 347; and clemency for R. Finney, 323–24, 331, 332, 335
Finney, Mary Jane, 11, 45, 117, 146, 147
Finney, Ronald T., 43–47, 51–52, 59; commodities-market speculations of, 4, 15, 30–31, 44, 65, 136–38; background of, 15–16, 121–35; state charges against, 23, 39–40, 49–50, 58; takes bonds to Chicago, 26, 27–28, 76, 167, 194–95, 197; banking irregularities by, 30, 38, 48–49, 54, 123, 189–94, 264–65; federal charges against, 39–40, 76, 77, 203; forgery of bonds by, 40–41, 163–67, 232, 235–38, 242–43, 250–58; and School Fund Commission, 44, 63–65, 136, 220–31; in jail, 167–69, 313–16, 317–19, 337; trial and appeal of, 170–76, 178–82; and Auditor's Office, 258–64, 266–67; writing by, 319–21, 337–38, 339; clemency and pardon for, 323–36, 339
Finney, Warren W., 14–15, 104–6, 113–16, 118–20, 127; and W. A. White, 11–12, 20, 107, 110, 148–49; telephone companies owned by, 11, 14, 107–10, 111–12; and Landon, 23–24, 117–18; state charges against, 40–41, 53–54, 144; civil suits against, 54, 144–45, 297–301; banking irregularities by, 66–67, 112, 124, 139–40, 141–44; federal charges against, 76, 77,

388

INDEX

203; electric company owned by, 110–11; trial and appeal of, 145–46, 152–62, 301–5; death of, 305–9, 316
Finney, Winifred (Mrs. Ronald), 16, 124–25, 139, 316–17, 321, 337
Finney County, Kans., 54, 102
Fort Scott Tribune, 86
Foster, Herbert, 224
Foulkes, A. S., 32
Frazier, M. D., 222–23
Fredonia Herald, 89
Fredonia Telephone Co., 77, 111
French, Will J., 55, 59, 285; as state auditor, 5–6, 22, 50, 165, 247–65; and Landon, 50–51, 118; impeachment of, 65–66, 67, 71, 72, 265–71

Garden City Telegram, 89
Garvin, Robert, 265, 270
Glick, George W., 81, 102
Goodell, Lester, 32, 49, 347; and R. Finney, 21, 58, 132; and T. Boyd, 34, 49, 58, 195; and R. Finney's trial, 170, 172, 175, 179–83; and Caldwell's trial, 207–13
Gourley, Byron, 255–56
Gove, Coryell, 195
Gove County, Kans., 252
Governor. *See* Landon, Alfred M.
Governor's executive order, 27–28
Grand-jury investigation, 75–77, 202–3
Graves, Roscoe, 302, 305
Graybill, J. W., 63, 244
Great seal of Kansas, 50, 65, 165, 262–64
Greene, Zula Bennington, 171–72, 208, 241, 242
Greenleaf, Jesse, 51–52, 136, 289
Greenwood County, Kans., 52
Griffith, Charles, 94, 127, 216
Guilfoyle, Matt, 85, 220, 283; on R. Finney, 29, 71; on impeachment, 32, 62, 67; as member of Board of Managers, 240, 245

Hamilton, John D. M., 22–23, 46, 188, 210, 277, 280
Hardin, Ray N., 60; and R. Finney, 6, 65–66, 260–62, 264, 267
Harner, Collis D., 76, 191–92, 203
Harris, Fred M., 49, 50, 59, 347; as special counsel to governor, 30–32, 43, 52; and Bloss Committee, 62, 64, 66, 69, 73, 74; on W. Finney, 161, 181–82; and Board of Managers, 240, 245; on bond scandal, 289, 292
Harris, Jack, 7, 44, 324

Harsha, May, 173–74
Harvey, Paul, 195; and R. Finney's trial, 170, 175, 179
Harvey, Randal, 265
Hatten, Mary A., 215
Haynes, Forrest, 53–54
Haynes, Lacy, 95, 147, 280
Heinz, Paul H., 28; as counsel for Caldwell, 28, 171, 208; and R. Finney, 170–71, 175–82, 328, 336
Helvering, Guy, 46, 170, 291
Hettie, Lee R., 126
Hill, Thurman, 282, 284
Hill Packing Co., 59, 131
Hilton, Elmer, 240–41
Hinsdale County, Colo., 187–88, 261, 302–3
Hinshaw, David, 45–46, 47
Hobbs, Charles, 130–31
Holton Recorder, 89
Hopkins, Richard J., 75–76, 94, 115, 116, 127, 203
House, Jay, 88
House Resolution 13, 71
House Resolution 12, 71
Howes, Cecil, 16, 94–95
Hungate, Otis E.: and Boyd's trial, 196, 198, 201–2; and Caldwell's trial, 207, 211
Hutchinson, Kans., 29, 39, 49, 138, 170–75
Hutchinson News, 7, 44, 324

Impeachment of state officials, 36–37, 62, 64–66, 70–73. *See also* Boynton, Roland; French, Will J.
Income Tax Association, 116
Independent Telephone Co. *See* Emporia Telephone Co.
Interim Legislative Committee. *See* Legislative Council

Jackson, Arthur S., 195, 346
Jackson Brothers, Boesel and Co., 39–40, 137, 191, 195, 332, 344
Jardine, William M., 56–58
Jayhawk Hotel: R. Finney's headquarters in, 15, 21, 29, 64, 120, 135–36
J. C. Darling Stamp Co., 53–54, 173, 207
Jochems, William D., 150
Johnson, Charles W., 143, 145
Johnson County, Kans., 22, 53, 167
Jones, A. R., 26, 27, 29

Kansan, 335–36
Kansans: reaction of, to bond scandal, 82–85, 168

389

INDEX

Kansas City, Kans., 21, 54
Kansas City Journal-Post, 92, 277, 302-3. *See also* Clugston, William G.; Ellet, Marion
Kansas City Star, 72, 73, 93-95, 271, 277. *See also* Howes, Cecil; Trigg, Fred
Kansas Farmer, 87
Kansas Home Telephone Co., 53, 77, 111, 154
Kansas Legislature: appropriations by, for investigations, 60, 75, 344-45; special session of, 62, 66, 68-75
Kansas Life Insurance Co., 128
Kansas School Fund. *See* School Fund
Kelsey, Jim, 260
Ketchum, Omar, 284, 289-90, 292-94
Kiowa News-Review, 89
Kirk, John E., 130, 190, 197
Kismet, Kans., 64-65, 224-25, 230, 231
Klinkenberg, Kathrine. *See* White, Kathrine (Mrs. William L.)
Knapp, Dallas, 37
Knightley, John, 43, 224, 233-35, 250-51
Koeneke, H. W., 55, 67, 69-70; and Finney banks, 24, 142-43
Kretsinger, W. S., 118

Lake City Times, 132
Lamb, Ehret E., 63-64, 227
Landon, Alfred M., 2-3, 16-17, 38, 50-51, 58-59, 82-85, 347; initiates investigation, 19-21, 30-32, 34-36, 61, 66; and W. Finney, 20, 23-24, 117-18; closes treasury, 26-28, 95; and new state treasurer, 56-58; on impeachment, 62, 68; and R. Finney, 229-32, 333-34; and 1934 campaign, 277-80, 288-89, 293-94
Landon, John, 50, 117
Landon, Peggy Anne, 16, 58-59, 117, 168
Landon, Theo C. (Mrs. Alfred M.), 59, 232
Laughlin, Ann, 289-90, 294
Leavenworth Times, 89, 276, 330
Legislative Council, 35-36; special investigating committee of (*see* Bloss Committee)
Leoti Standard, 89-90, 148, 283
Light, G. L., 71, 228-30, 347
Lindley, Ernest H., 244
Little, Donald C., 31, 240, 277
Logan, Austin, 197
Logan County, Kans., 29, 250-51, 256-57
Long, Bernice, 48, 194, 196, 200-202
Lundblade, Leon, 34, 196-97
Lyon County, Kans., 53-54, 75; deposits of, in Fidelity Bank, 34, 52, 142-43, 145

McCarty, Alonzo C., 9, 147, 297-98; and W. Finney's trial, 152-53, 157, 158, 159-61
McConnell, Hellen H. (Mrs. David W. Finney), 103
McDermott, George T., 40, 112
McDonald, George, 294
McGill, George, 283-84
McKeen, Carl, 38-39, 48, 189-91; federal charges against, 77, 202-3; and R. Finney, 191, 193-94, 255-56
Mackey, Tom, 234, 242-43
McLean, M. R., 17, 26, 28
McNeal, Tom, 293
Markham, W. T., 62-63, 242, 294; and R. Finney, 63-64, 136, 225-27
Marysville Advocate-Democrat, 85-86, 283
Matile, Jake, 162
May, Oscar P., 73, 265
Meadows, Lee, 60, 236, 237, 267
Mellot, Arthur J., 240
Melvin, George K., 240
Mensendieck Grain Co., 137
Miller, Charles E., 244, 268, 282, 283, 284
Miller, Dora, 57
Mitchell, Charles L., 29, 242-43
Mitchell-Hutchins Co., 137, 194, 197
Mitchner, Lillian M., 244
Mulvane, David W., 185, 190
Munger Ranch, 51, 134
Murdock, Victor, 92

National Bank of Topeka, 59, 76, 77, 231; forged bonds in, 19, 21, 26, 30, 38, 48-49, 139; warrants sold to, 252, 254, 255-56; claims against, 343-44. *See also* McKeen, Carl
National Old Line Life Insurance Co., 51-52
Needels, Robert, 141, 153, 154
Neosho Falls Post, 90
Neosho Falls State Bank, 15, 112, 123, 124, 143; forged bonds in, 21, 24, 40, 52; and Banking Board, 66-67; claims against, 299-300, 345
Neosho Falls Telephone Co., 104, 107, 154, 157
Newsweek, 88
Newton Kansan, 89
Norton, 22

O'Connor, J. F. T., 38, 49
O'Neil, Ralph T. ("Dyke"), 46-47, 130, 197, 210
O'Neil and Hamilton, 22, 46, 128

INDEX

101 Ranch Real Wild West Show, 133–34, 139
Ottawa Herald, 177

Paola Telephone Co., 53, 77, 111, 144, 154, 155
Parker, W. W., 220
Parsons Sun. *See* Reed, Clyde
Paulen, Ben, 56, 82, 244
Payton, John F., 72
Pedroga, Edward E., 240
Peggy of the Flint Hills. *See* Greene, Zula Bennington
Pennick, Ruth, 199
Peoples National Bank of Kansas City, Kansas, 187–88
Perkins, H. A., 263
Peterson, Carl J., 130
Pihlbad, Ernest, 56
Pink Rag, 86, 203
Pittsburg Sun, 97
Plain Talk, 55
Pottorf, Lucy M., 84, 257–58, 347
Powers, Ed, 294–95
Prater, F. A., 224–25
Prater, W. R., 224–25
Pratt County, Kans., 22, 53, 253–55, 267–68
Press: and bond scandal, 86–97
Prudential Investment Trust Co., 48

Ralston, W. C., 228, 234
Ratner, Payne, 323–24, 326
Reed, Clyde, 2, 82, 86, 94, 246; and W. Finney, 14, 115, 117, 142; and French, 248–49
Reed, Russell, 173
Reilly, W. D., 265, 269
Rhodes, J. J. ("Jake"), 294–95
Riegle, Wilford, 69–70
Riley County, Kans., 22, 257–58
Roach, Nell, 154, 156
Robb, George, 295
Rogers, George E., 285–86
Rooney, Mark, 49, 191–92, 197
Ross, M. A., 255–56
Rost, F. J., 207–8
Roulier, Leon, 71, 136; and Thomas County bonds, 230, 233–38, 242–43
Russell County, Kans., 22, 256
Ryan, Frank, 62–63, 65, 225–27, 242, 347

Sabetha Telephone Co., 53, 77, 111, 144, 155
St. John, John P., 101, 102
Salina, Kans., 29, 49, 170, 173
Samuel, Owen, 150, 298
Satanta, Kans., 223–24, 228–30, 231

Schenck, Clyde, 150, 162, 170
Schenck, John, 28; and W. Finney's trial, 150, 158–59, 160, 162; and R. Finney's trial, 170–76, 179
Schoeppel, Andrew, 328–29, 332, 334–35
School Fund, 32, 219. *See also* School Fund Commission
School Fund Commission, 71, 75; bonds owned by, 19, 21, 22, 38, 53; officers of, 33, 219; and bonds sold to, by R. Finney, 44, 64–65, 163–67, 220–31
Scott, Charley, 41
Seaton, Fay, 56
Secretary of state. *See* Cornell, E. A.; Ryan, Frank
Shearman, J. C., 50, 175, 208–9, 262–64
Shriver, J. H., 253–54, 268, 347
Shultz, A. L. ("Dutch"), 17, 29, 239; on R. Finney, 29, 65, 96–97
Sloan, Edward R., 150, 158, 302, 305
Smith, William A., 112, 182, 216, 303, 305; and clemency for R. Finney, 325–26, 327–29, 334–36
Southwestern Bell Telephone Co.: and forged check of, 53–54, 112, 158; and W. Finney's telephone companies, 107, 111–12, 149, 154–56, 158–59; claims of, against Fidelity Bank, 298–300
Stacey, W. A., 63
Stanley, William H., 33, 241–42; and bonds sold to School Fund Commission, 64–65, 219–20, 223–25, 227–28, 230
Stevens County, Kans., 22
Stiers, Garnet, 199, 264
Stites, O. R. ("Jack"), 22, 67, 117, 150
Stratton, Clif, 17, 87, 95, 292, 347; and Boyd, 25–26; on R. Finney, 46–47, 220–21
Superintendent of public instruction. *See* Allen, George A.; Markham, W. T.
Superior Printing Co., 173

Telephone User's Protective Association, 109
Templar, George, 265, 269
Thomas, Chester, 26
Thomas County, Kans., 29, 231, 232–38
Thompson, Charles W., 36
Time, 88
Tincher, Jaspar N. ("Poly"), 265, 267, 270
Topeka Capital, 17, 75, 95–96, 115, 201, 276; on impeachment, 73, 271–72; on R. Finney, 137, 169, 180–81, 230, 320. *See also* Capper, Arthur; Stratton, Clif
Topeka State Journal, 86, 276–77; on R. Finney, 47, 176–79, 183; on Boynton, 65, 73,

INDEX

239, 272; on French, 73, 265, 272; on Caldwell, 211–12. *See also* Shultz, A. L. ("Dutch")
Tracey, Vivian, 49–50, 135–36
Trapp, Charley, 86, 203
Treasurer. *See* Boyd, Tom
Treasury, state: investigation of, 19, 37–38, 192; closing of, 26–28, 95; reopening of, 54–58
Treasury Board, 47–48; officers of, 35, 74; and deposit in Fidelity Bank, 65, 67, 72, 264–65
Trigg, Fred, 79
Trusler, Harold, 47, 197, 237
Tucker, Edwin, 14–15, 107, 139
Tucker, Edwin Sparr ("Ted"), 107, 193–94, 197
Tucker, Howard, 107
Tucker, Mabel. *See* Finney, Mabel (Mrs. Warren)

Ullfers, C. A., 156

Veale, Tinkham, 40, 196–202
Voorhees, Joe, 6, 252–55, 259–60, 263–64, 266–67

Walker, Arthur, 240
Warren Mortgage Co., 124
Wedell, Hugo T. ("Dutch"), 31, 263, 266, 292, 347; and W. Finney's trial, 150–51, 155, 157–60, 162; and R. Finney's trial, 170–71, 179, 181–83
Wells, Seth, 56

Western Spirit, 282
Wetherton, Bertha, 63
What People Said (by William L. White), 91, 129, 318–19, 333
White, Carl, 56
White, J. R., 240
White, Kathrine (Mrs. William L.), 13–14
White, Mary, 11
White, Sallie L. (Mrs. William A.), 11, 95, 146–47, 309
White, William Allen, 9–11, 45, 54, 106, 119–20, 284–86; friendship of, with W. Finney, 11–12, 20, 107–9, 110, 145–49, 309; on W. Finney, 14, 115, 116–17, 308–11; on Boynton, 72–74, 216–17, 232, 238–39, 271, 279–80; and R. Finney, 134–35, 329–30
White, William Lindsay, 12–13, 46, 87, 94, 147; friendship of, with R. Finney, 13–14, 90–91; on R. Finney, 91–92, 181, 315–16, 340–41; and clemency for R. Finney, 322, 323–36. *See also What People Said*
Wichita, Municipal University of, 58
Wichita Beacon, 92, 201
Wichita Eagle, 75, 92–93
Wiggam, Jennie, 124–25
Wiggam, John H., 124
Wiggam, Winifred. *See* Finney, Winifred (Mrs. Ronald)
Winters, George, 258–59
Wood, George G., 90
Woodring, Harry, 2, 5, 46, 81, 229, 290–92
Woodson County, Kans., 52

Yates Center Telephone Co., 111

www.ingramcontent.com/pod-product-compliance
Lightning Source LLC
Chambersburg PA
CBHW020120240426
43673CB00038B/538